Guns for the Sultan

Military Power and the Weapons Industry in the Ottoman Empire

Gábor Ágoston's book contributes to an emerging strand of military history, which examines organized violence as a challenge to early modern states, their societies and economies. His is the first to examine the weapons technology and armaments industries of the Ottoman Empire, the only Islamic empire that threatened Europe on its own territory in the age of the Gunpowder Revolution. Based on extensive research in the Turkish archives, the book affords new insights regarding the early success and subsequent failure of an Islamic empire against European adversaries. It demonstrates Ottoman flexibility and the existence of an early modern arms market and information exchange across the cultural divide, as well as Ottoman self-sufficiency in weapons and arms production well into the eighteenth century. Challenging the sweeping statements of Eurocentric and Orientalist scholarship, the book disputes the notion of Islamic conservatism, the Ottomans' supposed technological inferiority and the alleged insufficiencies in production capacity. This is a provocative, intelligent and penetrating analysis which successfully contends traditional perceptions of Ottoman and Islamic history. It is certain to become a classic in the field.

Gábor Ágoston is Associate Professor in the Department of History, Georgetown University. His previous publications include *Hungary in the Seventeenth Century* (with Teréz Oborni, 2000).

Cambridge Studies in Islamic Civilisation

Guns for the Sultan

Military Power and the Weapons Industry in the
Ottoman Empire

GÁBOR ÁGOSTON

Georgetown University

CAMBRIDGE UNIVERSITY PRESS
Cambridge, New York, Melbourne, Madrid, Cape Town, Singapore, São Paulo

Cambridge University Press
The Edinburgh Building, Cambridge CB2 2RU, UK

Published in the United States of America by Cambridge University Press, New York

www.cambridge.org
Information on this title: www.cambridge.org/9780521843133

First published 2005

Printed in the United Kingdom at the University Press, Cambridge

A catalogue record for this book is available from the British Library

Library of Congress Cataloguing in Publication data
Ágoston, Gábor.
Guns for the sultan: military power and the weapons industry in the Ottoman Empire / Gábor Ágoston.
   p.   cm. – (Cambridge studies in Islamic civilization)
Includes bibliographical references (p. 248) and index.
ISBN 0 521 84313 8 (hbk. : alk. paper) – ISBN 0 521 60391 9 (pbk. : alk. paper)
1. Weapons industry – Turkey – History.   2. Turkey – History, Military.   I. Title.   II. Series.
HD9743.T92A36   2004   338.4′76234′09560903 – dc22   2004051106

ISBN-13 978-0-521-84313-3 hardback
ISBN-10 0-521-84313-8 hardback

To my family with love and gratitude

Without these munitions and artillery one cannot preserve any state, nor defend it, nor attack the enemy.

Venetian senate minute, June 16, 1489
(Quoted in English by Michael Mallett, "Siegecraft in Late
Fifteenth-Century Italy," in Ivy A. Corfis and Michael Wolfe eds., *The Medieval City under Siege* [Woodbridge, 1995], p. 247).

My Blissful Padishah. As your great lord knows, the main support of the Sultanic campaigns is gunpowder. Without gunpowder, the campaign is completely impossible ... Gunpowder is not like other things. If we fail to take measures concerning it and it is not produced in time, where there is a shortage of gunpowder, even if we have 100,000 gold coins, the amount shall be of no benefit. Where there is a shortage of gunpowder, even if there is a sea of gold coins, it cannot take the place of gunpowder. The defense of the fortresses and warfare takes place with gunpowder.

Grand Vizier Yemişçi Hasan Pasha's petition (*telhis*) from 1603
(Cengiz Orhonlu, *Osmanlı Tarihine Aid Belgeler: Telhisler* [*1597–1607*] [Istanbul, 1970], pp. 19–20).

Contents

Illustrations

Figures

Maps

Tables

Acknowledgments

This book has been researched, planned and written over a period of years and I owe a considerable debt to my teachers, friends and colleagues. Gyula Káldy-Nagy and Géza Dávid introduced me to the study of Ottoman history and paleography. Gyula Káldy-Nagy also played an important role in directing my interest towards the topic of the present book by drawing my attention to Abdülkadir Efendi's seventeenth-century manuscript, an unusually rich source for contemporaneous Ottoman military history. I cherish the memory of the late István Mándoky-Kongur, the last "nomad" of the Hungarian Turkologists, whose love and deep knowledge of everything related to the Turkic peoples profoundly shaped my professional life. The friendship of Pál Fodor and that of the late Ferenc Szakály have meant so much to me, and I miss their gentle criticism and encouragement. Teréz Oborni occupies a special place among my Hungarian friends. She was the first reader and critic of an earlier version of the book and her friendship has been precious ever since. I also thank Klára Hegyi, Ágnes Várkonyi and the late Géza Perjés for their comments on the dissertation which dealt with some of the issues examined in the book. The present book, however, is a rather different work.

In the past decade it has been my good fortune to have had the opportunity to return regularly to my beloved Istanbul and to carry on follow-up research in the archives that not only broadened and deepened the source base of the book but also raised important new questions. In the archives Mehmet Genç, İbrahim Sahillioğlu and the late Nejat Göyünç were generous with their time and knowledge when I faced difficulties in deciphering Ottoman documents. The companionship of my colleagues working in the archives made research an enjoyable daily activity and it is a pleasure to acknowledge them: İdris Bostan, Selim Deringil, Feridun Emecen, Caroline Finkel, İlber Ortaylı, Victor Ostapchuk, Ariel Salzmann and Fariba Zarinebaf-Shahr. I have spent long hours in the bookshops of Muhittin S. Eren and Rasim Yüksel who have been instrumental in locating old and new Turkish publications and who shared with me their knowledge, as well as the news and gossip, of Turkish academia and Ottoman studies. I am indebted to Hüseyin Özdeğer for the long conversations we have had on Ottoman history. Tuba Çavdar, Nejat Dinçel and Cemil Öztürk made sure that I did not lose touch with everyday life and that I felt at home in Istanbul.

I am also grateful to Jacob Roodenberg and Ted Largo, directors of the Dutch Historical and Archeological Institute in Istanbul, and to Tony Greenwood, director of the American Research Institute in Turkey, for the pleasant working conditions they provided. In England, I benefited from the friendship and hospitality of Kate Fleet (Skilliter Centre for Ottoman Studies, Newnham College, Cambridge) and Colin Heywood (School of Oriental and African Studies, University of London).

I have discussed some of the results of my research with colleagues and friends and I am indebted to my fellow-researchers in the archives and to Virginia Aksan, Jeremy Black, Colin Heywood, Ekmeleddin İhsanoğlu, Rhoads Murphey and Brett Steele for their support and stimulating comments. I am especially indebted to Colin Heywood for sharing with me his knowledge on the subject as well as his anecdotes regarding his mentor, Vernon J. Parry, whose ground-breaking studies inspired my research.

The book was written during my Georgetown years. The friendship of Dina and Alfred Khoury and the welcome extended to me by Georgetown University's History Department smoothed the transition from Budapest to Washington, D.C. I have been fortunate to meet new friends at Georgetown. The companionship and support of Jim Collins, Catherine Evtuhov, Andrzej Kamiński, John McNeill and Jim Shedel means a great deal to me. Many of them have read parts of the book at some stage of its life and offered valuable comments. Jim Collins and Andrzej Kamiński have read and critiqued the entire manuscript and I have immensely benefited from their insight and suggestions.

The positive reports and helpful comments of the two anonymous readers of Cambridge University Press are much appreciated. I am most grateful to my editor, Marigold Acland, for her early interest in this project and for being an ideal editor. I also thank my copy-editor, Carol Fellingham Webb, for her professionalism and careful work, as well as Andrew Timothy Gane, Jean Ranallo and Nadya Sbaiti who, at different stages of this work, labored to improve its language and style. Of course, any remaining flaws of the book are entirely mine.

Parts of the material used in the book were delivered as a paper at a conference held in 1999 at MIT's Dibner Institute for the History of Science and Technology and will appear in Brett Steele and Tamera Dorland eds., *The Heirs of Archimedes: Science and the Art of War through the Age of Enlightenment* (Cambridge, MA: MIT Press, forthcoming 2005), whereas other smaller sections were published in my "Ottoman Warfare in Europe, 1453–1826," in Jeremy Black ed., *European Warfare, 1453–1815* (London: Macmillan, 1999). I would like to thank the editors as well as MIT Press and Macmillan Press for permissions to use these materials in the book.

I am indebted to the staff of the following institutions: the Başbakanlık Ottoman Archives of Istanbul, the British Library, the libraries of Eötvös Loránd University, the Hungarian Academy of Sciences, Cambridge University and the School of Oriental and African Studies, and above all Georgetown University's Lauinger Memorial Library. Special thanks are due to the staff of the Interlibrary Loan Division of the latter who handled my requests expeditiously. Illustrations were provided by the Historical Gallery of the Hungarian National Museum, the Special Collections of Lauinger Memorial Library, Georgetown University and the Anne S. K. Brown Military Collection of Brown University Library. I thank the directors, curators and staff of these institutions for the permissions to reproduce the illustrations in the book.

I would also like to acknowledge the financial assistance of several institutions and foundations. Fellowships and grants from the Eötvös Loránd University and the George Soros Foundation, the Skilliter Centre for Ottoman Studies and the Andrew W. Mellon Foundation supported my research in Istanbul, London and Cambridge. A junior sabbatical and several Summer Academic Research Grants awarded by the Graduate School of Georgetown University greatly facilitated the completion of the book. To all of these institutions I offer my sincere gratitude.

It has been my parents' caring love that allowed me to pursue my dreams and turn them into my profession. They have supported my choices and let me go when my studies, research and profession took me to ever further lands: hard decisions on their parts and a token of true love for which I am grateful. My sister and her children have constantly reminded me that there exists another world outside the archives and libraries. This book could not have been completed without the support of my wife, Alíz, who not only managed our life almost single-handedly during our major transition from Hungary to the United States, but also read and commented on versions of the manuscript. It was the birth of our son that helped me put things into perspective and his crying at two in the morning that signaled the end of my busy days during the final revision of the book. This book is dedicated to my family with love and gratitude.

Notes on transliteration and place names

Ottoman terms have been rendered in their Ottoman Turkish spelling using the modern Turkish alphabet. Diacritical marks have been omitted. Words that have found their way into the English language (e.g., pasha) are used in their common English spelling. Regarding place names, I preferred the Ottoman forms used in the sources. However, internationally accepted place names (e.g., Belgrade) have been retained. Place names before the Ottoman conquest are used in their contemporary Hungarian, Slavic, etc. forms. To locate place names and their equivalents readers are referred to the index and to Donald Edgar Pitcher, *An Historical Geography of the Ottoman Empire* (Leiden, 1973).

Abbreviations

AK	Topçular Katibi Abdülkadir Efendi, *Tarih-i Al-i Osman*. Vienna, ÖNB, Handschriftensammlung, Codex Vindobonensis Palatinus Mxt. 130
AOH	*Acta Orientalia Academiae Scientiarum Hungaricae*
ArchOtt	*Archivum Ottomanicum*
BOA	Başbakanlık Osmanlı Arşivi (Prime Ministry's Ottoman Archives, Istanbul)
BSOAS	*Bulletin of the School of Oriental and African Studies*
BTTD	*Belgelerle Türk Tarih Dergisi*
CA	Cevdet Askeri
DBŞM	Bâb-i Defteri Başmuhasebe Kalemi Defterleri collection in the BOA
DBŞM BRG	Bâb-i Defteri Başmuhasebe Kalemi Defterleri Gelibolu Baruthânesi collection in the BOA
DBŞM BRİ	Bâb-i Defteri Başmuhasebe Kalemi Defterleri İstanbul Baruthânesi collection in the BOA
DBŞM BRS	Bâb-i Defteri Başmuhasebe Kalemi Defterleri Selanik Baruthânesi collection in the BOA
DBŞM TPH	Bâb-i Defteri Başmuhasebe Kalemi Defterleri Tophane-i Âmire collection in the BOA
DMKF	Bâb-i Defteri Mevkufat Kalemi collection in the BOA
DPYM	Bâb-i Defteri Piyade Mukabelesi Kalemi collection in the BOA
EI	*Encyclopedia of Islam* (new edition, Leiden and London, 1960–2002)
HK	*Hadtörténelmi Közlemények*
İA	*İslam Ansiklopedisi* (13 vols., Istanbul, 1965–1974)
İED	*İstanbul Enstitüsü Dergisi*
İFM	*İstanbul Üniversitesi İktisat Fakültesi Mecmuasi*
IHR	*International History Review*
IJMES	*International Journal of Middle Eastern Studies*
JESHO	*Journal of the Economic and Social History of the Orient*
JMH	*Journal of Military History*

JRAS	*Journal of the Royal Asiatic Society of Great Britain and Ireland*
JTS	*Journal of Turkish Studies*
Kavanin	"Kavanin-i Yeniçeriyan-i Dergah-i Ali" in Ahmed Akgündüz ed., *Osmanlı Kanunnameleri ve Hukuki Tahlilleri*, vol. 9/1 (Istanbul, 1996), pp. 127–268, facsimile, ibid., pp. 269–366.
KK	Kâmil Kepeci collection in the BOA
MAD	Maliyeden Müdevver Defterleri collection in the BOA
MD	Mühimme Defterleri collection in the BOA
OsmAr	*Osmanlı Araştırmaları/Journal of Ottoman Studies*
ÖNB	Österreichische Nationalbibliothek
POF	*Prilozi za orijentalnu filologiju*
TD	*İstanbul Üniversitesi Edebiyat Fakültesi Tarih Dergisi*
TDVİA	*Türkiye Diyanet Vakfı İslam Ansiklopedisi* (25 vols., Istanbul, 1988–)
TED	*İstanbul Üniversitesi Tarih Enstitüsü Dergisi*
TSAB	*Turkish Studies Association Bulletin*
TSMK	Topkapı Sarayı Müzesi Kütüphanesi
Turcica	*Turcica. Revue d'études turques*
VVM	*Vesnik Vojnog Muzeja*

CHAPTER 1

Introduction: firearms and armaments industries

The "discovery" of gunpowder, the appearance of firearms, and especially their mass employment in warfare was one of the most significant developments of the late Middle Ages. Gunpowder – a mixture of saltpeter, sulfur and charcoal – was first made in China in the seventh or eighth century AD and the first proper firearms were manufactured there from the 1280s onward. The first firearm "had three basic features: its barrel was of metal; the gunpowder used in it was rather high in nitrate; and the projectile totally occluded the muzzle so that the powder charge could exert its full propellant effect."[1] Within decades, gunpowder weapons had reached both Islamdom and Christian Europe, and by the first decades of the fourteenth century firearms were being used in European battlefields and sieges. By mid-century, firearms had reached Hungary and the Balkans, and by the 1380s the Ottomans were also acquainted with the new weapon. The Ottoman conquest of Constantinople was but one dramatic illustration of how, by the 1450s, cannons had become a decisive weapon in siege warfare. In the early fifteenth century, cannons were frequently being used aboard European ships and towards the end of that century shipboard artillery had already proved its value on the Mediterranean war galleys.[2]

The appearance of firearms and their mass employment in battles, sieges and by navies significantly changed the way states and empires waged wars. In order to remain militarily competitive in the gunpowder age, states needed cannons, cannon-proof fortifications, a sizable infantry armed with handguns, as well as navies with shipboard artillery. Organized violence between states and empires,

---

[1] Joseph Needham, *Gunpowder as the Fourth Power: East and West* (Hong Kong, 1985), pp. 14–15. Thanks to the monumental work of Joseph Needham and his colleagues, there appears to be a scholarly consensus regarding the place of origin and the direction of the transfer of knowledge of gunpowder from east to west. See Joseph Needham, Ho Ping-Yü, Lu Gwei-Djen and Wang Ling, *Science and Civilization in China, vol. V: Chemistry and Chemical Technology, pt. 7, Military Technology: The Gunpowder Epic* (Cambridge, 1986). From the latest literature see Alfred W. Crosby, *Throwing Fire: Projectile Technology through History* (Cambridge, 2002) and Kenneth Chase, *Firearms: A Global History to 1700* (Cambridge, 2003).

[2] Bert S. Hall, *Weapons and Warfare in Renaissance Europe: Gunpowder, Technology, and Tactics* (Baltimore, 1997); Carlo M. Cipolla, *Guns, Sails, and Empires: Technological Innovation and the Early Phases of European Expansion 1400–1700* (New York, 1965; reprint New York, 1996).

1

geographical exploration and overseas expansion led to an unprecedented arms race. In order to participate effectively in the attendant inter-state rivalry, monarchs had to create their indigenous weapons industries or supply the necessary weaponry and ammunition otherwise.[3] In the long run, the adequate and steady supply of weaponry and military hardware proved to be more important than (usually temporary) technological or tactical advantages. To be sure, superiority in weapons technology and tactics could occasionally have determined the outcome of individual battles or sieges, although weaponry in itself was hardly sufficient to win the day.[4] However, states and empires that wanted to achieve long-standing military prominence and maintain military pressure for decades had to possess weaponry and military hardware in substantial quantities and of acceptable quality.[5]

Arms and ammunition production required investment in capital, manpower, organizational skills and so forth. Apart from paying and feeding the troops, arms production and shipbuilding constituted the most burdensome challenge for early modern states, for "gunpowder weapons and their services may have added a third to the costs of a campaign."[6] Thus, the examination of the supply of weapons can significantly enhance our understanding regarding the military capabilities of states and empires. Comparative data and analyses concerning the supply of weaponry and ammunition of competing empires in the gunpowder age might illuminate issues pertaining to larger questions, such as the shifts in the balance of power.

The aim of this book is to understand the Ottoman weapons industry, the systems and methods by which the Sultans procured their armaments. The bulk of the content examines the Ottoman armaments industry in the sixteenth and seventeenth centuries. It was not only a crucial period of Ottoman conquests and of subsequent setback, but also an age which – at least in the major European theaters of war where the Empire was drawn into conflict – was characterized by siege warfare rather than by pitched battles. In these sieges the supply of artillery and gunpowder

---

[3] Geoffrey Parker, *The Military Revolution: Military Innovation and the Rise of the West, 1500–1800* (Cambridge, 1988; rev. 3rd edition, 1999); William H. McNeill, *The Pursuit of Power: Technology, Armed Force, and Society since AD 1000* (Chicago, 1982).

[4] Cipolla, *Guns, Sails, and Empires*, p. 28; McNeill, *The Pursuit of Power*, pp. 12–20, 36–40; Parker, *The Military Revolution*, p. 43; Jeremy Black, *A Military Revolution? Military Change and European Society, 1550–1800* (London, 1991), pp. 12–13; George Raudzens, "War-Winning Weapons: The Measurement of Technological Determinism in Military History," *Journal of Military History* 54 (1990), 403–33.

[5] The history of military conflicts provides many examples which show how the lack of adequate weaponry and ammunition might force policy-makers to compromise or delay military operations. The most recent example would be the case of the 1,000-pound "bunker-buster" bombs used against Taliban targets in Afghanistan in 2001 and 2002. In February 2002, Pentagon planners reminded politicians and the public that, despite the rhetoric of President Bush, it was unlikely that a war against Iraq would be started soon, because army and navy inventories "ran dangerously low." They suggested that it would take at least six months to replenish the stockpiles. See Walter Pincus and Karen DeYoung, "Anti-Iraq Rhetoric Outpaces Reality," *Washington Post* February 24, 2002, A1.

[6] J. R. Hale, *War and Society in Renaissance Europe 1450–1620* (London, 1985), p. 47.

was a crucial element of success, as was the defense of the Ottoman frontiers against the Sultans' Hungarian, Habsburg, Venetian and Safavid adversaries.[7]

Gunpowder technology, the Military Revolution thesis and the Ottomans

As can be seen from the two quotations that open this book, contemporary politicians, Europeans and Ottomans alike, were well aware of the significance of firearms. The spread of gunpowder weapons stirred passionate debate among intellectuals of the Renaissance.[8] Although no comparable debate in the contemporaneous Ottoman literature is detectable, it is noteworthy that the seventeenth-century Ottoman historian Ibrahim Peçevi included a small section about the manufacturing of black powder in his chronicle. Writing around 1640, Peçevi repeated the well-known European myth about Berthold Schwarz, perhaps following one of his Hungarian sources. What is more interesting, though, is the fact that Peçevi discussed the invention of "black powder" together with that of printing.[9]

Many European historians have considered the "discovery" of gunpowder and that of printing as the two most significant inventions of the late Middle Ages. Indeed, historians, especially in Europe, have long been fascinated with the "gunpowder epic." Many of them argued that "gunpowder blasted the feudal strongholds and the ideas of their owners," a notion that was shared by such authorities as David Hume (1711–76) and Adam Smith (1723–90). Johan Huizinga went even further when he wrote that "the rebirth of the human spirit dates from the discovery of firearms."[10] According to one of the most influential historical theses of the late twentieth century – Geoffrey Parker's Military Revolution theory – gunpowder weapons had far-reaching consequences regarding state formation and the power balance between states and civilizations. Parker substantially modified Michael Roberts's original conception of the Military Revolution. In Parker's version of the thesis, gunpowder weaponry and military technology occupy center stage. Since only monarchs possessed the necessary financial and organizational means to invest in cannon-proof fortresses (*trace italienne*) and to establish and maintain artillery corps of sufficient size to besiege these fortifications successfully,

---

[7] Until the 1680s, there were only three major field battles (in 1526, 1596 and 1664) that took place between the Ottomans and their Hungarian and Habsburg opponents in Hungary, the most important theater of Ottoman–European land confrontations during the sixteenth and seventeenth centuries. In that same period of time, the Hungarian frontier saw dozens of sieges, heroic defenses as well as considerable efforts of fortress building and modernization, especially on the Habsburg side.

[8] J. R. Hale, "Gunpowder and the Renaissance: An Essay in the History of Ideas," in J. R. Hale, *Renaissance War Studies* (London, 1983), pp. 389–420.

[9] İbrahim Peçevi (Peçuylu), *Tarih-i Peçevi* (2 vols., Istanbul, 1283/1866–67), vol. I, p. 83. It is known that Peçevi, who was born in Pécs, Hungary and spent most of his life on that frontier, used Hungarian sources while writing his own history of the Ottomans. From the latest literature see Pál Fodor, "Egy pécsi származású oszmán történetíró: Ibrahim Pecsevi," in Ferenc Szakály ed., *Pécs a törökkorban* (Pécs, 1999), pp. 107–31.

[10] For these statements see Hale, "Gunpowder and the Renaissance."

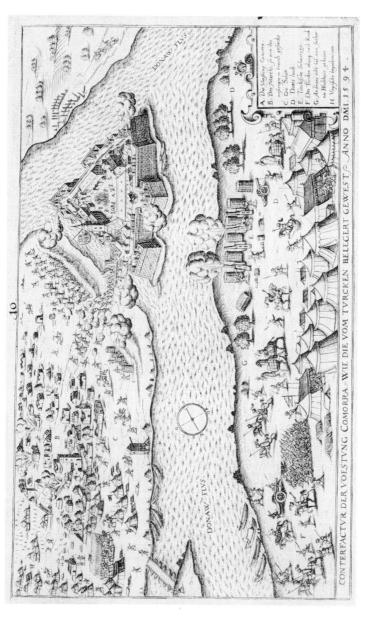

Figure 1 Planned and built by the Italian master-builder Pietro Ferabosco between 1552 and 1555, Komárom was the only major fortress built or modernized according to the *trace italienne* that the Ottomans could not conquer in Hungary. However, the reasons for Ottoman failure are manifold: besides the fortress's architecture, the width of the Danube that rendered Ottoman cannons on the far side of the river ineffective, steadfast defense, cold weather and the outbreak of typhus that killed some eight thousand besiegers all mentioned by contemporaneous sources. Engraving by Johann Sibmacher (1594).

Parker argues, cannons and the *trace italienne* eventually led to the strengthening of state power vis-à-vis the feudal lords and facilitated the emergence of centralized states. Similarly, superior firepower and ocean-going naval technology conclusively shifted the military balance towards Europe, and were responsible for establishing Europe's eventual hegemony over non-European civilizations, a process that many historians proudly label the "rise of the West."[11]

The nature and the impact of the Military or Gunpowder Revolution are disputable and have been hotly debated for decades.[12] While some historians rejected Parker's ideas, accusing him of technological determinism,[13] others incorporated them into their sweeping treatments of war and society. Students of warfare and military technology continue to examine the development of gunpowder and its role in the history of military conflicts and that of humankind. Military and economic historians have tried to determine the significance of European arms and ammunition production as well as the role of arms transfer and technological diffusion in the rise and fall of states, empires and civilizations.[14] Others are more cautious regarding the historical significance of military technology. In his recent works, Jeremy Black questioned the importance of military technology as a determining factor in the "fate of the continents" and offered important qualifications regarding Europe's global expansion, emphasizing the relationship and interactions between European technology, economy and state formation.[15] Despite criticisms of it, the Military Revolution thesis continues to exert considerable impact far beyond the works of historians and figures prominently in the appealing surveys on state formation and geopolitics.[16] In this generalist literature, Europe's "aggregate firepower"

[11] Parker, *The Military Revolution*; cf. also Cipolla, *Guns, Sails, and Empires*. See also my "Disjointed Historiography and Islamic Military Technology: The European Military Revolution Debate and the Ottomans," forthcoming in the *Ekmeleddin Ishsanoğlu Festschrift*.

[12] Several of the important studies are readily available in Clifford J. Rogers ed., *The Military Revolution Debate: Readings on the Military Transformation of Early Modern Europe* (Boulder, CO, 1995). See also Black, *A Military Revolution?*

[13] See, for instance, Bert S. Hall and Kelly DeVries, "The Military Revolution Revisited," *Technology and Culture* 31 (1990), 500–07.

[14] Cipolla, *Guns, Sails, and Empires*; David Ayalon, *Gunpowder and Firearms in the Mamluk Kingdom: A Challenge to a Mediaeval Society* (London, 1956; 2nd edition, London, 1978); John Francis Guilmartin, Jr., *Gunpowder and Galleys: Changing Technology and Mediterranean Warfare at Sea in the Sixteenth Century* (Cambridge, 1974; rev. edition Annapolis, MD, 2003; all references are to the 1974 edition); Volker Schmidtchen, *Bombarden, Befestigungen, Büchsenmeister. Von den ersten Mauerbrechern des Spätmittelalters zur Belagerungsartillerie der Renaissance. Eine Studie zur Entwicklung der Militärtechnik* (Düsseldorf, 1977); Andrew C. Hess, *The Forgotten Frontier: A History of the Sixteenth-Century Ibero-African Frontier* (Chicago, 1978); McNeill, *The Pursuit of Power*; Trevor N. Dupuy, *The Evolution of Weapons and Warfare* (New York, 1985); Kelly DeVries, *Medieval Military Technology* (Peterborough, Ontario, 1992); Hall, *Weapons and Warfare*; Crosby, *Throwing Fire*; Chase, *Firearms*.

[15] Jeremy Black, *War and the World: Military Power and the Fate of the Continents, 1450–2000* (New Haven and London, 1998); Jeremy Black, *European Warfare, 1494–1660* (London, 2002).

[16] See, e.g., Paul Kennedy, *The Rise and Fall of the Great Powers: Economic Change and Military Conflict from 1500 to 2000* (New York, 1989); Charles Tilly, *Coercion, Capital, and European States, AD 990–1990* (Oxford, 1990); Brian M. Downing, *The Military Revolution and Political Change: Origins of Democracy and Autocracy in Early Modern Europe* (Princeton, NJ, 1992); Keith Krause, *Arms and the State: Patterns of Military Production and Trade* (Cambridge, 1992). Even

and naval capability figure prominently and the far-reaching consequences that the proliferation of firearms brought about are usually accepted.[17]

While an increasing number of works present a more balanced and multi-causal, evolutionary (rather than revolutionary) explanation of European military changes, students of non-European history are lagging behind their Europeanist colleagues. The historiography of the Ottoman Empire, militarily the most sophisticated non-European adversary of early modern Europe, is a case in point. Given the significance of warfare in the history of the Ottoman Empire and that of the whole region once ruled by the Sultans, it is hard to understand that the Ottomans have until recently been sidelined by the flourishing literature of the New Military History.[18]

The Turkish archives are rich in material regarding Ottoman gun casting, salt-peter and gunpowder manufacturing, as well as shipbuilding, to name but the most important sectors of early modern war industry. Despite this, the history of Ottoman military technology and armaments industry is still *terra incognita* for students of European and Ottoman history.[19] This is difficult to understand given the Ottomans' military endurance against their European and Middle Eastern adversaries. As a result of the lack of relevant studies on Ottoman military technology and arms production, it is hardly surprising that sweeping (and often misleading) statements with regard to Ottoman (and Islamic) military technology and military capabilities are often repeated in the generalist literature. Of these, the notion of "Islamic conservatism," the ideas regarding the Ottomans' supposed technological inferiority, as well as the Empire's alleged insufficient production capacity and its putative dependence on imported European weapons and ammunition have proved to be the most persistent.

---

those authors who disagree with the thesis feel it necessary to reflect on it. See, for instance, Hendrik Spruyt, *The Sovereign State and its Competitors: An Analysis of Systems Change* (Princeton, NJ, 1994).

[17] I borrowed the term "aggregate firepower" from Jeremy Black.

[18] It was not until 1999 that the first general text on Ottoman warfare appeared. See Rhoads Murphey, *Ottoman Warfare, 1500–1700* (New Brunswick, 1999).

[19] The most recent handbook on Ottoman economic history (the first and only such undertaking published in English) hardly mentions the armaments industry. See Halil İnalcık and Donald Quataert eds., *An Economic and Social History of the Ottoman Empire, 1300–1914* (Cambridge, 1994), p. 465. Although some pioneering studies have been available for several decades, and in recent years there is a visible interest in the subject in Turkey, no monographic study of Ottoman weapons technology and war industries exists in any language. For the relevant studies by İsmail Hakkı Uzunçarşılı, Halil İnalcık, Djurdjica Petrović, Colin Heywood, Rhoads Murphey and Mücteba İlgürel see the bibliography. Although Birol Çetin's and Salim Aydüz's Ph.D. dissertations (on the eighteenth- and nineteenth-century gunpowder works, and on the sixteenth-century Istanbul cannon foundry, respectively) were not available to me during the writing of this book, an attempt has been made to include some of their findings during the final revision of this manuscript. Both are traditional institutional histories with valuable information. However, they lack the comparative approach, hardly use the relevant literature in foreign languages, and could have been more thoroughly researched, particularly Çetin's. Birol Çetin, *Osmanlı İmparatorluğu'nda Barut Sanayi, 1700–1900* (Ankara, 2001); Salim Aydüz, "Osmanlı Devleti'nde Tophane-i Amire ve Top Döküm Teknolojisi (XV–XVI. Yüzyıllar)," unpublished Ph.D. dissertation, University of Istanbul, 1998.

Although the present book tackles many of the above questions, its aim is not to present a simple counter-thesis to previous views, but rather to broaden the scope of our examination by a thorough assessment of Ottoman arms and ammunition production. Based on extensive research in the Turkish archives, this book offers new insights regarding the early success of an Islamic empire against its European adversaries and its subsequent military failure.

Apart from the military aspects, it is hoped that the book will enhance our understanding of the Ottoman economy in general. The weapons and ammunition industries along with the construction of vessels were the only major branches of the early modern Ottoman industry that were managed, controlled and financed by the state. While arms and ammunition production meant challenge and burden for the Ottoman state, war-related industries also could provide important stimuli for the general economy, and could play a significant role in improving existing technologies or acquiring new ones.

From a theoretical and methodological point of view, I follow the emerging literature of the New Military History, which is no longer confined to the narrow study of campaigns and sieges; rather, it examines organized violence as a major challenge to early modern states, their societies and economies. My research also owes much to the pioneering studies of Carlo Maria Cipolla, John Francis Guilmartin, Jr., Bert Hall, William H. McNeill, Geoffrey Parker, and Keith Krause, all of whom have examined the diffusion of gunpowder technology, European arms production and the arms trade. While these works proved to be valuable guides during my research, when it came to the Ottomans, they raised more questions than provided answers. Although my research eventually led me either to disprove or to qualify some of the theses put forward by my scholarly predecessors, they inspired me throughout the process of writing this book, for which I am indebted to all of them.

Challenging Eurocentric and Orientalist views

Following superficially understood Islamic doctrines, authors such as Kenneth M. Setton, Eric L. Jones and Paul Kennedy fault the "extreme conservatism of Islam,"[20] the "military despotism," which "militated against the borrowing of western techniques and against native inventiveness,"[21] or the "cultural and technological conservatism," for the failure of Islamic civilizations to keep pace with western

[20] Kenneth Meyer Setton, *Venice, Austria, and the Turks in the Seventeenth Century* (Philadelphia, PA, 1991), pp. 6, 100, 450. For its critique see Rhoads Murphey's review in *ArchOtt* 13 (1993–94), 371–83. Setton places too much emphasis on the impact of religion. He argues that "the Spanish were caught in an era of religious bigotry, the Turks in a renewal of Islamic fanaticism, and neither people could keep abreast of the technological innovations which had been altering European society from at least the mid-sixteenth century" (ibid., p. 6).
[21] E. L. Jones, *The European Miracle: Environments, Economies, and Geopolitics in the History of Europe and Asia* (Cambridge and New York, 1987), p. 181. (The book's third edition was published in 2003 showing that his Eurocentric views are still very much in demand.)

military technology.[22] Others advocate an East–West technological divergence and western technological superiority from the mid-fifteenth or late sixteenth century onward.[23] Along the lines of the traditional view of "Ottoman decline," some students of Middle Eastern history claim that "the Ottomans lagged behind the West in weaponry and fighting techniques" as early as the end of the sixteenth century.[24] In several of his works, Bernard Lewis repeats his notions concerning the Muslims' (chronologically unspecified) ignorance, their technological inferiority vis-à-vis the (unqualified) "West," as well as their continued reliance on "foreign" technology and know-how. The chronology and reasons for the failure of the "Islamic world" to keep up with the "West" are seldom presented and the successes of "Islamic war departments" are mentioned only cursorily, as if they were mere exceptions to the dominant picture of continuous decline, inferiority and setbacks.[25]

Examining the spread of firearms technology in Euro-Asia in chapter 2 shows that the adoption or rejection of firearms technology by Islamic societies had very little to do with Islam. Rather, it was a decision of the political and military elites of the respective societies, and was influenced by the social fabrics, economic capabilities, geopolitical realities and constraints, as well as by military and political objectives. The Ottomans were far from being prisoners of the "extreme conservatism of Islam" as suggested by the representatives of the traditional Eurocentric school. Chapter 2 provides ample cases regarding the continued Ottoman receptivity to new ideas and western military technology well into the seventeenth century. It also shows that the pragmatism of the fourteenth- and fifteenth-century Ottoman rulers made it relatively easy to adopt firearms technology and to come up with the organizational frameworks necessary to integrate and operate these weapons. Continuous military conflict with European armies equipped with firearms, as well as the existence of strong fortresses in the Byzantine Empire, in the Mediterranean and in Hungary, forced the Ottomans to adjust their weapons technology and tactics to these challenges. Military encounters with European troops and navies, as

---

[22] Kennedy, *Great Powers*, p. 12.
[23] Cipolla, *Guns, Sails, and Empires*, p. 98. Cf. Victor Davis Hanson, *Carnage and Culture: Landmark Battles in the Rise of Western Power* (New York, 2001), pp. 254–55, where he claims that "the Ottomans increasingly looked westward, not merely for additional slaves and plunder but also for European weaponry and manufactured goods."
[24] Arthur Goldschmidt, *A Concise History of the Middle East* (Boulder, CO, 2002), p. 140. Although the notion of "Ottoman decline" resurfaces from time to time in the generalist literature, very few students of the Empire would adhere to the traditional notion of decline nowadays. See Douglas A. Howard, "Ottoman Historiography and the Literature of 'Decline' of the Sixteenth and Seventeenth Centuries," *Journal of Asian History* 22, 1 (1988), 52–77; Douglas A. Howard, "With Gibbon in the Garden: Decline, Death and The Sick Man of Europe," *Fides et Historia* 26, 1 (1994), 22–34; Linda Darling, *Revenue-Raising and Legitimacy: Tax Collection and Finance Administration in the Ottoman Empire, 1560–1660* (Leiden, 1996), pp. 1–21; Cemal Kafadar, "The Question of Ottoman Decline," *Harvard Middle Eastern and Islamic Review* 4, 1–2 (1997–98), 30–75.
[25] Bernard Lewis, *Muslim Discovery of Europe* (London, 1982; reprint 1994), p. 223; Bernard Lewis, *What Went Wrong? The Clash between Islam and Modernity in the Middle East* (New York, 2002), p. 13.

well as contraband trade in weaponry, fostered the diffusion of military technology and know-how. When Ottoman technological receptivity was coupled with mass-production capabilities and superior Ottoman logistics, the Sultans' armies gained clear firepower superiority over their immediate European opponents by the mid-fifteenth century. Comparative data presented in the following chapters suggest that the Ottomans were able to maintain their firepower and logistical superiority against the Austrian Habsburgs and Venetians until the very end of the seventeenth century.

Chapter 2 also demonstrates that European–Ottoman military acculturation did not end in the sixteenth century. When at the end of the century Ottoman leaders realized that the Europeans outperformed the Sultan's soldiers in the use of hand-held firearms on the Hungarian front, the Grand Vizier and a clear-sighted observer both advocated the more massive use of firearms and encouraged the introduction of adequate countermeasures in tactics, along with suggestions for restructuring the army. The employment of European military experts (captives, renegades and adventurers) by the Ottomans continued into the eighteenth century. Since there were no revolutionary innovations in European firearms technology until the very end of the eighteenth century, the continuous (if somewhat delayed) transfer of European technology and know-how, and, more importantly, the Ottomans' logis-tical strength, were sufficient for keeping pace with Europe until the end of the seventeenth century.

Chapter 3 examines the weapons the Ottomans manufactured and used. The main objective of this chapter is to understand the bewildering terminology of Ottoman weapons and to offer a classification of Ottoman cannons that provides a basis for a comparative analysis of Ottoman and European cannons. Comparing Ottoman and European artillery pieces, the chapter challenges the notion that early modern Ottoman artillery was dominated by giant cannons, and shows that from the sixteenth through the eighteenth centuries the Ottomans used a large variety of cannons – from the smallest pieces that fired projectiles of 30–500 g to the largest *balyemez* and *şayka* guns of the cannon class firing shots of 31–74 kg in weight. In the fifteenth and early sixteenth centuries, while a number of exceptionally large bombards (hurling cut stones of more than 100 kg) were made and deployed in some of the Empire's key forts, medium- and small-caliber pieces were mostly pre-dominant in fortresses. Among the smallest pieces *şakalozes*, the Ottoman variant of the Hungarian *szakállas* and of the German *Hackenbüchse*, were the most popu-lar weapons – as were the *szakállas* in the Hungarian, Croatian and Austrian forts – and were the most practical and effective anti-personnel weapons deployed on both sides of the military border. Archival evidence demonstrates that the majority of Ottoman cannons designated as siege or battering guns (literally "castle-smasher" or *kale-kob*) were also considerably smaller pieces than is assumed in the gener-alist literature. Such guns fired projectiles of 15–20 kg in weight, and they are not only comparable to the European guns of the culverin/*Karthaun* class, but also were often smaller in caliber than some of the Spanish and Austrian siege cannons.

The most commonly used Ottoman "battering guns" (*darbzen*) fired shots of only 0.15–2.5 kg in weight. While the Ottomans – similarly to other Mediterranean nations – reserved some of their large stone-throwing pieces as center-line bow guns on their flagships, the majority of guns deployed aboard their galleons were small-caliber bronze pieces whose projectiles weighed between 3.7 and 8.6 kg. Most of the guns aboard the boats of the Ottoman river flotillas consisted of even smaller cast-iron guns that weighed only 20–40 kg and fired projectiles of usually less than 500 g.

In short, comparisons of Ottoman and Habsburg mortars as well as of Ottoman, Spanish and Venetian siege cannons and shipboard artillery suggest that Ottoman and European weapons were more similar than had been assumed. Since in the sixteenth and seventeenth centuries the Ottomans had continued to cast their large- and medium-caliber pieces of bronze – mainly because the Empire possessed abundant copper ore deposits – their guns were not only lighter than the cast-iron Austrian, Spanish or English pieces of similar caliber, but also safer. A comparative study of Ottoman hand firearms used by the Janissaries, that is, the Sultans' elite infantry troops, shows that they were similar to the muskets the Ottomans' Spanish and Venetian opponents used. For instance, the Ottomans adopted the Spanish *miquelet* lock. Despite these similarities, however, the chapter also reveals important differences, and argues that one field where the Ottomans lagged behind their European opponents was the lack of standardization. While standardization was hardly accomplished by the Europeans in general, the Austrians, and especially later the Russians, had considerably fewer caliber types within a certain class than the Ottomans did. This certainly made supply of ammunition a more difficult task in the Empire, and also hindered tactical reforms.

Chapters 4, 5 and 6 are devoted to the study of the Ottoman weapons industry: saltpeter and gunpowder manufacturing, and cannon casting. These chapters question the "dependency theory," which claims that the Ottomans failed to establish an indigenous arms industry capable of meeting the needs of the Sultan's army. According to Keith Krause the Ottomans were "third-tier producers" and "relied heavily on imported weapons and technologies."[26] Others have suggested that after the battle of Lepanto (1571), which saw the (almost total) destruction of the Ottoman navy and shipboard artillery, the Ottomans became more and more dependent on foreign, especially English and Dutch, imports of weaponry and gunpowder. When the channels of this arms trade clogged up in the 1660s, the Ottoman troops and navies experienced difficulties in their supply. This in turn led

---

[26] Krause, *Arms and the State*, pp. 48–52. These views are repeated by Jonathan Grant who claims that the Ottomans remained a "third-tier producer" country through the eighteenth century and possessed capabilities only comparable to their similarly "third-tier producer" immediate rivals (Hungary, Poland, and the medieval Balkan states). See his "Rethinking the Ottoman 'Decline': Military Technology Diffusion in the Ottoman Empire, Fifteenth to Eighteenth Centuries," *Journal of World History* 10, 1 (1999), 179–201. Geoffrey Parker in his earlier works also suggested that the Ottomans "experienced difficulty in mass-producing." However, in light of new research he modified his views and this statement was removed in the 1999 edition of his book. See Parker, *The Military Revolution*, p. 126 (in both editions).

to the decrease of Ottoman military abilities to wage war and this corresponded "with the beginning of decline in Ottoman naval fortunes."[27]

Based on unpublished production output accounts of the saltpeter and gunpowder works in Asia Minor, the Middle East and the Balkans, as well as on the account books of the Imperial Cannon Foundry in Istanbul, I argue that the Empire had abundant supply of those raw materials needed for the production of gunpowder and cannon. More importantly, the Ottomans were successful in creating the necessary organizational, industrial and financial frameworks capable of ensuring a prompt and efficient supply of raw materials to their gunpowder works and cannon foundries. These organizational and financial frameworks, and the ability of the Ottoman central and local authorities to adjust them according to the changing socio-economic conditions, enabled the Ottomans to achieve self-sufficiency in armament production and to maintain it for centuries – indeed, in certain sectors of the arms industry well into the eighteenth century.

Following an overview of saltpeter and sulfur deposits in Europe and the Ottoman Empire, chapter 4 examines the various forms of Ottoman saltpeter production. While the chapter gives the most comprehensive mapping of Ottoman saltpeter deposits to date, its main emphasis is on the various methods by which Istanbul supplied this most crucial ingredient of gunpowder. Sub-sections devoted to the *ocaklık* or service villages, and to the "Ottoman military entrepreneurs" constitute in the context of ammunition production the first attempt in the literature to understand the actual functioning of such crucial methods of Ottoman resource mobilization as the *ocaklık* and the *iltizam* systems. It is hoped that detailed examination of the *ocaklık* system – a widely used method by which the Istanbul government procured funds, labor and material for its industries and paid its garrisons – and of the tax-farms or *iltizam*s in the context of saltpeter and gunpowder production, will broaden our knowledge regarding this complex and not fully understood feature of Ottoman financial and economic history. While this study convincingly demonstrates that Ottoman saltpeter industries were generally able to provide this most important ingredient of gunpowder to the Ottoman gunpowder works, chapter 4 also indicates that by the seventeenth century there occurred important changes regarding the means by which the state procured the required amounts. The percentage of saltpeter supplied by the *ocaklık* or service villages declined considerably, forcing Istanbul to acquire more and more saltpeter from the domestic market, purchased at market price. This in turn was well in line with the general development of the Ottoman economy that was characterized by increased monetarization.[28]

Chapter 5 examines Ottoman gunpowder production and demonstrates that in the sixteenth, seventeenth and eighteenth centuries – a period during which the

---

[27] Rhoads Murphey, "The Ottoman Attitude towards the Adoption of Western Technology: The Role of the Efrencî Technicians in Civil and Military Applications," in Jean-Louis Bacqué-Grammont and Paul Dumont eds., *Contributions à l'histoire économique et sociale de l'Empire ottoman* (Leuven, 1983), pp. 292–93.

[28] On which see Şevket Pamuk, *A Monetary History of the Ottoman Empire* (Cambridge, 2000).

Ottoman Empire covered an area of more than 1.5–2.5 million square kilometers and extended from Buda to Basra – gunpowder was produced in almost all of the principal provinces. The chapter answers many of the questions regarding Ottoman production capabilities, as well as the quality of powder produced in the Empire. It demonstrates the Ottomans' self-sufficiency during the sixteenth and seventeenth centuries and shows that production levels adequately met the Empire's needs until the mid-eighteenth century. However, production levels then dropped considerably and from that point onward the Empire was forced to import ever larger quantities of powder from Europe. At the end of the eighteenth century, though, the government had reorganized powder production and modernized its gunpowder works, an undertaking that resulted again in establishing self-sufficiency.

Chapter 6 is devoted to the study of the Ottoman gun-founding technology and production capabilities. It overviews the major ore deposits and mining centers of the Empire, and concludes that in the sixteenth and seventeenth centuries the Empire was self-sufficient in copper, lead and iron, and had only to import tin. From the 1680s, however, even lead had to be bought from outside sources. In terms of cannon casting and the production of cannon balls, all available evidence suggests that the Empire managed to establish a robust ordnance industry that was capable of satisfying the needs of the Ottoman army and navy. The chapter also demonstrates that although Istanbul remained the major center of cannon casting in the sixteenth and seventeenth centuries, in the fifteenth and early sixteenth centuries *in situ* production was still important and the output levels of some of the provincial foundries could rival that of the Istanbul foundry. Archival evidence disproves the notion of the Ottomans' inability to mass produce and their supposed third-tier producer status. It also challenges the idea regarding ostensible Ottoman technological inferiority suggested by Eurocentric historiography.

While the concluding chapter briefly summarizes the evidence regarding the similarities and differences in the contemporaneous Ottoman and European military hardware, it suggests that differences in gun casting and gunpowder production had no significant ballistic effects. It contends that slight European technological superiority alone did not matter when the Ottomans could compensate for it with their enormous resources, remarkable production volumes and better logistics. In the sixteenth century the Ottomans' nearly inexhaustible human and economic resources enabled them to gain logistical and firepower superiority not only over their Muslim adversaries (such as the Mamluks in Egypt and the Safavids in Persia) but also over the Hungarians, the Austrians and the Venetians. In response to this Ottoman superiority the Austrian Habsburgs modernized their military and defense systems, and deployed more infantry firepower and artillery along their Ottoman frontiers. In this context, the Ottoman Turks were not slow and imperfect recipients of the "superior western" military technology and tactics, as most historians of the Eurocentric school maintain; rather they were important participants in the dynamics of organized violence in the Euro-Asian theater of war. This book suggests that understanding Ottoman weapons technology and war industry capabilities in a comparative framework will tremendously enhance our appreciation not only of the strengths and weaknesses of the Ottoman Empire, but also those of the Ottomans' European and Middle Eastern adversaries.

About the sources

Human, motivational and psychological dimensions of Ottoman warfare, as well as methods of combat and siege warfare, can be reconstructed from chronicles, most of which are either accessible in print or can be obtained from European and Turkish manuscript libraries. To collect quantitative data in large enough numbers on the basis of which one can construct broad generalizations regarding technology, industrial capability or logistics, requires frequent and prolonged research in the Ottoman archives. This study is based on such research. I have examined the hitherto neglected account books of the Ottoman gunpowder works and that of the Imperial Cannon Foundry in Istanbul.[29] Similar registers of some of the Ottoman copper and iron mines in the Balkans and Asia Minor, as well as inventories of weaponry and ammunition of major Ottoman fortresses from such diverse regions of the Empire as Hungary, the Balkans, Crete and Iraq, have also been used. Although some of the registers may contain errors, an attempt has been made to check and when needed correct their data. The utilization of large amounts of data from consecutive years covering crucial periods of Ottoman military engagements (also comparative data from relatively "peaceful" years) helped to reconstruct the major trends regarding both quantitative and qualitative issues of the Ottoman ordnance industry.[30]

Most of the accounts prior to the mid-seventeenth century may be found in the Finance Department's (Maliye) collections, for which no detailed catalogues have been published. The accounts were copied into registers several hundred pages in length that contain a wide range of financial records. The typewritten summary catalogues contain merely a few lines about these lengthy registers. As a consequence, researchers must examine each register from cover to cover, in order to find even a few pages of relevant accounts of the Empire's saltpeter and gunpowder works or cannon foundries and mines. The situation is more favorable from the second half of the seventeenth century on, because the accounts of the most

---

[29] These sources are either summary or detailed accounts and contain the following sets of data: (1) monetary receipts and deliveries of raw materials (saltpeter, sulfur, charcoal, copper and tin) and the fuel-wood; (2) the sources of the raw materials and the methods through which the workshops acquired them; (3) the quantity of gunpowder produced and the number and types of cannons cast; (4) raw materials that remained in stock; and (5) the quantity and the destination of deliveries of powder and ordnance. The more detailed accounts usually contain lists of tools and equipment that were used in the workshops.

[30] While summary data upon which my conclusions are based appear in the main text along with data that were used for illustrative purposes, the majority of the detailed figures are presented in the Appendix.

important gunpowder works and that of the Imperial Cannon Foundry survived among the holdings of the Supreme Financial Supervision Office (Muhasebe-i Evvel or Başmuhasebe Kalemi), which was responsible for controlling the afore-mentioned accounts.

Most of our sources were written in *siyaqat*, a special form of Ottoman chancery script. Reserved for financial record-keeping, the *siyaqat* script's distinctive feature is the omission of diacritical dots on the Arabic letters. As a consequence, readings and interpretations of Ottoman words might often be open to discussion.[31] The difficulties of the *siyaqat* script are frequently exaggerated and until recently only a fraction of Ottomanist historians were able or willing to read documents written in *siyaqat*, for training in it was limited both in Turkey and elsewhere. However, any historian can master the necessary skills, and with some practice should be able to read most of the documents written in *siyaqat* with relative ease. The situation is more complicated when one deals with special terminology of hitherto neglected topics. Whereas students of Ottoman financial and economic history can safely rely on published tax registers and treasury account books from such diverse parts of the Empire as Hungary, the Balkans, Asia Minor or Palestine, as well as on an impressive body of secondary literature (including paleographical handbooks, special dictionaries and glossaries of terms), researchers dealing with the Ottoman armaments industry are left largely alone with their difficulties in deciphering and understanding their sources. However, available documentary studies about European weapons technology and arms production as well as the collective wisdom of researchers working in the Istanbul archives not only were of great help, but made the task more enjoyable. I am thankful to all of my colleagues who at various points of my research offered suggestions and educated guesses, or challenged my readings and interpretations.

---

[31] Lajos Fekete, *Die Siyaqat-Schrift in der türkischen Finanzverwaltung* (2 vols., Budapest, 1955).

CHAPTER 2

Gunpowder technology and the Ottomans

Knowledge of gunpowder and firearms spread quickly within Euro-Asia, either by direct encounters with the Chinese or by way of trade. The Mongols were already acquainted with gunpowder and gunpowder-based devices starting from the 1230s, and from the mid-thirteenth century on they were instrumental in introducing these devices into Central Asia, Iran, Iraq and Syria. Firearms proper, however, probably were not used in Central Asia before the latter part of the fourteenth century.[1] By the reign of Shahruh (1405–47), the successor of Timur (or Tamerlane) who ruled over Transoxania, parts of Persia, Afghanistan and Azerbaijan, firearms were not only used in the region, but also manufactured there. In fact, the Timurids seem to have followed the general trend of the era. In 1434–35, a cannon founder by the name of Farruh cast a giant piece that is said to have fired huge cut-stone balls weighing at least 320 kg.[2]

References to early use of firearms in Islamdom (1204, 1248, 1274, 1258–60, 1303 and 1324) must be taken with caution since terminology used for gunpowder and firearms in late medieval Arabic sources is confused. Furthermore, most of these testimonies are given by later chroniclers of the fifteenth century whose use of terminology may have reflected their own time rather than that of the events they were writing about. While David Ayalon has concluded that artillery appeared in the Mamluk Sultanate only in the 1360s, recent research suggests that certain references to Granadan siege weapons in the 1320s and 1330s may be interpreted as cannon proper, although the evidence remains inconclusive.[3]

---

[1] See A. M. Belinickii, "O poiavlenii i rasprostaneii ognestrel'nogo oruzhia v srednei Azii i Irane v XIV–XVI. vekah," *Izvestiia Tadzhiskogo Filiala Akademii Nauk SSSR* 15 (1949), 21–35; Iqtar Alam Khan, "Coming of Gunpowder to the Islamic World and North India: Spotlight on the Role of the Mongols," *Journal of Asian History* 30, 1 (1996), 44.

[2] Belinickii, "O poiavlenii i rasprostaneii," p. 25. The weight of the shot is given as 400 *männ*. As all weights, the *männ*, too, varied from region to region. I calculated it against the standard *männ* in Iran and Asia Minor (799 or 834 g), and 400 *männ* = 320 or 333 kg. See Notes on weights and measurements.

[3] David Ayalon, *Gunpowder and Firearms in the Mamluk Kingdom: A Challenge to a Mediaeval Society* (London, 1956; 2nd edition, London, 1978), pp. 1–44. Cf. Weston F. Cook, Jr., *The Hundred Years War for Morocco* (Boulder, CO, 1994), pp. 60–66; G. S. Colin, "Barud," in *EI*, vol. I, pp. 1057–58; Ahmad Y. al-Hassan and Donald R. Hill, *Islamic Technology: An Illustrated History* (Cambridge, 1986), pp. 113–20.

Authorities agree that it was in Europe that the importance and advantages of firearms proper were fully recognized and where the new weapon made its most remarkable career, affecting the nature of organized violence for centuries to come. More importantly for our purposes, it was also the European countries that played the most significant role in the transmission of gunpowder technology to the Ottoman Empire and which, in the course of the sixteenth, seventeenth and eighteenth centuries, stimulated technological and military adjustments in the Empire, either via direct military conflicts or through a common pool of experts and by way of weapon trading.

Early references to the Europeans' use of guns (1284, 1313, etc.) are as uncertain as similarly early testimonies regarding the "first" use of firearms in other societies. However, it is generally accepted that guns appeared in European campaigns and sieges in the 1320s and 1330s. By the beginning of the fifteenth century shipboard artillery was also common, though guns may have appeared earlier on ships.[4] These early guns, however, were too small and too imperfect to cause any significant physical destruction, and it was not until the mid-fifteenth century that large wrought-iron and cast bronze cannons proved to be effective in siege warfare.[5]

The diffusion of firearms in the Ottoman Empire

Most of the earliest dates (1354, 1364, 1386 and 1389) with regard to the supposed use of firearms by the Ottomans, too, remain disputable, for these dates are usually single-sourced and are mentioned by chroniclers who wrote several generations after the events (Aşıkpaşazade d. after 1484, Neşri d. before 1520, Kemalpaşazade d. 1534 and Şikari d. 1584), and therefore may have projected the terminology of their own times when referring to earlier events.[6] Credible evidence suggests that

[4] There are several problems with the early references to shipboard artillery and many of the early dates (1336, 1338, 1340, etc.) suggested by Carlo Cipolla, Philippe Contamine, Fernand Braudel and others have recently been challenged. See John Francis Guilmartin, Jr., "The Early Provision of Artillery Armament on Mediterranean War Galleys," *The Mariner's Mirror* 59, 3 (1973), 259; Kelly R. DeVries, "A 1445 Reference to Shipboard Artillery," *Technology and Culture* 31, 4 (1990), 818–29.

[5] Carlo M. Cipolla, *Guns, Sails, and Empires: Technological Innovation and the Early Phases of European Expansion 1400–1700* (New York, 1965; reprint New York, 1996), pp. 21–22; Bert S. Hall, *Weapons and Warfare in Renaissance Europe: Gunpowder, Technology, and Tactics* (Baltimore, 1997).

[6] The earliest references are reviewed in Colin Heywood, "Notes on the Production of Fifteenth-Century Ottoman Cannon," in *Proceedings of the International Symposium on Islam and Science, Islamabad, 1–3 Muharrem, 1401 A. K.* (November 10–12, 1980), Islamabad, Government of Pakistan, Ministry of Science and Technology, 1981, pp. 58–61; reprinted in Colin Heywood, *Writing Ottoman History: Documents and Interpretations* (Aldershot, 2002), article XVI, pp. 3–9; V. J. Parry, "Barud," *EI*, vol. I, p. 1061; Gábor Ágoston, "Ottoman Artillery and European Military Technology in the Fifteenth to Seventeenth Centuries," *AOH* 47, 1–2 (1994), 19–26. Despite problems regarding the credibility of single-sourced data, Turkish historians seem to accept most of the earliest dates, however untrustworthy they may be. See, among others, Mücteba İlgürel, "Osmanlı Topçuluğun İlk Devri," in *Hakkı Dursun Yıldız Armağanı* (Ankara, 1995), pp. 285–93.

the Ottomans may have been acquainted with gunpowder weapons in the 1380s, that is, some sixty years after firearms had appeared in Western European sieges. Whereas the Central Asian and the Arab channels of transmission of firearms technology cannot be ruled out, the Balkans appears to have been the region that played the most crucial role in the diffusion of gunpowder technology to the Ottoman Empire. Having to face enemies already in possession of firearms facilitated the Ottomans' decision to adopt the new weapon.

Gunpowder weapons arrived in the Balkans from Italy with the Venetian–Hungarian rivalry over the Dalmatian coastal towns. Sources indicate that bombards were employed in the siege of Zara (Zadar, Iadra) in 1346, when Venice temporarily re-conquered the Dalmatian town from Hungary. Gunpowder weapons are first mentioned in Ragusa (Dubrovnik) in 1351, and in 1362–63 a local smith manufactured several small firearms called *spingarda*.[7] By 1378, guns had become regular weapons in the defense of the city, and Ragusa had soon acquired the status of a major center of firearms production in the peninsula from which other Balkan states got their guns. By 1380, gunpowder weapons were fairly commonly used in Bosnia, which, unlike Serbia, enjoyed prosperity and strength in the latter part of the century under King Trvotko I (r. 1353–91). The Serbians, whose empire broke up into several smaller units after the death of Uruš (r. 1355–71), imported guns from Venice in the 1380s, but started to manufacture their own firearms in the 1390s.[8] Besides the Balkan states, Byzantium also knew about the new weapon and firearms had been used there before the end of the fourteenth century (1390 and 1396–97), although most of these weapons were of Genoese origin.[9]

In the transmission of gunpowder technology from the Balkans to the Ottomans during direct military conflicts, Serbian and other vassal contingents from the peninsula fighting alongside the Ottomans, as well as trade in weaponry, played a role. Given the relatively small size of these early weapons, smuggling and transporting them would not have been a problem.[10]

It appears that in the first battle of Kosovo (1389), only the Ottomans' Christian opponents used firearms. However, at least two separate sources refer to the use of firearms by the Ottomans during the long-running siege of Constantinople between 1394 and 1402.[11] They used cannons against the walls of the city again in 1422, though unsuccessfully, and in 1430 in the siege of Salonica with success, but the new weapon gained tactical significance only in the 1440s, when the Ottomans fought several wars against the Hungarians. By this time, the Ottomans possessed cannons in some of their Balkan forts (such as Silistre and Niğbolu), and it was also

---

[7] Ágoston, "Ottoman Artillery," 21–22.

[8] Djurdjica Petrović, "Fire-arms in the Balkans on the Eve of and After the Ottoman Conquest of the Fourteenth and Fifteenth Centuries," in V. J. Parry and M. E. Yapp eds., *War, Technology and Society in the Middle East* (London, 1975), pp. 168–78.

[9] Mark C. Bartusis, *The Late Byzantine Army: Arms and Society, 1204–1453* (Philadelphia, 1992), pp. 335–36.

[10] The smallest bombards in Ragusa were 16–40 cm in length and the smallest *spingardas* weighed only 14 kg. See Petrović, "Fire-arms," pp. 173; Ágoston, "Ottoman Artillery," 22.

[11] Petrović, "Fire-arms," pp. 172–75.

around this time when they first used field artillery. In 1444, Ottoman artillerists "gave a hard time" to the Burgundian ships that tried to prevent the Sultan's Asian troops crossing into Europe at the Dardanelles, indicating that by this time Ottoman gunners were able to use their weapons not only against city walls and fortresses but also against such moving targets as galleys.[12]

We do not know when the Ottomans started to use guns aboard their ships. According to a Venetian report, the Ottomans had some sort of a fleet by 1374. An important further development was the conquest of the Turkish maritime principalities of Aydın and Menteşe under Bayezid I (r. 1389–1402) and the expertise the shipbuilders and sailors of these principalities provided the Ottomans with.[13] By the 1390s, the Ottomans possessed their first naval dockyards in Gelibolu (Gallipoli), initially with two pools for the construction of vessels.[14] The Ottomans also realized the importance of the Danube, and by the 1430s kept "a good hundred *fustas*" or smaller oared warships at Güvercinlik (Galambóc/Golubac) on the Danube below Belgrade, "for use in their incursion into Hungary."[15] Since the Hungarian forts, against which the Ottomans used these vessels, were "well furnished with" artillery, it can be assumed that the Ottomans too used some ordnance aboard their *fustas* which, when in Venetian hands, usually carried two or three small cannons.[16] Given later examples – such as the siege of Belgrade in 1456 – it can also be suggested that in this early phase of Ottoman shipboard artillery the weapons were used in amphibious warfare, which was these weapons' most common form of use aboard flotillas on the Danube, the Black Sea and the Mediterranean.

Although the Sultan possessed several giant cannons, his troops also valued mobility and through their wars against the Hungarians in the 1440s the Ottomans became acquainted with Christian battlefield artillery and the *Wagenburg* tactic. The *Wagenburg* or "wagon fortress," first used by the Hussites in Bohemia during the Hussite wars (1419–36), was a defensive arrangement of "war wagons" chained together, wheel to wheel. It was manned with crossbow-men and hand-gunners and was protected by heavy wooden shielding and by light artillery against cavalry assault. Altogether, 600 wagons, operated almost entirely by Czech mercenaries, were reported to have been employed in János Hunyadi's Balkan campaign of 1443–44 against the Ottomans. Such a mass employment of armed wagons and the *Wagenburg* tactic must have made quite an impact upon the Sultan's generals

---

[12] Parry, "Barud," p. 1061; Heywood, "Notes on the Production," pp. 3–9; from the earlier literature see Paul Wittek, "Appendix II: The Earliest References to the Use of Firearms by the Ottomans," in Ayalon, *Gunpowder and Firearms*, pp. 141–43. The Appendix, or a substantial part of it, was prepared by Vernon Parry, Wittek's former student and later colleague. Cf., Heywood, " Notes on the Production," p. 3, n. 5.

[13] Kate Fleet, "Early Turkish Naval Activities," in Kate Fleet ed., *The Ottomans and the Sea, Oriente Moderno,* 20 (81) n.s. 1 (2001), 132–35.

[14] By 1403 there were forty vessels in the Gelibolu arsenal. See Halil İnalcık, "Gelibolu," *EI,* vol. II, p. 984; Colin H. Imber, "The Navy of Süleyman the Magnificent," *ArchOtt* 6 (1980), 236; İdris Bostan, *Osmanlı Bahriye Teşkilatı: XVII. Yüzyılda Tersane-i Amire* (Ankara, 1992), p. 15.

[15] Heywood, "Notes on the Production," p. 8.   [16] Ibid.

and soldiers.[17] An anonymous contemporary Ottoman chronicle indicates that the Ottomans quickly learned how to besiege the *tabur*, that is, the Christian wagon camp, so named in Ottoman sources after the Hungarian *szekértábor*. In the battle of Varna (November 10, 1444), the Ottomans defeated the Crusaders' army and captured the Christian war wagons and weapons and acquired a strong knowledge of the *Wagenburg* tactics.[18] While the speed with which the Ottomans adapted their way of fighting to the new tactic of their Christian adversaries is remarkable, it should not surprise us, for the *Wagenburg* tactic was not that dissimilar from the Turks' Central Asian fighting traditions. Later, Ottoman experts introduced the *tabur cengi* or "the camp battle," that is, the new technique which relied on these war wagons, to the Safavids and Mughals, who called it *destur-i Rumi*, the Ottoman order of battle.[19] In the latter part of the sixteenth century, Lazarus Freiherr von Schwendi, the commander of the imperial forces in Hungary during the years from 1564 to 1568, observed that the Ottomans could use the *Wagenburg* system very successfully against his forces and that the Sultan's soldiers owed their military success to the *tabur*. Consequently, he urged the Emperor's troops to use war wagons, armed with double arquebus as well as with small cannons.[20]

It is possible that the Ottomans, like their Hungarian opponents, also used hand-held firearms on their wagons. Fifteenth-century Ottoman chroniclers mention *tüfenks* or handguns[21] with regard to events that had taken place in 1421, 1430 and 1442–44,[22] and *tüfenks* appear in weapons registers in the newly conquered Balkan fortresses around the mid-fifteenth century (e.g., 1455: Novoberda/Novo Brdo; 1468: Güvercinlik/Galambóc), though these weapons are likely to have been of western origin as were most of the soldiers who initially handled them.[23] Despite such early references, it is clear from our sources that small firearms became widely used only in the latter part of the fifteenth century, and that their usage was usually confined to siege warfare.

---

[17] Gábor Ágoston, "15. Yüzyılda Batı Barut Teknolojisi ve Osmanlılar," *Toplumsal Tarih* 18 (1995), 12–13.

[18] *Gazavât-i Sultân Murâd b. Mehemmed Hân İzladi ve Varna Savaşları (1443–1444) Üzerinde Anonim Gazavâtnâme*. Ed. Halil İnalcık and Mevlud Oğuz (Ankara, 1987), pp. 59–60, 68.

[19] Parry, "Barud," p. 1062 and Halil İnalcık, "The Socio-Political Effects of the Diffusion of Fire-arms in the Middle East," in Parry and Yapp, *War, Technology and Society*, p. 204.

[20] Vernon J. Parry, "La maniere de combattre," in Parry and Yapp, *War, Technology and Society*, p. 224.

[21] Known as early as 1075, the word *tüwek* originally meant "a blowpipe used to kill birds with small pebbles." Wittek, "The Earliest References," p. 143. From the mid-fifteenth century on, the term *tüfenk* was used as a general term for handguns referring to the arquebus and, later, to the musket.

[22] The early references are readily available in Mustafa Cezar, *Osmanlı Tarihinde Levendler* (İstanbul, 1965), pp. 156–58; Mücteba İlgürel, "Osmanlı İmparatorluğunda Ateşli Silahların Yayılışı," *TD* 32 (1979), 301.

[23] However, Muslim arquebusiers or *tüfenkçis* were already employed in these early years: in Novoberda their number (ten) matched that of the Christians. See Olga Zirojević, *Tursko vojno uređenje u Srbiji, 1459–1683* (Belgrade, 1974), p. 136. By the middle of the sixteenth century, Muslim *tüfenkçis* outnumbered their Christian colleagues in the Balkan and Hungarian fortresses. See Ágoston, "Ottoman Artillery," 27.

Ottoman archival sources provide further, although indirect, evidence for the Ottomans' early use of gunpowder weapons. On the basis of a cadastral survey, Halil İnalcık was able to date back the existence of cannoneers or *topçus* in the Empire to the reign of Çelebi Mehmed I (r. 1413–21). More recently, Idris Bostan found a summary *timar* register that mentions a *timar* revenue that had been given to a certain Ömer *topçu* in the time of Sultan Bayezid I (r. 1389–1402). Bostan is of the opinion that this indicates that Ottoman artillerists had already been organized into units under Bayezid I.[24]

While this might well be the case, the above piece of information – and similar sources that could possibly be unearthed in the future – suggests an even more important development. By the 1390s, the Ottoman central government had, on a permanent basis, employed cannoneers or *topçus* who possessed the necessary skills to handle these early guns. To remunerate these artillerists, the Ottoman government used the *timar* system, a well-known method of Ottoman resource mobilization and redistribution that also financed the provincial *timariot* cavalry, which – at least until the end of the sixteenth century – comprised the bulk of the Ottoman armed forces. Alongside these *timariot* cannoneers, the Ottoman government would, within a generation or so, employ *topçus* paid in cash and would make them an integral part of the Sultan's permanent household forces. While some of them were assigned to the most strategically important forts of the Ottoman realms, the main contingents of the permanent artillery corps were stationed in the Empire's center, along with other branches of the Sultan's standing army. As a consequence, the Ottoman artillery corps could be deployed by the Sultan with relative ease and swiftness. All this was in sharp contrast to most of the Ottomans' European opponents. In Europe, artillerists formed a transitory social category between craftsmen and soldiers and were usually hired by the state on a temporary basis to handle the weapons during campaigns. Their transformation from craftsmen to professional soldiers was closely related to a long evolutionary process that took place between 1500 and 1700, a process that has been labeled the emergence of the European fiscal-military state and of the standing army, one of the fiscal-military state's main instruments.[25]

There is nothing surprising regarding the somewhat belated Ottoman acquaintance with, and employment of, firearms. In the time when firearms were first used in European sieges, that is, during the 1320s and 1330s, the Ottoman principality was a rather negligible polity, even in a regional context. Historians should not

---

[24] İdris Bostan, "XVI Yüzyıl Başlarında Tophane-i Amirede Top Döküm Faaliyetleri," manuscript, to be published in the forthcoming Halil İnalcik *Festschrift*. See also Bostan, "A szultáni ágyúöntő műhelyben (Tophane-i Amire) folyó tevékenység a 16. század elején," *Aetas* 18, 2 (2003), 6. (My thanks to the author, who forwarded a copy of his article prior to its publication.)

[25] William H. McNeill, *The Pursuit of Power: Technology, Armed Force, and Society since AD 1000* (Chicago, 1982); Geoffrey Parker, *The Military Revolution: Military Innovation and the Rise of the West, 1500–1800* (Cambridge, 1988; rev. 3rd edition, 1999); Jeremy Black, *War and the World: Military Power and the Fate of the Continents, 1450–2000* (New Haven and London, 1998); Jan Glete, *War and the State in Early Modern Europe: Spain, the Dutch Republic and Sweden as Fiscal-Military States, 1500–1660* (London and New York, 2002).

be fixated on the often dubious references to the "first" use of firearms. The real question is not when firearms were first used but, rather, when they were employed effectively enough to have significant impact on the outcome of military conflicts. This did not happen until around the middle of the fifteenth century. By that time, the Ottomans were not only using the new technology routinely but, as the conquest of Constantinople in 1453 illustrates, were among those who did this with often notable efficacy. Ottoman cannoneers not only excelled in destroying the city's walls, thought to be impregnable, but also showed remarkable ship-killing skills when they effectively blocked the Dardanelles and the Bosporus.

We should not overestimate the role of early gunpowder technology. The change in military technique was slow to take root and new weapons were competing with old ones for decades everywhere in Europe; however, it is also true that cannons and hand firearms were the weapons of the future. The procurement of firearms and their ammunition, as well as the creation of specialized troops trained to handle the new weapons, was a major challenge that late medieval monarchs and societies had to solve if they wanted to remain players in the international political scene. In this regard, the Ottomans showed remarkable success, not least because of the flexibility of early Ottoman society and the pragmatism of its rulers. The assimilation of gunpowder technology into the Ottoman military and navy, the creation of a professional infantry equipped with hand firearms and the establishment of the Ottoman artillery corps are clear examples of this pragmatism and flexibility.

Integration of firearms into the Ottoman military

Handguns and the Janissaries

In the early years of the Ottoman state, the main constituent elements of the Ottoman army were the ruler's military entourage or guard, the cavalry troops of Türkmen tribes which had joined forces with the Ottomans and those peasants who had been called up as soldiers for military campaigns. The members of the military entourage – who were designated by the word *kul* or *nöker* – were the forerunners of the Sultans' salaried troops that by the fifteenth century had become the pillar of the Ottoman military organization. The troops of the Türkmen tribes that were in alliance with the Ottomans received a share of military booty and were granted the right to settle on conquered lands. In return, they had to provide men-at-arms in proportion to the amount of benefice in their possession. Later they became the *timar*-holding *sipahis*, that is, members of the provincial cavalry army whose remuneration was secured through prebends and who constituted another pillar of the Ottoman army.

Since the salaried troops of *kuls* and the cavalry contingents proved too few in number to fulfill the needs of a growing state, young volunteer peasant boys were taken on. These youths later formed the infantry *yaya* and cavalry *müsellem* units.

While during the campaigns they were paid by the ruler, at the conclusion of the campaign season they returned to their villages. The numerous campaigns soon required that this third component of the early Ottoman army be made permanent: the voluntary nature of the force was therefore abandoned and conscription was introduced during the military campaigns.[26]

Under Murad I (r. 1362–89) numerous changes were made in the organization of the salaried troops. These changes did not, however, affect the *timar*-holding *sipahi* cavalry that remained the bulk of the Ottoman army throughout the period under discussion. The *müsellems* were slowly replaced by the palace horsemen (who were also called *sipahis*) and the *yayas*' place was taken by the *azabs* – a kind of peasant militia serving as foot soldiers during campaigns, as well as in fortresses and on ships – and by the Janissaries. As a result, by the mid-fifteenth century the *yayas* and *müsellems* gradually became auxiliary forces, charged, respectively, with the restoration of military roads and bridges for the marching army, and, after the spread of cannons, with the transportation of ordnance.[27] The most significant measure was the establishment of the Janissary corps, the paid household infantry of the Sultans, and the creation of specialized corps for the manufacturing and handling of firearms.

The Ottomans recognized from the start that they needed to establish an independent army, a force that would stand above the various religious, cultural and ethnic groups. Such a force was provided by the Janissaries, the new army (*yeni çeri*), which was financed by the treasury and remained under the direct command of the Sultan. The replacement of Janissaries (and later of the members of the artillery corps and other specialized technical troops of the standing army) was ensured by the *devşirme* (collection) system, introduced probably also during the reign of Murad I. Under this system Christian males between fifteen and twenty years of age were periodically collected and then Ottomanized. Subsequently, they were trained for government service or eventually became members of the salaried central corps of the Sultan. The regulations concerning the *devşirme* were extensive and circumspect with regard to the physical and mental conditions of the youth, as well as their social status.[28] The *kul-devşirme* system created the highest and

---

[26] Halime Doğru, *Osmanlı İmparatorluğunda Yaya-Müsellem-Taycı Teşkilatı: XV. ve XVI. Yüzyılda Sultanönü Sancağı* (Istanbul, 1990), pp. 2–8.

[27] In addition, it was common for both corps to be employed in the mines where they were casting cannon balls. See Doğru, *Osmanlı İmparatorluğunda* pp. 8–13; Gyula Káldy-Nagy, "The Conscription of the Müsellem and Yaya Corps in 1540," in Káldy-Nagy ed., *Hungaro-Turcica: Studies in Honour of Julius Németh* (Budapest, 1976), pp. 275–81.

[28] Certain ethnic groups – like the Hungarians and Croatians or those who lived in the regions between Karaman and Erzurum – were excluded from the collection of *devşirme*. The Hungarians and Croatians were considered unreliable, while those belonging to the second group were suspicious because they were mixed with Georgians, Türkmens and Kurds. As for the restrictions: the officials charged with the collection of Christian boys could not gather the only child of a family, for the head of the household needed the son's help with cultivating his land in order to pay taxes to the *sipahi*. Similarly, they were not supposed to collect the sons of the village headmen "as they belonged to the lower classes"; the children of shepherds and herdsmen "as they had been brought up in the mountains so they were uneducated"; the boys of craftsmen since they did not fulfill their pledge for

most loyal pillars of support for the House of Osman. The Janissaries represented the corner-stone of the centralizing political technology of the Ottoman Sultans and provided the ruler with a permanent armed force well before similar standing armies were established in Western Europe.[29] This was an important development, for the Sultans using the Janissaries and the salaried cavalrymen of the Porte could claim a monopoly over organized violence, in sharp contrast to their European counterparts who had to rely upon and negotiate with local power-holders when they wanted to deploy armies that were operationally effective. It was especially true regarding the Austrian Habsburgs, the Ottomans' main adversary in Central Europe, who – following unsuccessful experiments under Maximilian I (1493–1519) – possessed the first permanent troops of any importance during the Thirty Years War (1618–48). Although some 15,000–20,000 men (nine infantry and ten cavalry regiments) were kept together after the war, it is generally accepted that the Habsburgs established their standing army only under Leopold I (r. 1658–1705).[30]

As already noted, the Janissaries, who numbered 2,000 in the first battle of Kosovo (1389) and were all equipped with bows,[31] started to employ hand firearms (designated by the general term of *tüfenk/tüfeng/tüfek* in our sources) under Murad II (r. 1421–51), but the number carrying handguns increased only towards the end of the fifteenth century. It seems that it was not until around the mid-sixteenth century that most of the Janissaries carried firearms. While the number of these troops was 12,000 in the early 1520s, only 3,000–4,000 arms-bearing Janissaries participated in the campaign against the Egyptian rebels in 1523. In the 1526 Hungarian campaign only 2,000 of them, under the command of the Grand Vizier, were armed with *tüfenks*.[32] It is likely that most of the Janissaries

soldier's pay; and the married boys, because their "eyes had been opened, and those cannot become the *kul* of the Padishah." Likewise, excluded from the child-levy were the orphans, because they were opportunist and undisciplined; those who were not in perfect health (e.g., were "cross-eyed"); those who spoke Turkish or were circumcised, for they could have been Turks and Muslims and thus their relatives could have demanded tax exemptions; those who were too tall or too short, because they were considered stupid and trouble-makers, respectively; and those who had been to Istanbul, for they did not have a sense of shame. *A janicsárok törvényei*. Trans. Pál Fodor (Budapest, 1989), pp. 6–10. Cf. also Colin Imber, *The Ottoman Empire, 1300–1650* (New York, 2002), pp. 134–42; Mücteba İlgürel, "Yeniçeri," *İA*, vol. XIII, pp. 385–95.

[29] This is not to say that European monarchs did not experiment with standing armies. In France, for example, Charles V (r. 1363–80) and later his grandson Charles VII (r. 1423–61) both established standing armies. However, these attempts brought only limited and temporary success. Based on the provincial nobility, the loyalty of these armies was often questionable: they frequently lapsed after the death of the king and they had to be supplemented by mercenaries. See James B. Collins, *The State in Early Modern France* (Cambridge, 1999), pp. 14–15.

[30] Eugen Heischmann, *Die Anfänge des stehenden Heeres in Österreich* (Vienna, 1925); Jürg Zimmermann, *Militärverwaltung und Heeresaufbringung in Österreich bis 1806. Handbuch zur deutschen Militärgeschichte, 1648–1939* (3 vols., Frankfurt am Main, 1965), vol. III, pp. 45–51; Philipp Hoyos, "Die kaiserliche Armee 1648–1650," in *Der Dreißigjährige Krieg* (Vienna, 1976), pp. 169–232; John A. Mears, "The Thirty Years' War, the 'General Crisis,' and the Origins of a Standing Professional Army in the Habsburg Monarchy," *Central European History* 21, 2 (1988), 122–41.

[31] Gyula Káldy-Nagy, "The First Centuries of the Ottoman Military Organization," *AOH* 31 (1977), 165.

[32] İbrahim Peçevi (Peçuylu), *Tarih-i Peçevi* (2 vols., Istanbul, 1283/1866–67), vol. I, pp. 78, 85. Cf. also Cezar, *Levendler*, p. 159. However, archival documents suggest that the number of *tüfenks*,

had firearms in the 1532 campaign. Based on information gathered from Turkish captives, a German pamphlet published in August 1532, presumably in Vienna, claimed that of 10,000 Janissaries present in the campaign some 9,000 were equipped with handguns, whereas the remaining 1,000 had only pole-arms.[33]

Venetian sources claim that it was only Sultan Murad III (r. 1574–95) who equipped all the Janissaries with muskets, although it is possible that this meant only the introduction of a new type of firearm. The Janissaries' traditional weapon, the recurved bow, remained an important and formidable weapon well into the seventeenth century, although the ratio of bows to muskets had changed significantly by the mid-1600s. For example, during the 1663–64 Hungarian campaign 10,982 *tüfenks* and only 861 bows (together with 56,530 arrows) were distributed to the troops from the Imperial Armory.[34] While the numbers might not include all the small firearms and bows used during the campaign, they certainly reflect the general picture, which is also corroborated by battle and siege narratives of the war.

The Janissaries' firepower, especially in the early sixteenth century, often proved to be fatal for the Ottomans' adversaries. These elite troops of the Sultan could fire their weapons in a kneeling or standing position without the need for additional support or rest, as is visible on a miniature depicting the battle of Mohács in 1526. From a contemporaneous Ottoman chronicle we learn that, during this battle, the Janissaries formed nine consecutive rows and they fired their weapons row by row. They were so effective that most European and Ottoman sources on Mohács attributed the Ottomans' success in the battle to the Janissaries' firepower and not to the cannons, in sharp contrast to later historians who usually claim that it was the Ottoman artillery that decided the fate of the Hungarians.[35]

According to existing regulations, the Janissaries had to practice twice a week to familiarize themselves with their *tüfenks*, but it seems that the drill had been abandoned by the beginning of the seventeenth century. Writing around 1606, the author of *The Laws of the Janissaries* (*Kavanin-i Yeniçeriyan*) was complaining that the members of the corps were no longer given powder for the drills and that the soldiers used the wick for their candles and not for their muskets.[36] On the other hand, it is apparent from other sources that, at least before

and perhaps that of *tüfenk*-bearing soldiers, could have been somewhat higher even in the early 1520s, especially in crucial military enterprises. An inventory of weapons and material that was transported to Rhodes in May 1522 lists 4,500 small *tüfenks* and 1,000 larger ones to be used on boats, as well as 4,800,000 and 150,000 bullets appropriate for each, respectively. Cf. Nicolas Vatin, *L'Ordre de Saint-Jean-de-Jérusalem, l'empire ottoman et la Méditerranée orientale entre les deux sièges de Rhodes (1480–1522)* (Paris, 1994), pp. 484, 488.

[33] István Bariska ed., *Kőszeg ostromának emlékezete* (Budapest, 1982), p. 121.
[34] MAD 3279, p. 175, data refer to the period from March 25, 1663 through June 24, 1664.
[35] Most of the Ottoman, Hungarian and western sources are conveniently available in Károly Kis ed., *Mohács Emlékezete* (Budapest, 1987). That the Janissaries were deployed in nine rows is mentioned by Celalzade Mustafa (d. 1567). Their firepower is emphasized by, among others, the Hungarian eyewitness István Brodarics (d. 1537), who also noted that the cannons did no harm to the Hungarians since their shots landed behind them. The miniature is reproduced in ibid., after p. 196.
[36] *A janicsárok törvényei*, p. 108.

major campaigns, the Janissaries did practice with their muskets.[37] Istanbul also urged the provincial governors to continue the shooting practices and to examine thoroughly the shooting skills of all the Janissaries serving in their respective provinces.[38]

While such orders from the 1560s and 1570s can be interpreted as signs of a more common problem, namely the deterioration of old Janissary discipline and skills, it is worth noting that European military commanders who fought against the Janissaries still respected their military prowess. Lazarus Freiherr von Schwendi, who was earlier quoted regarding the Ottomans' use of *Wagenburg* tactics and who was one of the best experts on the Ottoman military of his time, noted that the Janissaries, although having longer arquebuses than their adversaries in the Habsburg army, handled their weapons adroitly. Therefore, he emphasized the importance of arquebus as a counter to the Janissaries. He advised the Habsburg Emperor to enroll Spanish and Italian arquebusiers as well as "Schützen zu Ross," that is, horsemen equipped with this weapon.[39] Others seconded his views. In 1577, at a military conference in Vienna, most experts were of the opinion that "for the time being, hand firearms are the main advantage of Your Majesty's military over this enemy (i.e., the Ottomans)."[40] From the 1570s onwards the Austrian Habsburgs modernized their military along their Croatian and Hungarian frontiers using experience gained by the Spanish armies fighting in Flanders, troops considered by historians to be at the leading edge of contemporaneous military art. The proportion of Habsburg infantry soldiers carrying firearms while fighting in the Long Hungarian War of 1593 through 1606 against the Ottomans is said to have been as high as in the army of Flanders, in certain units even higher.[41] Even though the sources – the *Bestallungen* or recruitment contracts that stipulated the desired composition and equipment of troops intended to be hired – upon which such observations are based should be treated with greater skepticism, they signaled a change in deployed Habsburg firepower which the Ottomans were quick to notice. Hasan Kafi al-Akhisari (d. 1616), who participated in the battle of Mezőkeresztes in 1596, the single major field battle of the war, complained in his treatise – composed soon after the battle – that the Imperialists used the most modern types of arquebus and cannon and showed a distinct advantage over the Ottomans.[42] Other contemporaneous Ottoman observers made similar remarks. The Ottoman chronicler Selaniki Mustafa Efendi contended that the Ottomans "could not withstand

[37] AK, fol. 55a, regarding the preparations for the 1596 Hungarian campaign.
[38] MD 12, p. 209, no. 440, orders sent in 1571 to the governors of Van, Erzurum, Şehrizol, Baghdad, Basra, Damascus and Lahsa.
[39] Parry, "La manière de combattre," p. 225.
[40] Cf. István Geőcze, "Hadi tanácskozások az 1577-ik évben," *HK* 7 (1894), 658.
[41] József Kelenik, "The Military Revolution in Hungary," in Géza Dávid and Pál Fodor eds., *Ottomans, Hungarians, and Habsburgs in Central Europe: The Military Confines in the Era of Ottoman Conquest* (Leiden, 2000), p. 154, where he seems to place too much confidence in his sources.
[42] Mehmet İpşirli, "Hasan Kâfî el-Akhisarî ve Devlet Düzenine ait Eseri Usûlü'l-hikem fi Nizâmi'l-âlem," *TED* 10–11 (1979–80), 268. Also quoted from an older German translation by Parry, "La manière de combattre," p. 228.

Table 2.1 *Increase in the number of Janissaries*

Fiscal year	Number of Janissaries
1514	10,156
1526	7,886
1567–68	12,798
1609	37,627
1660–61	54,222
1665	49,556
1669	51,437
1670	49,868
1680	54,222

Sources: Gábor Ágoston, "Ottoman Warfare in Europe, 1453–1812," in Jeremy Black ed., *European Warfare, 1453–1815* (London, 1999), p. 135. The figure for 1514 is from Ömer Lütfi Barkan, "H 933–934 (M 1527–1528) Mali Yılına ait Bir Bütçe Örneği," *İFM* 15, 1–4 (1953–54), 312. The figure for 1680, given by Luigi Ferdinando Marsigli, *Stato Militare dell' Imperio Ottomano* (2 vols., Amsterdam, 1732.), vol. I, p. 68, may have been copied from an earlier Ottoman register.

the musketeers from Transylvania." In 1602, the Grand Vizier reported from the Hungarian front to the Sultan that "in the field or during a siege we are in a distressed position, because the greater part of the enemy forces are infantry armed with muskets, while the majority of our forces are horsemen and we have very few specialists skilled in the musket."[43]

The Ottoman government attempted to counterbalance in two ways. First, they increased the number of Janissaries armed with muskets. Second, they established formations of arms-bearing infantry troops generally known as *sekban, sarıca* and *tüfenkendaz,* hired from among the vagrants of the subject population, the *reaya* musketmen, and usually designated in the sources as *levend.*[44] The increase in the numbers of the Janissaries was quite significant.

Such increases, however, led to a decrease in quality of these elite troops. In addition, the salary burden was a source of financial distress in an empire that faced continuous treasury deficits from the early 1590s and already suffered from a cash-flow problem. Whereas the treasury had to pay all on the muster rolls, only a fraction of the Janissaries – 21,000 troops in 1697, for instance[45] – was actually mobilized for campaigns. On the other hand, during campaigns commanders could count on those who served in the provincial fortresses. Their numbers were significant,

---

[43] Cengiz Orhonlu, *Osmanlı Tarihine Aid Belgeler: Telhisler (1597–1607)* (Istanbul, 1970), pp. 70–71, nos. 60, 81. Quoted in English by İnalcık, "The Socio-Political Effects," p. 199.

[44] Caroline Finkel, *The Administration of Warfare: The Ottoman Military Campaigns in Hungary, 1593–1606* (Vienna, 1988), pp. 37–48.

[45] MAD 2731, p. 187, which is an account of 2,100 pack horses allocated to 21,000 Janissaries mobilized for the campaign.

especially in such strategically important forts as, say, Baghdad, Buda, Temeşvar, Özi and Kandiye or Hanya.[46]

The establishment of the *sekban* companies was to have other drawbacks in the longer term. As a result of the economic and social changes of the sixteenth century, details of which are still the subject of scholarly debate, thousands of peasants became deprived of home and country, and many of these became outlaws possessing firearms – despite all efforts on the part of the state to ban or restrict their use. During the Iranian and Hungarian wars the Istanbul government welcomed with open arms soldiers who knew how to use firearms and who could be recruited for a campaign or two and then discharged. However, these *sekbans* did not return to their villages after the campaigns. Instead, they joined the bandits or supported the uprisings in Anatolia, contributing to the general disorder and economic dislocation in the Empire.[47]

While the direct connection between the Hungarian wars and the so-called Celali revolts in Asia Minor is difficult to prove,[48] the war did have an important if indirect effect on the Ottoman military: Habsburg firepower increased the demand for firearms and for men-at-arms able to use them. However, the steps taken in response to the Habsburg challenge in Hungary did more to weaken the Empire's military capability in the long run than strengthen it. The swelling of the ranks of the Janissaries led to the decline of discipline and fighting skills. The employment of *sekban* and *tüfenkendaz* companies did not help to improve discipline and build troop cohesion either, as can be seen from the desertion of such troops at the battle of Mezőkeresztes in 1596. Furthermore, the need for *sekban* companies with firearms that were manufactured outside the state's control certainly did not facilitate the government's policy to curb the spread of firearms among its subject population, the *reaya*. The proliferation of firearms and the formation of bands of demobilized musketmen considerably weakened the state's ability to control violence.[49]

Nevertheless, the extent of Ottoman difficulties during the war should not be overstated. Desertion occurred on the Habsburg side, too. In 1596, during the siege of Eger, some 250 Christian soldiers defected from the garrison and "fled to the Sultan's camp and became Turk." In the summer of 1600, some 400–500 French and Walloon mercenaries of the garrison of Pápa offered their services to the Sultan,

---

[46] MAD 2732, pp. 5–19, gives the following figures for 1697–98: Baghdad: 3,352; Damascus: 406; Van: 755; Kerkük: 343; Temeşvar: 2,501; forts in Bosnia: 428; Bender: 357; Özi: 945; Limni: 204; Midilli: 179; Sakız: 218; Eğriboz: 2,043; Kandiye: 1,732; Hanya: 1,151; Resmo: 564; and so forth.

[47] Cezar, *Levendler*; William J. Griswold, *The Great Anatolian Rebellion, 1000–1020/1591–1611* (Berlin, 1983); Karen Barkey, *Bandits and Bureaucrats: The Ottoman Route to State Centralization* (Ithaca and London, 1994).

[48] İnalcık saw a direct connection between the Celali rebellions and the Long War in Hungary, but Caroline Finkel demonstrated that the majority of *sekbans* taken on in the war were not from Anatolia but from Bosnia and from Albania and therefore could not have been involved in the Anatolian rebellions. See Halil İnalcık, "Military and Fiscal Transformation in the Ottoman Empire, 1600–1700," *ArchOtt* 6 (1980), 283–337; Finkel, *Administration*, pp. 39–46.

[49] On which see Gábor Ágoston, "Az európai hadügyi forradalom és az oszmánok," *Történelmi Szemle* 4 (1995), 465–85.

whereas in 1601 several Italians fled to the Ottomans.[50] The employment of these European infantry musketmen during the remaining years of the war in Hungary and, later, at the mouth of the Danube against the Cossacks (in 1607) and in the eastern front against the Safavids (in 1610) offered further opportunities for the Ottomans to acquaint themselves with the latest European infantry tactics. Ottoman difficulties notwithstanding, the Sultan's troops did win the only significant battle of the war at Mezőkeresztes in 1596, which should cast some doubt on the effectiveness of Habsburg reforms and on the supposed decisiveness of increased Habsburg infantry firepower.

More importantly, the war was dominated by siege warfare in which the Ottomans still had the upper hand, as illustrated by the conquest of several Hungarian castles, including two modernized key forts (Eger and Kanizsa in 1596 and 1600, respectively). Apart from cavalry skirmishes, which remained a dominant feature of frontier life throughout the sixteenth and seventeenth centuries, major and medium-scale campaigns continued to be characterized by siege warfare, in which the Ottomans proved to be quite successful, not least because of the performance of the Ottoman artillery corps.

The artillery corps

It is not clear when the Ottoman artillery corps (*topçu ocağı*) was organized. If we consider that sources unearthed so far mention merely *timariot topçus* from the reigns of both Sultan Bayezid I (r. 1389–1402) and Çelebi Mehmed I (r. 1413–21), it is likely that a separate artillery corps as part of the salaried standing army was established only later, under Sultan Murad II (r. 1421–51),[51] well before such artillery units became an integral part of the armies of Europe. It appears that the unit of the gun carriage drivers or *top arabacıları* was established only in the second half of the fifteenth century. In the 1473 campaign against Uzun Hasan, the Ottomans had used carriages to transport certain types of ordnance, preceding the French who were the first in Western Europe to introduce mobile land carriages for heavy ordnance at the end of the century. In 1514, 372 gun carriage drivers were paid by the central treasury, which indicates that by that time the unit had become an integral part of the artillery corps.[52]

[50] Caroline Finkel, "French Mercenaries in the Habsburg–Ottoman War of 1593–1606," *Bulletin of the School of Oriental and African Studies*, 55, 3 (1992), 451–71; Péter Sahin-Tóth, "À propos d'un article de C. F. Finkel: Quelques notation supplémentaires concernant les mercenaires de Pápa," *Turcica* 26 (1994), 249–60.

[51] According to İsmail Hakkı Uzunçarşılı, the *topçu ocağı* was established under Murad I (r. 1362–89) or somewhat later. See Uzunçarşılı, *Osmanlı Devleti Teşkilatından Kapukulu Ocakları*, II: *Cebeci, Topçu, Top Arabacıları, Humbaracı, Lağımcı Ocakları ve Kapukulu Suvarileri* (Ankara, 1984), p. 36.

[52] Ömer Lütfi Barkan, "H 933–934 (M 1527–1528) Mali Yılına ait Bir Bütçe Örneği," *İFM* 15, 1–4 (1953–54), 312. The assertion that the unit of the *top arabacıs* was established as early as the end of the fourteenth century (Uzunçarşılı, *Cebeci, Topçu*, p. 97) is not tenable on the basis of current knowledge.

While the gun carriage drivers were responsible for transporting Ottoman ordnance to the battlefront, another unit called the *cebecis* or armorers had to take care of the Janissaries' bows, arrows, sabers, muskets, gunpowder, wick, musket bullets, and all the necessary trenching tools (pickax, shovel) the Janissaries needed during sieges. It was the *cebecis* who transported the weapons and tools to the front, distributed them to the Janissaries before the military engagements, and gathered them after the battle or siege. They were also responsible for the manufacturing, storage and repair of the weapons.[53] Among them there were craftsmen who were specialized in making muskets, gunpowder, shields and so forth.[54] In addition to Janissary weapons and trenching tools, the head of the *cebeci* corps (*cebeci başı*) was often charged with the task of providing the miners, sappers and various craftsmen who participated in the campaign with adequate tools.[55] He also supervised the making and storing of grenades, hand grenades and other ammunition – except, of course, cannon balls and gunpowder for cannons – and it was he who authorized their delivery.[56] When the task was urgent and the *cebecis* needed more workers in the workshops, they were given novices and war captives to help them.[57] The armorers were armed with firearms and participated in battles and sieges. They had other military obligations during campaigns, such as safeguarding river routes[58] and shipments of arms and gunpowder.[59]

It is difficult, in the absence of credible records, to ascertain when the corps of armorers was established, but it is assumed that it took place during the fifteenth century, perhaps under Mehmed II. The *cebecis* were part of the Sultan's salaried central troops and until the deterioration of the *devşirme* their recruitment was assured through this system. While the majority of the armorers were stationed in Istanbul, many served in the Empire's garrisons, usually for three-year terms, after which they were recalled to the capital, like the Janissaries, gunners and gun carriage drivers.[60] Some of them were paid from the central treasury and received their grain supplies also from the local state granary.[61] Others were paid from the provincial treasury or were remunerated with *timar* revenues of neighboring

---

[53] Uzunçarşılı, *Cebeci, Topçu*, pp. 3–12.   [54] MAD 7539, pp. 52, 57; DPYM 35132, p. 16.

[55] MD 74, p. 260, no. 675, ordering the *cebeci başı* to transport the necessary tools for 250 craftsmen and sappers, including 10 architects (*mimar*), 3 specialists responsible for repairing water conduits (*su yolcu*), 40 smiths (*demürci*), 87 masons and carpenters (*benna ve neccar*), 100 sappers (*lağımcı*) and 10 saw-makers (*erre-keşan*) who had been appointed for the 1596 campaign.

[56] MAD 9879, p. 13.

[57] AE Mehmed IV, no. 1119, regarding the provision of biscuits (*peksimed*) for 150 captives (*esir*) in the armorers' barracks in August 1674.

[58] AK fol. 52a, where he mentions that in the 1596 Hungarian campaign 1,000 *cebecis* were safeguarding the Danube.

[59] MAD 3527, p. 28, regarding 115 *cebecis* who guarded the shipment of gunpowder sent from Istanbul to Belgrade in the summer of 1685.

[60] MD 77, p. 74, no. 253, an order that recalled (in November 1605) the *top arabacıs* of İstolni Belgrad since they had completed their three-year service.

[61] MAD 2732, p. 4, records that seventy *cebecis* of the Porte in the defense of the fortress of Temeşvar in 1600–01 were given, from the state granary (*anbar-i miri*), 0.5 *kile* wheat per month per person, equal to 12.8–20.5 kg, depending on the type of *kile* the locals used.

Table 2.2 *The size of the Ottoman artillery corps, 1514–1769*

Date	1514	1527	1567	1574	1598	1609	1660	1669	1687	1698/99	1702	1738/39	1769
Topçu	348	695	1204	1099	2827	1552	2026	2793	4949	4604	1269	7279	1351
Top arabacı	372	943	678	400	700	684	282	432	670	1074	470	2274	180
Cebeci	451	524	789	625	3000	5730	4180	4789	3503	9629	2462	9877	3691
Total	1171	2162	2671	2124	6527	7966	6488	8014	9122	15307	4201	19430	5222

Note: Abdülkadir Efendi claims that for the 1593 Hungarian campaign 2,000 *cebecis* were appointed (AK fol. 5a); their number was raised to 3,000 for the 1594, 1596 and 1604 campaigns (AK fol. 20a, 57b, 191b). He gives the number of *top arabacıs* in the 1604 campaign as 150 (fol. 191a). His figures for gunners are 1,000 for 1593, 2,000 for 1596 and 1,700 for 1604 (ibid.). Before major campaigns Janissary novices were allocated to the gunners and armorers, as in 1596 when 150 novices (*acemi oğlan*) were given to them (AK fol. 59b).

Sources: Uzunçarşılı, *Cebeci, Topçu*, pp. 21, 70, 107; Káldy-Nagy, "First Centuries," p. 169 (for 1514, 1527 and 1567); Murphey, *Ottoman Warfare*, p. 45 (for 1574, 1609 and 1669); MAD 136 and AK (for 1598); DPYM 35162, pp. 5–7 (for 1698/99); DPYM 35218 (for 1738/39); DPYM 35273 (for 1769).

villages in the given province. Judging from available treasury accounts, theirs was the most numerous unit within the artillery corps.

Although payroll registers and central treasury records did contain errors, not least because the salaries of deceased soldiers were duly collected by their comrades[62] – a well-known practice in all early modern armies – they still provide the best available figures for reliable estimates regarding the strength of the various units of the standing army. These sources are especially good at reflecting major trends. Vacancies in the corps were usually filled from among the *acemi oğlans* or Janissary novices,[63] whose number is recorded in the central treasury accounts. It is more difficult, and for the whole Empire impossible, to estimate the number of gunners in provincial forts when vacancies in their ranks were filled on an *ad hoc* basis from among the garrison soldiers (*hisar eri*).[64] However, it is essential that we take into consideration their number and that we note that the figures presented in Table 2.2 do not include those gunners, armorers and gun carriage drivers who were stationed in the provinces and who were either paid from local provincial treasuries or remunerated with *timar* revenues. Because of the nature of the relevant source material and the absence of related studies it is unfeasible to come up with educated guesses regarding these troops. However, it is obvious from available data that we are dealing with very significant numbers. In twelve forts of the province of Buda in 1549–50, that is, some six to eight years after these garrisons had been captured by the Ottomans, there were 250 gunners. More than half of them were serving in Buda (106) and Pest (30).[65] Such figures also exclude all those who

[62] MD 70, p. 27, concerning such a problem with regard to gunners, armorers and gun carriage drivers in 1592.
[63] MD 6, p. 186, no. 401, regarding twenty-five *acemi oğlans* who were given to the gunners. Cf. also MD 10, p. 80, concerning the need for novices in 1571.
[64] MD 26, pp. 76, 95, regarding one such instance in the fort of Güvercinlik in July 1574.
[65] Asparuch Velkov and Evgeniy Radushev eds., *Ottoman Garrisons on the Middle Danube* (Budapest, 1996), p. 27.

were remunerated by *timar* revenues. Thus, the total number of cannoneers must have been much higher, especially later in the century.[66] In Yanık (Győr), the most important fortress in western Hungary close to Vienna which the Ottomans held from 1594 through 1598 and which was regarded as the bastion of Vienna and the Reich when in Habsburg hands, there were no fewer than 1,915 *cebecis*, including 643 newly recruited ones in 1594–95.[67] These *cebecis* were probably paid from the central treasury, as were many of the cannoneers serving in provincial fortresses. While they performed crucial services in their respective forts, they could also have been mobilized during campaigns, especially when they numbered several hundred, which was indeed the case in the strategically important forts.[68]

As can be seen from Table 2.2, the number of cannoneers and armorers increased rapidly from the late sixteenth century and the highest figures correspond to major troop mobilizations during major military undertakings. The number of cannoneers almost doubled under Süleyman's reign, which saw a series of major sieges both in Hungary and in Iraq. It rose again markedly at the peak of the Long Hungarian War (1593–1606), when it almost tripled. Another significant increase occurred in 1669, at the height of the Cretan war (1645–69), and their number almost doubled again during the Long War against the Holy League (1684–99). After the peace treaties of Karlowitz (1699) and Istanbul (1700), however, it declined sharply, arriving again at the level of the 1560s and 1570s. It rose once more during the war against Russia and Austria (1736–39), but the figure was surprisingly low in 1769, which saw the second year of the protracted Russo-Ottoman war of 1768–74. Even more spectacular was the increase in the ranks of *cebecis*, whose number in 1609 was more than nine-fold the figure of 1567, and increased significantly in 1698–99 and 1738–39, which reflects their growing importance during the protracted wars against the Habsburgs and Russia.

The surprisingly low figures of the gun carriage drivers are difficult to understand, given the importance of the work performed by these troops during military operations. It can at least partly be explained by the practice of recruiting new carriage drivers during campaigns,[69] and assigning hundreds of auxiliary *yaya* and *müsellem* troops, as well as *yörük* nomads, captives and peasants to the *top*

[66] In the 1570s and 1580s gunners comprised, depending on the size and strategic importance of the fort, 6–16 percent of the garrison. The total number of troops in the province of Buda paid from the local treasury at the same time varied between 10,000 and 11,000. In the 1650s, in Kanije (Kanizsa) there were 89 gunners and 25 *cebecis*. MAD 2113; MAD 6188; MAD 4457; MAD 2843.
[67] MAD 6151, pp. 149, 160–86. While most of the *cebecis* must have arrived with the troops of the 1594 campaign, several of them were from neighboring forts or established relationships within a very short time. Peçevi, who gives their numbers as 1,000 to 2,000, stated that most of them, as with the Janissaries, were living with their wives and families in Peçuy, Koppan and İstolni Belgrad, that is, in forts and towns 100 to 250 km to the east and south of Yanık. In fact, Peçevi claimed that the fortress was retaken by the Habsburg forces with relative ease in 1598 because of their absence (and because of the drunkenness of those who were present). Peçevi, *Tarih*, vol. II, p. 211.
[68] MAD 4321, pp. 596–620, for example gives the following figures regarding the number of *topçus* in 1694–95: Belgrade: 556 (476 old and 80 new recruits); Azak: 246; Kandiye: 198; Hanya: 156; Eğriboz: 190; Temeşvar: 190, etc.
[69] DPYM 35161/51, regarding the 219 newly conscripted *top arabacıs* in June 1698.

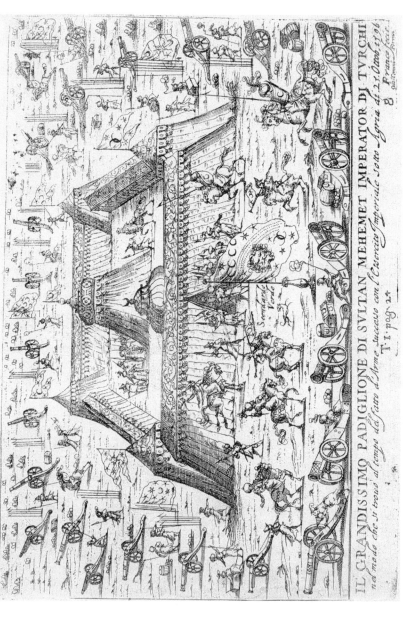

Figure 2 One of the tasks of Ottoman cannoneers was to protect the Sultan. Here the pavilion of Sultan Mehmed III at Eger (1596) is defended by Ottoman cannons. Notice the relative lightness of the cannons and their carriages. Engraving, published by Franco Giacomo.

arabacıs during campaigns in order to assist them in their strenuous task.[70] In addition, during campaigns craftsmen responsible for repairing carriage wheels and gun carriages were also helping them.[71] Also, it seems that it was not the *top arabacıs* but the officers (*çorbacıs*) of the cannoneers who were charged with the purchase of draft animals needed for the transportation of cannons. At least in certain cases when water buffaloes were purchased to pull the largest artillery pieces, further assistance came from shepherds who were hired for the duration of the campaign to take care of the animals.[72]

It is also clear that enrollment figures fluctuated considerably even within short periods of time according to military needs and availability of personnel. The number of gunners, for instance, was 4,604 in 1698–99, but rose to 5,084 by the next year. Of course, as in the case of the Janissaries, only a fraction of the gunners and armorers were mobilized for campaigns. For instance, there were 567 *topçus* and 2,110 *cebecis* in the returning army *en route* from Edirne to Istanbul in 1697,[73] whereas the figures regarding the total strengths of these corps were much higher (4,604 and 9,629, respectively) in the next year. While it is certain that many remained in Belgrade and Edirne, sources like this indicate that – as in the case of other troops – the Porte deployed only a fraction of their potential strength.

These difficulties notwithstanding, the overall numbers of the artillery corps are impressive, especially if one compares them with similar figures of the sixteenth- and seventeenth-century Spanish, Austrian and Russian armies. In 1563, the number of gunners in Spain was only 158, plus 50 staff and technical officers. Although by 1619 the figures increased to 297 and 92, respectively,[74] the Ottomans paid four times as many gunners as the Spanish government did. In Austria, the Viennese government had some 600 cannoneers on its payroll from the mid-1680s until the mid-1710s.[75] More numerous were the gunners in Russia, though available figures regarding the members of the artillery corps (*ludi pushkarskogo china*, or people of the cannon rank) are somewhat contradictory. The total number serving with the artillery was 4,215 in 1630, of whom about 2,700 were cannoneers (*pushkari*) and gunners operating smaller field pieces (*zatishniki*); it hardly changed until the mid-century (4,250 men in 1650), but it increased markedly to about 7,000 in the 1680s. However, one should note that the latter two figures included all

[70] MD 5, p. 304, no. 792; ibid., p. 305, no. 795, orders regarding the mobilization of the *Yörüks* of Selanik and Ofçabolu for the transportation and service of cannons for the 1566 campaign. Cf. also AK fols. 10b–11a.
[71] AK fol. 57b.
[72] MAD 3127, pp. 17, 26. In other instances, however, it was the head of the gun carriage drivers who was responsible for procuring horses needed for the cannons. MAD 2731, p. 188.
[73] MAD 2732, p. 4, is an account of expenditures dated October 30, 1697, regarding bread and other supplies for the gunners and armorers returning from the 1697 campaign.
[74] I. A. A. Thompson, *War and Government in Habsburg Spain, 1560–1620* (London, 1976), p. 340, n. 7.
[75] Anton Dolleczek, *Geschichte der österreichischen Artillerie von den frühesten Zeiten bis zur Gegenwart* (Vienna, 1887), p. 210.

Figure 3 During imperial campaigns hundreds of metric tons of gunpowder were shipped from the powder works to the theaters of war. Although for efficiency and economic reasons water transport was preferred, when it was not available powder and ammunition were transported on camels, horseback and on carts similar to these shown by Luigi Marsigli, *L'état militaire de l'empire ottoman,* 1732.

the servicemen within the artillery corps, not just cannoneers.[76] Another source asserts that the cannoneers numbered only 674 men in 1700, and that their number increased noticeably only in the eighteenth century: from 3,523 in 1712, to 12,937 by mid-century.[77] Compared with the Ottoman data, Austrian figures reflect possible Ottoman firepower superiority, which is, indeed, substantiated by other sources. Russian figures, on the other hand, signal a major shift in the balance of power between the two empires in the eighteenth century.

In the sixteenth century, Ottoman gunners, like the Janissaries, had to attend shooting drills, and it seems that a shooting-gallery (*talimhane*) was erected around 1572 in Istanbul.[78] The superiority of Ottoman gunners over their European adversaries is well illustrated by their record of capturing European forts with remarkable efficiency. For instance, between 1521 and 1566 only thirteen Hungarian garrisons were able to resist Ottoman sieges for more than ten days and only nine castles for more than twenty days. In this period only four fortresses were capable of withstanding Ottoman assaults (Kőszeg in 1532, Temesvár in 1551, Eger in 1552 and Szigetvár in 1556), but only Kőszeg was besieged by the main military force of the Sultan. Temesvár and Eger were attacked by the troops of the Grand Vizier, while Szigetvár was assaulted by the *beylerbeyi* of Buda. The defenders managed to withstand Ottoman sieges only if the siege started late in the year and the cold, rainy weather hindered the investment of the besiegers, as in 1551, when the siege of Temesvár started on October 17, a week before Ottoman troops were usually disbanded to their winter quarters for overwintering. It is then hardly a surprise that the siege lasted for only ten days. Another chance for the defenders was possible if the rescue forces arrived in time and attacked the besiegers, as in 1556 during the siege of Szigetvár. However, lack of troops and funds, as well as of political commitment on the part of Vienna, rendered such victorious defenses a rare occurrence in the sixteenth and seventeenth centuries, and brought only temporary success against the Ottomans. Three of the aforementioned fortresses were captured some years later – Temesvár in 1552, Szigetvár in 1566 and Eger in 1596 – a testimony that in the sixteenth century Ottoman siegecraft was superior to the Hungarian and Habsburg art of defense.[79]

Frequent sieges and defenses in Hungary and in the Mediterranean offered repeated opportunity for the Ottomans to remain informed about new developments in the art of European siegecraft. In connection with the 1596 siege of Eger, Ibrahim

[76] A. V. Chernov, *Vooruzhennye sily russkogo gosudarstva v XV–XVII vv* (Moscow, 1954), pp. 130, 167. It is also not clear whether these figures refer only to the central corps stationed in Moscow or also include the numbers of those serving in the towns and fortresses (*gorodovie pushkari*). Esper, who also gives the two latter figures, asserts that in the second part of the sixteenth century "there were three thousand men with the artillery." Cf. Thomas Esper, "Military Self-Sufficiency and Weapons Technology in Moscovite Russia," *Slavic Review* 28, 2 (1969), 193, 201.

[77] L. G. Beskrovnyi, *Russkaia armiia i flot v XVIII veke: Ocherki* (Moscow, 1958), pp. 43, 63.

[78] MD 10, p. 80, a decree sent to the Agha of Janissaries on December 16, 1571 commanded the addressee to find, in cooperation with the Şehremini, a suitable place for the purpose and to build the shooting-gallery.

[79] Marosi Endre, *XVI. századi váraink (1521–1606)* (Budapest, 1991), p. 32.

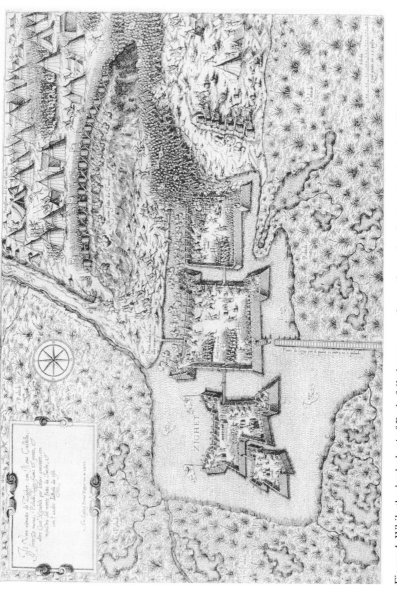

Figure 4 While the *beylerbeyi* of Buda failed to capture the partly modernized medieval castle of Szigetvár in 1556, Süleyman's forces took it on September 8, 1566, following a month-long siege. However, the Sultan did not see the surrender of the castle for he died on September 6. Notice the Ottoman siege batteries and their overwhelming firepower. The Siege of Szigetvár in 1566 by an unknown Italian artist (A. Lafreri?).

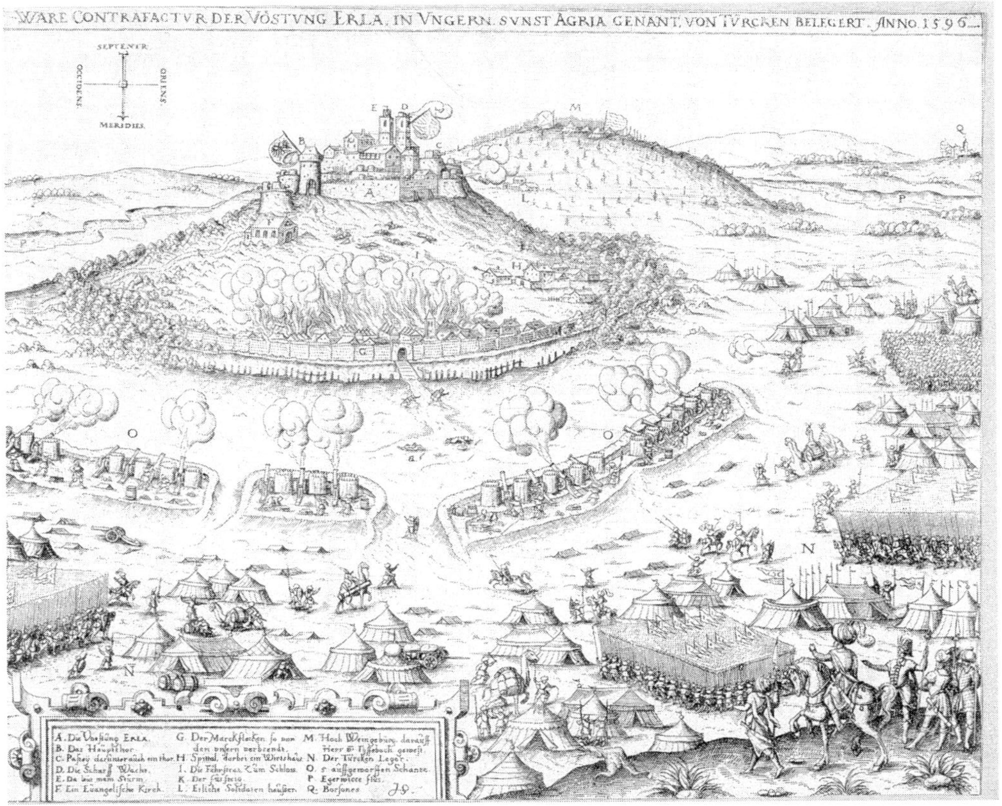

Figure 5 Although the castle of Eger was modernized and strengthened under the supervision of the Italian master-builder Ottavio Baldigara in the 1570s, hills towering above its eastern side rendered it vulnerable. The castle was conquered by Sultan Mehmed III's forces on October 13, 1596 following a three-week siege. The Siege of Eger in 1596 by Johann Sibmacher.

Peçevi, the Ottoman chronicler who spent a good deal of his life on the Hungarian frontier, recalled the firing techniques of his master, Mehmed Pasha, *beylerbeyi* of Anatolia. Mehmed Pasha was given eight battering guns (*kale kob*)[80] with which he besieged the fortress from the north. First he fired all the guns at the same time, aiming them at the very same point; then the guns were fired one by one, still aiming at the same point on the wall. The chronicler noted that Mehmed Pasha had learned this technique from the Christians during the 1595 siege of Estergon, and that other battering units followed his techniques.[81]

The Porte paid special attention to maintaining the fighting skills of its gunners, and ordered periodic examination of those serving in provincial garrisons. Those who had been found inept were to be replaced by trained gunners from the capital.[82] However, reports from various parts of the Empire indicate that local gunners, hired by fort commandants (*dizdars*) without thorough examination and without the approval of the head gunners, were often unskilled and had no knowledge of how to use properly the various types of ordnance at their disposal.[83]

It appears that by the late seventeenth century such complaints were more general and concerned not only the gunners serving in provincial fortresses but also those mobilized for campaigns. The situation was noticed by European observers too. Paul Rycaut stated that by then few of the *topçus* were "expert in their art" and were especially "ill practiced in the proportions and Mathematical part of the Gunners mystery." Therefore, "knowing their own imperfections in this exercise; when Christian Gunners are taken in the War, they entertain them with better usage than other Captives."[84] Such foreign experts did, indeed, continue to advise Ottoman gunners in the seventeenth century. In 1664, an English engineer "had supplied the most certain advantages for the progress of the Ottoman arms" in Hungary, whereas during the siege of Candia in Crete, an Italian gunner, named Cornaro, was helping the Turks.[85] Whether the transmission of possible new siege and defense techniques through such channels was still enough at the end of the seventeenth century is open to question.

[80] For the various types of Ottoman cannons see chapter 3.
[81] Peçevi, *Tarih*, vol. II, p. 193.
[82] MD 10, p. 269, no. 419, regarding the gunners in the forts in Cyprus (December 1570). Another order sent to the *beylerbeyi* of Erzurum in 1558 is reproduced in Uzunçarşılı, *Cebeci, Topçu*, p. 78.
[83] MD 28, p. 36, no. 86, and MD 31, p. 108, no. 265, orders regarding incompetent gunners in the fortress of Moton on the Morea in October 1576 and in July 1577, which indicate that the problem persisted for a while. A similar order sent to the *beylerbeyi* of Egypt in October 1577 commands that vacant posts of gunners in the fortresses of the province should, in the future, be given to qualified *topçus*. MD 28, p. 86, no. 205. Yet, one must take into consideration the possible distortion caused by the apparent tension between the *topçu başıs* and *dizdars* regarding the right and practice of appointing gunners. In addition to the above orders see also MD 5, p. 303, no. 788, concerning the situation in the fort of Bodrum in January 1566.
[84] Paul Rycaut, *The History of the Present State of the Ottoman Empire* (London, 1686), p. 200.
[85] Horatio F. Brown ed., *Calendar of State Papers and Manuscripts, Relating to English Affairs, Existing in the Archives and Collections of Venice, and in other Libraries of Northern Italy*, vol. XXXIII (London, 1932), p. 276, no. 379.

Bombardiers and miners

In addition to the cannoneers there were other specialized troops, most notably the bombardiers and sappers, whose service was indispensable during sieges. It is not known when the unit of the bombardiers or *humbaracıs*[86] was established but it could have happened either toward the end of the fifteenth century or in the sixteenth. It seems that the bombardiers did not comprise separate corps; instead they were allocated to the gunners and armorers. Those who operated the mortars firing bombshells belonged to the cannoneers, while those who were charged with the manufacturing of the bombs worked together with the *cebecis*.[87] While these were part of the salaried central troops and stationed in the capital in the barracks of the gunners and armorers, the majority of the bombardiers were *timariots*, that is, were remunerated by prebends and served in provincial garrisons. The number of bombardiers paid from the central treasury was rather modest compared with the cannoneers or armorers. Only fifty bombardiers were assigned to the Ottoman troops in the time of the 1594 and 1596 Hungarian campaigns that saw two significant and successful sieges, those of Győr and Eger, respectively, but they could obtain some assistance from the bombardiers serving in the border fortresses of Hungary.[88] Since the *humbaracıs* are missing from the best-known seventeenth-century works that give specific numbers of the various units of the Ottoman army (Ayni Ali, Tarhoncu Ahmed Pasha), it is assumed that by the seventeenth century the separate unit of the bombardiers within the Sultan's salaried central troops ceased to exist.[89]

On the other hand, it is known that salaried bombardiers served also in provincial border fortresses. Since they were often paid from local state revenues, such men are missing from the central treasury accounts, records on which Ayni Ali and others based their works. Furthermore, as noted, the majority of them received their salaries in the form of *timar* revenues. Whatever the case may have been, it seems that by the end of the seventeenth century many of them lacked the necessary skills. In June 1683, it was reported that the thirty salaried *humbaracıs* serving in Buda had no skills and knowledge in the art of *humbaracılık*, that is, in making and using bombshells. At the same time in Belgrade, all the four *timariot* bombardiers

---

[86] The word comes from *humbara* or *kumbara* (itself a loanword from Persian) meaning a bomb made of iron and containing explosive materials. The word *humbaracı* refers to those who fired these explosive shells from mortars, as well as to those who manufactured the bombs. Cf. also Uzunçarşılı, *Cebeci, Topçu*, p. 117.

[87] For instance, in 1687 the regiment (*cemaat*) of bomb-makers or bomb-casters (*rihteciyan-i humbara*) consisted of 21 casters of bombs, 344 powder-makers and 14 miners. Cf. Ahmet Halaçoğlu, "Humbaracı," *TDVİA*, vol. XVIII, p. 349.

[88] AK, fols. 20a, 57b. According to the roll-call register of 1549, there were eleven *humbaracıs* in Buda, three in Peşte and five in Vişegrad. Cf. Velkov and Radushev, *Ottoman Garrisons*, p. 27. Together with the *timariots*, the total number of bombardiers serving in Hungary at the time of the 1594 campaign could have matched that of the *humbaracıs* of the Sultan's household army mobilized for the campaign.

[89] Cavid Baysun, "Kumbaracı," *İA*, vol. VI, p. 982.

were reported to have been untrained.[90] The ineptitude of Ottoman bombardiers was also noticed by Marsigli. The reforms in the 1730s under the French renegade Claude-Alexandre Comte de Bonneval, known in the Empire as Humbaracı Ahmed Pasha, brought only limited success. The new corps of bombardiers was established by Ahmed Pasha in 1735, and it consisted of 300 Bosnians, trained and organized along western lines. Together with 300 *timariot* bombardiers, the total number of *humbaracıs* reached 600. Stationed permanently in the capital, the bombardiers and their officers were, for the first time in the history of the corps, trained in military engineering, ballistics and mathematics.[91] However, the corps was allowed to lapse after its founder's death in 1747, and was not revived until the more thorough military reforms under Selim III (r. 1789–1807), and especially under Mahmud II (r. 1808–39).

More numerous were the *lağımcıs*, that is, the miners and sappers, whose significance during sieges can only be compared to that of the cannoneers. Like the bombardiers, the sappers comprised two groups: those who served under the head armorers and belonged to the Sultan's salaried household army, and those who were stationed in the provinces and remunerated by *timars*. Their number fluctuated according to military needs and when it was considered insufficient, especially before major campaigns and sieges, miners and sappers from the Empire's mining centers were recruited for the job. When in 1453 Mehmed II realized that he had an insufficiently trained workforce to dig mines under the walls of Constantinople, he was bound to fetch professional miners from Novo Brdo in Serbia. Ottoman Novoberda, along with such well-known mining centers of the peninsula as Kratova, Srebreniçe or Zaplana, remained a valuable recruiting area for miners during sixteenth- and seventeenth-century campaigns.[92] In the sixteenth century the number of miners and sappers must have increased, for in the 1593 and 1596 campaigns 200 and 500 *lağımcıs*, respectively, were mobilized.[93] The seventeenth-century Ottoman traveler Evliya Çelebi claimed that in the late 1630s no fewer than 5,000 sappers lived in the capital, the majority of whom consisted of Armenians from Kayseri. Marsigli, too, pointed out that most of the miners and

---

[90] The phrase used in both cases is "humbara sanatında asla maharetleri ve malumatları olmayub." MAD 2931, p. 70. Cf. Meryem Kaçan Erdoğan, "II Viyana Seferi'nde Osmanlı Ordu'sunun Kullandığı Silahlar ve Mühimmatının Temini," in Güler Eren ed., *Osmanlı*, vol. VI (Istanbul, 1999), p. 664, who also used the document.

[91] These subjects were taught by, among others, another French renegade, Mühendis (Engineer) Selim, who while in France had been educated in military engineering and fortress building. See Mustafa Kaçar, "Osmanlı İmparatorluğunda Askeri Sahada Yenileşme Döneminin Başlangıcı," in Feza Günergun ed., *Osmanlı Bilimi Araştırmaları* (Istanbul, 1995), pp. 209–25; Abdülkadir Özcan, "Humbaracı Ahmed Paşa," *TDVİA*, vol. XVIII, pp. 351–53; Avigdor Levy, "Military Reform and the Problem of Centralization in the Ottoman Empire in the 18th Century," *Middle Eastern Studies* 18 (1982), 232.

[92] MD 5, p. 648, no. 1820, where the *kadıs* of Novoberda, Kratova, Srebreniçe, Vulçitrin, Blasniçe (?) and Zaplana are ordered to send trench-diggers and sappers in connection with the 1566 campaign.

[93] AK fols. 7a, 57b. On the other hand, an imperial order regarding the 1596 campaign mentions only 100 *lağımcıs* but this number referred only to those who were under the command of a certain architect, called İsmail. MD 74, p. 10, no. 25.

Figure 6 On October 7, 1594, a week after he had captured Győr (Raab), "the bastion of Vienna," Sinan Pasha besieged Komárom, the center of the Habsburg Danube flotilla and the second most important Hungarian fortress on the Danubian waterway leading to the Habsburg capital. Along with Ottoman cannoneers the Sultan's miners and sappers worked hard. However, the defenders constantly harassed them and their use of countermines rendered the Ottomans' labor inefficient, forcing the Pasha to abandon the siege on October 25, just before Kasim's day (October 26), which traditionally marked the end of the Ottoman campaign season. Engraving, published by Franco Giacomo (Giovanni).

sappers were Armenians, Greeks and other Christians from Bosnia.[94] Although in the seventeenth century the discipline of the Ottoman troops deteriorated compared with the previous century, it appears that within the technical corps the situation was better.[95] As for the skills of the sappers, Marsigli – who, while working in the Ottoman siege works as a captive in 1683, could observe them closely – praised the Sultan's Armenian miners, noting that they were not only more experienced and more industrious than their colleagues in the Austrian army, but also more effective. Unlike the sappers in the Habsburg army, these Ottoman-Armenian miners and sappers "were working in a sitting position," and "consequently they carried out the same work in just half of the time and with half of the effort" of their Christian counterparts.[96]

Given the importance of the art of siegecraft and of defense along the Empire's borders in the period under discussion, the service rendered by the Janissaries, gunners, armorers, bombardiers and sappers proved to be indispensable. This is true even if one recalls that during field battles and never-ending skirmishes cavalry forces dominated the engagements.[97] Indeed, it was the artillery and the mines that opened breaches in the walls of forts or demolished them, and it was the cannons, mortars and the Janissaries' firepower that broke the spirit of the defenders. Without them sieges and defenses were doomed to fail. It was also essential that the weapons be up to the job and that Ottoman cannoneers be informed about the latest developments in siege warfare. Despite claims to the contrary, it seems that, at least until the end of the seventeenth century, the Ottomans managed to keep pace with their European opponents in the art of siegecraft and defense. All this was possible because the Ottomans, contrary to allegations about their supposed "Islamic conservatism," remained receptive to new ideas and technologies and continued actively to participate in the technological dialogue of the time. Essential players in this dialogue were those craftsmen and military experts who, migrating from one place to another, shared their skills and spread new techniques, thus creating a fairly similar body of knowledge regarding the manufacturing and handling of firearms.

Foreign experts: the human pool of military acculturation

As with all thriving empires throughout history, the fifteenth- and sixteenth-century Ottoman Empire was a place that attracted people with all sorts of skills and agendas. This imperial appeal was further facilitated by the wealth and economic prosperity of the Empire, the splendor of its capital, the military successes of its rulers, the prospects for upward social mobility, and the relative tolerance shown

[94] Uzunçarşılı, *Cebeci, Topçu*, pp. 131–32.
[95] One indication of this is the low rate of desertion. In 1664, for instance, only eight sappers deserted and another eight failed to show up for the campaign. See MAD 3774, p. 130.
[96] Andrea Veress, *Il Conte Marsili in Ungheria* (Budapest, 1931), p. 26.
[97] On this see Parry, "La manière de combattre," p. 242; Murphey, *Ottoman Warfare*, p. 35.

by the Ottomans towards non-Muslims in an age when Europe saw the expulsion and forced conversion of Iberian Jews and Muslims from Spain and Portugal, religious intolerance, persecution, torture and execution of those who happened to have beliefs other than the official religion of the state.

Envied and feared as they were, the Ottoman Sultans were also known to value skills and knowledge, especially if those skills were related to military matters. The Empire was blessed with some unusually talented rulers. The personal interest of Mehmed II in military affairs was so widely known in Europe that authors of military treatises dedicated their works to him and rulers who wanted to gain his support or simply desired to maintain good relations with him dispatched their own military experts to the Sultan. A manuscript copy of Roberto Valturio's (1413–84) *De re militari* was sent to the Sultan by Sigismundo Malatesta in 1461, despite recurring attempts at prohibiting the transfer of up-to-date military knowledge to the "infidels," mainly by the Papacy and by countries at war with the Ottomans. However, in this particular case the alertness of the Venetians did work. Malatesta's man was arrested en route to Istanbul by the watchful Venetians and the book was confiscated, along with a map of the Adriatic.[98] Yet, it was impossible to seize all such books, for there was no iron curtain between Christendom and Islamdom in the early modern era. It is probable, for example, that Mehmed II acquired a copy of Ser Mariano di Giacomo Vanni's (1381–*c.* 1458) *Tractatus* before the siege of Constantinople.[99]

While these and similar military treatises may have played some role in the diffusion of European military techniques to the Ottomans, the knowledge brought to Istanbul by European military experts was of more significance. There were many ways by which European military technicians, craftsmen and soldiers ended up in the Ottoman foundries, naval arsenals and in the army. Certain military experts and adventurers from Europe offered their services to the Sultans hoping for a better salary and advancement in their social status. A known example of this type is Master Orban, "a Hungarian by nationality," and perhaps German by birth, "a very competent technician," whose cannons played a crucial role in the capture of Constantinople in 1453.[100]

Others were forced to work for the Ottomans, like the Christian smiths, stone-carvers, carpenters, masons, caulkers and shipbuilders in the conquered Balkan

---

[98] Franz Babinger, "Mehmed II., der Eroberer, und Italien," in Babinger, *Aufsätze und Abhandlungen zur Geschichte Südosteuropas und der Levante* (2 vols., Munich, 1962), vol. I, p. 197. Thus, it is doubtful whether Mehmed could have ever read the book, as is usually asserted. The Palace Library in Istanbul owned a copy of the book's 1472 edition. However, the provenance of this book is dubious. One possibility is that it arrived in Istanbul during the lifetime of Mehmed. Another is that the book was obtained only in 1526 when, after the battle of Mohács, Süleyman seized King Matthias's famous library, the Bibliotheca Corviniana, which possessed at least two copies of Valturio's book. On this see Balogh Jolán, *A művészet Mátyás király udvarában* (Budapest, 1966).

[99] Franz Babinger, "An Italian Map of the Balkans, Presumably Owned by Mehmed II," *Imago Mundi* 8 (1951), 8–15.

[100] Ágoston, "Ottoman Artillery," 27. Feridun Emecen, *İstanbulun Fethi Olayı ve Meseleleri* (Istanbul, 2003), pp. 37–38.

fortresses, towns and mines. Ottoman pragmatism and flexibility not only enabled these craftsmen to continue their former occupations, but often rewarded them with privileges. Through them the Ottomans acquainted themselves with Serbian and Saxon technologies of ore mining, for the latter had been introduced into the Balkans by miners from Saxony in the thirteenth and fourteenth centuries.[101] The population of mining towns and of entire regions was predominantly, and in the fifteenth century exclusively, Slavic. No wonder Ottoman technical language regarding ore mining is full of German and Slavic terms.[102]

Some European technicians were captured in wars and raids, and when the Ottomans discovered their skills they forced them to use those for the benefit and glory of the Sultans. This is what happened to Jörg of Nuremberg, who was captured in 1460 while working in Bosnia as *Büchsenmeister* or cannon founder. Jörg subsequently worked for twenty years for the Ottomans. When he eventually managed to escape, his skills and his knowledge in matters related to the Turks and their military art made him a valuable expert in Rome, where he continued to work as *Büchsenmeister* in Papal service.[103]

Craftsmen also arrived in Istanbul through a state-organized mass resettlement policy, known in the Ottoman Empire as *sürgün*, which aimed at invigorating the economic life of the capital city. Selim I is known to have resettled all the craftsmen of Tabriz in 1514 to Istanbul, although their exact number is difficult to estimate. While contemporaneous chroniclers and the keeper of the campaign's daybook claimed that Selim took with him some 1,700–2,000 craftsmen, including sword-makers, *cebecis*, bow-makers and so forth, a recently discovered register mentions only 110 craftsmen and bureaucrats, though it may contain only a portion of all the resettled ones.[104] Commercially dynamic groups, such as the Greeks, Jews and Armenians, were also occasionally resettled.[105]

Europeans who traveled to Istanbul were especially struck by the great number of Christians who worked in the Istanbul foundry and arsenal. Nicolaos de Nicolay, who visited the Ottoman capital city in 1551, pointed out that these western technicians "to the great detriment and damage of the Christianitie, haue taught the Turkes diuers inuentions, craftes and engines of warre, as to make artillerie, arquebuses, gunne pouder, shot, and other munitions."[106] Vincente Roca in his *History*, first

[101] See, among others, Robert Anhegger, *Beiträge zur Geschichte des Bergbaus im osmanischen Reich* (Bern, 1945), pp. 90–109; Mihailo J. Dinić, *Za istoriju rudarstva u sredjevekovnoj Srbiji i Bosni* (Belgrade, 1955), vol. I, pp. 1–27; N. Filipović, "Das Erbe der mittelalterlichen sächsischen Bergleute in den südslavischen Ländern," *Südost – Forschungen* 22 (1963), 192–233.
[102] Adem Handžić, "Rudnici u Bosni u drogoj polovini XV stolječa," *POF* 26 (1976), 7–41.
[103] A. Vasiliev, "Jörg of Nuremberg: A Writer Contemporary with the Fall of Constantinople (1453)," *Byzantion* 10 (1935), 205–09.
[104] For the chroniclers, see M. C. Şehabeddin Tekindağ, "Selim-nameler," *İstanbul Üniversitesi Edebiyat Fakültesi Tarih Dergisi* 1 (1970), 214; Tekindağ, "Yeni Kaynak ve Vesikaların Işığı Altında Yavuz Sultan Selim'in İran Seferi," *TD* 17, 22 (1967), 72. For the register, see Hüseyin Arslan, *Osmanlı'da Nüfus Hareketleri (XVI. Yüzyıl)* (Istanbul, 2001), pp. 325–33.
[105] J. Hacker, "The Sürgün System and Jewish Society in the Ottoman Empire during the Fifteenth to the Seventeenth Centuries," in Aron Rodrigue ed., *Ottoman and Turkish Jewry: Community and Leadership* (Bloomington, IN, 1992), pp. 1–65.
[106] Nicolaos de Nicolay, *The Nauigations into Turkie* (London, 1585), fol. 130v.

published in 1556, claimed that the Jews expelled from Spain taught the Ottomans "most of what they know of the villainies of war, such as the use of brass ordnance and of fire-locks."[107] Others added that the Ottomans learned the construction and use of gun carriages from the Jews and Marranos. While the role of Jews in the transmission of military techniques to the Ottomans should not be overstated, Ottoman and Jewish sources indicate that their assistance cannot be denied, either. Jewish blacksmiths are recorded in the 1517–18 accounts of the Imperial Cannon Foundry at Istanbul, which mention that Jewish iron-workers or blacksmiths (*ahengeran-i Yahudiyan*) together with an unspecified number of (apparently non-Jewish) hammer-smiths (*çeküççiyan*) and bellows-workers (*körükçiyan*) manufactured thirteen wrought-iron cannons.[108] A sixteenth-century Jewish author, Elijah Capsali, was of the opinion that Selim I "loved the Jews very much because he saw that by means of them he would beat nations and kill great kings, for they made for him cannons and weapons."[109]

Sources show that there were many experts working at the Imperial Cannon Foundry or Tophane-i Amire from different nations of Europe, and that Jews were a minority. The Savoyan traveler Jerome Maurand, who visited Istanbul in 1544, reported that at the foundry there were forty or fifty Germans employed by the Sultan to cast cannon. The French ambassador to Istanbul, d'Aramon, added that in 1547–48, several French, Venetian, Genoese, Spanish and Sicilian experts worked at the Tophane.[110]

The contribution of European technicians to the Ottoman arms industry and weapons technology should not be exaggerated. We have noted in the Introduction that Eurocentrists and Orientalists alike tend to overstate the importance of foreign technicians in the Ottoman Empire, using such examples to prove the putative Ottoman inferiority and dependence upon western technology. However, a closer look at the history of Ottoman weapons technology and that of early modern technology transfer raises serious doubts about such oversimplified statements. To begin with, one must remember that even in the Empire's European fortresses, where the Ottomans "inherited" dozens of Christian arquebusiers and gunners, there were several Muslim *tüfenkçis* and *topçus*, working together with their Christian colleagues, as early as the middle of the fifteenth century. Their numbers increased rapidly and the proportion of Christian to Muslim artillerymen had changed in favor of the latter by the sixteenth century. Mehmed II is also known to have had several Turkish craftsmen working independently of Master Orban during the siege of Constantinople. Similarly, it is unlikely that during the siege of Belgrade in 1456 all the cannons were operated by German, Italian,

---

[107] Bernard Lewis, *The Jews of Islam* (London, 1984), pp. 134–35.

[108] KK 4726, p. 45. I am indebted to İdris Bostan for drawing my attention to this document.

[109] Charles Berlin, "A Sixteenth-Century Hebrew Chronicle of the Ottoman Empire: The Seder Eliyahu Zuta of Elijah Capsali and its Message," in Charles Berlin ed., *Studies in Jewish Bibliography, History, and Literature in Honor of T. Edward Kiev* (New York, 1971), p. 36.

[110] Heywood, "Notes on the Production," p. 61. The ambassador himself assisted the Ottomans during the siege of Van in 1548, when giving advice to the Ottoman artillerists on how to direct fire against the walls of the fortress. As a result of his advice – so we are told – the garrison soon surrendered.

Hungarian and other European artillerymen, as European sources would like us to believe. Given the large number of cannons (150–300) there should have been dozens, if not hundreds, of Turkish artillerists present.[111] We have seen that in the 1520s, almost 700 *topçus* were on the Sultan's payroll, and hundreds must have served in provincial garrisons who were paid either from the local treasuries or from *timar* revenues.

However, it seems that Christian and Jewish blacksmiths and casters could have played a considerably more important role at the Istanbul foundry. Given the fact that the number of Muslim cannon founders working at the Imperial Cannon Foundry was around 50–60 in the sixteenth century, the employment of seven Christian and thirteen Jewish blacksmiths in the 1510s, charged with forging wrought-iron pieces,[112] or the service of a dozen or so foreign casters could have had significant impact on Ottoman forging and casting technology. Since the art of casting rested on accumulated experience transmitted from caster to caster rather than on scientific knowledge, even limited numbers of foreign founders who had brought something new with themselves to the Ottoman capital could have introduced it to the Istanbul foundry. Yet, the employment of foreign military technicians and artisans was not unique to the Ottomans. It was a well-established practice all over Europe.

Most of the artillerymen employed in medieval Hungary were of German and (to a lesser degree) of Italian origin. Apart from western technicians, in the sixteenth century a considerable number of Slav and Gypsy artisans from the Balkan peninsula, who had escaped from Ottoman rule, served the Hungarian kings, building ships and making swords, guns, projectiles and gunpowder.[113] As late as the first decades of the sixteenth century Venice also relied on foreign, mostly German, gunners, and the situation had changed only in the mid-sixteenth century after the establishment of the *scuole de' bombardieri* or training schools for gunners in its major cities.[114] Another example is Spain, which also lacked native cannon founders in the sixteenth century. Spanish monarchs were repeatedly forced to employ Italian, German and Flemish foundrymen. "I do not think," the Venetian ambassador to Spain wrote in 1557, "there is another country less provided with skilled workers than Spain." [115] This lack was one of the main problems afflicting the Spanish war industry. In 1575 at the Malaga foundry the casting of guns had to be delayed since none of the cannon founders was able to cast cannon without help. Skilled founders had to be imported from Germany. When it turned out that they

---

[111] Ágoston, "Ottoman Artillery," 27–30. Even the smallest pieces required two gunners to handle them.

[112] İsmail Hakkı Uzunçarşılı, "Osmanlı Sarayı'nda Ehl-i Hıref (Sanatkarlar) Defteri," *BTTD* 11, 15 (1981–86), 50.

[113] Gábor Ágoston, "Muslim–Christian Acculturation: Ottomans and Hungarians from the Fifteenth to the Seventeenth Centuries," in Bartolomé Bennassar and Robert Sauzet eds., *Chrétiens et Musulmans à la Renaissance* (Paris, 1998), pp. 293–301.

[114] M. E. Mallett and J. R. Hale, *The Military Organization of a Renaissance State: Venice c. 1400 to 1617* (Cambridge, 1984), p. 403.

[115] Cipolla, *Guns, Sails, and Empires*, pp. 33–34; Thompson, *War and Government*, p. 235.

were heretics (i.e., Protestants) they were arrested. The work at the foundry could start only after the newly invited Catholic masters from Innsbruck had arrived.[116] The first blast furnaces for casting iron ordnance in Spain were erected with the help of master founders from Liège and Luxembourg.[117] The case was similar in Portugal which, despite its ephemeral great power status in the sixteenth century and its role as "prime diffuser of new weaponry to Asia and Africa," remained largely dependent upon foreign technology and imported weaponry.[118]

The French also set up their cannon foundries and arms centers in the fifteenth century with the help of foreign technicians from Italy and Liège. Despite all efforts, however, France experienced shortages in armaments and remained partially dependent on foreign supplies.[119] Russia's case under Peter the Great is all too well known to repeat the story here. Suffice to say that foreign craftsmen played a crucial role in establishing the Russian arms industry. Under Ivan III (r. 1462–1505) Italian technicians had trained their Russian colleagues in the techniques of casting bronze cannon, and the famous Tula arms factory was established by Andries Vinius, a Dutchman who ran the enterprise until 1647 and, according to his contract, employed and trained Russian workers. After one year of unsuccessful experiment with direct management under the state armorer, in 1648 the enterprise was given again to two Dutchmen for twenty years.[120]

One can rightly point out that all the above examples come from countries that developed only "weak or enclave arms industries" or were "able to reproduce and adapt technology but not to innovate," in other words, from countries that were classified by Krause as second-tier and third-tier arms producers, respectively.[121] However, the history of early modern technology transfer provides ample evidence that even the leading, so-called first-tier arms producer countries were dependent, for shorter or longer periods, upon foreign expertise and know-how. This is especially true with regard to the early phase of their arms industries. England's "quasi-monopoly" of cast-iron ordnance between 1540 and 1620 owed much to French cannon founders and iron-workers. Thanks to their assistance, by the second half of the sixteenth century a strong English ordnance industry had come into existence. From this time onward English technicians as well as English

---

[116] Ibid., p. 243.

[117] In 1613 Jean Curtuis from Liège agreed to set up a cast-iron foundry in Spain and to supply the Spanish armada and fortresses with cast-iron ordnance. His contract also required him to train Spanish craftsmen in the art of casting iron artillery. Although the costs of initial tests with the local ore led to his bankruptcy, his plant in Liérganes was consolidated by his successor, Georges de Bande, a Luxembourger, and by 1630 Spain was self-sufficient in cast-iron ordnance. However, as a result of financial problems and the collapse of demand following the destruction of the Spanish armada in 1639 the production stopped and it was not until the eighteenth century that production in the plant recommenced. Yet it was again with the help of foreigners, for the attempt to train local craftsmen had failed. See David Goodman, *Spanish Naval Power, 1589–1665: Reconstruction and Defeat* (Cambridge, 1997), p. 147.

[118] Keith Krause, *Arms and the State: Patterns of Military Production and Trade* (Cambridge, 1992), pp. 49–50.

[119] Ibid., p. 46.   [120] Esper, "Self-Sufficiency," p. 199; Krause, *Arms and the State*.

[121] Ibid., p. 46.

artillery were much in demand throughout the Continent. Sweden's cast-iron ordnance industry, which dominated the European arms market from the 1620s until
the late eighteenth century, was also established with considerable foreign assistance. The blast-furnace technology was introduced to Gustavus Adolphus's country by Louis de Geer and Willem de Basche, two master founders from Liège, and
by their Liégeois iron-workers.[122]

In short, inviting and employing foreign technicians was the major means
throughout Europe to acquire new technology. The help of craftsmen from countries that were considered to be on the cutting edge of technology at a certain point
in time was inevitable for countries not yet familiar with the techniques, if they
were to establish their indigenous arms industries. The Ottomans were very much
part of this transfer of early modern weapons technology.

What made the Ottoman case unique, though, was that it was ideally placed
for technological diffusion. While miners from the mining centers of medieval
Serbia, Bosnia, Greece and Asia Minor brought their knowledge of metallurgy into
Istanbul, Muslim blacksmiths added their knowledge of metalworking techniques
of the Islamic East that produced the world-renowned Damascus blades. Istanbul,
with its Turkish and Persian artisans and blacksmiths, Armenian and Greek miners
and sappers, Bosnian, Serbian, Turkish, Italian, German, and later French, English
and Dutch gun founders and engineers, as well as with its Venetian, Dalmatian and
Greek shipwrights and sailors, proved to be an ideal environment for "technological
dialogue."[123]

The Ottoman navy, naval ordnance and acculturation

Another field where this technological dialogue was apparent was the Ottoman
navy, which, at the same time, was a major instrument of Ottoman amphibious
warfare and also played a crucial role in the transportation of heavy ordnance
and ammunition. Under Mehmed II and Bayezid II (r. 1481–1512) the Ottomans
acquired the common naval technology of the Mediterranean. Despite initial experiments with round-ships in the late fifteenth century, the long war galley remained
the most important vessel on Mediterranean waters. Following their Venetian and
Spanish Habsburg rivals, the Ottomans also adopted the galley as their principal
vessel.[124]

The size of the Ottoman navy was already impressive in the latter part of the fifteenth century. The Ottomans employed some 200 ships, including 64 galleys, during their campaign against Belgrade in 1456,[125] while in 1470 against Negroponte

[122] Cipolla, *Guns, Sails, and Empires*, pp. 32–37; Goodman, *Spanish Naval Power*, p. 147; Krause,
Arms and the State, p. 42.
[123] The phrase is taken from Arnold Pacey, *Technology in World Civilization: A Thousand-Year History*
(Oxford, 1990).
[124] Imber, "The Navy of Süleyman the Magnificent," 214–17.
[125] Ágoston, "La strada che conduceva a Nándorfehérvár (Belgrade): L'Ungheria, l'espansione
ottomana nei Balcani e la vittoria di Nándorfehérvár," in Zsolt Visy ed., *La campana di mezzogiorno. Saggi per il Quinto Centenario della bolla papale.* Budapest, 2000, p. 239.

they mobilized 280 galleys and *fustes* or small galleys. During their operation against Caffa in 1475, which resulted in the conquest of Crimea and the subjugation of the Crimean Khanate, the Ottomans employed some 380 boats, of which 120 were galleys and the rest *"fuste, barche, pantarenee."*[126] By this time the Ottomans could operate two large armadas independently. In May 1480, an Ottoman fleet of 104 vessels (including 46 galleys) arrived at Rhodes under the command of Mesih Pasha, a member of the Byzantine Palaiologos family. At around the same time, another Ottoman armada of 28 galleys and 104 light galleys and transport vessels, under the command of Gedik Ahmed Pasha, left the Straits and landed at Otranto on July 28.[127] In 1496, Marino Sanudo the younger claimed that the Ottomans had 100 galleys, 50 *fustes*, 50 *grippi* (Ottoman *ağribar*, smaller vessel than the *fusta*), three galleasses, two carracks and two smaller carracks called *barzotti*. In the battles of Lepanto in 1499 and of Modon in 1500, the Ottoman fleets are said to have numbered 260 and 230 ships, respectively.[128] However, one should note that the bulk of the Ottoman navy consisted of lighter galleys that "could not stand in formal battle against the heavier, well-armed galee sottili of the Christian West."[129]

At the beginning of the sixteenth century, apart from the Ottoman Empire, only Venice and the Knights of Rhodes possessed regular fleets in the Mediterranean. The existence of a navy facilitated the Ottomans' conquest of a vast area that extended from Syria through Egypt to Morocco; they were also able to expel the Portuguese from the Red Sea. According to a report submitted by Andrea Gritti, the Venetian *Bailo* in Istanbul, Bayezid II had at least 150 ships of different types at his disposal in ports across the Empire (Galata, Gelibolu, Avlonya in the Adriatic, and Volissa on the western side of Chios).[130]

Gelibolu, their first naval arsenal, remained an important shipyard for the construction and repair of Ottoman ships.[131] Nevertheless, by the beginning of the sixteenth century the Istanbul Naval Arsenal (Tersane-i Amire) on the shore of the Golden Horn, inherited from the Genoese of Galata and expanded under the reign of Selim I, had become the principal center of Ottoman shipbuilding and

---

[126] Heywood, "Notes on the Production," p. 8.

[127] Colin Imber, *The Ottoman Empire, 1300–1481* (Istanbul, 1990), pp. 248–50.

[128] John H. Pryor, *Geography, Technology, and War: Studies in the Maritime History of the Mediterranean, 649–1571* (Cambridge, 1992), p. 180.

[129] Ibid., pp. 169–70.

[130] Palmira Brummett, *Ottoman Seapower and Levantine Diplomacy in the Age of Discovery* (New York, 1994), pp. 89–121; cf. also Andrew C. Hess, "The Evolution of the Ottoman Seaborne Empire in the Age of Oceanic Discoveries, 1453–1525," *American Historical Review* 75, 7 (1970), 1892–1919; Hess, *The Forgotten Frontier: A History of the Sixteenth-Century Ibero-African Frontier* (Chicago, 1978).

[131] Between 1496 and 1498 there were twenty galleys, five galiots (*kalyatas*, which is the Turkicized form of the Italian word *galiotta*), eight *kayıks* and twenty-five *sandals* (small rowboats carried by ships, with only seven to twelve pairs of oars) constructed at Gelibolu. In addition to these newly made ships, nineteen galleys, five gun ships (*top gemisi*) and twenty-four horse ships (*at gemisi*, for the transportation of horses) were repaired. See Bostan, *Bahriye*, p. 16. On the types of ships used by the Ottomans see ibid., pp. 83–97; Svat Soucek, "Certain Types of Ships in Ottoman-Turkish Terminology," *Turcica* 7 (1975), 233–49; Henry Kahane, Renée Kahane and Andreas Tietze, *The Lingua Franca in the Levant: Turkish Nautical Terms of Italian and Greek Origin* (Urbana, 1958; reprint Istanbul, 1988) and Pryor, *Geography*, pp. 67–68.

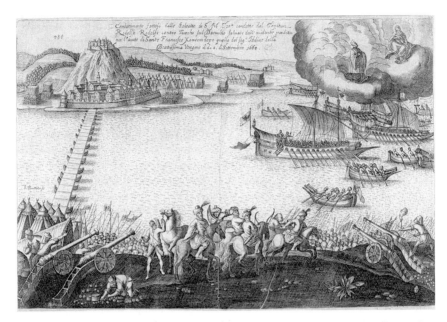

Figure 7 Strategically located on the Danubian waterway, Estergon was a key fortress in the defense of Ottoman Buda, and also a site of shipbuilding activity. Engraving by Gaspar Bouttats.

maintenance. In the 1550s, 250 ships could be constructed or repaired there at a time.[132]

In addition to Gelibolu and Istanbul, there were arsenals at Izmit on the Sea of Marmara, at Sinop and Samsun on the Black Sea, at Suez in the Red Sea, and at Birecik and Basra on the Euphrates and the Shatt al-Arab, respectively. If one includes the smaller shipyards, the number of Ottoman shipbuilding sites is close to seventy for this period. For instance, on the Danube, in addition to the most important arsenals of Rusçuk, Niğbolu and Vidin, ships were constructed at Güvercinlik, Semendire, Belgrade, İzvornik, Alacahisar (Kruşevac), Pojega, Mohaç, Buda and Estergon. The capacity of some of these shipbuilding sites was impressive.[133]

[132] Imber, *The Ottoman Empire, 1300–1650*, pp. 292–93. The number of galleys actually constructed was, however, fewer. Between 1610 and 1664, the shipwrights of the Tersane constructed 180 new galleys and 59 *baştardas* or large galleys, and repaired 413 galleys and 102 *baştardas*. See Bostan, *Bahriye*, p. 98.

[133] Ibid., pp. 17–29. In 1545 the *sancakbeyi* of İzvornik was ordered to construct 150 ships, whereas in 1565 the *sancakbeyi* of Semendire had to prepare 200 smaller transport vessels and 50 *şaykas* for Süleyman's campaign against Hungary. For the same campaign the *sancakbeyi* of İzvornik was instructed to build 16 *şaykas* and 200 vessels for the transportation of provisions. See Imber, "The Navy of Süleyman the Magnificent," 269–77; Jusuf Gülderen, "Turska brodogradilišta na Dunavu i njegovim pritokama u drugoj polovini XVI veka," in Vasa Čubrilović ed., *Plovidba na Dunavu i njegovim pritokama kroz vekove* (Belgrade, 1983), pp. 179–91. For the 1596 campaign, 500 *şaykas* were built (AK fol. 54a).

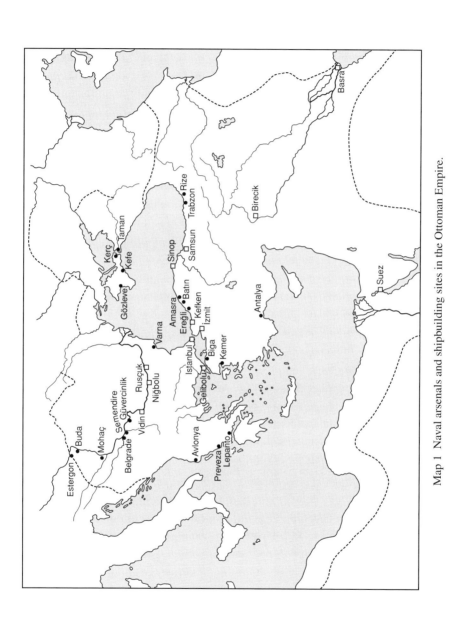

Map 1 Naval arsenals and shipbuilding sites in the Ottoman Empire.

The Mediterranean fleet under the command of the Grand Admiral, who also held the governorship of the province of the Archipelago, was the core of the Ottoman navy. Operating independently of this main fleet, there were smaller squadrons under the command of the captain of Kavala who patrolled the northern Aegean; the *sancak* governors of Lesbos and Rhodes, the latter commanding the vital sea routes between Egypt and Istanbul; the admiral of Egypt, who controlled both the Egyptian fleet based in Alexandria and the Suez fleet; and the captain of Yemen, who guarded the entry to the Red Sea. In addition, smaller flotillas operated on the Danube and its tributaries as well as on the Tigris, Euphrates and the Shatt al-Arab. The fighting power of such flotillas was not negligible. On the Shatt al-Arab in 1698–99, there were sixty frigates (*firkate*) with seventy *levends* aboard each ship, which meant a fighting power of 4,200 troops.[134]

Ordnance and ammunition, especially heavy stone cannon balls, were transported on special ships, called gun ships (*top gemisi*) and stone ships (*taş gemisi*). For the transport of gunpowder the Ottomans used special "covered" (*örtülü*) boats. In 1488, in the Ottoman fleet there were about ten gun ships and it seems that their number remained about the same in the sixteenth century. They were regularly repaired and when need arose for more, even local dockyards were able to build them.[135] Judging from available data, it is safe to say that the vessels at the government's disposal in the sixteenth and seventeenth centuries were capable of transporting hundreds of cannons of various calibers as well as the necessary ammunition. Ships carrying cannon balls could transport 2,000 cast-iron shots each.[136] When the Ottoman army marched against its Hungarian and Habsburg enemies, the cannons were transported via the Black Sea until Varna, where they were loaded on carts.[137] Apart from the Black Sea, the Danube, the Tigris and the Euphrates were all instrumental in the transportation of heavy armaments, as well as of victuals. During the 1596 campaigns, for instance, besides 200 transport ships for grain, 120 *şaykas* and 50 other boats suitable for the transportation of artillery pieces were mobilized and loaded with cannons and ammunition.[138] However, rivers were only partially navigable or ran in the wrong direction. During campaigns against the Habsburgs, the Danube waterway was used only from Rusçuk (or Belgrade) up to Buda (or Estergon); thus cannon and ammunition shipped from Istanbul via the Black Sea to Varna were transported on carts from Varna to Rusçuk (or to Belgrade), where they were again loaded on ships.[139]

The number of artillery pieces aboard Ottoman ships varied according to the type and size of the vessel. In 1488, the ordnance aboard various ships was as follows:

---

[134] MAD 975, pp. 15, 17.

[135] In 1497–98 in the Gelibolu arsenal five, and in the late 1520s in the Galata arsenal ten to twelve, gun ships were regularly repaired every year. In 1557, two gun ships were made in Varna. Cf. Bostan, *Bahriye*, pp. 16, 6–7, 26.

[136] A. S. Beygu, "Köprülüler Devrinde Kiği Demir Madenlerinde Yapılan Top Güllelerinin Avrupa Seferleri için Erzurum'dan Gönderilmesine ait Üç Vesika," *Tarih Vesikaları* 2, 11 (1943), 336.

[137] AK fols. 53b, 55b, 57b, 66a, 190b, etc.   [138] AK fol. 66a.

[139] MD 5, p. 288, no. 743; MAD 2758, pp. 45, 87 (for the more common Varna–Rusçuk route in 1566 and 1697, respectively); and AK fols. 53b, 206a (for the Varna–Belgrade route in 1596 and 1604).

Table 2.3 *Ottoman oar-ships and shipboard artillery*

	Length (m)	Thwarts	Oars	Rowers per oar	Crew per ship	Fighting men per ship	Crew plus fighting men	Guns per ship	Shots per ship
Oar-ships									
Frigate/*firkate*		10–17		2–3		80–100		7	200
Galiot/*kalyata*	32–36	19–24				220		7	255
Galley/*kadırga*	42	25–26	49	4–5	200–245	100–150	330	3–13	200
Bastarda/*baştarda*		26–36		5–7	290–340				
Admiral's galley /*Paşa baştardası*	53–55	36	72	7	500	216	800	11–13	
Galleass/*mavna*	49	26	52	7	364	150	600	24	
Oar-ships on river flotillas									
Chaika/*şayka*	13–25				20	21	43		
işkampoye		13			35		74	7	100

Note: The length is given in the sources and the related literature in *zira*. I have calculated with the architect or mason *zira* (*arşun*) which was 0.758 m. Figures are rounded. Figures for crew are estimates based on actual numbers employed. Cf. Bostan, *Bahriye*, and for data from 1610–11, 1612–13, 1620–21 and 1648–49 see Murat Çızakça, "Ottomans and the Mediterranean: An Analysis of the Ottoman Shipbuilding Industry as Reflected by the Arsenal Registers of Istanbul, 1529–1650," in Rosalba Ragosta ed., *Le genti del mare Mediterraneo*, vol. II (Naples, 1981), p. 785.

Sources: Bostan, *Bahriye*, pp. 83–89; Soucek, "Certain Types," 233–49; Imber, "The Navy of Süleyman the Magnificent," 211–82; MAD 2732.

barça eighty-three, *ağribar* forty-five, *kadırga* thirteen, *kalyata* seven and *kayık* five guns.[140] Apart from the main fleet, the firepower aboard Ottoman naval flotillas was also considerable. In 1697–98, 311 guns of various types were deployed on the *firkates*, *kalyatas* and *işkampoyes* operating near Özi.[141] In 1698–99, no fewer than 928 bronze and cast-iron guns of various sizes were sent from Istanbul to Baghdad for the Shatt al-Arab flotilla.[142]

Besides cannons, the firepower of Ottoman ships was further enhanced by musket-bearing troops, the *timar*-holding *sipahis* and their retinues (*cebelü*), Janissaries, *azabs* and *levends*, who comprised the crew. Prior to the battle of Lepanto (1571), Ottoman galleys had only 60 fighting men, a number that was raised to 150 after the battle. As in the land forces, the majority of troops on Ottoman galleys consisted of *timar*-holding *sipahis*, followed in importance by the Janissaries. It is clear that the major difficulty the Ottomans faced after Lepanto, when

---

[140] Bostan, *Bahriye*, p. 174, where the number of guns aboard the *ağribar/iğribar* is mistakenly given as twenty-nine. Cf. İsmail Hakkı Uzunçarşılı, *Osmanlı Devletinin Merkez ve Bahriye Teşkilatı* (Ankara, 1984), pp. 512–13, where the document is reproduced. Imber, who also uses the document, thinks that the large number of ordnance aboard the *barças* (*bargia*) and *ağribars* indicates that these vessels were used for artillery transport. See his *Ottoman Empire* (2002), p. 291.

[141] MAD 2732, p. 39. The distribution of artillery was as follows: bronze *koğuş*: 3; cast-iron *koğuş*: 44; and smaller cast-iron *saçmas*, 264. For Ottoman types of guns see chapter 3.

[142] MAD 975, p. 16. The distribution of ordnance was as follows: 60 *koğuş* guns (of which 41 were of 1.5-*okka* and 19 of 1-*okka* caliber), 120 flanking guns (*top-i yan*) (of which 92 were of 0.5-*okka* and 28 of 100-*dirhem* caliber), four mortars (two 24-*okka* and two 14-*okka* pieces), 18 *saçmas*, 24 *eyneks*, apparently of bronze, as well as 230 cast-iron *saçmas* and 472 cast-iron *eyneks*.

Table 2.4 *Ottoman sailing ships and shipboard artillery*

Sailing ships	Length	Number of masts	Number of holds	Guns per ship
Barza/bargia/ *barça*				83
Galleon/*kalyon*	33–49	3	2	58–80
Galleon/*kalyon*		3	3	80–130

Source: Bostan, *Bahriye*, pp. 94–96.

they undertook the rebuilding of their entire navy that had been destroyed in the battle, was not to build the ships but rather to man them with troops. After the battle, a deliberate attempt was made to augment the firepower of the troops and equip even the *timar*-holding *sipahis*, of whom some 4,400 men were called up for the newly constructed galleys (and to staff some coastal forts). The *sipahis* were threatened with losing their fiefs if they did not bring a musket or bow. Orders sent to the *sancak* governors made clear that any *sipahi* "who did not know it already" had "to learn the use of the musket." Yet, judging from the growing numbers of musket-bearing volunteers, drafted from the provinces for the galleys in 1572 and later, it seems that muskets were never fully accepted by the *sipahis*. As already noted, the spread of firearms among the *reaya* was quite common by this time, and the government was more than happy to hire them, even promising *timars* to them if they excelled in naval campaigns. It seems that it was they, along with 3,000 Janissaries drafted in 1572, who provided most of the firepower aboard the galleys.[143]

It has been suggested that from the late sixteenth century onward Ottoman military mastery was in decay at the Mediterranean. While it is true that by the 1580s proponents of the land forces had gained the upper hand vis-à-vis those who wanted to strengthen the navy in order to further Ottoman maritime ambitions, the navy remained an integral part of the Ottoman military machine. It is also true that by this time Ottoman galleys had become vulnerable to the heavily armed sailing ships of the northwestern European powers, which could outfight the galleys. However, this was also true for the Ottomans' traditional Mediterranean adversaries, the Venetians and Spaniards, who were also galley powers. Compared with them, the Ottomans remained a capable and formidable naval power, and when the demarcation lines moved, they usually did in favor of the Ottomans. In the Mediterranean the galley retained its role as transport vessel, and remained a useful means of coastal patrol and amphibious warfare.[144]

If the Ottomans still could match their galley power adversaries in the Mediterranean it was because they continued to participate in the diffusion of new naval and

[143] Colin Imber, "The Reconstruction of the Ottoman Fleet after the Battle of Lepanto, 1571–1572," in Imber, *Studies in Ottoman History and Law* (Istanbul, 1996), pp. 85–101, especially pp. 96–98.
[144] John Francis Guilmartin, Jr., *Gunpowder and Galleys: Changing Technology and Mediterranean Warfare at Sea in the Sixteenth Century* (Cambridge, 1974).

military technology. In this process, renegades and Christian adventurers, as well as the Barbary corsairs, the vassals of the Porte, all played significant roles. In his famous work on the history and geography of Algiers, Diego de Haëdo, a Spanish Benedictine and a captive in Algiers from 1579 to 1582, listed thirty-five corsairs who owned galleons in Algiers in 1581. Of the thirty-five ship owners three were sons of renegades and twenty-two were renegades: six Genoese, three Greeks, two Spaniards, two Venetians, two Albanians, one Hungarian, one Frenchman, one 'judeo de nacion', one Corsican, one Calabrian, one Sicilian and one Neapolitan. Only ten of them were Turks. Given such a cultural variety among the Barbary ship owners, it is hardly surprising that the corsairs provided the Ottomans with an invaluable reservoir of naval experts. The employment of hundreds of these renegades in the Mediterranean facilitated military acculturation and resulted in a common military and nautical knowledge of the region. The Turkish naval vocabulary of Italian and Greek origin mirrors this "cultural unity" of the Mediterranean.[145]

Seventeenth-century sources also suggest that the Ottomans continued to rely on naval and military men who came from a common pool of experts of the Mediterranean and the Adriatic. Thus, they had a good chance of employing technology that was not dissimilar to the technology used by their Venetian and Spanish opponents. The Ottoman admiral in 1645, Yusuf Pasha *alias* Yosef Masković, was a renegade from the Veneto-Ottoman frontier of Dalmatia. He successfully commanded the Sultan's fleet during the first landing in Crete (1645), which ended with the surrender of Canea (Hanya).[146] When in 1669 an English ship captured a small vessel from Algiers off the southern Mediterranean coast of Spain, the English found that its captain was a certain Ali Reis, a renegade from Lübeck. There were several other renegades serving Ali as well. Ottoman chronicles and personal accounts also mention some celebrated defectors and Christian renegades in the service of the Ottoman Sultans.[147] In addition, the Ottomans seized Christian captives during major battles at sea as well as during raids against Spanish and Venetian coastal cities and Spanish presidios in North Africa. These provided the Ottoman navy with thousands of European oarsmen.[148]

Apart from renegades and captives, the Christian subjects of the Sultans with special military and naval skills were also employed en masse. Whereas in 1529–30 most of the workers of the Istanbul Naval Arsenal were Muslims, by the mid-seventeenth century Greeks from Istanbul and the Archipelago had become the

[145] Kahane et al., *Lingua Franca*.
[146] Kenneth Meyer Setton, *Venice, Austria, and the Turks in the Seventeenth Century* (Philadelphia, 1991), p. 116. Cf. also Rhoads Murphey's review article of Setton's book in *ArchOtt* 13 (1993–94), 374.
[147] Rhoads Murphey, "The Ottoman Resurgence in the Seventeenth-Century Mediterranean: The Gamble and its Results," *Mediterranean Historical Review* 8 (1993), 196.
[148] After the Venetian victory at the battle of the Dardanelles in 1656, the galley slaves aboard the eleven captured Ottoman vessels comprised 194 Poles, 60 Germans, 51 Spaniards, 92 Frenchmen, 182 Italians, 43 Sicilians, 26 Neapolitans, 106 Greeks, 143 Hungarians, 119 Muscovites and 1,087 Ukrainians. See M. Fontenay, "Chiormes turques au XVIIe siècle," in Rosalba Ragosta ed., *Le genti del mare Mediterraneo* (Napoli, 1981), p. 890.

principal workforce. Among the Sultans' oarsmen and sailors we also find many Christians. The fighting force of the Ottoman navy, however, remained predominantly Muslim and Turk, for Christian *forsas* could not be trusted in battles.[149]

Given the presence in the Ottoman navy of many Christians from different parts of the Mediterranean, it is hardly surprising that the Ottomans shared naval and weapons technology with their Mediterranean adversaries. Impressed by the Venetian galleasses at the battle of Lepanto, that is, by the heavy galleys which could fire broadsides as opposed to the traditional galleys that fired only from the bows, the Ottomans were quick to imitate them. During the reconstruction of the Ottoman navy they built at least three galleasses at Sinop and one or two in the Istanbul arsenal.[150] To match their Venetian adversaries, the Ottomans began to build galleons as early as the fifteenth century, though they were mainly used as transport ships until the mid-seventeenth century, when, during the Cretan war, the Porte began using them as warships. Yet, it was only from the 1680s onward that galleons became standard warships in the Ottoman navy.[151] By the second half of the seventeenth century the high-board ships, similar to the ones used in the Atlantic, were also to be found in the Ottoman navy. Initially, the Ottomans would charter or requisition such ships from the northerners, that is, from the Dutch and English. Later, however, such high-board ships were built at the Istanbul arsenal. Visiting there in March 1692, Luigi Ferdinando Marsigli witnessed:

> Everywhere I went to the seashore, I saw the construction of warships according to the most exact proportions maintained by the most experienced Christian maritime nations. The construction of these vessels was directed by Christians dressed in European clothing who, cane in hand, commanded the workers by means of interpreters.[152]

Marsigli credited the innovation to Köprülüzade Fazil Mustafa Pasha, who held the office of Grand Vizier between 1689 and 1691, and who was advised in matters concerning shipbuilding by Mehmed Ağa, a Christian renegade from Livorno. After he had produced a scale-model of a high-board sailing ship, Mehmed Ağa not only persuaded the Grand Vizier of the superiority of this new type of ship, but also procured skilled Italian shipwrights to build new ones.

Conclusion

In the light of the Ottomans' experience with firearms, notions concerning the "extreme conservatism" of Islamic societies[153] are hardly tenable. Above we have

---

[149] Murat Çizakça, "Ottomans and the Mediterranean: An Analysis of the Ottoman Shipbuilding Industry as Reflected by the Arsenal Registers of Istanbul 1529–1650," in Ragosta, *Le genti del mare*, pp. 784–87.

[150] Imber, "The Reconstruction," p. 88.

[151] Bostan, *Bahriye*, p. 94; Imber, *The Ottoman Empire* (2002), p. 291.

[152] Allan Z. Hertz, "Armament and Supply Inventory of Ottoman Ada Kale, 1753," *ArchOtt* 4 (1972), 98–99.

[153] Setton, *Venice, Austria, and the Turks*, pp. 6, 100 and 450; E. L. Jones, *The European Miracle: Environments, Economies, and Geopolitics in the History of Europe and Asia* (Cambridge and

seen that, after a somewhat belated start, the Ottomans proved quite successful in integrating gunpowder technology into their armed forces and navy. They
established centralized and permanent troops specialized in the manufacturing and
handling of firearms well before such permanent units appeared in the armies of
their opponents. Direct military conflicts, prohibited trade in weaponry and the
employment of European military experts ensured relatively smooth dissemination of up-to-date technologies and military know-how in the Sultan's realms. As
long as these channels of military acculturation remained open, as they did until the
end of the seventeenth century and in certain cases even after that, it was virtually
impossible to gain significant technological superiority over the Ottomans. In fact,
after the introduction, in the 1420s, of the corned powder that resulted in greater
penetrating force of hand firearms, which in turn led to the increased importance
of infantry troops armed with these weapons and prompted significant reorganization of the armed forces in Europe[154] – and as we have seen in the Ottoman
Empire, too – there were no major technological innovations in the period under
discussion that would have had decisive tactical significance. It is quite clear that
the Ottomans not only successfully adopted and integrated gunpowder technology
into their armed forces and navy, but until the seventeenth century remained a
strong "gunpowder empire," indeed stronger than their immediate neighbors, both
Christian and Muslim.

The oft-cited counter-argument, that is, the reluctance of the *sipahis* to adopt
firearms, has very little to do with Islam. Rather, it can be explained in terms of the
mentality, social status and military tradition of the light-armed *sipahi* horsemen,
the nature of war the Ottomans fought on their eastern front, as well as the inadequacy of early firearms for the mounted warrior. The *sipahis* regarded the use of
firearms as beneath their dignity. Their attitude is well illustrated by an incident
when some 500 mounted Christians, armed with muskets, routed 2,500 *sipahis* in
Croatia. When the Grand Vizier, Rüstem Pasha, was furious at them, the informant
who brought the news replied: "You do not take a right view of the matter. Did you
not hear that we were overcome by the force of firearms? It was fire that routed
us, not the enemy's valour. Far different, by heaven, would have been the result
of the fight, had they met us like brave men."[155] By no means was the *sipahis*'
attitude unique. The Mamluk and Safavid warrior aristocracies maintained very
similar stances, as did the feudal knights in Italy, France, Germany, Spain, and
England.[156]

New York, 1987; 3rd edition 2003), p. 181; Paul Kennedy, *The Rise and Fall of the Great Powers:
Economic Change and Military Conflict from 1500 to 2000* (New York, 1989), p. 12.

[154] Hall, *Weapons and Warfare*, pp. 69–73; Parker, *The Military Revolution*, pp. 6–44.

[155] Charles Thornton Forster and F. H. B. Blackburne Daniell eds., *The Life and Letters of Ogier
Ghiselin de Busbecq Seigneur of Bousbecque Knight, Imperial Ambassador* (2 vols., London,
1881), vol. I, p. 243; cf. Cezar, *Levendler*, p. 160; Ronald C. Jennings, "Firearms, Bandits, and
Gun-control: Some Evidence on Ottoman Policy towards Firearms in the Possession of Reaya,
from Judicial Records of Kayseri, 1600–1627," *ArchOtt* 6 (1980), 341.

[156] For European examples, see J. R. Hale, "Gunpowder and the Renaissance: An Essay in the History
of Ideas," in Hale, *Renaissance War Studies* (London, 1983), pp. 389–420.

One should also note that before the introduction of the wheel-lock mechanism, firearms were not only impractical but also utterly unsuitable for cavalrymen. Introduced first in Italy about 1520, firearms with wheel-lock mechanisms were unfamiliar to the Ottomans until 1543, when in the siege of Székesfehérvár (Hungary) they confiscated several wheel-lock pistols from German horsemen.[157] Although a report dated 1594 states that the soldiers of the Sultan had not yet adopted the pistol,[158] this does not mean that the *sipahis* did not use firearms at all. As noted, after the battle of Lepanto, those *sipahis* who were called up for serving in the Ottoman navy had to be armed with arquebuses. Other sources indicate that they did use pistols in the seventeenth century.

Apart from the Ottomans, the history of firearms in the Mamluk kingdom and in Safavid Persia, though in a different way, also challenges beliefs about "Islamic conservatism." The Mamluk and Safavid experiences with firearms suggest that when Muslim societies were slow to integrate gunpowder technology or when they failed to arm certain units of their armed forces with firearms, it had very little to do with religion and was rather, as in the "West," a result of more complex issues.

David Ayalon has convincingly demonstrated that the Mamluks became acquainted with firearms too early (in the 1360s) and thus their experience with the new weapon, still in its infancy, "had been most disappointing." These early cumbersome weapons were unsuitable to traditional Mamluk tactics characterized by the mobility of the cavalry, who rejected the use of firearms, as did cavalry forces elsewhere for longer or shorter periods.[159]

The Safavid experience with firearms is even more illustrative. Although the myth that firearms technology was introduced to the Safavid Empire in the late 1590s by two Englishmen, Sir Anthony and Sir Robert Sherley, has long been discredited,[160] it resurfaces in popular works and in studies by Orientalists who – ignoring the abundant evidence regarding the use of firearms in the region and by overstating the role of these two English adventurers in modernizing the Persian army under Shah Abbas the Great (1587–1629) – perpetuate the notion of Islam's allegedly "inherent conservatism." In fact, it is known that the predecessors of the Safavids, the Akkoyunlus – whose empire (1378–1508) controlled Mesopotamia and much of present-day Iran – were familiar with firearms and did use them, especially after the shocking defeat they suffered at the hands of the Ottomans in 1473, when, in the battle of Bashkent (Otluk-beli), the Ottomans had proved the advantages of the new weapon.[161] The Safavids, too, used firearms even before the foundation of their empire under Ismail I (1501–24), and arquebus (*tofak*) and

[157] Parry, "La manière de combattre," p. 250.   [158] Parry, "Barud," p. 1064.
[159] Ayalon, *Gunpowder and Firearms*, pp. 98, 107–08.
[160] Roger Savory, "The Sherley Myth," *Iran* 5 (1967), 73–81.
[161] The Akkoyunlus used firearms in 1478 and 1485. In fact, in the latter case, the sources mention heavy battering cannon (*tup-i giran*) with which the Akkoyunlus besieged the Georgian fort of Akhiska (Akhatsikhe). Cf. ibid., pp. 78–79; Vladimir Minorsky, "La Perse au XVe siècle entre la Turquie et Venise," in his *The Turks, Iran, and the Caucasus in the Middle Ages* (London, 1978), pp. 12–13.

cannon (*tup*) "constituted an integral, albeit small part" of Safavid armament.[162] However, it was only after the battle of Çaldıran (1514) – where the Safavids faced, for the very first time, the devastating firepower of an enemy – that the Safavid leadership decided to arm its troops with cannons and arquebuses in a more systematic manner and on a much larger scale than had previously been the case. That is, the main stimulus was, as it had been for the Ottomans in the fifteenth century, the need to adjust to an enemy already well armed with gunpowder weapons.

The reasons for the dominance of traditional, non-gunpowder weapons are manifold, but religion, again, played a very modest role, if any at all, in delaying the integration of firearms into the Safavid army. Of greater importance were perceptions of honor and of manliness among the traditional Safavid warrior aristocracy, the different nature of warfare in the region, the physical environment of Persia, and the lack of natural resources needed for the manufacturing of weapons and ammunition.

Just like the Ottoman *sipahis* and the feudal lords in Europe, the Safavid warrior aristocracy regarded the use of firearms as against the idea of honor and manliness. Unlike the Ottomans, who very early in their wars in the Balkans faced enemies already in the possession of firearms, the Safavids' enemies, except for the Ottomans in the west, lacked firepower. Even after Çaldıran, where the Safavids suffered a crushing defeat, they were able to deny decisive Ottoman victory not by the deployment of cannons and musketeers, but by avoiding pitched battles and by using their scorched earth tactics. Both worked against the Ottomans and neither required artillery.

Nor was artillery essential for monopolizing the means of organized violence and for subduing possible alternative centers of power in a country that lacked fortified towns where rebels could have found refuge. The absence of wheeled transportation and of navigable rivers, as well as the land-locked nature of the country, made it extremely difficult to move large artillery trains. The Safavids were also handicapped by the scarcity of raw materials needed for the casting of cannons and the manufacturing of gunpowder.[163]

However, when the Safavids faced recurring Ottoman attacks, they proved quite capable of adjusting their armed forces to those of their Ottoman opponents. Two years after Çaldıran, Shah Ismail created a corps of musketeers (*tofangchi*) whose number is said to have reached 8,000 by 1517 and varied between 15,000 and 20,000 in 1521, although these figures should be treated with great caution. Whereas the Safavids used no artillery at Çaldıran, Shah Ismail supposedly had 100 cannons in 1517. Artillery remained a standard weapon throughout the century, though used mainly during sieges and thus referred to in the sources as *qal'eh-kub*

---

[162] For specific examples during the reigns of Haydar and his son, Shah Ismail, see Willem Floor, *Safavid Government Institutions* (Costa Mesa, CA, 2001), p. 176.

[163] Rudi Matthee, "Unwalled Cities and Restless Nomads: Firearms and Artillery in Safavid Iran," in Charles Melville ed., *Safavid Persia: The History and Politics of an Islamic Society* (London, 1996), pp. 389–416.

or "castle-smasher."[164] The reorganization of the artillery and musketeers was a major element of the Safavid military reforms under Shah Abbas.[165]

Ottoman, Mamluk and Safavid experiences with firearms all suggest that the integration of gunpowder technology was a complicated matter and that the modes, timing, success or failure of it depended on historical, social, economic and cultural factors, as they also did in Europe. There is very little peculiar to Islam in this process. All these empires were rather pragmatic in their decisions. Unquestionably, among the three empires, the Ottomans proved to be the most successful in this undertaking, indeed more successful – at least until the end of the seventeenth century – than all their neighbors, Muslims and Christians alike.

---

[164] Floor, *Safavid Government*, pp. 176–200. Some of the figures regarding the number of cannons possessed by Ismail or deployed in certain sieges are obvious exaggerations of contemporaneous Persian and European chroniclers.

[165] His permanent army is said to have had, among others, a corps of artillery 12,000 strong with 500 cannons, as well as 12,000 infantrymen armed with muskets. See L. Lockhart, "The Persian Army in the Safavī Period," *Der Islam* 34 (1959), 89–98.

CHAPTER 3

Cannons and muskets

As noted in the Introduction, scholars of the Eurocentric and Orientalist schools alike have made wild generalizations regarding the Ottomans' supposed technological inferiority, as well as their military capabilities and performance. They introduced the idea of an East–West technological divergence that supposedly occurred around the mid-fifteenth century. From that point onward, the Ottomans allegedly continued to rely upon their heavy and clumsy ordnance, whereas European monarchs opted for smaller and thus more mobile and tactically efficient weapons. Similarly, these European weapons are believed to have been superior to those of the Ottomans. Seeking explanation for the Ottomans' putative preference for giant weapons and for their supposed failure to manufacture up-to-date weapons, historians usually point at cultural differences, the lack of private capital and entrepreneurship, and the relative conservativeness of the prevailing command economies of Asian empires.

A short glance at the literature will suffice to illustrate that such assumptions regarding Ottoman weapons technology have been based on random and often atypical evidence without respect for chronology. Following contemporary narrative sources' obsession with giant Ottoman cannons,[1] when writing about Ottoman artillery, nineteenth- and twentieth-century historians are content with mentioning some of the most often cited Ottoman monster-guns (e.g., the cannons at the Tower of London and at the Dardanelles) and usually neglect to provide corrective descriptions of smaller pieces frequently designated by the same names.[2] In so doing, they further the myth of Ottoman technological inferiority and obsolescence.

---

[1] See, for instance, Baron de Tott's description of and experience with "an enormous Piece of Ordnance, which would carry a Marble Ball of eleven hundred pounds weight" that he found on the walls of the Dardanelles castle. Baron de Tott, *Memoirs of Baron de Tott* (London, 1785; reprint New York, 1973), book iii, pp. 66–69. Although Tott suggested that this piece "no doubt, had not its equal in the Universe," it will be seen later that similar large bombards, forged or cast mainly in the fifteenth century, could also be found in Europe and, though obsolete, were treated as prestige weapons. On Tott see Virginia Aksan, "Breaking the Spell of the Baron de Tott: Reframing the Question of Military Reform in the Ottoman Empire, 1760–1830," *IHR* 24, 2 (2002), 253–77.

[2] To prove "the obsession of the Turks with huge guns" Cipolla, who also cites Baron de Tott's experience with the large piece of the Dardanelles, mentions a large fifteenth-century Ottoman cannon (weighing more than 18 tons) that was presented in 1867 by Sultan Abdülaziz to Queen

In addition to the general problems of Orientalist and Eurocentric approaches, the literature regarding Ottoman weapons technology suffers from serious method-ological deficiencies. Of these the most important are:

1 lack of understanding of the bewildering terminology of Ottoman guns and thus of the various types of Ottoman artillery pieces;
2 lack of any attempt to compare Ottoman and European pieces and thus failure to understand the similarities and differences between guns employed by the Ottomans and by their European adversaries; and
3 ignorance of the rich archival material preserved in the Ottoman archives with regard to the technical characteristics of individual guns upon which more solid conclusions can be drawn.

In order to address the deficiencies in the literature the present chapter seeks a better understanding of the ways the Ottomans classified their firearms. To avoid the most common mistake of earlier studies, that is, their reliance on accidental evidence, an attempt has been made to collect statistical data in sufficient quantity regarding the main types of firearms used by the Ottomans.[3] Such sources are more abundant regarding artillery pieces than hand firearms, and this chapter reflects the nature of the source material by concentrating on ordnance. Given the abundance of the sources regarding Ottoman artillery pieces and the structure of this book, the Ottoman ordnance industry and its production capabilities will be discussed in a separate chapter following the study of Ottoman saltpeter and gunpowder industries.

There are several ways one can classify early modern ordnance. One can study the technological make-up of the weapons, that is, whether they were wrought-iron pieces or were cast of bronze, copper or iron. Another way is to differ-entiate between flat-trajectory guns and high-trajectory mortars. The Howitzer, invented by the Dutch in the seventeenth century, was an in-between category.[4] Although flat-trajectory guns included a perplexing variety of artillery pieces from the smallest to the largest ones, by the sixteenth century in most European coun-tries two main classes of guns had appeared: large-caliber siege and fortress guns (*cannon/Karthaun*) and longer, culverin-type medium- and small-caliber guns (*culverins/Schlangen*).[5] The three main classes (mortars, cannons and culverins)

Victoria and can be seen today in the Tower of London. He also mentions another large stone-shooting piece of 19 tons in weight that was cast in 1533 and later captured by the Portuguese. Carlo M. Cipolla, *Guns, Sails, and Empires: Technological Innovation and the Early Phases of European Expansion 1400–1700* (New York, 1965; reprint New York, 1996), pp. 95–96.

[3] The overwhelming majority of data were gathered from the official account books of the Imperial Cannon Foundry in Istanbul and from registers of weaponry of major Ottoman castles from such diverse regions of the Empire as Iraq, Hungary, the Balkans and Crete.

[4] They fired projectiles, mainly shells, at medium-high trajectory, were lighter and hence more mobile than mortars, yet still capable of throwing large shots.

[5] Local classifications could and did vary. In Spain, for instance, which otherwise followed the Germans, the heaviest guns were the *pedreros*. Shorter and heavier than the cannons, *pedreros* are listed together with mortars in the same class by Luis Collado, author of the late sixteenth-century artillery manual, *Platica Manual de la Altilería* (1592). Collado's three main classes of Spanish artillery were (1) culverins, (2) cannons and (3) *pedreros* and mortars.

were used as early as the fifteenth century,[6] but there were several types of guns within each class.

Despite repeated attempts to impose standards, guns in the sixteenth and seventeenth centuries were notable for their individuality throughout Europe. "All our great pieces of one name are not of one weight, nor of one height in their mouths," complained Cyprián Lucar in 1587.[7] Guns with similar characteristics could be listed under different names in different forts.[8] Languages and local customs added to the confusion, as is shown, for example, by comparing weapons inventories of the same castle compiled in different languages.[9] Even when broad standardizations, based on the weight of the projectile, were introduced in Europe, guns of the same caliber could vary in terms of the weight or length of the barrel. Guns designated by a particular type name varied considerably in caliber, especially in Italy and Spain.[10] Guns referred to by a particular type name in sixteenth- and seventeenth-century weapons' tables in England, France and in the Austrian Habsburg lands appear to have shown fewer discrepancies, but there were several names for sub-types, and the usage of these names was inconsistent.[11] To add to our confusion, guns of similar names were not of the same caliber in different countries. For instance, the caliber of Italian and Spanish culverins varied greatly. Although the usual English culverin of 1592 was the 17.5-pounder, culverins from 10- to 18-pounders are known from sixteenth-century England.[12] Understanding contemporary weapons terminology and thus the characteristics of various types of guns is essential if we are to embark on a comparative examination of the Ottoman weapons technology. Failure to do so may, and did indeed, lead to false generalizations.[13] The following attempt at classification of Ottoman artillery pieces should

---

[6] A rudimentary classification, reflecting the three classes, is visible in Emperor Maximilian I's famous *Zeugbücher* that recorded all the weapons of his *Zeughäuse* or weapons storehouses established in Innsbruck, Vienna, Graz, Osterwitz, Görz, Breisach and Lindau. See Gerhard Kurzmann, *Kaiser Maximilian I. und das Kriegswesen der österreichischen Länder und des Reiches* (Vienna, 1985), pp. 125–38.

[7] Colin Martin and Geoffrey Parker, *The Spanish Armada* (London, 1988), p. 215.

[8] "What is a *pasabolante* in Granada would appear much like a *bonbarda* in Chinchilla, and even the bombard seems to have been no more standardised than having a barrel between six and fifteen palms in length and firing a stone of 'two palms' (Chinchilla), 'nine pounds and a half' (Almería), or to be more exact, 'like that of a *culebrina*' (Alcázar de Madrid)." James D. Lavin, *A History of Spanish Firearms* (London, 1965), p. 40.

[9] Habsburg Hungary provides ample examples for alternate classifications of similar guns in the very same castles as well as regarding inconsistencies in Latin-, German- and Hungarian-language inventories.

[10] In sixteenth-century Italy, *colobrina*s could be 14-, 16-, 20-, 30-, 50- and 120-pounders. At the end of the sixteenth century, Luis Collado listed 24-, 25-, 30-, 40- and 50-pounder *culebrina*s in Spain.

[11] Thomas Smith's book from 1628 listed 37-, 32- and 24-pounder demi-cannons the weights of which were 2,721, 2,540 and 2,268 kg (6,000, 5,600 and 5,000 lb).

[12] Wilhelm Gohlke, *Geschichte der gesamten Feuerwaffen bis 1850* (Leipzig, 1911), pp. 50–51; O. F. G. Hogg, *English Artillery, 1326–1716* (London, 1963), pp. 26–29.

[13] The dispute among scholars regarding the superiority-inferiority issues of the English and the Spanish armadas and their ordnance is a case in point. The dispute, which often reflected nationalist bias, was, to a large extent, due to lack of understanding of contemporary naval and weapons terminology. Until the late 1980s it was thought that Spanish ships carried more heavy guns of the cannon type (believed to be less effective) while the English had more culverin-type medium-caliber

be treated with the same caution with which historians consider similar efforts regarding European ordnance.[14]

From the beginning the Ottomans applied their own terminology to their guns. Although many of the gun names in the Empire derived from European types of guns, an apparent sign of acculturation, Ottoman pieces differed from guns of similar European names, and these differences seem to have been more profound than dissimilarities among European guns of the same kind.

Bombards

Wrought-iron pieces were the first guns to appear in Europe and among the Ottomans. Manufactured of wrought-iron bars, they were fitted together longitudinally like the staves of a barrel and bound together with heated iron hoops. They had a detachable powder chamber and were loaded from the rear. Although initially small and rude pieces, these wrought-iron breech-loaders had evolved into large hooped bombards by the late fourteenth and especially by the fifteenth century. The largest ones had a bore diameter of 50–80 cm, weighed from about 6,000 to about 16,000 kg and fired large cut stone projectiles weighing from 150 to 700 kg. Because of their enormous size and weight it was extremely difficult to transport and maneuver these giant bombards, and their use remained limited to sieges and defense of castles. Some of these heavy stone-throwing wrought-iron pieces found their way into the Mediterranean galleys as center-line bow guns towards the end of the fifteenth century.[15]

The Ottomans followed suit and also produced their monster wrought-iron pieces. It seems that – unlike most of their European adversaries, who had abandoned the production of such giant pieces by the beginning of the sixteenth century – the Ottomans still manufactured a limited number of such massive pieces in the 1510s and perhaps even later. There was a special group of Ottoman blacksmiths (*cemaat-i topçiyan-i ahengeran* or *topçiyan-i haddadin*) responsible for forging wrought-iron pieces. Their number varied from eight to twenty-nine from

pieces. However, recent studies have argued that the opposite is more likely to have been the case and that the mistake is due to lack of understanding of the relevant names of guns. The guns listed as culverins aboard the English fleet were in fact cut-down versions of the culverin that had distinct cannon proportions (they were shorter and heavier than true culverins), yet still listed as culverins, for the English retained the name "culverin" for these shortened pieces. The Spaniards, on the other hand, referred to these shortened versions as *medios canones*, reserving the term *culebrina* for their true culverins. Thus, weapons registers would mistakenly suggest that the English had mainly light and long culverins whereas the Spaniards carried more heavy and short *canones*. See David Lyon, "Ordnance," in M. J. Rodríguez-Salgado ed., *Armada, 1588–1988* (London, 1988), p. 173.

[14] For an earlier attempt at classification, see Gábor Ágoston, "Ottoman Artillery and European Military Technology in the Fifteenth to Seventeenth Centuries," *AOH* 47, 1–2 (1994), 15–48. Salim Aydüz relies heavily on my article, largely follows its logic, and uses many of its sources, often without referring to it. See his 'Osmanlı Devletinde Tophane-i Amire ve Top Döküm Teknolojisi (XV–XVI. Yüzyıllar)' unpublished Ph.D. dissertation, University of Istanbul, 1998, pp. 311–63.

[15] John Francis Guilmartin, Jr., "The Early Provision of Artillery Armament on Mediterranean War Galleys," *The Mariner's Mirror* 59, 3 (1973), 259–64.

Table 3.1 *Large wrought-iron bombards in fifteenth-century Western Europe*

Name	Place of origin	Date	Weight of piece (kg)	Length of piece (cm)	Bore diameter (cm)	Weight of shot (kg)
Pumhart von Steyr	Steyr				80	697
Faule Mette	Braunschweig	1411	8,228	290	76	409
Dulle Griet	Ghent		16,400	501	64	350
Mons Meg	Mons/Flanders	1449	6,040	404	50	130–150

Sources: Data are from Robert D. Smith and Ruth Rhynas Brown, *Bombards: Mons Meg and her Sisters* (London, 1989); W. Gohlke, *Feuerwaffen*, pp. 26–29; Kelly DeVries, *Medieval Military Technology* (Peterborough, Ontario, 1992), pp. 150–52; Bert S. Hall, *Weapons and Warfare in Renaissance Europe: Gunpowder, Technology, and Tactics* (Baltimore, 1997), pp. 59–60. Modern estimates given by Smith and Brown are calculated on the basis of the bore of the gun, allowing 1–2 cm for windage, and assuming a specific gravity of stone of 2.6 (ibid., pp. 48–49.)

the late 1490s through 1527.[16] In 1517–18 Muslim and Jewish blacksmiths made twenty-two wrought-iron cannons at the Istanbul Imperial Foundry. Of these, the largest four were 714 cm (32 *karış*) long; nine were 558 cm (25 *karış*) long; and nine shorter cannons with an average length of 491 cm (22 *karış*). These Ottoman guns were longer than most European bombards and, given their average weight (6,210 kg), they were amongst the heaviest cannons known to contemporaries,[17] though the shorter ones probably were not heavier than Emperor Maximilian I of Habsburg's (r. 1493–1519) largest bombards that weighed some 5,600–7,280 kg.[18]

However, by the early sixteenth century, following, and in many respects preceding the European trend, the majority of Ottoman ordnance was not made on the forge, but was cast at the foundry. Single-piece cast bronze guns, made with an integral powder chamber and firing either stone balls or cast-iron projectiles, were safer than guns made of wrought iron. They could be cast thicker and thus were able to withstand the higher pressure of the larger powder charges cast-iron projectiles required. They were especially popular aboard ships, for they were less subject to corrosion. By the first decades of the sixteenth century bronze artillery had become regular pieces as center-line bow guns aboard the Mediterranean war galleys.[19] The Ottomans started to cast bronze cannon very early and some of their bronze pieces proved to be decisive during the siege of Constantinople in 1453.

[16] Ömer Lütfi Barkan, "H 933–934 (M 1527–1528) Mali Yılına ait bir Bütçe Örneği," *İFM* 15, 1–4 (1953–54), 310. Aydüz, "Tophane-i Amire," 294–95.

[17] İdris Bostan, "XVI Yüzyıl Başlarında Tophane-i Amirede Top Döküm Faaliyetleri," based on KK 4726, p. 45, manuscript, to be published in the forthcoming Halil İnalcık *Festschrift*. See also Bostan, "A szultáni ágyúöntő műhelyben (Tophane-i Amire) folyó tevékenység a 16. század elején," *Aetas* 18, 2 (2003), 12. For the Ottoman *karış* see Notes on weights and measurements.

[18] Kurzmann, *Kaiser Maximilian*, p. 125. This calculation is based on the Viennese *Pfund*, for which (and for other pounds used in the Empire) see Notes on weights and measurements.

[19] John Francis Guilmartin, Jr., *Gunpowder and Galleys: Changing Technology and Mediterranean Warfare at Sea in the Sixteenth Century* (Cambridge, 1974), pp. 157–58.

Figure 8 Fifteenth-century Ottoman bombard. Mistakenly identified as *darbzen*, this huge bronze bombard is 424 cm long, weighs 15 metric tons and fired shots of 285 kg in weight. It is assumed that it was used during the 1453 Siege of Constantinople. It was certainly one of the largest pieces the Ottomans cast in the middle of the fifteenth century. Military Museum, Istanbul.

Following Master Orban, Ottoman cannon founders cast a couple of giant pieces in the fifteenth century. One of Mehmed II's bronze cannon from 1467 weighed 17,500 kg.[20]

Given the enormous size of these cannons, the Ottomans often transported the raw materials with them and cast their cannons *in situ* before sieges, as was the case before, among other examples, the sieges of Salonica (1430) and the Hexamilion walls at the Isthmus of Corinth (1446) and the 1478 siege of Škodra. In the latter case, Daud Pasha who commanded the Rumelian army had, Angiolello recalled, "a great quantity of metal carried on camels for casting bombards, because it would not have been possible to carry large cannon through the rugged mountains and narrow passes on the way through Serbia and Albania."[21] These large bombards proved instrumental in breaching the walls of the Byzantine, Balkan and Hungarian fortresses. The effectiveness of cannon during the siege of Constantinople in 1453 is usually accepted, although some deny the role of cannons or have qualified their significance.[22] Other examples, however, clearly demonstrate the effectiveness of

[20] Gohlke, *Feuerwaffen*, p. 30.
[21] Quoted by Colin Imber, *The Ottoman Empire, 1300–1481* (Istanbul, 1990), p. 237.
[22] Hans Delbrück, *History of the Art of War*, vol. IV: *The Dawn of Modern Warfare*. Trans. Walter J. Renfroe, Jr. (Lincoln and London, 1990), p. 35; Kelly DeVries, "Gunpowder Weapons at the Siege of Constantinople, 1453," in Yaacov Lev ed., *War and Society in the Eastern Mediterranean, 7th–15th Centuries* (Leiden, 1997), pp. 343–62.

Ottoman artillery. All sources seem to agree that the large stone-throwing bombards of the Ottomans, though only seven in number, were remarkably effective against the walls of Otranto, which fell to Gedik Ahmed Pasha's forces on August 11, 1480 after an eleven-day siege. The siege itself was unusually swift, considering that it took four-and-a-half months in the next year for the Duke of Calabria to recapture Otranto, despite the fact that the latter siege was directed by one of the best contemporaneous European experts in siege warfare, Scirro Scirri.[23]

Nevertheless, it is true that cannons alone could not do the job, and other factors – the availability and the quality of infantry who stormed the breaches made by cannon-fire, leadership, and so forth – were likely to be as important as guns in the fifteenth century, as the examples of the failed Ottoman sieges of Belgrade (1440 and 1456), Škodra (1478) and Rhodes (1480) demonstrated. That cannons alone were not war-winning weapons is demonstrated by the 1456 siege of Belgrade. Mehmed II's twenty-two large bombards, whose bore diameter is said to have been about 60 cm, caused such destruction that, according to one eyewitness, after two weeks of heavy bombardment "the castle resembled not a fortress but a plain." Yet other factors, among which the most important was the timely arrival of János Hunyadi's relief forces and their successful assault on the besiegers, denied Ottoman victory.[24]

Mortars

By the second half of the fifteenth century, heavy and relatively short mortars that fired projectiles with parabolic trajectories had become a useful addition to the siege trains. Initially they fired large stone balls, but the most effective projectiles of the mortars were the explosive shells. The Venetians may have used primitive bombs as early as 1376. Robertus Valturius's *De re militari* (1472) – which may or may not have been familiar to Mehmed II, as we have seen – contains illustrations of bombs, which has led some historians to claim that these projectiles had appeared by the late fifteenth century.[25] Bombs filled with powder or a composition of saltpeter, sulfur, gunpowder and melted pitch, however, appeared regularly in continental warfare only after 1550. They remained the preferred ammunition for mortars in the centuries to come. These incendiary shells, sailing over walls and landing on rooftops, set ablaze magazines, barracks and buildings and had devastating effects on the besieged castles and towns. With smaller explosive shells that required even smaller powder charges, the mortars could be made with thinner

---

[23] Michael Mallett, "Siegecraft in Late Fifteenth-Century Italy," in Ivy A. Corfis and Michael Wolfe eds., *The Medieval City under Siege* (Woodbridge, 1995), pp. 251–53. One should not forget, however, that by the spring of 1481 the Ottomans had considerably strengthened the fortifications of the captured city. Some even claimed that the Ottoman fortification marked the beginning of genuine cannon-proof fortifications in Western Europe. This latter claim, though, has been challenged (ibid.).

[24] Gábor Ágoston, "La strada che conduceva a Nándorfehérvár (Belgrade): L'Ungheria, l'espansione ottomana nei Balcani e la vittoria di Nándorfehérvár," in Zsolt Visy ed., *La campana di mezzogiorno. Saggi per il Quinto Centenario della bolla papale* (Budapest, 2000), pp. 244–46.

[25] Delbrück, *Art of War*, vol. IV, p. 33.

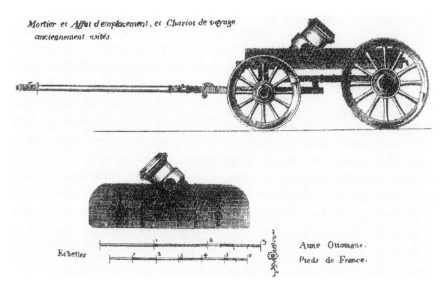

Mortier et Affut d'emplacement, et Chariot de voyage anciennement usités.

Echelles

Arme Ottomane.

Pieds de France.

Figure 9 The Ottomans are said to have used mortars as early as the 1453 siege of Constantinople. Ottoman mortar on its carriage. Mahmud Raif Efendi, *Tableau des nouveaux reglemens de l'empire ottoman*, Constantinople, 1798.

walls which gave them relatively high mobility. In the period under discussion, mortars were made in all sizes: the very large pieces threw stone balls, while the smallest ones hurled hand grenades.[26]

A contemporaneous source claims that the Ottomans first used mortars with parabolic trajectories during the siege of Constantinople to destroy enemy ships that closed the Golden Horn. In fact, European military historians tend to date the use of mortars from this date, crediting the Ottomans with developing and introducing this new type of gunpowder weapon.[27] Contemporary sources, indeed, confirm that by the middle of the fifteenth century the Ottomans used mortars routinely and with expertise. Giovanni da Tagliacozzo's eyewitness account of the 1456 siege of Belgrade mentioned seven huge mortars that hurled their "stone shots one Italian mile high."[28] Such European sources are especially precious, for the relevant Ottoman terminology is somewhat confusing.[29]

[26] Christopher Duffy, *Fire and Stone: The Science of Fortress Warfare, 1660–1860* (London, 1996), pp. 122–25; Trevor N. Dupuy, *The Evolution of Weapons and Warfare* (New York, 1984), pp. 104–05.
[27] During the siege, Sultan Mehmed urged his cannon-makers to make a different type of cannon which could fire its shot "to a great height, so that when it came down it would hit the ship." Kritovoulos, *History of Mehmed the Conqueror*. Trans. Charles T. Riggs (Westport, CN, 1954), 51. See also Steven Runciman, *The Fall of Constantinople, 1453* (Cambridge, 1965), p. 98; DeVries, "Gunpowder Weapons," p. 360; Aydüz, "Tophane-i Amire," p. 363. Dupuy asserts that mortars "were known from the very beginning of the gunpowder period." Dupuy, *Weapons and Warfare*, p. 104.
[28] Ágoston, "La strada," p. 244.
[29] It is possible that the term *havayî* (*top*), that is, "mortar gun," was used to denote longer mortars of the *Steinbüchse* type, a descendant of large stone-throwing bombards used in the Austrian Habsburg lands, while, especially later, the term *havan* was used for shorter mortars.

The assertion of Turkish historians that the Ottomans used mortars firing explosive shells at the sieges of Škodra (1478) and Rhodes (1480), and that an independent unit was set up towards the end of that century in order to manufacture such bombs and to operate the mortars firing explosive shells, needs further investigation, although the claim is not implausible.[30] References to fires caused by projectiles fired from either cannons or mortars during sieges are inconclusive, for the Ottomans used other weapons and projectiles (burning arrows, as well as burning projectiles and red shot fired from cannons) to set ablaze besieged towns and castles.[31] At the 1480 siege of Rhodes, for instance, the Ottomans used *carcasses*, that is, clay "eggs" "filled with a burning mixture of pitch, pinewood, charcoal and tow" hurled by the spoon-shaped arm of their *mangonel*. The "wild fire" these projectiles caused could not be extinguished with water, but only "with vinegar, urine or glue."[32] The Ottomans used all kinds of explosive devices in siege warfare. It is difficult, in the absence of the original text, to tell what kind of device the Ottomans used in the 1521 siege of Belgrade. An Arab eyewitness who served in the army of Mustafa Pasha had this to say about the device in his poem:

> They are attacking with maroons, which fly off when ignited, when high up they are surrounded by the usual wreath of fire, then fall back faster than they ascended, and burst. But first they spin like an accelerated mill and then explode into seventy or more or fewer pieces. It is, of course, only an approximate estimation. Each of these shards breaks and cuts and smashes what it hits, and each is lethal, except the ones rendered harmless by God himself. But it happens rarely. The fire of these splinters set every wet and dry object around them aflame. A horrible thing![33]

Some of the devices described above must have been bombshells, for in the 1522 siege of Rhodes the Ottomans used them in the thousands. An inventory of weapons and war material sent for the siege in May 1522 lists 4,580 bombs, of which 3,080 pieces were made of earth (*çömlek*) while the remaining 1,500 bombs were explosive shells (*serpme*).[34]

By the mid-sixteenth century *humbaracı*s were present in several major Ottoman forts.[35] This indicates that by that time mortars firing bombshells had

[30] İsmail Hami Danişmend, *İzahlı Osmanlı Tarihi Kronolojisi* (4 vols., Istanbul, 1971), vol. I, p. 340; Ahmet Halaçoğlu, "Humbaracı," *TDVİA*, vol. XVIII, pp. 349–50.

[31] See, for instance, the descriptions of the sieges of Eger (1552 and 1596) and Szigetvár (1556 and 1566).

[32] Eric Brockman, *The Two Sieges of Rhodes, 1480–1522* (London, 1969), p. 45.

[33] Janicsek István, "Egy arab szemtanú Belgrád megvételéről, 1521," *HK* 31 (1930), 103. Quoted by Ferenc Szakály, "Nándorfehérvár, 1521: The Beginning of the End of the Medieval Hungarian Kingdom," in Géza Dávid and Pál Fodor eds., *Hungarian–Ottoman Military and Diplomatic Relations in the Age of Süleyman the Magnificent* (Budapest, 1994), p. 65. Whereas in Janicsek's Hungarian translation the device is called a "petard," the translator of Szakály's original Hungarian article rendered it as "maroon".

[34] Nicolas Vatin, *L'Orde de Saint-Jean-de-Jérusalem, l'Empire ottoman et la Méditerranée orientale entre les deux sièges de Rhodes (1480–1522)* (Paris, 1994), pp. 483, 486, 490.

[35] As we have seen there were nineteen *humbaracı*s in three Ottoman forts in Hungary in 1549.

become regular weapons in the defense of fortresses. Mortars firing explosive shells (*havan-i humbara*)[36] were made in various calibers. In the 1690s the most popular ones fired explosive projectiles of 30, 43, 44 and 98 kg in weight and are designated in our sources as 24-, 35-, 36- and 80-*okka* mortars.[37] Due to their shorter barrel and thinner tube, mortars were lighter than cannons of the same caliber. The average weight of a 35-*okka* caliber mortar was 636 kg (11.78 *kantar*) in 1693–94, that is, they were lighter than the smaller, 30-pounder European mortars that weighed 680 kg (1,500 lb).[38]

In the early eighteenth century in Praviște, which was one of the major bomb-producing centers in the Empire, bombshells were still cast in eight different calibers that ran from 22-*okka* (27 kg) through 90-*okka* (111 kg). It seems that the pieces most in demand were those of 45-*okka* (55 kg) and 85-*okka* (104 kg) calibers.[39] Nevertheless, there were mortars firing much smaller explosive shells. Among the 12,589 bombshells taken into inventory in the port of Kavala in 1717, the most numerous were those that weighed only 4, 18 and 23 kg (3, 14, and 18 *okka*).[40]

As in sixteenth-century Europe, mortars in the Ottoman Empire, too, comprised a minority of the artillery train. In 1517–19, of the 673 guns and mortars cast in the Tophane, only two (0.3 percent) were mortars. Of the 685 guns listed in the fortress of Rhodes after its conquest in 1522, only three (0.4 percent) were mortars.[41] Similarly, Ottoman chronicles refer to mortars very rarely in the sixteenth century.[42] The ratio of mortars to cannons, however, could and did alter according to changing military situations. In the 1690s, when the Ottomans were forced to become engaged in pitched battles in the Hungarian theater of war against the forces of the Holy League and thus needed mainly lighter field artillery pieces,

---

[36] MAD 4428, p. 24, ordering eighteen such mortars from Istanbul during the preparations for the 1685 campaign.

[37] MAD 5432, p. 11; DBŞM TPH 18610. As indicated in the Notes on weights and measurements, throughout this book I calculate with the following: until the end of the seventeenth century one *okka* = 1.2288, and consequently one *kantar* = 54 kg; regarding eighteenth-century data, one *okka* = 1.2828, and one *kantar* = 56.4 kg. Figures in kg in the tables and in the text are rounded for clarity and expediency.

[38] MAD 5432, p. 11. For the European mortars see Dupuy, *Weapons and Warfare*, p. 103.

[39] MAD 4415, pp. 8, 30–33. Of these bombs 2,000 and 1,610 pieces, respectively, were made. The total weight of the shells exceeded 332 metric tons. In 1708, the Praviște works stored 1,000 bombshells from 34-*okka* (43.62 kg) through 44-*okka* (one-*kantar* or 56.44 kg) caliber. See KK 5185, p. 1. The number of bombshells amassed and used in late seventeenth-century campaigns is impressive. According to an account of the Imperial Ammunition House, which covers the period from September 7, 1687 through January 15, 1689, the *Cebehane* received 12,000 large bombshells (*tane-i humbara-i kebir*), of which 10,000 pieces were sent to the campaign. KK 4738, p. 8.

[40] MAD 4456, p. 43. Cf. also Appendix.

[41] Bostan, "Top Döküm Faaliyetleri," based on KK 4726, pp. 30–31. Taking into consideration the other castles of the island the ratio is 848 to 8, and the percentage of mortars is still less than one percent.

[42] For example, the term *havayî top* is mentioned only once (in connection with the siege of Malta, 1556) by the Ottoman chronicler Selanikî Mustafa Efendi (d. after 1600), who is often specific regarding the different types of weapons used in the Ottoman army. Selanikî Mustafa Efendi, *Tarih-i Selânikî*. Ed. Mehmed İpşirli (2 vols., Istanbul, 1989), vol. I, p. 6.

Figure 10 Mortars like this fired either stone shots or explosive shells and were an essential part of the Ottoman siege train. Military Museum, Istanbul.

there were years (e.g., 1695–96) when they did not cast a single mortar. When they did manufacture mortars, their number was not that impressive.[43]

A comparison of Ottoman and Habsburg mortars shows that, contrary to received wisdom, Ottoman mortars were not larger than the ones used by their opponents. As can be seen from the data presented in Table 3.2 the Ottomans used mortars of a great variety of calibers. The largest were the 85-*okka* through 200-*okka* caliber pieces that hurled stone balls of 104–246 kg in weight. Yet, the majority of Ottoman mortars were smaller pieces, the 14-*okka* through 45-*okka* caliber ones that fired balls weighing 17–55 kg, and as the eighteenth century wore on, small-caliber pieces became the dominant types. In 1771–72 only 14-, 18- and 32-*okka* caliber mortars were cast in the Tophane; they fired shots weighing 18, 23 and 41 kg.[44] While even the medium-sized Ottoman mortars might seem too large, such large pieces were not unusual in the armies the Ottomans confronted, either.

[43] The distribution of the output was as follows: 1691–92: one mortar and 297 cannons (0.3 percent); from 1693 through 1695: 24 mortars and 649 guns (3.4 percent); 1696–97: 16 mortars and 1,306 guns (1.2 percent); 1697–98: 16 mortars and 255 cannons (5.9 percent). See MAD 5432, p. 29b; MAD 173, p. 16b; MAD 2732, p. 32. Yet in other years the percentage of mortars was considerably higher. In 1712–14, for instance, the ratio of mortars to cannons was 15 to 88 (14.5 percent), though the relatively small number of cannons cast at this time may distort the picture to a certain extent. DBŞM TPH 18618. Two decades later, an inventory of the Tophane listed 450 guns of various sizes and only 32 mortars (6.6 percent). See MAD 2677, p. 21; cf. also Appendix.

[44] MAD 2677, p. 21; DBŞM TPH 18645, p. 23; DBŞM TPH 18693, p. 3. See also Appendix.

Table 3.2 *Ottoman and Habsburg mortars in the 1680s and 1690s*

	Date	Caliber (weight of shot in lb)	Caliber (weight of shot in *okka*)	Weight of shot in kg
Habsburgs	1683M	30, 60, 100, 200, 300		15/20, 30/41, 50/68, 100/136, 150/205*
Habsburgs	1683V	15, 20, 28, 60, 150, 200		8, 11, 16, 34, 84, 112
Habsburgs	1686B	30, 60, 70, 100, 150, 200, 300, 400		17, 34, 39, 56, 84, 112, 168, 224
Ottomans	1680s and 1690s TPH		14,18, 20, 24, 32, 36, 45, 80, 85, 120, 180, 200	17, 22, 25, 29, 39, 44, 55, 98, 104, 147, 221, 246
Ottomans	1686B	5, 8, 30, 34, 35, 40, 60, 65, 66, 70, 100, 200		3, 4, 17, 19, 20, 22, 34, 36, 37, 39, 56, 112
Ottomans	1696–97 TPH		24, 36, 80, 180	

Notes: Abbreviations for the Habsburgs: 1683M = mortars listed in Michael Miethen's *Artilleriae receptor praxis* (1683); 1683V = mortars used during the defense of Vienna in 1683; 1686B = mortars used in the siege of Buda in 1686; for the Ottomans: 1680s and 1690s TPH = mortars cast in the Tophane; 1686B = mortars listed in Habsburg inventories of Ottoman Buda after its reconquest in 1686; 1696–97 TPH = mortars cast in the Tophane in 1696–97.
Data in kilograms are rounded; Miethen used the Nurenberger pound, but it is difficult to calculate his figures in kg for handbooks give two separate kg equivalents (0.509 kg and 0.682). Hence the double figures in kg after Miethen's data (marked with *). All other Habsburg data are calculated in Viennese pounds. As elsewhere, for pre-eighteenth-century Ottoman data 1 *okka* = 1.2288 kg.
Sources: Habsburg data are from Dolleczek, *Geschichte der österreichischen Artillerie*, pp. 155–56, 207; György Domokos, "Várépítészet és várharcászat Európában a XVI–XVII. században," *HK* 33, 1 (1986), 83; Domokos, "Buda visszavívásának ostromtechnikai problémái," *HK* 106, 1 (1993), 54–58; Ottoman data are from MAD 5432, p. 11; MAD 4415, pp. 30–33; DBŞM TPH 18610, etc. See also Appendix.

In fact, they were similar to the mortars used in the Austrian army in the 1680s and 1690s. It should also be remembered that for defensive purposes contemporaries used larger mortars, since in forts the problems regarding their transportation and maneuvering were limited. In 1683, during the second Turkish siege of Vienna, the defenders used 15-, 26-, 28-, 60-, 150- and 200-pounder mortars. By the late seventeenth century 300-pounder mortars were rare, but during the 1686 siege of Buda the Habsburgs used even larger, 400-pounder pieces which would throw shots of 224 kg in weight. Such large-caliber mortars were rare. According to the various weapons inventories compiled by the Habsburg authorities after the re-conquests of Buda, the Ottomans had no such giant pieces in Buda, although in 1696–97 they cast one 180-*okka* caliber mortar in Istanbul that fired shots of 221 kg. But the Ottomans had few such large mortars, as can be seen from output figures of the Imperial Cannon Foundry. Although they weighed 3,888 kg (72 *kantar*), they were not heavier than the 200-pounder European mortars that weighed on average 4,500 kg.[45]

In terms of caliber and weight of the projectile Ottoman mortars were not that dissimilar from the Habsburg pieces. In terms of standardization, though, the Ottomans seem to have lagged behind their Habsburg opponents. All data indicate that the Ottomans used a greater variety of mortars than the Habsburgs. While the Habsburgs were also far from achieving real standardization, they used only six to eight different calibers during the 1683 defense of Vienna and the 1686 siege of Buda. At the same time, the Ottomans had twelve different types of mortars at their disposal in 1686, and the number of mortar types they cast in the 1690s was about the same. In short, it was not the supposed larger size of their mortars that caused problems for the Ottomans, but the lack of standardization. The same appears to be true with regards to their cannons.

Large guns of the cannon class

Contrary to the widespread notion in European literature, the Ottomans also participated in the European trend toward smaller field guns, starting in the early sixteenth century: in fact, the majority of their cannons were small and medium-caliber pieces (see chapter 6). Like their European opponents, they continued to manufacture larger siege and fortress guns, but those cast in the sixteenth and seventeenth centuries were much smaller than the giant bombards of the fifteenth century. Mid-sixteenth-century sources indicate that, in a similar way to their European contemporaries, the Ottomans distinguished between large siege cannons and smaller field pieces. Sixteenth-century Ottoman military specialists considered 8- to 22-*okka* caliber guns firing projectiles of 10–27 kg in weight suitable for both campaigns and sieges.[46] Cannons of 14- and 16-*okka* caliber that fired shots of 17 and 20 kg in weight are specifically referred to in the sources as battering guns or *kale-kobs* (from the Persian *qal'eh-kub*).[47] Although the majority

[45] MAD 173, p. 16b; Dupuy, *Weapons and Warfare*, p. 103.
[46] When preparing for the 1566 Hungarian campaign, the *beylerbeyi* of Buda was ordered in November 1565 to examine all the cannons in Buda that fired projectiles of 11–22 *okka*. (MD 5, p. 223, no. 566.) Later, in June, he was ordered to bring altogether thirty pieces of siege guns: five 16-*okka*, nine 14-*okka*, five 11-*okka*, six 10-*okka* and five 8-*okka* pieces. (MD 5, p. 667, no. 1874; cf. also MD 5, p. 599, no. 1658.)
[47] AK fol. 133b, regarding the request of ten pieces of *kale-kob* guns firing 14- and 16-*okka* shots for the siege of Kanizsa in 1600. The Persian word *kob* means beating, striking or who beats or strikes, hence *qal'eh-kub* means battering gun or "castle-smasher." As we have seen in the previous chapter, in the Safavid army, where cannon were mainly used for sieges, cannons were often called *qal'eh-kub*. Abdülkadir Efendi, who served as the scribe of the armorers and artillerists, provides

Table 3.3 *Ottoman, Spanish and Austrian siege cannons*

Name	Country	Translation	Caliber/weight of shot (*okka*/lb)	Weight of shot in kg
Kale-kob	Ottoman	Fort-smasher	12, 14, 15, 16	15, 17, 18, 20
Culebrina	Spain	Culverin	30, 40, 50	14, 18, 23
Canon de abatir	Spain	Siege cannon	32	15
Doble canon	Spain	Double cannon	48	22
Canon de batería	Spain	Battering cannon	60	28
Quebrantamuro or lonbarda	Spain	Wall-breaker or lonbard	70–90	32–41
Ganztze Karthaun	Austria	Full *Karthaun*	48	27
Dreiviertel Karthaun	Austria	Three-quarter *Karthaun*	36	20
Halbe Karthaun	Austria	Half *Karthaun*	24	13

Note: Figures in kg are rounded and calculated with the Spanish pound of 0.46 kg and the Viennese pound of 0.56 kg.

Sources: Dolleczek, *Geschichte der österreichischen Artillerie*; Albert Manucy, *Artillery through the Ages* (Washington, DC, 1949; reprint 1985), p. 34, following Luis Collado, *Platica Manual de la Artillería* (Milan, 1592).

of the *kale-kob*s remained large 14-, 15- and 16-*okka* caliber pieces, in the seventeenth century there were also smaller, 12-*okka* caliber guns that used 15 kg balls.[48] As can be seen from Table 3.3, these Ottoman battering guns – based on the weight of the shot they fired – can be compared to the large European culverins and siege cannons.[49]

Apart from the generic name of *kale-kob* borrowed from the Persian language, the Ottomans used several types of siege or fortress guns. Among these, the most often used types were the *şayka*, *balyemez*, *bacaluşka* and *kanon* guns.

Şayka

"Guns throwing stone balls that are too large to be carried by humans are called *şayka*s," reported Evliya Çelebi in the middle of the seventeenth century. He also noted that "Such guns cannot be put on carriages and transported to campaigns but

the most valuable information regarding sixteenth- and seventeenth-century Ottoman ordnance. On Abdülkadir Efendi and his work, see Markus Köhbach, "Der osmanische Historiker Topçilar Katibi Abdü'l-qadir Efendi. Leben und Werk," *OsmAr* 2 (1981), 75–96.

[48] MAD 3150, pp. 110–11, an inventory of several Cretan fortresses from 1666 which lists *kale-kob* guns firing 16-, 15-, 14- and 12-*okka* projectiles.

[49] The larger *kale-kob*s would be close to the 40-pounder Spanish *culebrinas* and the 32-pounder siege cannons (*canon de abatir*), and the 41-pounder English bastard cannons, but were larger than the 36-pounder Austrian *Dreiviertel Karthaun*. However, they fired lighter shots than the Spanish double cannons (48 lb), battering cannons (*canon de batería*, 60 lb) or the English cannon and serpentine cannon (60 and 53 lb). The 12-*okka kale-kob*s can be compared to the 30-pounder Spanish *culebrinas* and *culebrina relas*, the 32-pounder siege cannon (*canon de abatir*), and to the 24-pounder Austrian *Halbe Karthaun*.

Table 3.4 *Types and calibers of* şayka *guns, 1560s–1740s*

	Caliber (weight of ball in *okka*)	Weight of ball (kg)
Large *şaykas*	28, 36, 42, 44, 45, 50, 55	34, 44, 52, 54, 55, 61, 68
Medium-sized *şaykas*	20, 22, 24	25, 27, 30
Small *şaykas*	0.5, 2, 2.5, 5, 10, 12, 14	2.5, 3, 6, 12, 15, 17

Sources: Vienna, ÖNB Mxt., 599 (Buda castle, 1565); MAD 3448, p. 248 (fort of Selanik, 1659–60); MAD 3150, p. 125 (fort of Eğriboz, 1666); DBŞM Dosya 1, vesika 13 (Istanbul, Saray garden, 1500); MAD 3992, p. 19 (fort of Semendire, 1687); DBŞM TPH 18617, p. 4. and DBŞM TPH 18618, pp. 20–25 (Tophane, 1712–14); DBŞM TPH 18637, p. 27 (Tophane, 1732–33); DBŞM TPH 18645, p. 22 (Tophane, 1737–38); DBŞM TPH 18645, p. 23 (Tophane, 1736–40).

only slid on sleighs and installed at castles. No one in the world, but the Ottomans have cannon of this kind." In his description of the Imperial Cannon Foundry at Istanbul, he mentioned *şayka*s large enough to enclose a man.[50]

These cannons were named after the *şayka* (Slavic *chaika* or "seagull") boats that were usually equipped with three guns.[51] This seems to contradict Evliya Çelebi's description of these guns as so enormous. The contradiction, however, is easily resolvable: initially *şayka* guns may have been used on *şayka* boats sent to defend river mouths. Later they were carried from these boats into riverside forts, which enabled the Ottomans to install *şayka* guns of ever larger bore sizes. Archival sources also reveal that *şayka* guns were made with various bore sizes. Evliya Çelebi, obsessed with size and numbers, mentioned only the largest pieces.

The Ottomans differentiated between large, medium-sized and small *şayka* guns, often without specifying their calibers.[52] While in certain cases the above distinction was made according to the caliber of the piece, in other cases it was the length of the barrel that determined whether a particular piece was designated as large, medium or small.

The length of the *şaykas* also shows a great variety. The shortest pieces were 176, 198 and 264 cm (8, 9 and 12 *karış*) long, whereas the longest ones to be found in inventories were 396, 418, 440 and 462 cm (18, 19, 20 and 21 *karış*) in length. In addition to these small and long pieces, our sources also list 308, 330 and 352 cm (14, 15, and 16 *karış*) long *şaykas*.[53] In the early eighteenth century 44-*okka*

[50] Evliya Çelebi, *Evlia Cselebi török világutazó magyarországi utazásai 1600–1664*. Trans. Imre Karácson, ed. Pál Fodor (Budapest, 1985), p. 361; Evliya Çelebi, *Seyahatname* (10 vols., Istanbul, 1314/1896–97), vol. I, p. 437.

[51] On which see Victor Ostapchuk, "The Human Landscape of the Ottoman Black Sea in the Face of the Cossack Naval Raids," in Kate Fleet ed., *The Ottomans and the Sea, Oriente Moderno* 20 (81) n.s. 1. (2001), 41–43.

[52] MD 27, p. 58; DMŞM TPH 18599, regarding large and medium-sized *şayka* guns in the castle of Semendire in 1575 and 1689–90, respectively.

[53] MAD 3448, p. 248; MAD 3150, p. 125; DBŞM Dosya 1, vesika 13; MAD 3992, p. 19.

caliber *şaykas* weighed around 4,060 kg (72 *kantar*), while the smaller 36- and 22-*okka* pieces weighed 3,666 and 2,707 kg (65 and 48 *kantar*), respectively.[54]

In addition to *şaykas* deployed as siege and fortress cannons, large *şayka* guns were also used aboard Ottoman ships. In 1697–98, the eight large *şayka* guns that were to be deployed aboard the Ottoman flagship, the admiral's galleon, each fired 61 kg (50 *okka*) marble cannon balls.[55] In 1732 and again in 1736–40, *şayka* guns throwing 56 kg (44 *okka*) shots were designated as *şayka-i kalyon*, that is, *şaykas* to be used aboard *kalyons*, the Ottoman equivalent of the Mediterranean galleon or sailing warships.[56] However, there were considerably smaller *şayka* pieces aboard Ottoman ships, used mainly to flank the main centerline bow guns. In 1698, a *şayka* weighing only 378 kg (7 *kantar*) is mentioned as a flanking gun (*top-i yan şayka*).[57]

The data suggest several conclusions. *Şaykas* showed a great variety regarding their caliber and size. Calibers ran from the smallest 2-*okka* pieces to the largest 50-*okka* pieces in the sixteenth and seventeenth centuries, though 2-, 2.5- and 5-*okka* caliber pieces were rare. Although large European siege/fortress guns of the cannon class were divided into several sub-types, in most European countries the number of these sub-types was much smaller than in the case of Ottoman *şaykas*. One obvious exception was Spain, Istanbul's main adversary in the Mediterranean, whose armada used a great variety of guns of the cannon class from the smallest 2-pounders to the largest 60-pounders in the sixteenth and seventeenth centuries.[58]

While the 176 cm long 5-*okka* (6 kg) caliber pieces (listed in 1666 in the castle of Eğriboz) can be considered small *şaykas*, the 264 cm long 44-*okka* (54 kg) caliber piece in the same castle, although still relatively short, belonged to the largest-caliber *şaykas*. The 462 and 396 cm (21 and 18 *karış*) long *şaykas* that fired cannon balls of 52 and 55 kg (42 and 45 *okka*) in weight (Selanik, 1659–60) or the 44-*okka* caliber *şaykas* with barrels of 440 and 418 cm (20 and 19 *karış*) in length (Semendire, 1687) appear to have been among the largest *şaykas* recorded in seventeenth-century sources.[59]

The sources also show that during the eighteenth century the Ottomans considerably reduced the various types of *şaykas*. In 1732, in the storehouse of the Imperial Cannon Foundry we find only 14- and 44-*okka* caliber *şaykas*. Guns in the first category are designated as "campaign *şaykas*" (*şayka-i sefer*), that is to say, field *şaykas*, while the latter were part of the Ottoman shipboard ordnance, designated as *şaykas* for galleons (*şayka-i kalyon*).[60] In the late 1770s, newly cast guns designated as large *şaykas* were mainly 44- and 22-*okka* caliber and fired shots of 56 and 28 kg in weight. Equally important is the observation that by

[54] MAD 2652, p. 25; MAD 2679, p. 4.
[55] MAD 2732, p. 43. The galleon was provided with 400 such big cannon balls.
[56] MAD 2677, p. 21; DBŞM TPH 18645, p. 23.   [57] MAD 2730, p. 7.
[58] Sources mention 2-, 3-, 4-, 5-, 7-, 8-, 9-, 10-, 12-, 16-, 18- and 40-pounder cannons at Castillo de San Marcos in 1683. Manucy, *Artillery*, p. 47.
[59] MAD 3448, p. 248; MAD 3150, p. 125; MAD 3992, p. 19.   [60] MAD 2677, p. 21.

Table 3.5 Balyemez *guns in the seventeenth and eighteenth centuries*

	Caliber (weight of ball in *okka*)	Weight of ball (kg)
*Balyemez*es/Evliya Çelebi	25, 30, 40, 50, 60	31, 37, 50, 61, 74
*Balyemez*es/in inventories	5, 7, 9, 11, 14, 16, 18, 20, 22	6, 9, 11, 14, 17, 20, 22, 25, 27

Sources: DBŞM CBH 18368, pp. 12–14 (fort of Baghdad, 1681); DBŞM TPH 18597, p. 7, and MAD 3448, p. 230 (fort of Belgrade, 1659–60); DBŞM TPH 18598, p. 3 (Tophane, 1685–86); DBŞM TPH 18696, p. 2 (Tophane, 1775–76).

this time these large *şayka*s comprised only a tiny percentage of newly cast guns, merely 6 percent (four pieces out of sixty-four guns) in 1779–80.[61]

Balyemez

Cannons called *balyemez*, a name of uncertain origin, were large siege guns, similar to the *şayka* guns with which they are occasionally listed.[62] It appears, however, that most *balyemez* guns were closer to the medium- and small-caliber *şayka*s. Evliya Çelebi, whose interest in curious objects and events is well known, mentioned *balyemez*es firing shots of 31, 37, 50, 61 and 74 kg (25, 30, 40, 50 and 60 *okka*) in weight. He also noted that there existed only four examples of the largest 60-*okka* caliber gun in the whole Empire: "there are two large ready guns at present in the gate section at the fortress of Akkirman; another cannon of Süleyman Han using 60 *okka* iron balls at the fortress of Ösek, and another one at the river Drava."[63] Archival sources, however, refer to significantly smaller *balyemez*es.[64]

In addition to *balyemez*es used as fortress guns, the Ottomans also employed this particular type of weapon as siege cannons.[65] Like *şayka*s, *balyemez*es were also to be found aboard Ottoman ships. In 1538 twenty *balyemez* cannons, firing shot of 25 kg (20 *okka*), were cast of bronze for the Ottoman navy.[66]

In short, Ottoman sources refer to large siege/fortress cannons by the term *balyemez*. The largest pieces, mentioned by chroniclers and above all by Evliya

---

[61] DBŞM TPH 18707, p. 10.

[62] DBŞM CBH 18368 pp. 12–13. Regarding the various etymologies of the word see Ágoston, "Ottoman Artillery," 33–34.

[63] *Evlia Cselebi török világutazó*, p. 361.

[64] Confiscated Christian pieces were given special terminology by the Ottomans. There is a bronze cannon from Venice called *balyemez* on display in front of the Military Museum (Askeri Müze) in Istanbul, being 9 *karış* long and weighing 1,188 kg (22 *kantar*) as confirmed by the inscription on its barrel. Subsequent measurements showed that it is 208 cm long and has a bore diameter of 23.5 cm (Inventory no. 342). Another bronze gun from Venice recorded as a *balyemez* was 191 cm long and its bore diameter was 23.5 cm (Inventory no. 262).

[65] In July 1684, preparations were made to send fifteen pieces to Belgrade before the coming of the winter. See MAD 4428, p. 23.

[66] Cengiz Orhonlu, "XVI. asrın ilk yarısında Kızıldeniz sahillerinde Osmanlılar," *TD* 12, 16 (1961), 14.

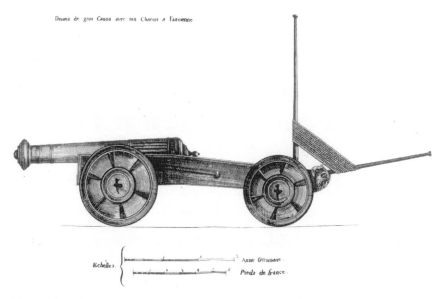

Figure 11   Mahmud Raif Efendi refers to this large cannon as "old *balyemez* or *cannon de batterie*." It was about 3.5 m long and judging from the approximate diameter of the cannon ball this large piece must have fired shots of some 27–35 kg in weight. Mahmud Raif Efendi, *Tableau des nouveaux reglemens de l'empire ottoman*, Constantinople, 1798.

Çelebi, threw stone balls that weighed 31–74 kg (25–60 *okka*), and would corre-spond to the largest (68–162-pounder) European bombards and *pedreros*. Such large pieces, used almost exclusively as fortress guns, were the heritage of the fifteenth century and were seldom made after the mid-sixteenth century. Archival sources mention much smaller pieces, 5–22-*okka* caliber *balyemez*es that fired mostly cast-iron projectiles weighing 6–27 kg. These Ottoman pieces would roughly correspond to 14–59-pounder European guns. Even these smaller *balyemez* pieces were a rarity by the late seventeenth century. Of 104 guns cast in the Istanbul foundry in 1685–86 there were only two *balyemez* cannons: one 14-*okka* and another 11-*okka* piece. Other inventories show a similar picture.[67]

Bacaluşka

Perhaps the most popular and widely used Ottoman siege/fortress guns were the *bacaluşka*s, also denoted by the terms of *baciliska, bacaluşka, bacaloşka,*

---

[67] MAD 4028, pp. 86–91; DMŞM TPH 18597, p. 7; DMŞM TPH 18598, p. 3; see also Appendix for output figures of the Istanbul foundry.

Table 3.6 Bacaluşka *guns in the sixteenth century*

	Caliber (weight of ball in *okka*)	Weight of ball (kg)
Small *bacaluşka*s	1, 4, 6, 11	1, 5, 7, 14
Large *bacaluşka*s	14, 16, 18, 20, 22, 23	17, 20, 22, 25, 27, 28

Sources: Vienna, ÖNB Mxt. 599; MD 5, p. 615, no. 1709; MD 5, p. 521, no. 1428; AK fols. 3b, 19a, 21b, 52a, 53b, 67b–68a, 102a.

badaluşka, badoluşka, badoloşka and *bedoloşka* in Turkish sources, which reflect the distorted name of the European basilisk.[68] As can be seen from Table 3.6, small *bacaluşka*s ran from one-*okka* through 11-*okka* caliber and fired projectiles of 1–14 kg in weight. Those from 14-*okka* caliber through 23-*okka* caliber were considered large *bacaluşka*s, and fired shots weighing 17–28 kg.[69]

The length of the *bacaluşka*s ranged between 198–220 and 396–440 cm. Larger pieces were usually 440 and 396 cm (20 and 18 *karış*) long, though occasionally, especially at the beginning of the sixteenth century, there were also considerably longer pieces.[70] Short pieces were 198 and 220 cm (9 and 10 *karış*) long, though still could fire relatively large projectiles of 22 kg (18 *okka*) in weight, like the ones listed in Eğriboz in 1666.[71]

The largest pieces exceeded 11 tons in weight. One such big basilisk (*top-i bacaluşka-i buzurg*) weighing 11,340 kg (210 *kantar*) was transferred to the Istanbul Imperial Cannon Foundry for recasting in the early 1520s. This cannon, however, must have been a *bacaluşka* rarity, since the average weight of the basilisks cast at the Istanbul foundry between 1522 and 1526 was only 4,193 kg (77.65 *kantar*).[72] In addition to Istanbul, local cannon foundries were also capable

---

[68] Henry Kahane, Renée Kahane and Andreas Tietze, *The Lingua Franca in the Levant: Turkish Nautical Terms of Italian and Greek Origin* (Urbana, 1958; reprint Istanbul, 1988), pp. 99–100. Cf., e.g., Spanish, Portuguese and Catalan *basilisco*.

[69] The 1565 inventory of Buda enumerates the following basilisks, referring to them as *badoloşka*: two pieces of 22-*okka* caliber together with 400 iron cannon balls, two pieces firing 18-*okka* balls together with 1,000 iron shots, two pieces using 16-*okka* balls with 500 iron cannon balls and 14 pieces of 14-*okka* caliber together with their 4,000 iron shots. At the same time in the castle of Peşte (Pest) one *badoloşka* firing shots of 16 *okka* and one infidel (*kâfirî*) basilisk throwing cannon balls of 18 *okka* were entered into inventory. In Peçuy (Pécs) the inventory lists one 20-*okka* basilisk, while another 14-*okka* piece in the castle of Şikloş (Siklós) is referred to as *şâhî badaloşka* (Vienna, ÖNB Mxt. 599).

[70] In 1517–19, for instance, the Ottoman founders cast sixteen such large basilisks in Istanbul that were 550 cm (25 *karış*) and 660 cm (30 *karış*) long. See KK 4726, pp. 6ff. Yet, these pieces appear to have been unusually large *bacaluşka*s. See Bostan, "A szultáni ágyúöntő műhely," 12.

[71] MAD 3150, p. 125.

[72] Colin Heywood, "The Activity of the State Cannon-Foundry (Tophane-i Amire) at Istanbul in the Early Sixteenth Century According to an Unpublished Turkish Source," *POF* 30 (1980) p. 209–16. Reprinted in Heywood, *Writing Ottoman History: Documents and Interpretations* (Aldershot, 2002), article XV, p. 215.

of casting relatively large basilisks. In 1543, a Persian cannon founder from Tabriz cast, in the Buda foundry within ten days, a 396 cm (18 *karış*) long, 20-*okka* caliber bronze *bacaluşka* that could fire 25 kg shots.[73]

Similarly to their *şayka* and *balyemez* guns, the Ottomans used their basilisks as siege guns. There were at least seventeen *bacaluşka*s, mainly of 16- and 14-*okka* caliber, deployed during Sultan Süleyman's 1566 siege of Szigetvár.[74] Before the 1593 Hungarian campaign, fifteen *badoloşka*s firing shots of merely 5 kg (4 *okka*) in weight were cast in Buda under the supervision of Mustafa Ağa, *kethüda* of the cannon founders of Istanbul who had been sent from the capital to Hungary.[75] During the 1594, 1596 and 1598 campaigns, the Ottoman troops employed several basilisks firing mostly 14 and 17 kg (11 and 14 *okka*) shots to besiege the Hungarian forts.[76]

The sixteen giant basilisks (660 cm and 550 cm long) cast in 1517–19 in Istanbul, and the enormous piece of over 11 metric tons, may have been similar to those that were mentioned in European sources in connection with the Ottoman–Portuguese encounter at Jiddah in 1517.[77] It appears, however, that the majority of Ottoman basilisks were smaller pieces whose caliber ran from 11-*okka* through 22-*okka*. Ottoman basilisks were smaller in caliber than most of the Spanish *basilisco*s, which threw large shots of 80 lb and up. Thus, it is also probable that contemporary Spanish sources (and perhaps Portuguese and Venetian ones too), not being familiar with the Turkish names of guns, referred to large Ottoman *şayka*s and *balyemez*es as *basilisco*. For instance, the huge 150- and 200-pounders that the Ottomans used during the 1565 siege of Malta are likely to have been *şayka*s and *balyemez*es, rather than Ottoman basilisks. The Spaniards' terminology was all the more natural, for the *basilisco* seems to have been the largest siege/fortress gun found aboard Spanish galleys. However, by referring to Ottoman *şayka*s and *balyemez*es as *basilisco*, these sources misled later historians, who, based on their testimony, depicted Ottoman *bacaluşka*s as the largest Ottoman pieces, which they were not.[78]

Kanon

Together with basilisks Ottoman inventories mention a type of gun referred to as *kanon* or *kanun*, which is the Turkish equivalent of the term cannon used in many forms in European languages (*canon, cannone, canone*). While in certain

---

[73] Thúry József, *Török történetírók* (2 vols., Budapest, 1896), vol. II, p. 346.

[74] MD 5, p. 615, no. 1709; MD 5, p. 521, no. 1428; Selânikî Mustafa Efendi, *Tarih-i Selânikî*, ed. Mehmed İpşirli (2 vols., Istanbul, 1989), vol. I, p. 27. See also Ágoston, "Ottoman Artillery," 38–39.

[75] AK fols. 3b, 52a.   [76] AK fols. 19a, 21b, 67b–68a, 102a.

[77] Guilmartin, *Gunpowder and Galleys*, p. 167.

[78] With regard to Lepanto, European sources used their own type names for captured Ottoman pieces. The deciphering of this European terminology needs further research.

documents the two terms, that is, *bacaluşka* and *kanon*, are used as synonyms, in other cases the *kanon* appears to have been used for smaller 11-*okka* caliber basilisks.[79] Thus, while the Spanish, English and French terms referred to guns that varied greatly in caliber, the Ottomans used the term *kanon* mainly for 11-*okka* caliber (and occasionally for smaller) pieces. In this respect, Ottoman *kanon*s were close to sixteenth-century Spanish siege cannons (the 32-pounder *canon de abatir*), the English demi-cannons, and the seventeenth-century Austrian *Halbe Karthaun*.

Medium- and small-caliber guns of the culverin type

Kolunburna

The guns mentioned as *kolunburna, kolumburna, kolomburina, kolumburina, kolunburina*, and *kolunburuna* in Ottoman sources were lighter field guns. It is easy to identify the culverin used in European sources behind this Turkish term.[80] Like European culverins, Ottoman *kolunburna*s varied in size. Sixteenth-century inventories mention *kolunburna*s whose caliber ran from 1.5-*okka* through 7-*okka* that fired projectiles from 2 to 9 kg in weight.[81] Seventeenth-century sources recorded pieces from 2-*okka* through 10-*okka* caliber, and occasionally 11-, 14- and 16-*okka* guns that used shots from 2 to 20 kg in weight. Their lengths were 220, 264 and 330 cm (10, 12 and 15 *karış*).[82]

In terms of caliber, the Ottomans had more small-caliber culverins than their Spanish and Italian adversaries, although the question of terminology arises, because the Spaniards gave different names (*falcone, pasavolante, media sacre, sacre* and so forth) to their smaller pieces of the culverin class. This means that we should include the *falcones, pasavolantes* and other smaller guns of the culverin

[79] In December 1565, in the castles of Buda and Peşte there were seventeen *kanon*s firing projectiles of 11 *okka* in weight along with 1,400 stone cannon balls, while in the castle of Istolni Belgrad the inventory lists four 11-*okka* Turkish (Türkî) *kanon*s along with 1,900 cannon balls. In the fortress of Estergon, the same inventory mentions one 11-*okka* piece, referred to as *şâhî kanon*, and another infidel *kanon* of the same caliber along with 450 and 390 projectiles, respectively (Vienna, ÖNB, Mxt. 599).

[80] Cf., for example, Spanish *culebrina*, Provençal *colobrina*, Italian *colubrine*, French *couleuvrine*, etc. Kahane et al., *Lingua Franca*, pp. 175–76.

[81] Vienna, ÖNB, Mxt. 599. At the same time they list several infidel (*kafiri*) *kolunburna*s firing 4, 5, 6 and 11 kg (3, 4, 5 and 9 *okka*) projectiles.

[82] MAD 3150. p. 125. Cf. also ibid., pp. 110–11: the 1666 inventory of Eğriboz which listed the following *kolunburna*s: three bronze *kolunburina*s being 10 *karış* long and throwing shots of 2 *okka* in weight, one 15 *karış* long 5-*okka* caliber piece, a 12 *karış* long gun firing projectiles of 2 *okka* in weight and another 12 *karış* long bronze cannon firing 10 *okka* shots, both referred to as *şâhî kolunburna*. In September 1681, fifteen *kolunburina*s throwing 2, 3 and 5 *okka* shots were taken into the inventory at the castle of Baghdad. See DBŞM CBH 18368, pp. 7 and 12–13.

Table 3.7 Kolunburnas *in the sixteenth and seventeenth centuries*

	Caliber (weight of ball in *okka*)	Weight of ball (kg)	Length of gun (cm)
Sixteenth century	1.5, 2.5, 5, 7	2, 3, 6, 9	
Seventeenth century	2, 3, 4, 5, 6, 7, 9, 10, 11, 14, 16	2, 4, 5, 6, 7, 9, 11, 12, 14, 17, 20	220, 264, 330

Source: Vienna, ÖNB, Mxt. 599; MAD 3150, p. 125; DBŞM CBH 18368, pp. 7 and 12–13.

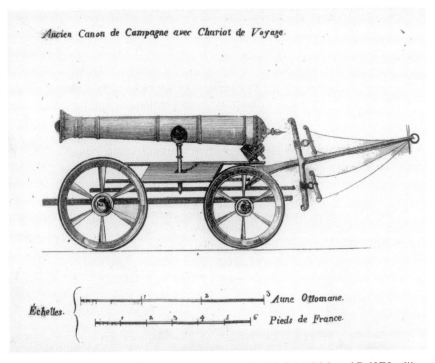

Ancien Canon de Campagne avec Chariot de Voyage.

Échelles.   *Aune Ottomane.*
Pieds de France.

Figure 12 Old Ottoman field piece on its carriage. Provided that Mahmud Raif Efendi's drawing reflects actual dimensions and diameter, this gun was about 2.6 m long and could have fired projectiles of 13–15 kg in weight. It was similar to the *kolunburnas*, despite the fact that Mahmud Raif Efendi talks about *şahis* in his text. Mahmud Raif Efendi, *Tableau des nouveaux reglemens de l'empire ottoman*, Constantinople, 1798.

type when comparing Ottoman *kolunburnas* with Spanish culverins. Even when one includes these Spanish pieces, it becomes readily obvious that – contrary to general belief – Ottoman pieces were not larger than Spanish culverins. Similar conclusions can be drawn regarding the weight of Ottoman culverins. The four *kolunburnas* cast at the Tophane in the spring of 1604 weighed 810 kg

(15 *kantar*).[83] Compared with European culverins these were very light pieces, given the fact that English culverins around the same time weighed 2,041–2,087 kg and even the demi-culverins weighed 1,360–1,542 kg, that is, almost twice as much as Ottoman *kolunburna*s. The weight difference is, however, understandable, for the Ottoman pieces were cast of bronze while the English ones were of cast-iron. Still, this does not change the fact that Ottoman culverins were much lighter than their English namesakes, and were closer to the lighter field guns called *saker*s (weighed 635 kg), a notion that goes against the orthodoxy regarding the supposed clumsiness of Ottoman pieces.

Darbzen

Guns designated as *darbzen*, *zarbzen* or *zarbuzan* were the most popular and widely used types of ordnance the Ottomans deployed during their campaigns. Although the word's meaning is "battering gun," and the majority of guns the Ottomans used during sieges were indeed *darbzen*, these light pieces were also deployed in large numbers in battles as field guns. Three types, namely big (*şâhî*), medium-size (*miyâne*) and small (*küçük*), are distinguished in the sources.[84] According to a sixteenth-century Turkish source small *darbzen*s (*zarbuzan-i küçük*) fired balls of 920 g (300 *dirhem*s) in weight, the medium-size *darbzen*s (*zarbuzan-i vasat*) used projectiles of 1.23 kg (1 *okka*) in weight and the big *darbzen*s (*zarbuzan-i büzürg*) fired 2.5 kg (2-*okka*) shots.[85] However, the smallest *darbzen*s were even lighter. The barrel of these small pieces was 132–154 cm long and weighed only 54 kg (one *kantar*), and they fired projectiles of merely 150 g or 50 *dirhem*s.[86] These small guns were also easy to transport; two of them could be mounted on one horse.[87] Longer and heavier *darbzen*s also existed, such as several 308 cm long pieces, made in two parts, manufactured in the 1510s.[88] Before the Mohács campaign, between 1522 and 1526, fifteen *darbzen*s weighing 73 kg (1.35 *kantar*) were cast in Istanbul. *Darbzen*s usually exceeded this small size: 625 small *darbzen*s weighing on average 162 kg (3 *kantar*) and 355 large *darbzen*s weighing on average 432 kg (8 *kantar*) were cast in Istanbul.[89]

---

[83] MAD 2515, p. 3. Salim Aydüz, "Cıgalazade Yusuf Sinan Paşa'nın Şark Seferi için Tophane-i Amire'de hazırlanan toplar ve Tophane-i Amire'nin 1012 (1604) yılı gelirgider muhasebesi," in Feza Günergun ed., *Osmanlı Bilimi Araştırmalrı*, vol. II (Istanbul, 1998), p. 49.

[84] İsmail Hakkı Uzunçarşılı, *Osmanlı Devleti Teşkilatından Kapukulu Ocakları*, vol. II: *Cebeci, Topçu Top Arabacıları, Humbaracı, Lağımcı Ocakları ve Kapukulu Suvarileri* (Ankara, 1984), p. 50.

[85] L. Fekete, *Die Siyāqat-Schrift in der türkischen Finanzverwaltung* (Budapest, 1955), p. 695, n. 6.

[86] MD 7, p. 423, no. 1215; ibid., p. 485, no. 1401; cf. Uzunçarşılı, *Cebeci, Topçu*, p. 50.

[87] MD 7, p. 422, no. 1214.

[88] Bostan, "A szultáni ágyúöntő műhelyben (Tophane-i Amire) folyó tevékenység," 12, where Bostan also mentions a 374 cm long *darbzen*.

[89] Heywood, "The Activity of the State Cannon-Foundry," pp. 212 and 214–15. At the same time, numerous damaged scrap *darbzen*s were delivered to the foundry for melting down and recasting. Some weighed 5.5 *kantar* (297 kg) on average, while others were only 4 *kantar* (216 kg).

Figure 13 Small-caliber guns were often transported on horseback or on camels. Luigi Marsigli, *L'état militaire de l'empire ottoman*, 1732.

Ottoman sources sometimes use the term *darbzen* to denote much larger guns as well. The forty-six large *darbzens* (*darbzen-i şâhî*) cast in the spring of 1604 as part of the preparations for Sinan Pasha's eastern campaign weighed 540 kg (10 *kantar*) each.[90] The most important characteristics of *darbzens* are summarized in Table 3.8.

[90] MAD 2515, p. 3; see also Aydüz, "Cıgalazade Yusuf Sinan Paşa'nın Şark Seferi," p. 149. The cannons put on display in the garden of the Military Museum at Istanbul and entered into the inventory as *darbzens* include a 360 cm long Italian piece from 1592, which weighed 31 *kantar* and 30 *okka* (1,711 kg), had a bore diameter of 11 cm and was capable of throwing shots of 3 *okka* in weight. We also know of a somewhat bulkier gun registered as a *darbzen*, which was made in Austria in 1684 with a length of 214 cm, the bore of the barrel being 15 cm in diameter (Inventory no. 146). Both are exceeded in size by an Ottoman *darbzen* cast by Hayreddin bin Abdullah in 1531, the inscription of which describes its weight as 40 *kantar* (2,160 kg) and its length as 16 span. Subsequent measurements show its length to be 357 cm and the bore of its barrel 26 cm in diameter (Inventory no. 10). Because in the last few examples guns were named *darbzen* not

Table 3.8 Darbzens *in the sixteenth and seventeenth centuries*

Caliber (*dirhem/okka*)	Weight of ball (g/kg)	Weight of gun (kg)	Length of gun (cm)
50, 100, 150, 200, 300 *dirhem*, and 1, 2 *okka*	154, 307, 461, 614, 921g and 1.2, 2.5 kg		
		54, 73, 162, 432, 540	
			88,110, 132,154, 352

Sources: MD 7, p. 7, no. 32; ibid., p. 423, nos. 1215 and 1216; ibid., p. 485, no. 1401; DBŞM Dosya 1, vesika 13; MAD 2515, p. 3; Heywood, "The Activity of the State Cannon-Foundry."

Many guns of this type, relatively easy to transport, were used by the Ottomans in their campaigns. A significant number of *darbzen*s cast between 1522 and 1525 were employed in the battle of Mohács. The reports in narrative sources of hundreds of cannon being present with the Ottoman army during major Sultan-led campaigns, therefore, relate mainly to these small field guns.[91] Selânikî stated that 280 large *darbzen*s were carried by the Ottomans against Szigetvár in the 1566 campaign.[92] According to Abdülkadir Efendi, the Istanbul foundry started to cast 300 large *darbzen*s in December 1595 in preparation for the 1596 Hungarian campaign.[93] Such large *darbzen*s required three artillerymen to operate.[94] *Darbzen*s were to be found aboard Ottoman ships, too. As we have already noted, it is not clear whether the thirty-two *darbzen*s (twelve big and twenty small) listed on the *barça*s in 1488 were flanking guns or artillery pieces transported on these ships. It is probable though that the ones aboard the *ağribar*s (four pieces), *kadırga*s (four pieces) and *kalyata*s (two pieces) were used as shipboard ordnance.[95]

Şâhî

Ottoman sources use the word *şâhî* to designate the larger version of a given gun; however, they also use the term to refer to very light and small guns. Dictionaries tell us laconically that the *şâhî* is "an ancient form of brass muzzle-loading cannon," or an old, long field gun.[96] They were indeed relatively long pieces, especially

by contemporary sources but by experts from museums at later dates, I have reservations about accepting and considering them as typical. Contemporary narrative and archival sources apparently referred to much smaller guns by the term *darbzen*.

[91] Hungarian captives who escaped from the Ottoman camp reported that most of the Ottoman cannon were pulled by two or four horses. Cf. Jenő Gyalókay, "A mohácsi csata," in *Mohácsi emlékkönyv 1526* (Budapest, 1926), pp. 197–98.

[92] Selânikî Mustafa Efendi, *Tarih-i Selânıkî*, vol. I, p. 27. The Nuruosmaniye manuscript of this chronicle, however, mentions only 180 *darbzen*s. Cf. ibid., vol. II, p. 867.

[93] AK fols. 53a–b, 55b and 57b.

[94] Uzunçarşılı, *Cebeci, Topçu*, p. 52. Uzunçarşılı, however, does not distinguish *şâhî darbzen*s from guns called *şâhî*.

[95] İsmail Hakkı Uzunçarşılı, *Osmanl Devletinin Merkez ve Bahriye Teşkilatı* (Ankara, 1984), p. 512.

[96] *New Redhouse Turkish-English Dictionary* (Istanbul, 1988), p. 1045.

Table 3.9 Şâhî *guns, sixteenth through eighteenth centuries*

Caliber (*dirhem/okka*)	Weight of ball (g/kg)	Weight of gun (kg)	Length of gun (cm)
50, 80, 100, 150, 200, 300 *dirhems* and 1, 1.25, 1.5 (3, 5[a]) *okka*	154, 245, 307, 460, 614, 922 g and 1.3, 1.5, 1.8 (3.7, 6.1[a]) kg		
200 *dirhem*	641 g	169	110
1 *okka*	1.2 and 1.3	324–338 and 378–395	
1 *okka*	1.3 kg	508 and 621	
			242, 330

Note: [a] These caliber guns were rare.
Source: DBŞM CBH 18368, pp. 12–13; MAD 177, fols. 42a, 61a–b; DBŞM TPH 18643, p. 12; MAD 2730, p. 7; MAD 2652, p. 25; DBŞM TPH 18618; MAD 5448, p. 2; MAD 2679, pp. 2–11; DBŞM TPH 18617, p. 4; DBŞM TPH 18637, p. 27; DBŞM TPH 18641, pp. 18, 24; DBŞM TPH 18652, p. 17; DBŞM TPH 18655, p. 19; DBŞM TPH 18671, p. 19.

considering their very small calibers. Weapons inventories from the latter part of the seventeenth century list 242 and 330 cm long *şâhî* guns.[97] The great majority of them were very small-caliber pieces firing shots ranging from 150 grams to 1.8 kg in weight.[98] The weight of these guns could have varied according to the length of the barrel. The minimum and maximum weight of the 0.5-*okka* caliber and 110 cm long *şâhî*s cast in Istanbul in 1736 varied from 159 to 182 kg, the average being 169 kg.[99] Several of the 1-*okka* caliber *şâhî* guns weighed around 325–395 kg, though the ones cast in Istanbul in 1704–05 and 1712–14 weighed considerably more, around 510 and 620 kg, respectively.[100] While the above data represent the majority of *şâhî* guns, occasionally we can find larger pieces firing 4 and 6 kg (3- and 5-*okka*) projectiles.[101]

The smallest pieces: *saçma, eynek, prangı, misket* and *şakaloz* guns

Saçma guns were among the smallest Ottoman pieces and, as the name suggests, often fired grapeshot.[102] They were such small pieces that inventories usually treated them separately from other cannons. The average weight of the *saçma*

[97] MAD 3448, p. 248; MAD 3150, pp. 111, 125.
[98] DBŞM CBH 18368, pp. 12–13; MAD 177, fols. 42a, 61a–b.
[99] DBŞM TPH 18643, p. 12.   [100] MAD 2730, p. 7; MAD 2652, p. 25; DBŞM TPH 18618.
[101] In 1686, for instance, 300 *şâhî* cannon balls weighing 5 *okka* each were delivered to the Ottoman fortress of Kanije in Hungary (MAD 5448, p. 2). On display in front of the Military Museum at Istanbul there is a copper *şâhî* gun from the era of Sultan Mehmed IV (r. 1648–87); 303 cm long, the bore of the barrel is 11 cm in diameter and it fired balls of 3 *okka* in weight (Inventory no. 24). There is a similar *şâhî* gun from the era of Mustafa III (r. 1757–74), made of copper, with an 11 cm barrel bore, a length of 281 cm, which also used shots of 3 *okka* in weight (ibid., no. 35). The cannons on display include several such guns, which fired shots of 1–3 *okka* in weight, and an Italian gun again called *şâhî* (ibid., nos. 37, 38, 401, 314 and 324).
[102] V. J. Parry, "Barud, IV: The Ottoman Empire," *EI*, vol. I, p. 1064.

guns cast at the Tophane in 1687–88 and in 1695–96 was around 35.6 kg. Those cast in 1704–05 weighed around 42 kg, while the two pieces cast in 1697–98 were much heavier, almost 190 kg each.[103] *Saçma*s were among the favorite naval guns: of the 311 guns aboard the 15 *kalyata*s, 19 *firkate*s and 25 *işkampoye*s dispatched to Özi on the Black Sea in 1697–98, 264 pieces (85 percent) were cast-iron *saçma* guns.[104] The 924 guns sent from Istanbul to Baghdad for the *kapudan* of the Shatt al-Arab navy in 1698–99 had a lower proportion of *saçma* guns, 248 pieces (27 percent), of which 230 were cast iron.[105]

Even smaller were the guns called *eynek*. Sixty-two *eynek* guns cast at the Tophane in 1695–96 weighed only 22.7 kg on average, while those cast in 1697–98 weighed just 11.5 kg.[106] Eleven medium-sized (*miyane*) *eynek* guns, enlisted in the castle of Selanik in 1659–60, fired projectiles of 461 g (150 *dirhem*s) in weight.[107] They were used mainly aboard ships operating on major rivers of the Empire. Several of them were deployed on the *kalyata*s and *firkate*s of the Danube fleet.[108] Of the shipment of guns mentioned above for the Shatt al-Arab navy, 496 pieces, that is, 54 percent of the total, were small-caliber *eynek*s. The overwhelming majority (472 pieces) of the *eynek*s were cast-iron pieces.[109]

*Prangı*s were among the smallest Ottoman guns, usually firing shots of 50 *dirhem*s or 150 g. These small pieces could easily be cast in local foundries. For instance, from October 31, 1499 until August 26, 1500, 206 *prangı*s were made in Avlonya. This comprised 72 percent of the guns cast there during the Venetian–Ottoman war of 1499–1503.[110] Guns referred to as *misket* in Ottoman sources also belonged to the smallest-caliber weapons that fired 150-, 100- and 50-*dirhem* projectiles in the seventeenth and eighteenth centuries.[111] Their proportion within Ottoman ordnance varied greatly, comprising from just 1 percent to 12 percent of the guns cast in the Tophane.[112]

Ottoman sources often mention guns called *şakaloz, şakloz, şakolos, şakalos, şakulos, şakulus, sakolos, sakalos, çakaloz, çakalos* or *çakanoz*. The word is a loan from Hungarian, where *szakállas* was the name of the *Hackenbüchse*.[113] The *szakállas* (*puska*) is the Hungarian equivalent of the Latin (*pixis*) *barbata* or "hook gun" and refers to a large-caliber hand firearm with a hook. The hook served to fix the weapon firmly to the rampart in order to take the firearm's heavy recoil. Unlike Hungarian *szakállas*, Ottoman *şakaloz*es are said to have been set on stock (*kundak*) and transported by gun carriages. However, some of the Ottoman *şakaloz*es must have been large hand firearms similar to European hook guns or *Hackenbüchse*. The sixty *şakaloz* listed in the inventory of the castle of Seçen in Hungary in December 1565 fired projectiles as small as 31 g (10 *dirhem*s), whereas the five

[103] MAD 1361, p. 17; KK 5654, p. 16; MAD 2652, p. 25; MAD 2732, p. 32. See also Appendix.
[104] MAD 2732, p. 39. [105] MAD 975, p. 16.
[106] KK 5654, p. 16; MAD 2732, p. 32. See also Appendix. [107] MAD 3448, p. 248.
[108] DMŞM TPH 18601, p. 15. [109] MAD 975, p. 16.
[110] Bostan, "Top Döküm Faaliyetleri," based on AE, Bayezid II, no. 41.
[111] MAD 2677, p. 21; DBŞM TPH 18615, p. 20 [112] See Appendix.
[113] Parry, "Barud," p. 1062; Gábor Ágoston, "Muslim–Christian Acculturation: Ottomans and Hungarians from the Fifteenth to the Seventeenth Centuries," in Bartolomé Bennassar and Robert Sauzet eds., *Chrétiens et Musulmans à la Renaissance* (Paris, 1998), 292–303.

pieces in the castle of Hollókő used 37 g (12-*dirhem*) balls.[114] These were really very small weapons given the fact that even the Janissary muskets, as well as the Spanish ones, fired bullets weighing more than 50 g.

*Şakaloz*es were the favorite guns in Ottoman fortresses as were *szakállas*es in the Hungarian castles. As we shall see later, almost half of the guns listed in 1536 in the castle of Belgrade were *şakaloz*es. In the same year, in the castle of Semendire there were 900 *şakaloz*es which were listed not among the cannons but among the hand firearms. In smaller castles of the Empire along with one or two larger pieces these were the only firearms the defenders could depend on.[115] On the other side of the frontier, in the Hungarian castles *szakállas*es composed a considerable part of weaponry. There were 4,500 *szakállas*es in forty-six Hungarian castles listed in an inventory of 1577.[116]

These small pieces were close-range weapons and as the name *misket* indicates were very close to the muskets in every respect. Like the muskets, they were anti-personnel weapons, often loaded with scrap iron. Except for the smaller *şakaloz*es, however, they still needed more than one person to operate them. In terms of effectiveness, the Janissary muskets, especially the heavy rampart muskets, rivaled these smaller pieces.

Janissary muskets

We know very little about the first portable firearms the Ottomans used. These weapons probably reached the Ottomans either by trade or as a consequence of their wars against Europeans in the Balkans and the eastern Mediterranean. While it is most probable that the word *tüfenk* that appears in Ottoman weaponry-registers of certain Balkan forts in the middle of the fifteenth century refers to the matchlock arquebus, it is not known if these weapons were operated by the serpentine-lock or by the more advanced form of the matchlock mechanism.[117]

Western sources suggest that Bayezid II (r. 1481–1512) provided the Janissaries – whose number had probably reached 10,000 by the 1470s – with more effective firearms.[118] The Venetian report probably referred to the introduction of the more advanced form of the matchlock gun, but it is impossible to tell

---

[114] Vienna, ÖNB, Mxt. 599.

[115] This was the case, for instance, in Simontornya, Ozora and Endrék in Hungary (see Vienna, ÖNB, Mxt. 599).

[116] József Kelenik, "Szakállas puskák XVI. századi magyarországi inventáriumokban," *HK* 35, 3 (1988), 509.

[117] The earliest matchlock mechanism known as the serpentine-lock is said to have appeared in the first part of the fifteenth century. It was an S-shaped piece of metal fixed to the stock – another important innovation of these early guns – with a central pivot and was used to fire the gun. The upper part of the S-shape lock held the burning match, while the lower part functioned as a trigger. When the soldier pulled the lower part of the serpentine-lock he lowered the match into a pan which contained the priming powder to fire the gun.

[118] Parry, "Barud," p. 1061.

whether this new version of the matchlock was imported from Europe or developed by the Ottomans themselves. In this respect it is worth noting that historians of technology credit the Ottomans with perfecting the serpentine mechanism.[119] Venetian sources also mention that Murad III (r. 1574–95) equipped all the Janissaries with muskets. This source undoubtedly refers to the even more advanced weapon, the matchlock musket, first introduced in the early sixteenth century by Spanish soldiers who, fighting in Italy against heavily armored troops, realized the need for more powerful weapons. The musket was larger than the arquebus; it had a longer barrel and could shoot heavier projectiles with the same or higher velocities. This combination proved effective against the shock of heavily armored adversaries. Spanish muskets weighed 8 kg or more, had bore diameters of 18–22 mm, and fired lead bullets of 56–57 g. John Francis Guilmartin has suggested that the "process that produced the Turkish musket of the sixteenth century must have closely paralleled that which produced its Spanish equivalent," for "the tactical stimuli and technological results were remarkably similar."[120] Indeed, there are some similarities between Spanish and Ottoman hand firearms.

Well into the seventeenth century the Janissaries used the matchlock musket (*fitilli tüfenk*), although from the late sixteenth century more and more flintlock muskets (*çakmaklı tüfenk*) were manufactured with the Spanish *patilla*-lock. It was an advanced form of flintlock, known from the nineteenth century as the *miquelet*-lock, most probably after the weapons (and lock mechanism) that the Spanish Miqueletes or mounted fusiliers used. It spread throughout the Mediterranean and the Balkans, not least because of the Ottomans, who adopted it at an early date. Since early flintlocks were not as reliable as the matchlock (the flint became worn, hit the pan at the wrong angle, or fell out of the finger piece, and therefore failed to strike enough sparks to ignite the powder in the pan), the Ottomans, like the Western Europeans, also used combination locks, referred to commonly by Europeans as the Vauban-lock after about 1688.[121]

In siege warfare or in defending fortresses the Ottomans employed the eight-sided or cylinder-barreled heavy matchlock musket. Known as *metris tüfengi* or trench gun, it had a 130–160 cm long barrel and bore diameters of 20–29 mm, though there were pieces with larger bore diameters (35 and 45 mm) often used for firing shells. When European sources claimed that Ottoman handguns were heavier than European ones, they probably referred to these trench guns which they certainly could have seen during Ottoman sieges.

Yet, generalizations made on the basis of such European sources should be treated with caution, for alongside these heavy muskets the Janissaries also used

---

[119] This perfected serpentine-lock arquebus appeared in Western Europe around the middle of the fifteenth century but its most reliable version was not introduced until the early sixteenth century.

[120] Guilmartin, *Gunpowder and Galleys*, pp. 149, 276.

[121] These latter *tüfenk*s must have been similar to the Turkish musket that was captured during the second siege of Vienna in 1683 and later kept in the Dresden museum. See József Borus, "Modern haditechnika és régi fegyverek a török háborúkban (1663–1698)," in Kálmán Benda and Ágnes R. Várkonyi eds., *Bécs 1683 évi török ostroma és Magyarország* (Budapest, 1988), p. 159.

Table 3.10 *Heavy Janissary trench guns*

Date (century)	Lock mechanism	Barrel length (cm)	Caliber (mm)	Inventory no.
16th	matchlock	148	22	8825
Early 17th	matchlock	128	44	2307
16th–17th	matchlock	139.5	25	9090
16th–17th	matchlock	137.5	20	9089
Late 17th	matchlock	122	28	8786
16th	*miquelet*-lock	147	29	9017
17th	*miquelet*-lock	131	26	8896
17th–18th	*miquelet*-lock	122	35 (havan)	8392
Late 18th	*miquelet*-lock	232	21.9	3043
17th–18th	*miquelet*-lock	143.5	21.6	5844

Note: Not all the weapons are cataloged as *metris tüfengi*; however, their characteristics would allow us to classify them among the heavier Janissary muskets.
Source: Examples are from the Istanbul Military Museum (Askeri Müze). Cf. Aysel Çötelioğlu, *Askeri Müze Osmanlı Dönemi Ateşli Silahlar Kataloğu* (Istanbul, n.d.).

smaller and lighter *tüfenks*. In 1567, the Janissaries in the fortress of Belgrade used muskets that fired bullets (*tüfenk fındığı*) of 12 and 15 grams.[122] Similar weapons – each firing 12 g bullets – were used in Ottoman Egypt.[123] Muskets manufactured in state workshops and used in Baghdad in 1571 fired 15 g bullets.[124] Given the weight of the lead bullets these weapons had a caliber of 13 and 14 mm or so and are likely to have been similar to the smaller Janissary *tüfenks*, used in field battles. These latter muskets were usually 115–140 cm long, weighed merely 3–4.5 kg and had bore diameters of 11, 13, 14 or 16 mm (and rarely 19 or 20 mm). The characteristics of these Janissary *tüfenks* were very similar to those of the weapons the Janissaries' European adversaries used. The "typical" matchlock handgun in sixteenth-century European armies was 120–150 cm long, weighed 2.5–4.5 kg, and had a caliber of 14–18 mm.[125]

Regarding the quality of Ottoman muskets our sources are contradictory. A former Janissary, who around 1606 wrote the most detailed description of the corps, complained that the muskets manufactured in state-operated workshops (*miri tüfenk karhaneleri*) in Istanbul were of inferior quality compared with those obtainable from private gun-makers: "nothing good can be expected from them anymore," he lamented. He also claimed that the *tüfenkçi*s or musket-makers,

[122] MD 7, p. 198, no. 539, speaks about projectiles of 4–5 *dirhem* in weight. Until the end of the seventeenth century I calculate with the *Tebrizi dirhem* (3.072 g) and thereafter with the *Rumi dirhem* (3.207 g); for details see Notes on weights and measurements.
[123] In late December 1567, 2,500 such muskets were sent from Istanbul to Egypt together with 5 million projectiles of the said caliber. MD 7, p. 219, no. 609.
[124] MD 12, p. 488, no. 934 (*5-dirhem atar miri tüfenk*).
[125] Kelenik, "Szakállas puskák," 126. The characteristics of the "typical" sixteenth-century arquebus were very similar: it weighed 4.5 kg and had a bore diameter of 15 mm or so. Cf. Guilmartin, *Gunpowder and Galleys*, p. 149.

Table 3.11 *Janissary* tüfenks

Date (century)	Lock mechanism	Barrel length (cm)	Caliber (mm)	Inventory no.
16th–17th	matchlock	120	16	406
16th–17th	matchlock	150	16	8925
16th–17th	matchlock	133	19	9086
Late 17th	matchlock	144	11	21626
16th	*miquelet*-lock	132	19	9053
17th	*miquelet*-lock	141	19	1371
17th–18th	*miquelet*-lock	154	13	1890
17th–18th	*miquelet*-lock	147	16	10410
17th–18th	*miquelet*-lock	151	17	1900
18th	*miquelet*-lock	123	13	81
18th	*miquelet*-lock	115	15	13607
18th	*miquelet*-lock	116	16	8821
18th	*miquelet*-lock	136	13.5	4177

Note: The Ottomans also used longer (140–175 cm) muskets with bore diameters of 11, 13, 14 and 16 mm.
Source: Examples are from the Istanbul Military Museum (Çötelioğlu, *Askeri Müze*, passim).

although still on the Sultan's payroll, ceased to manufacture the weapons and that the new recruits were not given muskets anymore.[126] Raimundo Montecuccoli, on the other hand, claimed that the metal of the Turkish muskets was of good quality and that their range and force were greater than those of the Christian muskets, a claim that historians of technology seem also to accept. The latter suggest that Ottoman musket barrels were stronger and more reliable than European ones because Ottoman gun-makers used flat sheets of steel – similar to that of the Damascus blades – which were coiled into a spiral. This method produced great strength in the barrel that could withstand higher explosive pressure.[127] Consequently, Ottoman muskets did fire larger projectiles, a case that is often mentioned by European observers, though, as noted above, these sources probably referred to the larger fortress or trench Janissary guns.

The Ottoman authorities seem to have shared the assessment of the 1606 author, because they attempted to acquire arquebuses and muskets from abroad, most notably from England and Holland, despite the strict prohibitions of the Papacy and the vigilance of the Spanish and Venetian armadas. One of the largest-known shipments of weapons and gunpowder was intercepted in November 1605, when the ships of the Princes of Savoy and Malta held up an English vessel whose cargo included 700 barrels of gunpowder, 1,000 arquebus barrels, 500 arquebuses for horsemen and 2,000 sword blades. While this cargo was successfully seized, we

[126] *A janicsárok törvényei*, trans. Pál Fodor (Budapest, 1989), p. 69; İsmail Hakkı Uzunçarşılı, *Osmanlı Devleti Teşkilatından Kapukulu Ocakları*, vol. I: *Acemi Ocağı ve Yeniçeri Ocağı* (Ankara, 1984), p. 366.
[127] Arnold Pacey, *Technology in World Civilization: A Thousand-Year History* (Oxford, 1990), p. 80.

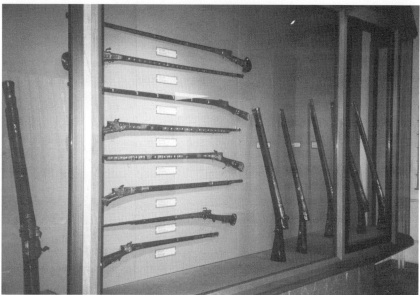

Figure 14   It was often the Janissaries' firepower that decided the fate of battles. Janissary muskets. Military Museum, Istanbul.

can be sure that other shipments did find their way to the Ottoman capital and port cities, as is apparent from Venetian and other ambassadorial reports from Istanbul.[128] What is less clear is whether the Ottomans tried to import arquebuses from England because their own stockpiles had run low as a consequence of the long and protracted wars against the Safavids (1578–90 and 1603–12) and the Hungarians and Habsburgs (1593–1606), or because they considered English arquebuses superior to the Janissary *tüfenks*.

Apart from muskets, the Janissaries also used hand grenades, especially during sieges. Although hand grenades were occasionally fired from specially designed Janissary *tüfenks* and from smaller mortars, they were usually thrown by hand. The amount amassed in the Imperial Ammunition House (Cebehane) and distributed to the troops during campaigns was impressive. In the summer of 1678, during Kara Mustafa Pasha's Çehrin campaign, the Cebehane got 23,520 hand grenades, as preparations for further campaigns against Russia were underway.[129] At the height of the war against the Holy League, in the period of September 7, 1687 through January 15, 1689, no fewer than 164,000 hand grenades (126,500 regular hand grenades or *tane-i humbara-i deste* and 37,484 hand grenades made of glass or *şişe-i humbara-i deste*) were delivered to the Cebehane.[130] This Ottoman stockpile of 1688 thus doubled or tripled the hand grenade supply brought by the Habsburg troops and their allies to the siege of Buda in 1686.[131]

Conclusion

Data presented in this chapter and the Appendix demonstrate that the Ottomans used all sorts of guns from the largest *şaykas* and *balyemeze*s to the smallest *şahi*, *saçma*, *prangı*, *eynek*, *misket* and *şakaloz* guns, often firing projectiles of merely a few grams. Eyewitness accounts show that the Ottomans deployed hundreds of smaller guns during their campaigns. Similarly, even during sieges the majority of their ordnance consisted of smaller pieces, and large siege artillery, though considerable in number by contemporary standards, comprised no more than 10 percent of the Ottoman siege train. This was the case even during the sieges of

---

[128] Gábor Ágoston, "Merces Prohibitae: The Anglo-Ottoman Trade in War Materials and the Dependence Theory," in Kate Fleet ed., *The Ottomans and the Sea*, *Oriente Moderno* 20 (81) n.s. 1 (2001), 177–92. The rivals of the Ottomans also imported hand firearms. In 1570, Spain imported 6,000 arquebuses from the Netherlands and 20,000 arquebuses from Italy. Cf. I. A. A. Thompson, *War and Government in Habsburg Spain, 1560–1620* (London, 1976), pp. 230–41.

[129] MAD 4040, p. 131. The total weight of the shipment was 18.5 metric tons, that is, the hand grenades weighed 0.79 kg (0.64 *okka*) on average.

[130] KK 4738, p. 8. Of these, 27,500 and 17,030 pieces, respectively, were sent to the army and fortresses and the rest remained in the *Cebehane*.

[131] The various figures given in contemporary sources regarding the number of hand grenades used in 1686 during the siege of Buda are: 52,082–54,106 (Giovanni Paolo Zenarolla) and 84,000 (*Kriegstagebuch Karls von Lothringen über die Rückeroberung von Ofen*). See György Domokos, "Buda visszavívásának ostromtechnikai problémái," *HK* 106, 1 (1993), p. 56.

Constantinople or Belgrade, that is, as early as the mid-fifteenth century, an era dominated by giant bombards.

The situation was different with regard to fortress guns. It seems that the Ottomans deployed the majority of their large pieces on the ramparts of their fortresses. Large pieces figured prominently, especially in their key forts that had particular strategic importance, such as Belgrade, Buda, Baghdad, or the forts of the Dardanelles that protected the capital city. Some of these guns were obsolete, giant pieces. However, even in these fortresses medium- and small-caliber pieces predominated.

As for Ottoman shipboard artillery, here too the overwhelming majority of guns consisted of medium- and small-caliber pieces, though ordnance varied greatly depending on the types of vessel. On their flagships, just like the Spaniards and other Mediterranean nations, the Ottomans preserved some of their large stone-throwing pieces as center-line bow guns (*baş topu*). The admirals' *kalyon*s, or galleons, carried large *şayka* guns as late as the mid-eighteenth century. In 1736–39, the Ottoman flagship carried eight pieces of 112-pounders and 22 pieces of 48-pounders,[132] which would correspond to 42- and 18-*okka* caliber Ottoman guns. However, the majority of guns deployed aboard galleons were 7-, 5- and 3-*okka* pieces, along with small-caliber cast-iron *saçma*s and *eynek*s, at least in the latter part of the seventeenth century. In 1696–97, some 303 pieces were deployed aboard the galleons of the Ottoman Black Sea armada: 200 iron *eynek*s, 100 iron *saçma*s, two 5-*okka* caliber iron pieces and one 3-*okka* caliber gun, also of cast iron.[133] In 1697–98 the government ordered 112 guns for two newly built galleons (*kalyon*). Of these, 60 pieces were 7-*okka*, 40 pieces 5-*okka* and 12 pieces 3-*okka* caliber guns, firing projectiles of 9, 6 and 4 kg.[134] *Kadırgas*, that is, the most popular type of Ottoman war galleys with twenty-five or twenty-six oar-benches, carried one large center-line piece and two small-caliber flanking guns in the late seventeenth century. In 1696–97, 9-*okka* caliber guns firing shots of 11 kg were used as center-line cannons, while 1.5-*okka* caliber guns were deployed as flanking (*yan*) pieces aboard Ottoman *kadırgas*. Smaller ships had smaller-caliber guns. In the same years we find 5-*okka* and 1.5-*okka* caliber iron guns along with iron *saçma*s and *eynek*s aboard the somewhat smaller Ottoman *kalyatas* (*galiotta*) operating on the Black Sea. Aboard the smaller *işkampoye* ships that had probably no more than thirteen oar-benches and were mainly used on rivers and in the Black Sea, we find small cast-iron *saçma*s and *eynek*s. *Saçma* and *eynek* guns were the most popular types of guns aboard ships operating on the Danube and Shatt al-Arab as well, and there were plenty of them aboard *firkate*s, too. Another tendency we must note is that the Ottomans, not unlike their adversaries, had deployed large numbers of cast-iron pieces aboard their ships by the late seventeenth century.[135]

[132] Daniel Panzac, "Armed Peace in the Mediterranean 1736–1739: A Comparative Survey of the Navies," *The Mariner's Mirror* 84, 1 (1997), 44. Similarly, in 1696–97 the *kapudan paşa's kalyon*s had 44- and 16-*okka* caliber *şayka* guns. MAD 173, p. 17a and Appendix.

[133] MAD 173, p. 17a.   [134] MAD 2732, p. 42.

[135] MAD 173, pp. 16b–17a, and Appendix.

One main difference though remained: whereas cast-iron guns of all calibers were to be found aboard European vessels, the majority of the medium- and big-caliber guns on Ottoman ships were of bronze and only the smallest pieces were cast of iron.

Though the tendency in Europe was to cast lighter guns, large stone-throwing cannons were not unknown either, especially in countries the Ottomans confronted in the sixteenth century. Among the guns Venice sent to Padua in 1509 and 1510 there were several cannons that fired projectiles of 12, 15 and 30 kg (40, 50 and 100 Venetian pounds). Though the majority of newly cast guns in the late sixteenth and early seventeenth centuries consisted of longer-barreled 20- and 40-pounder culverins, the Venetians also cast larger pieces firing balls of 24 and 30 kg (80 and 100 Venetian pounds). In 1625 they experimented with a huge bronze piece which threw stone balls of 75 kg (250 Venetian pounds).[136] While in the Austrian army stone shots were generally omitted after the mid-seventeenth century, the Austrian Habsburgs retained their large early and mid-sixteenth-century pieces in their fortresses in Hungary and Austria until the end of the seventeenth century.[137]

With regard to hand firearms Janissary *tüfenk*s closely resembled the muskets their Spanish and Venetian opponents used. Although the history of *tüfenk* manufacturing and trade needs further research, on the basis of our present knowledge, it seems that it was not the lack of weapons, but rather the spread of hand firearms in Asia Minor, the Balkans and the Arab lands that caused problems for the Istanbul government. This proliferation of firearms was a result of the manufacturing of *tüfenk*s in private workshops outside government control, as well as of the illicit trade in firearms. Given the fact that the quality of firearms from these two latter sources, that is, from trade and private manufacturing, appears to have been better than those made in the imperial workshops, it was not easy to shut down these sources. Although it seems that the Ottoman Empire was largely self-sufficient in the manufacturing of *tüfenk*s, available evidence does not offer similar estimates for pistols and flintlock mechanisms. Sporadic sources, however, indicate that they may have had a different story.

Given their significance and bulk, it was the production of gunpowder, cannons and their ammunition and not that of hand firearms that constituted the major challenge for states in the gunpowder age. To what extent the Ottomans were able to meet this challenge is the topic of the next chapters.

[136] M. E. Mallett and J. R. Hale, *The Military Organization of a Renaissance State: Venice c. 1400 to 1617* (Cambridge, 1984), pp. 397–98.
[137] Anton Dolleczek, *Geschichte der österreichischen Artillerie von den frühesten Zeiten bis zur Gegenwart* (Vienna, 1887), p. 179.

CHAPTER 4

Saltpeter industries

This and the following two chapters examine the availability of strategic minerals in the Empire and the most significant branches of the Ottoman ammunition
and weapons industry: the production of saltpeter and gunpowder, and the manufacture of cannons. It is hoped that by analyzing archival documents that offer
the most precise figures yet published on Ottoman production of these three vital
commodities, the following pages provide the foundation for a verifiable framework of comparative Ottoman military industrial capabilities. These chapters try to
rectify the undifferentiated presentation of former studies regarding early modern
Ottoman munitions and armament production. They challenge Keith Krause's and
Jonathan Grant's claim that the Ottoman Empire was a "third-tier producer" that
possessed capabilities only comparable to its similarly "third-tier producer" immediate rivals (Hungary, Poland and the medieval Balkan states), and "relied heavily
on imported weapons and technologies." They also contest Rhoads Murphey's
suggestion that the Ottomans, especially in the seventeenth century, relied on
Dutch and English imports, and that the absence of English gunpowder supplies
from the 1660s onward considerably restricted Ottoman military capability.[1] As
will be seen in the following chapters, detailed production figures available in
Ottoman archives tell us a much different story about Ottoman military industrial
production.

Raw materials: saltpeter

Saltpeter occurred as a natural deposit in many parts of India, Arabia and
China, because they possessed suitable climatic conditions (high temperature and
humidity) necessary for its formation. Most of Europe, however, is deficient in

---

[1] Keith Krause, *Arms and the State: Patterns of Military Production and Trade* (Cambridge, 1992),
pp. 48–52; Jonathan Grant, "Rethinking the Ottoman 'Decline': Military Technology Diffusion in the
Ottoman Empire, Fifteenth to Eighteenth Centuries," *Journal of World History* 10, 1 (1999), 179–201;
Rhoads Murphey, "The Ottoman Attitude towards the Adoption of Western Technology: The Role of
the Efrencî Technicians in Civil and Military Applications," in Jean-Louis Bacqué-Grammont and
Paul Dumont eds., *Contributions à l'histoire économique et sociale de l'Empire ottoman* (Leuven,
1983), pp. 292–93.

this most important ingredient of gunpowder, and natural deposits of peter could be found only in a handful of places, most notably in Spain, Hungary, Galicia in Poland-Lithuania, and in Russia. Without purification, such crude saltpeter was usually unsuitable for making gunpowder, for it was contaminated with calcium salt and contained only a small percentage of potassium nitrate. As a consequence, saltpeter had to be extracted in other ways in England, Germany, France and in northern Europe.[2]

Northern Europeans practiced scraping saltpeter from the walls of houses or extracting saltpeter from manured soils from the fourteenth century onward. They also created artificial saltpeter pits and, later, niter beds, descriptions of which are known from the late fourteenth-century German manuscript, the so-called *Hausbuch* from Konstanz (1390), and from Lazarus Ercker's *Beschreibung allerfürnemisten mineralischen Ertz und Bergwerksarten* (Prague, 1574), respectively. Ercker also gives the best contemporaneous woodcut illustration of the *Salpetergarten*. Europeans also used saltpeter barns, wooden sheds where soil was mixed with manure and composted waste. Despite these efforts, Western Europeans did not successfully create artificial niter beds that made significant contributions to domestic saltpeter supplies until the second half of the eighteenth century. Before the discovery of the Chilean source, India provided a substantial portion of the saltpeter used in Europe.[3]

The saltpeter deposits of the Ottoman Empire

In contrast to the territories of the major Western European states, Ottoman lands had abundant saltpeter deposits.[4] In the European part of the Empire, saltpeter had been produced near Üsküb and Priştine already in the fifteenth century, and production was continued in these sites in the sixteenth century.[5] From the mid-sixteenth century the sources mention other production centers in the Balkans: the *sancak* of Silistre,[6] and the villages of the district of Çirmen near Edirne,[7] which had the advantage of being close to the Maritza River. In the latter part of the sixteenth century saltpeter was also manufactured in Filibe, Tatarpazarı, and in the environs

---

[2] Ottomar Thiele, *Saltpeterwirtschaft und Saltpeterpolitik. Eine volkswirtschaftliche Studie über das ehemalige europäische Saltpeterwesen* (Tübingen, 1905), pp. 8–9; Joseph J. Needham, Ho Ping-Yü, Lu Gwei-Djen and Wang Ling, *Science and Civilization in China vol. V: Chemistry and Chemical Technology, pt. 7, Military Technology: The Gunpowder Epic* (Cambridge, 1986), p. 95.

[3] English domestic production of saltpeter ended in 1667, and was used only as a last resort thereafter. See H. C. Tomlinson, *Guns and Government: The Ordnance Office under the Later Stuarts* (London, 1979), pp. 111–12; see also Needham et al., *Science*, p. 95; Bert S. Hall, *Weapons and Warfare in Renaissance Europe: Gunpowder, Technology, and Tactics* (Baltimore, 1997), p. 75.

[4] An earlier, rather short, list of saltpeter deposits in the Ottoman Empire is given in Vernon J. Parry, "Materials of War in the Ottoman Empire," in M. A. Cook ed., *Studies in the Economic History of the Middle East* (London, 1970), p. 222. Birol Çetin, *Osmanlı İmparatorluğu'nda Barut Sanayi, 1700–1900* (Ankara, 2001), pp. 45–49, briefly discusses the raw materials of powder, but his data are exclusively from the nineteenth century.

[5] MD 6, p. 492, no. 1071.   [6] MD 14, p. 155, no. 220.   [7] MD 10, p. 1.

of Hırsova, a village on the banks of the Danube in the *sancak* of Semendire.[8] By the seventeenth century thousands of families in hundreds of villages were making peter for the gunpowder mills of Selanik and Istanbul. In the late seventeenth and early eighteenth centuries, saltpeter was being produced in the following judicial districts: Selanik, Yenice-i Vardar, Vodena (Voden), Avrathisar, Ağustos (Njeguš), Siroz (Ser), Zihna, Florina (Lerin), Nevrokop, Monastir (Bitola), Dırama (Drama), Temürhisarı (Demir-Hisar),[9] Filibe and Tatarpazarı.[10] The local *kadı* registers mention several additional saltpeter production sites: Köprülü (Veles), Serfice, Melnik, Cumapazarı (Džuma Pazar), Üsküp, Štip, Cumaya (Džumaja), Petriç (Petrič), Doyran, Kara Su, Prilep, Koçani (Kočani), Kumanovo, Kiçevo (Kičevo) and Karaferye (Ber).[11] In 1679 the gunpowder works of Temeşvar got their peter from as many as thirty-eight *kaza*s situated in the province of Temeşvar and in the *sancak*s of Semendire and Sirem.[12]

To the north of the Danube, in Hungary saltpeter could again be found in great abundance. Indeed, Hungary, where saltpeter had been produced since the fifteenth century, possessed some of the richest saltpeter deposits in Europe. Within several years of conquering Hungary, the Ottomans began making saltpeter at numerous locations (Buda, Gyula, Csanad, Temeşvar, etc.).[13] The 1679 report of the Temeşvar gunpowder mills indicates that at that time saltpeter was being produced in each of the province's twelve judicial districts.[14]

In Asia Minor, in the sixteenth and seventeenth centuries, Güzelhisar, a village on the Asian shores of the Bosphorus, was probably the closest saltpeter-producing village to the capital.[15] Saltpeter was also found in Kütahya in the province of Anadolu,[16] in the *kaza* of Karahisar-i Sahib (Afyonkarahisar) to the southeast,[17] and the *kaza*s of Lazkiye (Denizli) and Gököyükü to the southwest of the latter.[18] Perhaps the most important saltpeter-producing province in Asia Minor was Karaman, where by the early 1570s, thirteen production plants were in operation.[19] Later, saltpeter was produced here in the *sancak*s of Akşehir, Konya, İçil, Niğde, Aksaray, Kayseri and Kırşehir, as well as in places such as Kilisehisar in the *kaza*

---

[8] MD 14, p. 155, no. 220. Between fifty and sixty carts of saltpeter earth could be processed here daily.

[9] MAD 10305, p. 194 (1696–97); MAD 10312, pp. 202, 328 and 410 (for the 1720s).

[10] DBŞM 844.

[11] Milka Zdraveva, "Der Abbau von Schwefel und Salpeter in Makedonien zur Zeit der osmanischen Herrschaft und deren Verarbeitung zu Schwarzpulver," *Südost-Forschungen* 39 (1980), 108; Djurdjica Petrović and Dušanka Bojanić-Lukać, "Dobivanja šalitre u Makedoniji od polovine XVI do polovine XIX veka," *VVM* 10 (1964), 31.

[12] KK Mevkufat 2682, f. 22a–b. The source lists the *kaza*s of Niş, Resava, Kuçanya (Kučanja), Pojarofça (Požarofca), Ahram (Hram), Güvercinlik, Valyevo, Belgrad, Semendire, Ujiçe (Užice), Çaçak, Pojegacık, Graguyefça (Kragujevac) and Rudnik in the *sancak* of Semendire; whereas in the *sancak* of Sirem the *kaza*s of Mitrofça, İrig, Gragurofça, Varad, Zemun, Nemçe, Morovit', İlok and Valkovar are mentioned.

[13] MD 3, no. 1343; MD 7, no. 1420; MD 14, no. 1107; MD 7, p. 418; MD 9. no. 7.

[14] KK Mevkufat 2682, f. 22a. The source lists the *kaza*s of Temeşvar, Verseç (Versec), Pançova, Çanad, Beçkerek (Becskerek), Orşova (Orsova), Çakova, Lipova (Lippa), Modava, Gyula, Yanova (Jenő) and Şebeş-Lugoş (Sebes-Lugos).

[15] MD 5, p. 477, no. 1287.   [16] MD 24, p. 307, no. 832.   [17] MD 24, p. 117, no. 321.

[18] MD 7, p. 94, no. 248.   [19] MD 24, p. 101, no. 275.

of Niğde,[20] Develi, Larende, Şarkışla, Bozok, Sarmısak, Çırlavuk, Kemerhisar, Koçhisar, Budak Özü and Ürgüp.[21] In the province of Dulkadır, which lay to the east of Karaman, saltpeter was found in various places in the middle of the sixteenth century, including the *sancak*s of Maraş and Malatya.[22] Saltpeter was also produced in the *sancak*s of Erzurum, Malazgirt and Oltu in the northeastern province of Erzurum, which was established in 1535.[23]

Further to the east, Diyarbekir (the center of a province established in 1515) had become a major regional economic and logistical center by the middle of the sixteenth century.[24] In 1566 the governor general of Diyarbekir informed the government in Istanbul that there were no local saltpeter deposits and that this important ingredient of gunpowder had never been produced in Diyarbekir. Notwithstanding his report, the government, then preparing for a Hungarian campaign, ordered him to investigate the possibility of saltpeter production.[25] A decree issued in November 1575 indicates that by that time production of saltpeter was successfully underway in the area. Although the saltpeter earth deposits of the *sancak* of Deyrirahbe had been exhausted, sufficient quantities of high-quality saltpeter were still available in other *sancak*s of the province.[26] Saltpeter deposits were found in the province of Van, one of the most easterly provinces of the Empire, where villages in the *kaza* of Ahtamar, as well as several other localities, produced saltpeter.[27] Production of saltpeter in the Van area reached about 21,600 kg (400 *kantar*) per annum in the mid-1570s.[28] In the 1560s, saltpeter was also discovered in the Empire's most easterly province, the *beylerbeyilik* of Şehrizol.[29]

In the Arab lands saltpeter was to be found in the *sancak* of Hama and in the *kaza*s of Antakya, Şizer, Riha (Ruha), Sermin, Bakras, Muarra and Ekrad, all in the province of Aleppo (established in 1516).[30] The quality of Aleppine saltpeter did not always satisfy the Istanbul officials: they found one shipment in the 1680s to be too salty and too arid.[31] In the middle of the sixteenth century the *sancak* of Birecik in the same province became a center of saltpeter production. In Iraq, Basra was one of the major centers of production. In 1566 81,000 kg (1,500 *kantar*) of refined saltpeter were being held there. Elsewhere in Iraq, deposits of saltpeter were found in and around Vasit. Since they were closer to Baghdad than to Basra, the saltpeter produced here went to the gunpowder works of the former city.[32] Another major supplier of saltpeter and gunpowder in the Middle East was Egypt, where in the mid-sixteenth century seventy villages produced saltpeter for the gunpowder workshops in Cairo.[33]

[20] MD 31, p. 362, no. 804.
[21] MAD 5392, p. 26; MAD 5472, pp. 2–6; MAD 5685, pp. 2–9; MD 6, p. 492; MD 14, nos. 146, 147, 149, 150 and 151.
[22] MD 9, p. 83; MD 24, p. 122, no. 337.   [23] MD 27, p. 375, no. 897.
[24] MD 5, p. 233, no. 600.   [25] MD 5, p. 380, no. 1012.   [26] MD 27, p. 57, no. 143.
[27] MD 27, p. 263, no. 618. The order mentions the *baruthane* or gunpowder works that was operating in that region.
[28] MD 24, p. 23, no. 68.   [29] MD 6, p. 597.
[30] MD 9, p. 85.   [31] DBŞM 449, p. 5.
[32] MD 5, p. 319, no. 831; p. 233, no. 599.
[33] Muzaffer Erdoğan, "Arşiv Vesikalarına Göre İstanbul Baruthaneleri," *İED* 2 (1956), 118.

Sulfur

Sulfur is to be found in many volcanic regions of Europe, especially in Sicily, which in the early modern era supplied the whole continent. Vannoccio Biringuccio (1480–1539), the author of *Pirotechnia*, the classic sixteenth-century treatise on metals and metallurgy, mentioned that sulfur was "excavated from open mines because if the miners should try to extract it in any other way they could not endure to stay inside the mines on account of the great heat and unendurable odor that it gives out."[34] The sulfur in Sicily is mixed with limestone, and the sulfur content was usually between 20 and 40 percent.[35]

There were several methods of extracting sulfur from the sulfurous soil. Both Biringuccio and Georgius Agricola (the author of the *De re metallica*, the other sixteenth-century bestseller on minerals and metals) discussed in detail the more sophisticated methods using furnaces and tabulated vessels for the extraction of sulfur by distillation.[36] However, the method most commonly used in Europe and in the Ottoman Empire for recovering sulfur from ore was the wasteful "calcaroni" method. The pyrites were arranged in a large compact heap and covered with moistened ash. Initial combustion was provided by burning firewood, but later the combustion of the sulfur provided the necessary heat. The melted sulfur was collected on a prepared floor. This process could recover only about 60 percent of the sulfur.[37]

Sulfur was not available for the Ottomans in such ample quantities as saltpeter. The lands in the vicinity of the Dead Sea, the province of Van, Moldavia and the island of Melos supplied some.[38] In the European parts of the Empire, sulfur was mined and processed in Macedonia, especially in the villages near Ohri, which supplied sulfur to the gunpowder works of Istanbul and Selanik.

The Ottoman need for the raw materials of munitions sometimes led to fraud, because Ottoman subjects working in the ammunition and armaments industries were exempted from irregular wartime taxes. In the hope of obtaining tax exemptions many men undertook work that they were subsequently unable to fulfill. In 1572, the inhabitants of the village of Leskofçe in the *sancak* of Ohri were to be exempted from payment of the *tekalif-i örfiyye*, the customary or irregular wartime taxes,[39] in return for producing 8,100 kg (150 *kantar*) of sulfur per annum.

---

[34] Vannoccio Biringuccio, *The Pirotechnia of Vannoccio Biringuccio: The Classic Sixteenth-Century Treatise on Metals and Metallurgy*. Trans. Cyril Stanley Smith and Martha Teach Gnudi (New York, 1990), p. 86.

[35] Arthur Marshall, *Explosives I: History and Manufacture* (London, 1917), p. 70.

[36] Biringuccio, *Pirotechnia*, pp. 88–90; Georgius Agricola, *De re metallica*. Trans. Herbert Clark Hoover and Lou Henry Hoover (New York, 1950), pp. 578–81.

[37] Marshall, *Explosives*, pp. 69–70; Maurice Daumas, *A History of Technology and Invention*. Trans. Eileen B. Hennessey (2 vols., New York, 1969), vol. II, p. 183.

[38] Parry, "Materials of War," pp. 221–22.

[39] The *tekalif-i örfiyye* were the customary taxes, i.e., taxes different from the regularly levied taxes that had legal basis. The *tekalif-i örfiyye* seem to have been synonymous with the *avarız-ı divaniyye*, which was the generic term for the irregular wartime taxes that, by the seventeenth century, had more or less regularly been levied. The *avarız* system provided effective means for the provisioning of the Ottoman army, on which see Caroline Finkel, *The Administration of Warfare: The Ottoman*

A report by the local *timariot* cavalrymen, however, pointed out that there were no sulfur deposits on the lands belonging to the village and that the local inhabitants had no knowledge of extracting sulfur from ore. Moreover, it transpired that the inhabitants had hoped that, by producing the sulfur, they would be exempted from payment of the *avarız* taxes and would not have to dispatch their young men to be rowers for the fleet. Further inquiries revealed that, although the villagers had in fact found some sulfur, the Porte did not consider sulfur production in the area to be very good business. The methods used by the villagers for extracting the sulfur from the ore were very wasteful. The report stated (doubtless with some exaggeration) that while 8,100 kg (150 *kantar*) of sulfur had been extracted, another 81,000 kg (1,500 *kantar*) had been wasted because of the primitive methods used, which amounted to the burning of sulfur on fires.[40]

The local *kadı* registers indicate that in the seventeenth century the Macedonian sulfur producers supplied considerable amounts of sulfur to the gunpowder mills of the peninsula and the capital. From the 1660s until the first decade of the nineteenth century, they supplied about 32,400–34,020 kg (600–630 *kantar*) of sulfur each year.[41] Since the proportion of sulfur in gunpowder produced by the Ottomans fluctuated between 12.5 and 15.5 percent, in the late seventeenth century, the above amount was sufficient for the production of about 205–270 metric tons (3,800–5,000 *kantar*) of gunpowder, or between a quarter and a third of the total estimated gunpowder output of the major gunpowder works of the Empire in the sixteenth and seventeenth centuries. Contemporary calculations suggest that Ottoman imperial campaigns of the late seventeenth century required at least 540 metric tons or 10,000 *kantar* of gunpowder, so Macedonian sulfur production would have been able to provide between 40 and 50 percent of the needed amount. The sulfur mines in the district of Ohri were obliged to supply a fixed amount of sulfur each year to the gunpowder workshops of Selanik. The sulfur mines, as well as the sulfur that was shipped from the mines to Selanik, are referred to in our sources as the *ocaklık* of the gunpowder works.[42] The *ocaklık* of Ohri provided approximately 19,000–25,000 kg sulfur a year to the gunpowder works at Selanik in the 1690s.[43]

In Asia Minor, in the province of Van, the main producers of sulfur were Erciş, on the northern shore of Lake Van, and the *sancak* of Hakkari, to the south of the lake. In 1570 the Porte was informed that the raw material for sulfur production in Erciş had come from Iran, and that 108 metric tons (2,000 *kantar*) had been produced in the *sancak* of Hakkari. The Porte immediately ordered that the sulfur should be brought as quickly as possible on hired draught animals to the port in Trabzon, and from there by sea to Istanbul. Later, however, it became apparent

Military Campaigns in Hungary, 1593–1606 (Vienna, 1988), pp. 130–43, and the literature cited there. It was also instrumental regarding the procurement of raw material and manpower for the Ottoman war industry plants, on which see later in this chapter.

[40] MD 16, no. 241.   [41] Zdraveva, "Der Abbau von Schwefel und Salpeter," p. 107.

[42] The *ocaklık*s were special funds or permanent in-kind contributions by which the Empire secured the necessary raw materials and supplies for its armaments industries. See the section on *ocaklık*.

[43] Sources mention 15,800–20,000 *okka*s in the 1690s and 12,500 *okka*s in the 1720s. MAD 3620 and MAD 10312, respectively. For detailed data see Appendix.

that the amount of sulfur produced in Hakkari was considerably less than the amount mentioned in the preliminary reports. The governor general also stated that the consignment was very expensive indeed: to transport one *batman* of sulfur (7.2–23 kg) cost more than 11 *akças*.[44] Owing to the campaign against Cyprus, the Ottoman government had a particular interest in locating all potential sources of sulfur and in encouraging gunpowder production by all means. The authorities instructed the governor to resolve the issue of delivery and to find out about a sulfur mine called Karagüden, where sulfur had been produced under the Safavids. The *beylerbeyi* had to discover whether this latter sulfur mine was now on Safavid or Ottoman territory.[45]

The Porte also attempted to keep a record of all sulfur reserves and dispatch these supplies to the gunpowder mills. In early 1576, 16,200 kg (300 *kantar*) of sulfur were requested from Aleppo for the gunpowder mills in Basra. Several months later, however, Basra had still not received the requested amount of sulfur, and therefore a renewed order urged that the consignment be sent.[46] Sulfur was also mined in the *sancak* of Kastamonu. Between 1697 and 1699, 31 percent of the sulfur supplied to the Istanbul *baruthane* came from Kastamonu.[47]

Many Ottoman gunpowder mills had to obtain sulfur from distant sources. Gunpowder mills in Ottoman Hungary brought in sulfur from other parts of the Empire: in late 1565, when preparations were underway for Süleyman's final campaign, sulfur was brought in from Belgrade for gunpowder to be produced in Buda.[48] A year later, central authorities instructed the *sancakbeyi* of Semendire to buy up any sulfur he could lay his hands on.[49] In the second half of the seventeenth century, sulfur was transported on several occasions to the Temeşvar *baruthane* from Istanbul (about 38,880 kg in 1673 and 1674).[50] The gunpowder mills in Izmir received several consignments of sulfur from Selanik: in 1697, for example, more than 18,400 kg (15,000 *okka*) of sulfur were transported to Izmir.[51]

Charcoal

Until the introduction of a more efficient cylinder method of charcoal production in the late eighteenth century, charcoal was made by the controlled and slow burning

[44] According to İnalcık the standard *batman* was 23 kg, but it is not clear in what period this was the case. Halil İnalcık and Donald Quataert eds., *An Economic and Social History of the Ottoman Empire, 1300–1914* (Cambridge, 1994), p. 987. A source from 1566, regarding the province of Dulkadır in Asia Minor, indicates that in that region one *batman* was about 7.2–7.5 kg (MD 5, p. 469, no. 1259).

[45] MD 10, p. 28; Ahmed Refik, *Osmanlı Devrinde Türkiye Madenleri (967–1200)* (Istanbul, 1931), pp. 7–8, doc. 12.

[46] MD 27, p. 227, no. 523, and p. 388, no. 932.

[47] DBŞM 19085, p. 14. The amount was 17,317.5 *okka* or 21,280 kg.

[48] MD 5, nos. 666, 667. Until the 1570s, the gunpowder mills in Habsburg Hungary brought in the sulfur needed for gunpowder production from Poland and from the hereditary provinces of Austria.

[49] MD 5, p. 665, no. 1868.   [50] KK Mevkufat 2628, fol. 22b; MAD 4527, p. 11.

[51] MAD 10305, p. 138. From time to time, some of the sulfur stored at Selanik was taken to Istanbul. DBŞM 642.

of selected wood to extract water and volatile compounds.[52] Although Biringuccio was of the opinion that the best charcoal was made of willow, he noticed that there were "some who make charcoal out of hazelnut instead of willow, some out of grapevine twigs, some of laurel, some of the shells of pine cones, some of oyster twigs of which baskets are made, some of young elder, and some of reeds." He also added that "all charcoals that are made of soft wood with much pith and woods that are thin, young, and without hard knots are good for this process."[53]

Early modern Europeans made charcoal from a great variety of types of wood. For a long time alder-wood was widely used for making charcoal for black powder, but later other kinds of softwoods were also used. The English preferred dogwood for rapid burning powder types of small grain, but they used alder, willow and hazel for larger powders.[54] In Germany alder and willow, in Austria alder and hazel, in France black alder, in Spain oleander, yew, willow, hemp stems and vine, and in Italy hemp stems were used.[55]

The Ottomans produced charcoal from kinds of wood that were called *karaağaç* (black wood) which they understood as wood from non-fruit-bearing trees. According to Vernon Parry, in Asia Minor above all oak was used for this purpose. In Lebanon charcoal was made from willow and in Syria from poplar.[56] Surviving account books seem to indicate that willow was the most popular wood for charcoal production in the Empire.[57] Iznikmid shipped 1,260 sacks of charcoal to Istanbul's gunpowder workshops between August 1696 and January 1699, and a further 14.6 metric tons (11,880 *okka*) between November 1701 and November 1703.[58] To ensure a continuous supply of charcoal to the gunpowder workshops, the Ottoman authorities protected the willow forests and banned the cutting down of trees near the charcoal burners.

In Europe the wood was generally cut in the spring because its sap contained less inorganic matter in that season. Furthermore, the proportion of ash in the wood was smaller at that time of the year and it was easier to strip off the bark – which also contained considerable quantities of ash. The wood was generally left to dry for 18–36 months.[59] Like their European contemporaries, the Ottomans protected both the raw wood and the charcoal from rain.[60]

The burning of charcoal required appropriate expertise, but this was far from universal. The activities of the charcoal burners were supervised by *kömürci başıs*, who might also be chosen from among the artillerymen like Mehmed *topçu* who was appointed in 1574 to head the charcoal burners of the Sapanca area. In addition

[52] Jenny West, *Gunpowder, Government and War in the Mid-Eighteenth Century* (London, 1991), p. 174.
[53] Biringuccio, *Pirotechnia*, pp. 413–14.
[54] Marshall, *Explosives*, p. 67; West, *Gunpowder*, p. 175.   [55] Marshall, *Explosives*, p. 67.
[56] Parry, "Materials of War," p. 221.
[57] DBŞM 598, p. 6; DBŞM 642, pp. 5–6; DBŞM 844, pp. 5–6; MAD 7488.
[58] DBŞM 19085, p. 2; MAD 7488, p. 3. The region was in fact one of the most important suppliers of timber to the Istanbul Arsenal, too. Cf. İdris Bostan, *Osmanlı Bahriye Teşkilatı: XVII. Yüzyılda Tersane-i Amire* (Ankara, 1992), pp. 102–03.
[59] Marshall, *Explosives*, p. 67.   [60] MD 29, p. 41, no. 96.

to supervising the production of charcoal, Mehmed was ordered to build a store-house (*anbar*) where large quantities of charcoal could be stored. Just as in the case of gunpowder, the storage of charcoal required particular care, because without proper protection the charcoal could be damaged by moisture, as happened in a storehouse poorly constructed by Mehmed's predecessor.[61]

The Ottoman authorities and saltpeter production

Like many of its European rivals, the Ottoman government declared the production of weapons and munitions a state monopoly, took an active part in mapping the resources of the Empire and controlled the production of peter and gunpowder. To ensure government monopoly over saltpeter, the Porte tried to place villages with saltpeter deposits under the supervision of the treasury. Where such locali-ties had been given to *timar*-holders, they were attached to the crown lands and the *timar*-holders were compensated.[62] Under Sultanic decrees, the search for and production of saltpeter were usually the tasks of the provincial and district gover-nors (*beylerbeyi*s and *sancakbeyi*s).[63] They had to inform Istanbul whenever new sources of saltpeter were discovered and if they became aware that saltpeter had been produced in their respective territories before the Ottoman conquest.[64] While overseeing the manufacturing of peter was part of their job, Ottoman governors also had a financial interest in saltpeter production, for Istanbul rewarded their service with salary increases.[65]

Both cooperation between local and central authorities and local initiatives played roles in mapping the peter resources of the Empire and in increasing pro-duction outputs. When production in Erzurum had met with obstacles in 1576 owing to a water shortage, a local saltpeterman (*güherçile üstadı*), called Behram, suggested that the production site should be moved to Oltu, where water was suf-ficient and peter could be produced for nine months per year as opposed to three months in Erzurum. Behram thought that the change of location would still be worthwhile, even though the transport of saltpeter from Erzurum to Oltu would

[61] MD 24, p. 98, no. 268.
[62] MD 3, p. 449, no. 1343; MD 7, p. 492, no. 1420; MD 5, p. 450, no. 1205. See also my "Ottoman Gunpowder Production in Hungary in the Sixteenth Century: The *Baruthane* of Buda," in Géza Dávid and Pál Fodor eds., *Hungarian–Ottoman Military and Diplomatic Relations in the Age of Süleyman the Magnificent* (Budapest, 1994), pp. 149–59.
[63] MD 7, nos. 1149, 1593, 2299; MD 14, no. 142. Sometimes the *defterdar*s (treasury chiefs) and *kadı*s (judges) were responsible in their place.
[64] MD 5, no. 1205; MD 14, no. 1107. Occasionally they also had to provide local saltpeter producers with the tools and raw materials they needed.
[65] In December 1567 the annual income of the *beylerbeyi* of Buda, Sokollu Mustafa Pasha, was increased by 80,000 *akça*s and that of the *sancakbeyi* of Nógrád by 20,000 *akça*s, in recognition of their efforts in the field of saltpeter production. MD 7, p. 194, no. 525. This was almost a 10 percent increase for Sokollu Mustafa Pasha, given the fact that he had taken up his post in 1566 with a yearly income of 924,000 *akça*s. See Géza Dávid, "Incomes and Possessions of the Beglerbegis of Buda in the Sixteenth Century," in Dávid, *Studies in Demographic and Administrative History of Ottoman Hungary* (Istanbul, 1997), p. 107.

result in additional costs.[66] Since Oltu had been integrated into the Ottoman provincial administration only in the 1550s, the proposal shows how quick the Ottomans were in drawing immediate economic benefits from newly conquered territories.[67]

The Ottomans employed various means of procuring saltpeter. The two most important forms were state-run workshops, usually run within the tax-farming (*iltizam*) system, and saltpeter produced by service or *ocaklık* villages in return for tax exemptions. When these two forms of production could not satisfy the demand, Istanbul had to purchase the needed amount of peter. This took two forms: purchase of saltpeter at fixed price, which was a form of irregular taxation, and purchase of peter at the market price.[68]

The earliest data at our disposal from the fifteenth century suggest that the Ottoman government – like many of its European contemporaries – sought to establish control over production of this strategically important raw material, and production was overseen by state commissioners. In areas close to the gunpowder works or *baruthane*s the state established several saltpeter production workshops. It then arranged for production to be supervised and controlled, ensuring sufficient financial funds to cover production costs.

Several of the originally state-run saltpeter production centers were later oper-ated as modest commercial enterprises. Entrepreneurs, usually members of the Ottoman ruling groups, called *askeri*, undertook – in return for income and privileges – to produce certain amounts of saltpeter annually. Sometimes the entrepreneurs found the deposits of saltpeter earth themselves and then offered to start production under certain conditions. At other times, the entrepreneurs took over plants established by the state, and then set about production either alone or in cooperation with several business partners (*şerik*). In such cases, the Ottoman *iltizam* or tax-farming system served as a model for the operation.

The other widely employed method was the parceling out of saltpeter produc-tion among thousands of saltpeter-manufacturing families in the so-called *ocaklık* villages, so named after the widely used method by which the government pro-cured funds, labor and material for its industries and paid its garrisons. In return for their services the villages were exempt from the extraordinary wartime taxes known as the *avarız*.

While the functioning of the state-run saltpeter plants will be examined using the case study of the saltpeter works in the province of Karaman, the example of hundreds of Macedonian *ocaklık* or service villages that produced saltpeter for the gunpowder mills in Selanik will illustrate this second method. This will be followed by a brief description of saltpeter purchases.

---

[66] MD 27, p. 375, no. 897. The additional cost was 7 *akça*s per *kantar* (54 kg).

[67] In 1578, the Porte decided to leave Oltu as a hereditary *sancak* in the hands of the Georgian princes. Istanbul's flexibility allowed the Ottoman armaments industry to benefit from local supplies of raw materials. Dündar Aydın, *Erzurum Beylerbeyiliği ve Teşkilatı* (Ankara, 1998), pp. 256–57.

[68] It seems that the methods changed little in the centuries to come, for similar means were used in the nineteenth century. See Çetin, *Barut Sanayi*, p. 50.

Saltpeter production and the Ottoman military entrepreneur

In the sixteenth and seventeenth centuries members of the Ottoman ruling groups (*askeri*) often functioned as military entrepreneurs, managing revenue collection as well as military industrial plants, operated within the tax-farming or *iltizam* system, a well-known method of revenue collecting in the Mamluk Sultanate of Egypt, the Ottoman Empire and Mughal India. In the Ottoman Empire the state delegated its rights to collect taxes from certain tax sources (*mukataa*) to tax-farmers (*mültezim*) for a determined tenure.[69] Tax farmers acquired the rights to collect taxes through a state auction at which the highest bidder was awarded the job. In anticipation of future revenue, the tax-farmers agreed to pay lump sums, that is, the auction price, as well as yearly installments to the treasury.[70]

While the *iltizam* has usually been discussed in connection with revenue collecting, it is clear from the sources that the management of saltpeter and gunpowder production often took place within the same system. In 1574 the saltpeter works (*güherçile karhaneleri*) of Van were being managed by Hacı Çavuş, whom sources refer to as *emin* or *mübaşir*, terms that, in this case, referred to an entrepreneur.[71] Since Hacı Çavuş was running the enterprise together with several of his associates (*şerik*), it seems we are dealing with a business partnership similar to those established in the fields of revenue collecting or shipbuilding.[72] Hacı Çavuş and his associates undertook to produce 64,800 kg (1,200 *kantar*) of saltpeter within three years.[73] Since their term (*tahvil*) was drawing to a close,[74] a man called Ahmed Çavuş submitted an offer to the authorities in April 1574 in which he expressed his desire to take over the management of the saltpeter works from Hacı Çavuş. He promised to increase the production output by 43,200 kg (800 *kantar*), producing a total of 108 metric tons (2,000 *kantar*) of peter in a three-year term. Ahmed belonged to the *timar*-holding cavalry and one of his conditions was that he should receive an increase in revenue of 10,000 *akça*s per annum. He also requested his appointment to the rank of the *ağa* of the *azab*s of the fortress of Van. A further condition was that his business partner, Mevlana Hacı Iskender, who had once been the *kadı* but was now apparently without any post, should be appointed as

---

[69] Although the tenure could range from several days to twelve years, the usual term was three years.
[70] İnalcık and Quataert eds., *An Economic and Social History*, pp. 64–66; Mehmet Genç, "İltizam," *TDVİA*, vol. XXII, pp. 154–58; Linda Darling, *Revenue-Raising and Legitimacy: Tax Collection and Finance Administration in the Ottoman Empire, 1560–1660* (Leiden, 1996); Murat Çizakça, *A Comparative Evolution of Business Partnerships: The Islamic World and Europe, with Specific Reference to the Ottoman Archives* (Leiden, 1996), pp. 140–59.
[71] In revenue collecting, *emin*s were government officials who managed the *mukataa*s that had not been sold off and remained under treasury control, but the words *emin* and *mübaşir* often indicated the agents of entrepreneurships. In certain instances the word *emin* denoted the head of a business and *mübaşir* a subordinate agent. The distinction, however, is not always consistent and the sources often use *emin* and *mübaşir* interchangeably to mean entrepreneur. Darling, *Revenue-Raising*, p. 129.
[72] Çizakça, *Business Partnerships*, pp. 86–131.   [73] MD 24, p. 3, no. 8.
[74] MD 24, p. 76, no. 209.

kadı of Bitlis and have his former salary raised by 12 *akças* per day. Abdülkerim, a *müderris* or an instructor at a *medrese* school, who was also to be Ahmed's business partner, should be given a wage increase of 10 *akças* per day and be appointed as *kadı* of Muş.[75] Clearly, Ahmed Çavuş was asking for quite a lot in return for an increase in saltpeter production, and the Porte ordered the *beylerbeyi* of Van to make a thorough investigation of his offer and capabilities. Istanbul's primary interest was whether Ahmed Çavuş and his associates were capable of manufacturing the promised 2,000 *kantar* of saltpeter and why the current agents (that is Hacı Çavuş and associates) had undertaken to produce just 1,200 *kantar* of saltpeter.[76]

Another entrepreneur with similarities to Hacı Çavuş and Ahmed Çavuş was a *timariot* called Mehmed who had discovered, at some time before 1574, the saltpeter mine (*güherçile madeni*) in the *kaza* of Deyrirahbe in the province of Diyarbekir. He had begun production at the mine, managing the works as a *mültezim*. Nevertheless, Zeynelabidin, who was the former *sancakbeyi* of the *sancak* of Kabur in the same province, set his eyes on the works and obtained management rights from the Istanbul Finance Department (*Maliye*). The form of his management, however, was not *iltizam* but *emanet*, and Zeynelabidin worked the mine as a paid state official. The discoverer and founder of the works, Mehmed, naturally disputed the change. Since the decision had been taken at the Finance Department in Istanbul, Mehmed traveled to Istanbul and took his complaint to the Imperial Divan. After hearing his case, the Divan ordered the governor general and treasury chief of Diyarbekir to examine the matter and to determine which operational form was most likely to guarantee saltpeter production and to benefit the state.[77]

It is clear that some military men saw a business opportunity in saltpeter production. Aware of the importance of saltpeter to the Ottoman army and navy, they attempted to achieve promotions for themselves and their fellows by holding out the prospect of higher production outputs. While most men achieved promotion by risking their lives on the battlefield, there were always some who attempted to achieve the same through service on the home front. The work was not only much safer, but it also had the advantage that one did not have to leave family and family businesses.

Military entrepreneurs such as Hacı Çavuş, Ahmed Çavuş or Mehmed were not the only ones to draw benefit from saltpeter production. The fortress soldiers and retired *sipahis*, as well as military auxiliaries, who labored in the saltpeter works and therefore received various bonuses and exemptions, were very happy to work in the munitions industry, thereby avoiding being drafted to fight military campaigns. The latter group found a valuable ally in the "military entrepreneurs"

---

[75] Ahmed Çavuş also requested that each year twenty of the border fortress soldiers of Van should be allowed to work in the saltpeter works, receiving tenure (*gedük*) for their services. Finally, one of the conditions listed by Ahmed Çavuş was that the authorities should provide him with a boat that might be used on Lake Van in order to transport wood needed in the production process.

[76] MD 24, p. 3, no. 8; p. 23, no. 68.   [77] MD 24, p. 290, no. 792.

and had few qualms about obtaining exemptions from the military campaigns by
bribing the local authorities.

The state and the military entrepreneurs: the saltpeter
works in Karaman

In regions rich in saltpeter Istanbul established saltpeter works that were managed
either by state employees or by tax-farmers who were often the highest administra-
tors, treasury chiefs (*defterdar*) and judges (*kadı*) of provinces where the saltpeter
and gunpowder works were situated. In 1638–39, Yakub Efendi, the province's treasury chief, and Kudretullah Efendi, the *kadı* of Niğde, were running the Karaman
saltpeter works. Kudretullah Efendi was also a *müfettiş*, that is, an inspector, and
as such he was Yakub Efendi's partner in the business.[78] In total the two undertook
to produce 178.2 metric tons (3,300 *kantar*) of raw saltpeter per annum.[79] The
main entrepreneur was the province's treasury chief who supervised the production at more than half a dozen saltpeter works and was to produce 108 metric
tons (2,000 *kantar*), whereas his partner was responsible for just two production
plants and for the manufacturing of 70.2 metric tons (1,300 *kantar*) of peter. The
saltpeter works of the province of Karaman had previously produced 118.8 metric
tons (2,200 *kantar*) of peter per year, and the two entrepreneurs raised the output
to 178.2 metric tons, by opening new production plants. Moreover, it seems that
Yakub Efendi, in true entrepreneurial spirit, also made some investments and built
a gunpowder mill in Bor.[80]

Although two years later Yakub Efendi was still running the saltpeter works
and the gunpowder mills,[81] by that time complaints against his business conduct
had been lodged in Istanbul. One of the accusations was that he had failed to
pay off peasants supplying saltpeter earth and firewood to the plants.[82] Allegedly
he had demanded a so-called "entry duty" of 2 *akça*s per pack-load from the
peasants and committed other abuses which forced the peasants to flee the area,
causing significant losses to the treasury.[83] In the eyes of Istanbul, however, the

---

[78] Although the sources do not use the term *iltizam* when referring to the enterprise, they do mention
the terms of *deruhde* (assumed, undertaken) and *taahhüd* (an undertaking or contract), which are
used synonymously with *iltizam*. Moreover, details in the accounts leave no doubt as to the nature
of the enterprise.

[79] MAD 5472, pp. 2–3, 6–7.

[80] This is recorded in a much later source dated 1670–71 that deals with the repair of the *baruthane* in
that year. See AE Mehmed IV, no. 2397.

[81] MAD 5392, pp. 43–44.

[82] They should have received 4 *akça*s for each pack-load (*yük*). The actual weight of the *yük* varied
greatly depending on the type of pack animal and on the kind of goods that were carried. See Halil
İnalcık, "Yük (Himl) in the Ottoman Silk Trade, Mining, and Agriculture," in his *The Middle East
and the Balkans under the Ottoman Empire: Essays on Economy and Society* (Bloomington, 1993),
pp. 432–60. Since a later source claims that peasants supplying saltpeter earth and firewood are paid
4 *akça*s per *kantar* (54 or 56 kg) the *yük* used in the region could have weighed close to a *kantar*.

[83] MAD 5392, p. 49.

most serious complaint was doubtless that Yakub Efendi had failed to fulfill his contractual responsibilities and that his gunpowder deliveries of 110.5 metric tons (90,000 *okka*) had usually been delayed, even though the *defterdar* received the necessary funds and equipment from the state. It seems the complaints did have an effect. By the following year, Yakub Efendi was neither the *defterdar* of Karaman nor the entrepreneur running the saltpeter works in the province.[84]

Before we draw any wider conclusion from the accusations, we should remember that the complaints against Yakub Efendi have survived in a letter whose aim (as in other situations of a similar type) was to obtain support for another entrepreneur interested in the business. This new entrepreneur was Murad who lived in the nearby *sancak*-center of Niğde and who had formerly been the "holder" or occupant (*mutasarrif*) of the *sancak* of Celbe. Concerning Murad, the application merely recognizes that he is an honest and religious person who had accomplished his tasks and benefited the state in all his earlier state offices. Murad pledged that should he win the business he would have regard for the peasants, demanding just half of the saltpeter earth and firewood required by Yakub Efendi. Moreover, unlike Yakub Efendi, he would duly pay the 4 *akças* that the peasants were owed for each pack-load of saltpeter earth. A weakness in his offer, however, was that, as against Yakub Efendi who had undertaken the production of 110.5 metric tons (90,000 *okka*) of gunpowder per annum, Murad – perhaps because he had a more realistic view of local conditions – undertook to produce 98.3 metric tons (80,000 *okka*) of powder.[85] The accounts of the Karaman gunpowder works stemming from a later period show that Murad both won the business and became Yakub Efendi's successor as *defterdar* of the province, and was still running the saltpeter works as contractor in 1650–51.[86]

In 1637–38 in total 178.2 metric tons (3,300 *kantar*) of raw saltpeter were produced in the Karaman plants which cost 1,257,000 *akças*.[87] Since total revenues of the province had amounted to just 2,390,000 *akças* in 1636–37,[88] the costs of saltpeter production in Karaman were 53 percent of the previous year's revenues. Adding to this the cost of transporting the saltpeter from the production plants to the gunpowder works of Bor (170,000 *akças*), and an extraordinary amount of 500,000 *akças* that was spent on the construction of the gunpowder works in Bor, we arrive at the total cost of 1,927,000 *akças*, which is 80 percent of the province's total revenues in the preceding year. Although the production output in 1637–38 was unusually high (178.2 metric tons versus the usual 118.8 tons or 2,200 *kantar*), the costs have never been as low as 23 percent of the province's

---

[84] MAD 5685, p. 9.   [85] MAD 5392, pp. 49–50.
[86] MAD 5685; MAD 12778.   [87] MAD 5472, p. 2.
[88] Rhoads Murphey, *Regional Structure in the Ottoman Empire* (Wiesbaden, 1987), pp. 188–89. Regarding saltpeter production the source contains only two short notes which state that the 500,000 *akças* of income derived from taxes paid by the pensioner *sipahi*s and the *sipahi-zade*s and the 150,000 *akças* of revenue derived from the Sultanic crown lands of Suğla were used to cover the costs of saltpeter production (ibid., pp. 52–55). Nevertheless, in the Appendix, the publisher of the source only mentions the former and claims that the amount spent on the preparation of saltpeter was just 23 percent of the total income of the province (p. 216).

revenue, a percentage indicated in the province's *mukataa*-register. They usually fluctuated between 35 and 42 percent in the seventeenth century.[89]

The method used to finance the saltpeter works of Karaman was called *ocaklık*. In order to cover production costs, certain taxes in the province were used to establish a separate cash fund, the *ocaklık*. Although the system of *ocaklık* funds and of *ocaklık* villages was a broadly used means of procuring funds, labor and material in many sectors of the Ottoman industry and financing, the *ocaklık* has been a rather neglected topic in Ottoman studies.[90] Nor were *ocaklıks* examined in a comparative manner, although in early modern Europe similar methods were also commonly used.[91] Apart from the Arsenal, it was in the Ottoman munitions and weapons industries where the *ocaklık* system was most generally employed by the authorities to ensure the continuous procurement of raw materials. In the province of Karaman extraordinary *avarız* taxes (known as the *bedel-i mütekaidin*), the province's poll-taxes (*cizye*) and various government revenues (*mukataas*) were used as more or less permanent cash funds, designated as *ocaklıks* of the plants, to cover the costs of saltpeter production.[92] Using the above system, the Karaman saltpeter plants could produce almost 119 metric tons of peter in the 1630s, which had fallen to about 98 metric tons by 1695–96.[93]

The nature of the enterprise

The individuals operating the saltpeter and gunpowder works within the *iltizam* system were entrepreneurs only in a limited sense, and they cannot be compared to the wealthy military entrepreneurs of the Thirty Years War or to the Jewish

---

[89] MAD 5472, pp. 1–6; MAD 5685, p. 6; MAD 5392, p. 26. All of this suggests that we should exercise great care when drawing conclusions from data provided in the *mukataa*-registers. Such data should be compared with other sources before any conclusions concerning the financial situation or economic activity of a given province are drawn.

[90] It is symptomatic that the term appears only once in the 1,000-page-long handbook of Ottoman economic and social history; see İnalcık and Quataert, *An Economic and Social History*, p. 461. *Ocaklıks* were also used to satisfy the timber needs of the imperial maritime arsenal, to secure the provisions for the Sultan's kitchen, larder and stables, as well as to finance payment of garrison troops. See Nejat Göyünç, "Yurtluk-Ocaklık Deyimleri Hakkında," in *Prof. Dr. Bekir Kütükoğlu'na Armağan* (Istanbul, 1991), pp. 269–77, which is the only study on the subject.

[91] To cover the operational costs of the saltpeter and gunpowder plants, the French government also designated certain royal revenues or raised special taxes in the respective provinces. See John U. Nef, *Industry and Government in France and England, 1540–1640* (Ithaca, NY, 1964), pp. 61–65.

[92] MAD 5392, p. 26; MAD 5472, pp. 2–7; MAD 5685. In 1637–38 the authorities approved the transfer of a sum of 1,957,990 *akças* to Yakub Efendi and Kudretullah Efendi in order to cover the costs of operating the saltpeter works. Yakub Efendi sought to cover the costs of producing 2,000 *kantars* of saltpeter out of the revenue (*mahsul*) of the *sancak* of Akşehir (100,000 *akças*), his own areas (*bakiye*: 314,000 *akças*) and the poll-tax levied on displaced persons (*cizye-i perakende-i Karaman*: 356,000 *akças*). His associate, Kudretullah Efendi, covered the costs of producing 1,300 *kantars* of saltpeter out of the taxes of the retired *sipahis* of the *sancak* of Niğde (100,000 *akças*), money remaining from construction work in Niğde (100,000 *akças*) and the poll-tax levied on displaced persons in the province.

[93] MAD 3774, p. 14; MAD 4527, p. 13; DBŞM 40877. See Appendix.

army contractors of the 1680s and 1690s who financed and supplied the Habsburg forces during their wars against the Ottomans and France.[94] Students who have examined the *iltizam* in connection with revenue collecting have pointed out that it may not be considered private enterprise in the European sense, largely because of the tight state control of the system.[95] However, the extent of state control should not be exaggerated. On many occasions the Finance Department had no information whatsoever about activities in the more distant saltpeter works, which would indicate that local entrepreneurs enjoyed considerable freedom of activity and that the administrative checks of the center were of limited use.

An example regarding saltpeter manufacturing in Erzurum in the late 1570s might illustrate this point. In September 1577, the Istanbul government, having not received any report from Erzurum for a while, instructed the saltpeter inspector in that province (the *kadı* of Karahisar) to review the accounts of the saltpeter works and to answer the following questions regarding how many of these works were operating within the *iltizam* system; which *mukataa*s were covering the operating costs and how much money had been transferred; which plants had received saltpeter boilers (*kazgan*) and equipment (*alat*) and how many/much had they been given; how much saltpeter there was in the various production plants; how much of the saltpeter had been delivered to the gunpowder works; and, finally, how much gunpowder had been delivered to which fortresses.[96] The questions raised by the central government demonstrate just how little information was available in Istanbul about saltpeter and gunpowder production in Erzurum. Such examples, of which there are plenty, appear to substantiate recent skepticism concerning the views of earlier scholars who had stressed the omnipotence of the Istanbul government and point to the often surprisingly limited nature of Istanbul's administrative authority in the provinces. Similarly, such cases suggest a certain degree of independence on the part of the contractors.

In larger plants the entrepreneurs used the financial and human resources of the Ottoman state as well as the apparatus and facilities that the state put at their disposal. All of this hardly means, however, that we should refrain from considering men such as Hacı Çavuş, Ahmed Çavuş, Yakub Efendi and their associates as entrepreneurs. They frequently played a key role in establishing new saltpeter works, and often contributed their own capital towards such operations, supplementing the frequently insufficient financial resources that were allocated to them

[94] Of the latter group the best known are Samuel Oppenheimer (1630–1703), the *Oberhoffaktor* or *Oberkriegsfaktor* of Emperor Leopold, and his partner, Samson Wertheimer (1658–1728), who later established his own business independent of Oppenheimer's. In addition, we should also mention Lazarus Hirschel, Oppenheimer's main agent in Hungary, who supplied the Imperialists during their sieges of Buda (1686) and Belgrade (1688). Cf. Max Grunwald, *Samuel Oppenheimer und sein Kreis. Ein kapitel aus der Finanzgeschichte Österreichs* (Vienna and Leipzig, 1913); Ferenc Szakály, "Oppenheimer Samuel müködése különös tekintettel magyarországi kihatásaira," *Monumenta Hungariae Judaica* 14 (1971), 31–78; David Kaufmann, *Samson Wertheimer, der Oberfactor und Landesrabbiner (1658–1728) und seine Kinder* (Vienna, 1888).
[95] Darling, *Revenue-Raising*, p. 124.   [96] MD 31, p. 300, no. 665.

and thereby undertaking a certain business risk. Occasionally the state would settle its debts in kind: in the form of gunpowder produced or with saltpeter and other raw materials left over from the production, calculating the value of such materials in a way that was profitable for the state. Equally significant was the fact that in using the money of the *mültezim*-entrepreneurs the state received an interest-free loan, which it could use to finance its military industrial works.

The question of state control and security mechanisms

Naturally, the state attempted to include security mechanisms in the system. One of the guarantees was the entrepreneur himself. Most of these men were high-ranking members of the ruling *askeri* class: treasury chiefs, judges, members of the *timariot* provincial cavalry, or local garrison soldiers. All of them received their salaries from the state. In theory, therefore, the control of the state was assured. Where there was incompetence or negligence, the state could recall the men from their posts, thereby depriving them of their salaries or prebends. Similarly, the state could, in theory, cover any damages caused from these sources.

Another guarantee was surety. The military entrepreneurs operating saltpeter works within the *iltizam* system were required to find guarantors (*kefil*), persons who agreed to stand as sureties. Regarding the case of Hacı Çavuş and Ahmed Çavuş, the task of the *beylerbeyi* of Van was to determine not just whether Ahmed Çavuş was really capable of producing the promised amount (2,000 *kantar*) of peter but also the identities of Ahmed's guarantors. If Ahmed proved unable to fulfill his offer or if he ran off with the state's money, then the guarantors would have to redress the state for any losses arising.

When it came to revenue collecting, a further security was the use of inspectors. At first *nazır*s were chosen from among the local *kadı*s, but from the mid-sixteenth century on, we find that the *nazır* was frequently the nominee of the tax-farmer: often a *çavuş* (messenger) or possibly a member of the provincial cavalry or the standing army. Nevertheless, the state continued to maintain its control with the assistance of the *müfettiş*es, who served as financial inspectors for whole provinces or regions and were, almost everywhere, *kadı*s.[97] The system worked in a similar manner in the field of saltpeter and gunpowder production. Here too, we encounter the *nazır*s, most of whom were *çavuş*es. Similarly, the *müfettiş*es were inspectors for whole provinces, and in most known cases the *kadı*s performed this function.

Nevertheless, since many of the *müfettiş*es were also associate entrepreneurs in the saltpeter works of a region, it is doubtful as to whose interests these inspectors really served. We do not know how well founded the accusations against Yakub Efendi really were. At any rate, the sources indicate that the negligence and excesses of Yakub Efendi did not deter the *müfettiş* from becoming Yakub's partner in the enterprise for several years.

---

[97] Darling, *Revenue-Raising*, p. 131.

Misuse of authority, embezzlement and fraud

The Porte had every reason to be cautious. Some entrepreneurs failed to supply the promised amount of peter, but took the money allocated to them to cover their operational costs. There were also cases of embezzlement and theft.[98] Sometimes entrepreneurs took off with the money transferred to them for purchasing saltpeter. In 1695 Ibrahim from Urfa, Kara Ibrahimzade and Mahmud from Kayseri undertook to procure for the gunpowder mill in Istanbul the 98 metric tons (80,000 *okka*) of peter that were due in that year from the province of Karaman. Our source leaves no shadow of doubt that the three men undertook the task as a business partnership (*ber vech-i iştirak*). The Chief Accounting Bureau (Baş Muhasebesi) transferred to them the sum of 5,100,000 *akça*s to cover the purchase of peter. Nevertheless, the Porte soon became aware that Ibrahim, who had previously been the intendant of the Imperial Icehouse (*buz emini*), had caused nothing but losses to the treasury in all of his previous posts. It seemed certain, the report stated, that his present undertaking would lead only to the squandering of state resources. On receiving this information, the Porte immediately ordered the removal of the contract from Ibrahim and his associates and the confiscation of all monies transferred to them. The local authorities were instructed to detain Ibrahim and his business partners and to dispatch them under arrest to the capital, where they would be called to account.[99]

At first sight the case appears to be a rather simple one: Ibrahim was unfit for the assignment, because he had already won a whole variety of state commissions but had always failed to accomplish his tasks, and the state had regularly lost out as a result. But the matter becomes more suspicious when we observe the presence in the background of an earlier contractor, who also wished to acquire the business in question. Our source merely notes that this second man was commendable, and most suitable for the task of purchasing saltpeter. However, it seems likely that this former *mübaşir* sought to regain his lost business with the assistance of the local authorities. Below, we shall see that production of peter in Karaman frequently took place beyond the control of the state and the local authorities and very often illegally. Those involved in saltpeter production attempted to evade the state buyers, who purchased at the official price. Thus they concealed their stocks, selling them to merchants at the market price. All of this would seem to suggest that Ibrahim's failure should be linked not just to his own negligence but also to the general situation of saltpeter production in Karaman at the end of the seventeenth century.

We are left in less doubt by the report about Mustafa, the saltpeter *emin*, and his abuses of power. In March 1571, the inhabitants of the judicial districts of Bolvadin, Seferihisar, Şuhud, Eskişehir, Seyidgazi and Barçınlu (all in the province

[98] MD 24, p. 125, no. 347, regarding the *emin* of the saltpeter works in Aksaray who, in 1574, stole five *batman*s of saltpeter, probably then selling it to merchants.
[99] MAD 10142, p. 241.

of Andolu) went to Istanbul to complain about Mustafa, who had been running a saltpeter plant that he himself had founded four years earlier. The people of these districts objected to the fact that four or five times a year Mustafa ordered them to work in the saltpeter plants, and also demanded firewood, carts, sacks and camels, without ever paying for them. He had been taking advantage of the peasants like this for four years and had even collected money from them for firewood and day laborers. Nevertheless, the government was probably more troubled by the claim that Mustafa was spending neither the money collected from the peasants nor the state revenues transferred to him on saltpeter production, but was squandering the money (*ekl ü bel*, literally "eating and swallowing"). He had production halted, and for a long period each year the saltpeter works lay idle.[100] Mustafa was obviously seeking to use saltpeter production to get rich, and to climb up the social ladder. His father had once been the commander (*dizdar*) of the distant Malazgirt fortress, while Mustafa himself had already been the saltpeter agent responsible for several *sancak*s, perhaps even the whole province.[101]

The workforce: day laborers, auxiliaries, garrison soldiers and retired *sipahi*s

Some of the saltpeter workers were tax-paying subjects (*reaya*) of nearby villages, whom the authorities ordered from time to time to labor in the saltpeter works. In the seventeenth century, however, service could often be avoided through payment.[102] In addition to the day laborers, military auxiliaries (*yaya* and *müsellem*) also were used in the saltpeter plants. In the spring of 1566, while preparations were underway for Süleyman's Hungarian campaign, the *müsellem*s of Aydın were ordered to work in the mines of Bilecik, whereas the *yaya*s had to take part in bridge construction. It seems, however, that saltpeter and gunpowder production were priorities, and fifty of the *müsellem*s on duty and one hundred of the *yaya*s of Aydın were ordered with the usual six months' provisions to the saltpeter works in Güzelhisar.[103]

Garrison soldiers were also employed in saltpeter production and in other military industrial activities. We find them in the saltpeter works of the provinces of Karaman, Kütahya and Erzurum, and they were also present elsewhere. In 1574 fortress soldiers were working in each of the thirteen saltpeter plants of the province of Karaman. About seven or eight soldiers were working in each of the plants, but

---

[100] Unfortunately the source does not tell us whether Mustafa was running the saltpeter works as a state employee or a contractor, that is, whether, in this case, the term *emin* should be understood as the agent of an enterprise.

[101] MD 12, p. 283, no. 580. The districts mentioned in the decree belonged to the *sancak*s of Sultanönü (Eskişehir, Seyidgazi) and Karahisar-i Sahib/Afyonkarahisar (Bolvadin, Şuhud, Barçınlu), both in the province of Anadolu. Cf. Feridun Emecen, "Afyonkarahisar," *TDVİA* vol. 1, p. 444, and Yusuf Oğuzoğlu and Feridun Emecen, "Eskişehir," *TDVİA* vol. XI, p. 400.

[102] MAD 9829, p. 31, regarding the Karaman works in 1633.

[103] MD 5, p. 477, no. 1287. In June 1571 one hundred of the *müsellem*s of Çirmen were ordered to serve in the saltpeter works in the *kaza* of Çirmen. MD 10, p. 1.

in the two largest workshops (Kayseri and Kilisehisar) there were ten soldiers. Their task was to transport saltpeter earth and firewood, to guard the saltpeter stocks,[104] and to provide a military escort for the deliveries, which they neglected occasionally.[105]

Another group also used in saltpeter production comprised retired *sipahi*s and the sons of *sipahi*s (*mütekaid sipahi*s and *sipahi-zade*s). In the province of Karaman, a register of such men was compiled in 1574. They were then drafted to work in saltpeter production within a system that was similar to that of the *müsellem*s and other auxiliary military corps.[106] Not all of the *sipahi-zade*s were willing to fulfill their obligations. The *sipahi-zade*s of the *sancak* of İçil took advantage of the reorganization of the provincial administration that came with the occupation of Cyprus to wriggle out of their duties. Before the occupation of Cyprus the *sancak* had formed part of the province of Karaman, and resident *sipahi-zade*s had worked in the local saltpeter works. When the *sancak* was attached to the newly created province of Cyprus the *sipahi-zade*s refused to work in the plants. However, the Porte ordered them to continue their service.[107]

*Mütekaid sipahi*s and *sipahi-zade*s also sought exemptions from the work by paying compensation money (*bedel-i güherçile*) or by hiring substitutes (also called *bedel*) to take their place in the saltpeter works. This was a well-established practice among the *yaya* and *müsellem* auxiliaries, but the government tended to reject service-redemptions (through the provision of substitutes or payments) if Istanbul needed the men or if they had no evident reason for their exemption. When in 1576 several of the *mütekaid sipahi*s and *sipahi-zade*s failed to report for work in the Karaman plants, sending instead substitutes whom they had hired for 7 *akça*s a month, the Porte rigorously instructed the saltpeter inspector of the province to end the practice and to compel the *mütekaid sipahi*s and *sipahi-zade*s to take up their places in the saltpeter works.[108]

One of the reasons for using the *müsellem*s and the *mütekaid sipahi*s was to save on costs. When, in 1566, saltpeter production was being considered in the

[104] MD 24, p. 101, no. 275.
[105] Refik, *Türkiye Madenleri*, p. 12, no. 19, regarding soldiers who escorted a saltpeter shipment from Karaman in 1572, several of whom left the transport causing some loss of peter.
[106] One in every ten *mütekaid sipahi*s or *sipahi-zade*s was required to be on duty (*eşkünci*). These men were then obliged to serve in the local saltpeter works on a rotational basis (*nöbet ile*) (MD 24, p. 24, no. 70). In some places, for instance in the *kaza* of Kayseri, it appears that the on-duty *mütekaid sipahi*s and *sipahi-zade*s were obliged to work in the saltpeter works only every second year (MD 24, p. 18, no. 51). It seems that (at least in Karaman) young men under eighteen were exempt from service (MD 24, p. 24, no. 70).
[107] Refik, *Türkiye Madenleri*, p. 12, no. 20. If the *sipahi-zade*s so preferred, the Porte was willing to allow them to work in the saltpeter works of Cyprus rather than in those of Karaman. Istanbul showed flexibility, but it was not prepared to let the *sipahi-zade*s evade their obligations.
[108] MD 27, p. 364, no. 870. The sources also show, however, that the officials attempted occasionally to employ them when they had no right to do so. In March 1574, the *sipahi*s living on crown lands near Kayseri complained that they were being ordered to work in the saltpeter plants each year, while the *mütekaid sipahi*s and *sipahi-zade*s were required to perform similar services only once every second year. The Porte decreed that the men in question should be obliged to work once every second year on a rotational basis. MD 24, p. 18, no. 51.

province of Dulkadır, test production demonstrated that if saltpeter was prepared using wage laborers, then the cost of 1 *kantar* was 135 *akça*s. If the *müsellem*s and *mütekaid sipahi*s did the work, then the cost was just 90 *akça*s. Naturally, the Porte chose the second alternative.[109] The use of the *müsellem*s and *mütekaid sipahi*s in saltpeter production, however, was beneficial not just to the Porte but also to the men concerned, who received numerous advantages and privileges.

Saltpeter production and exemptions

Why was it worthwhile for the peasants and, in particular, the soldiers to labor in the saltpeter works? The peasants often had little choice in the matter, for the authorities simply ordered them to go to the saltpeter works where they performed forced labor – just as they did when strengthening fortifications or building roads and bridges. However, just as in the case of these construction projects and major public works, most of the men working in saltpeter production were day laborers. In some regions saltpeter production was the only possible form of work apart from work in agriculture, and it provided a living for many people, although provincial saltpeter plants employed fewer people than the mines or the Istanbul military-industrial complexes. Nevertheless, for the 150–160 day laborers (*irgad*) who, over a period of four to five months per year, excavated and transported saltpeter for 15–16 *akça*s per day in the works of the province of Karaman, or for the 50–60 day laborers who worked in the larger plants, saltpeter production was an important source of income.[110]

But the real advantage of participating in saltpeter production was tax exemptions. As we shall see later, in the Balkans hundreds of saltpeter manufacturing villages were exempted from payment of the *avarız* taxes. Participation in the production of peter was also beneficial for *mütekaid sipahi*s and *sipahi-zade*s. Those working in the saltpeter plants were exempted from payment of the peasant family taxes (*resm-i çift*, *bennak* and *caba*) as well as the sheep tax, beehive tax and *avarız* tax.[111]

These exemptions, however, were not always respected. In April 1573, eleven retired *sipahi*-sons (*mütekaid sipahi-zade*s) from the Akdağ and Zamantu judicial districts went to Istanbul to complain about the abuses of the local *timariot*s who

---

[109] MD 5, p. 469, no. 1259. The decree gives the amount of peter in both *batman* and *kantar* which indicates that in the mid-sixteenth century in the province of Dulkadır 1 *batman* was about 7.2–7.5 kg, and that we cannot calculate with the standard *batman* of 23 kg. See Notes on weights and measures.

[110] MAD 3774, p. 201.

[111] MD 24, p. 24, no. 70. According to standard practice, families who possessed a full *çift* or *çiftlik*, that is a peasant farm workable by a pair (*çift*) of oxen, had to pay the *çift* tax. Those who owned less than half a *çift* were called *bennak* and paid the *bennak* tax, whereas those who were even poorer or landless (*caba*) had to pay the *caba* tax. İnalcık and Quataert, *An Economic and Social History*, p. 149. The only tax levied on those who worked in the saltpeter plants was the tithe due to the local *sipahi* or "landlord" (*sahib-i arz*), regarding which they were given certificates (*berat*) by the governor. MD 24, p. 24, no. 70.

demanded that the former – despite their service in the saltpeter plants of Zamantu – pay the regular taxes imposed on the ordinary tax-paying subjects of the Empire (*rüsum-i raiyyet*). The Porte launched an inquiry into the matter, and the *kadı*s of the two judicial districts involved in the matter were ordered to compile detailed registers with information about the *sipahi-zade*s working in the saltpeter work-shops. The registers would then serve as the basis for any disputes arising in the future.[112] A similar register was compiled in the following year covering the whole of the province of Karaman. All of this was, of course, in line with government interests. Unauthorized taxation of the *sipahi-zade*s and other workers employed in the saltpeter works led to their going into hiding, which had a negative effect on output.

Those who participated in saltpeter manufacturing could also obtain exemp-tion from military campaigns. When in the spring of 1574 the Porte ordered the *müsellem*s of Karaman province to join the Tunis campaign, the *kadı*s of Karahisar and Develü in the province informed the government that implementation of the command would cause considerable stoppages and damage in saltpeter produc-tion, for the *müsellem*s in question were working in saltpeter works. Should only half of the men leave for the campaign, the remaining *müsellem*s could not ensure continuity of production, because those who would remain were the weak and the old, or young boys incapable of producing saltpeter. To drive their message home, the *kadı*s went on to argue that the *nazır* of the *mukataa* was also using the *müsellem*s in the management of local tax-farms, and thus their departure for the campaign would negatively affect the collection of revenues, too. The *kadı*s' letter convinced the government in Istanbul, and the *müsellem*s concerned were exempted from participation in the campaign.[113]

The decree demonstrates, on the one hand, that saltpeter production was suffi-ciently important for the government to grant exemptions from the campaigns. On the other hand, it is apparent that those involved in saltpeter production attempted to take advantage of their situation and to avoid mobilization with reference to this work. Without doubt, they also benefited. Saltpeter production enabled them to continue their usual lives and tend to the family farms. Although the decree cited above contains no such reference, it would come as no surprise to find out that in return for their exemption from the campaign the *müsellem*s, as well as other social groups performing similar military auxiliary tasks in the hinterland, were on occasion willing to offer bribes to the *kadı*s supporting their requests. Given the long and problematic history of service and campaign exemptions, our suspicion is not without foundation.

The *kadı*s of Develü and Karahisar requested and received campaign exemp-tions not only for the *müsellem*s mentioned above but also for the fortress troops of their respective castles. The example of the soldiers of the two fortresses was followed by other fortress troops in the province. Soldiers working in the two largest of the thirteen saltpeter plants of the province (Kayseri and Kilisehisar)

[112] Refik, *Türkiye Madenleri*, pp. 15–16, no. 26.   [113] MD 24, p. 54, no. 154.

requested exemptions from the campaign. As in the case of the *müsellem*s, here too the local authorities argued that if the soldiers in question went to the campaign then only the weak, the old and the young, who were unfit for the manufacturing of peter, would remain. In this instance, the Porte was more circumspect, granting exemptions to the men working at the two production plants only. The requests of the other troops were turned down and they were to take part in the campaign.[114]

Service (*ocaklık*) villages

Like many of its early modern rivals, the Ottoman government suffered from a lack of ready funds. For this reason, it attempted to organize the payment of soldiers' salaries, the production of weaponry and ammunition, and the construction and upkeep of its navy and fortresses in such a way that the financing of these tasks should require the smallest possible amounts of cash. This aim was well served by the Ottoman land-tenure system, with whose assistance the Empire was able to arm one of early modern Europe's largest cavalries. In the field of military-industrial production and shipbuilding, one such solution to the shortage of cash was the system of "service villages" – a system not unknown in medieval and early modern Europe – as well as the Ottoman method of financing called the *ocaklık*. The Ottoman government expected the inhabitants of villages lying close to the saltpeter fields, forests, gunpowder mills, mines, fortresses, bridges, mountain passes, etc., to produce saltpeter, chop wood, burn charcoal and prepare gunpowder, or work in the mines and on castle fortifications, or on the maintenance or protection of bridges and mountain passes. In return, as we have seen, the inhabitants of such villages were exempted from payment of the irregular wartime taxes (*avarız-i divaniyye*).

In Ottoman fiscal practice the *avarız-i divaniyye* was the generic term for extraordinary levies in cash, in kind and in service, whose main objectives were to assist the campaigns of the imperial army and navy, to pay the Empire's garrison troops, and to finance other war and state-related institutions and services.[115] Thus, *avarız* taxes were distinct from the regularly levied *şeri* and *örfi* taxes (*rüsum-i şeriyye* and *rüsum-i örfiyye*), which had been based on religious and customary law, respectively.[116] The nature and the amount of such regular taxes, as well as the methods by which they had to be assessed and collected, were described in

---

[114] MD 24, p. 101, no. 275.

[115] The first part of the term *avarız-i divaniyye* emphasized that these taxes were "the opposite of regular or basic (taxes)," while the second part of the term referred to the fact that such extraordinary wartime taxes could only be levied by the order of the Imperial Council (Divan). *Avarız* taxes were also referred to by our sources with the terms of *tekalif-i divaniyye* and *tekalif-i örfiyye*. Avdo Sučeska, "Die Entwicklung der Besteuerung durch die Avarız-i divaniye und die Tekalif- örfiye im Osmanischen Reich während des 17. und 18. Jahrhunderts," *Südost-Forschungen* 27 (1968), 89–130.

[116] Ömer Lütfi Barkan, "Avarız," *İA*, vol. II, pp. 13–19; Halil Sahillioğlu, "Avarız," *TDVİA*, vol. IV, pp. 108–09.

detail in the Ottoman law codes or *kanunname*s. Irregular taxes, however, had no such legal bases and were levied by imperial orders reflecting the Sultan's right and capability, not dissimilarly to his European counterparts, to mobilize the resources of the state in an emergency.

When the Ottoman state faced unexpected challenges, mostly during wartime, and its regular revenue sources were insufficient to provide for the army's increased needs of food, fodder and war material, the state had no choice but to mobilize its resources by using extraordinary methods and to levy irregular taxes that could be in-kind or cash taxes, as well as campaign-related services. In such cases the Empire's needs were assessed Empire-wide by the Imperial Council, then, using the cadastral surveys and other documents available to the decision-makers in the capital, the quotas were distributed throughout the Empire. The Empire was divided into tax-units called *avarızhane*s, especially instituted for the collection of extraordinary taxes. Unlike the regular household units (*hane*) that were used for the collection of the regular taxes and which referred to what might be called "family households" consisting usually of the parents and children,[117] the *avarızhane*s or "tax-houses" were the merger of a number of family household units whose actual number varied from region to region and from time to time, depending, among other things, on the wealth of the households. In principle, the tax-paying subjects of the Empire were to contribute according to their capabilities and were thus classified by the authorities as "wealthy" or "best quality" (*ala*); "of average wealth" (*evsat*); and "poor" or "the least wealthy" (*edna*). Since all the *avarızhane* units were levied the same amount of tax, where the families were poorer the number of real *hane*s that made up the *avarızhane* was greater. Whereas in the sixteenth century (at least in certain parts of the Empire) one *avarızhane* consisted of only one regular family household, in the seventeenth century it could encompass as many as fifteen regular *hane*s.[118]

The obligatory saltpeter production of the service or *ocaklık* villages was also levied according to the *avarızhane* units. In Macedonia (where the first data concerning saltpeter production stem from the mid-fifteenth century) in 1664, in the judicial districts of Monastir and Veles 520 *avarızhane*s manufactured saltpeter, each tax-house being responsible for providing about 37 kg (30 *okka*) of peter per year. From 1669 *avarızhane*s in the *kaza*s of Siroz, Zihna, Melnik, Temürhisari, Cumapazari and Nevrekop were also producing 24.5 kg (20 *okka*) of saltpeter per *avarızhane*. It seems, however, that these service villages were unable to satisfy

[117] Nejat Göyünç, "Hane Deyimi Hakkında," *TD* 32 (1979), 331–48, and "Hane," *TDVİA*, vol. XV, pp. 552–53.
[118] Barkan, "Avarız," p. 15; Feridun Emecen, *XVI. Asırda Manisa Kazası* (Ankara, 1989), p. 124; Darling, *Revenue-Raising*, p. 87; Suraiya Faroqhi, "Finances," in İnalcık and Quataert eds., *An Economic and Social History*, p. 533, where she translates the *avarızhane* as "tax house." On the size of the *avarızhane*s in the sixteenth century see Emecen, *XVI. Asırda Manisa Kazası*, p. 124, n. 43. Some examples with regard to seventeenth-century *hane/avarızhane* ratios: Kayacık kazası in 1646, 3:1 (ibid., p. 161); the *sancak*s of Konya, Niğde, Beyşehir and Aksaray in 1643–44, 10:1; Karahisar-i Sahib (Afyonkarahisar) in 1709, 4:1, 5:1; see Lütfi Güçer, *XVI–XVII Asırlarda Osmanlı İmparatorluğunda Hububat Meselesi ve Hububattan Alınan Vergiler* (Istanbul, 1964), p. 73, n. 68b.

the needs of the Selanik gunpowder works. Thus, villages from the judicial districts of Üsküp, Ştip, Cumaya, Petriç, Doyran, Yeniçe-i Vardar, Karasu, Prilep, Koçani, Kumanovo, Dırama, Avrathisar, Kiçevo, Vodena, Selanik, Ağustos and Karaferye had to join them, and participate in the manufacturing of peter, producing 20–30 *okka* of saltpeter per *avarızhane*, in lieu of the *avarız* tax. The annual amount of saltpeter thus produced was between 111 and 166 metric tons (90,000–135,000 *okka*).[119] This equaled (and in some years even exceeded by one-third) the production output of the Karaman saltpeter works. The number of these *ocaklık* villages[120] changed several times according to the fluctuating gunpowder needs of the army, as well as according to the capabilities of the subjects. In 1688–89, during the war against the troops of the Holy League, in the *sancak* of Köstendil 790 households were required to produce 24.5 kg (20 *okka*) of saltpeter per *avarızhane* for the gunpowder works in Selanik.[121] Ten years later, however, the sources no longer mention the saltpeter villages of the *sancak* of Köstendil. By that time saltpeter for the Selanik gunpowder mill was being produced in villages in the *sancak*s of Selanik and Paşa (Edirne) which manufactured 53,335 kg of peter.[122]

The manner in which the system worked can be reconstructed as follows. A commissioner (*mübaşir*) would arrive in the central *kaza* of a *sancak* with the imperial command (*ferman*) that stipulated the amount of peter to be manufactured. The *ferman* would be recorded by the district *kadı* in the court protocol (*sicil*) and the court would summon to its building the leaders of the *sancak* and representatives of the towns and villages. Their task was to divide up the amount specified in the *ferman* among the tax-paying units in accordance with the capacities of the villages, usually based on the number of *avarızhane*s. Once divided among the various villages and *avarızhane*s, the amounts were then recorded in a so-called *tevzi defter*, or distribution register. A copy of this register was then placed in the local *kadı*'s records, while the original copy remained with the saltpeter commissioner. The collection of saltpeter was then made on the basis of this register and the entire business was coordinated by the saltpeter commissioner. The saltpeter collected from the district of the territory was then supplied to the gunpowder works, in our case to those of Selanik.[123]

---

[119] Zdraveva, "Der Abbau von Schwefel und Salpeter," 108; also see Petrović and Bojanić-Lukać, "Dobivanja šalitre u Makedoniji," 31.

[120] The standard expression is: ". . . *baruthanesine ocaklık olan kazalar*"; cf. e.g. MAD 10312, p. 328, order sent to the *kadı*s of Selanik, Ağustos, Avrathisar, Vodena and Yeniçe-i Vardar.

[121] DMKF 27640, p. 2; 15,800 *okka*, i.e. more than 20 metric tons, of refined saltpeter from this source found its way to the *baruthane* of Selanik.

[122] MAD 10305, p. 194. In the *sancak* of Selanik there were 1,164.5 saltpeter-producing *avarız* households who lived in the *kaza*s of Selanik, Yeniçe-i Vardar, Vodena, Avrathisar and Ağustos, and produced 20,737 *okka* of saltpeter, while the 1,133 *avarızhane*s in the *kaza*s of Siroz, Zihna, Florina, Nevrekop, Monastir, Dırama and Temürhisari, all situated in the *sancak* of the Paşa, produced 22,667 *okka* of saltpeter. With minor changes, the same districts were supplying saltpeter to Selanik in the 1720s, when the *baruthane* received from this source between 34,225 and 43,200 kg (26,680–33,680 *okka*) of saltpeter depending on how many settlements were manufacturing the saltpeter (MAD 10312).

[123] Petrović and Bojanić-Lukać, "Dobivanja šalitre u Makedoniji," pp. 30–31.

The above system resembled that of the French prior to 1665. In the sixteenth century the domestic requirements of peter in France were determined by royal officials, and the quotas were assigned to the provinces. These quotas in turn were parceled out to the towns, each being responsible for manufacturing a specified quantity of peter. The system of collecting saltpeter closely resembled that of the collection of the *taille*, the most important direct tax, and of the salt tax (*gabelle*). As in the Ottoman Empire, saltpeter makers in France also were given a number of privileges, the most important of which was the exemption from paying the *taille*.[124]

The monetary redemption of saltpeter production

By the beginning of the eighteenth century, an increasing number of saltpeter-producing villages were redeeming their obligation to supply saltpeter in money. In 1720–21, each of the saltpeter villages of the *sancak* of Selanik had redeemed its obligation to supply saltpeter. Instead of producing saltpeter they were paying 375 or 475 *akças* per *avarızhane*. Owing to monetary redemption, the gunpowder workshop received somewhat less saltpeter: from the tax of 741.5 *avarızhanes* 16.5 metric tons of saltpeter could be bought.[125] If – as under the old system – the villages had given in kind 20 *okka* of saltpeter per *avarızhane*, then the gunpowder mill in Selanik would have received from the same source 19 metric tons of saltpeter.

In the late seventeenth century, there was also an evident reduction in the number of *avarızhanes* required to supply peter. The number had dropped from 1,164.5 to 741.5 in the above case, which meant a loss of almost 37 percent of the *avarızhanes*.[126] The only way the government could avert the reduction of the supply of saltpeter was to raise the amount paid by each *avarızhane* in lieu of salt-peter to such an extent that it was able to purchase the quantity of saltpeter that had previously been supplied, or find supplementary funds that could be used for the purchase of saltpeter. It is evident from the sources that the Porte tried to find the most effective solution, and the monetary redemption of the supply of saltpeter was not applied everywhere.[127] To be sure, the outcome of these experiments depended

[124] Nef, *Industry*, p. 60. On taxes, see James B. Collins, *The State in Early Modern France* (Cambridge, 1999), pp. 16–21.
[125] MAD 10312, p. 202.   [126] Ibid.
[127] MAD 10312, p. 410. In April 1714, Ahmed III abolished the requirement upon the villages of the *kaza* of Monastir to supply saltpeter in kind or to pay redemption. Instead, he ordered that the villages should pay the *avarız* tax. Within three years the resultant sum doubled. Nevertheless, the Porte appears not to have been satisfied with the new system because a decree of February 1721 restored the old system, and the villages of the *kazas* of Monastir, Nevrekop, Dırama, Temürhisari and Zihne had to supply the saltpeter to Selanik in kind once again (in total 13,666 *okka*). However, some saltpeter producers attempted to redeem their obligation to supply saltpeter through payment. In September 1723, the *kaza* of Siroz received permission to pay 1,750 *guruş* to the *nazır* of the Selanik gunpowder mill in lieu of 7,000 *okka* of saltpeter. A further order issued at the end of November, however, withdrew the previous permission and once again obliged the inhabitants of the *kaza* to supply the saltpeter in kind.

on many factors, among which the changing power relations between the authorities (both central and local) and the representatives of the saltpeter manufacturing villages deserve further study.

The advantages and disadvantages of *ocaklık* villages

By making the production of determined amounts of saltpeter the task of specific regions, the Porte was able to guarantee a steady supply of this most important ingredient of powder. Thus, in theory, the financial problems of the treasury could not disrupt the supply of peter and powder. This is an important point, given that in many European countries, where governments often had to purchase saltpeter for cash, a shortage of funds rapidly led to prolonged stoppages in the production of saltpeter and gunpowder, as was the case in Spain in the late 1570s and early 1580s when saltpeter and gunpowder production had been at a standstill for months and years.[128]

But the *ocaklık* system had its own limits, too. A decline in local revenue sources set aside for the saltpeter works negatively affected production as did decrease in the population of the saltpeter villages. Furthermore, although the *ocaklık* system assured continuous production of a fixed amount of saltpeter, in general the system proved inflexible and incapable of adapting to unexpected change. Thus when military conflicts dragged on for years or even decades (as in the late sixteenth and late seventeenth centuries), or when the Ottoman Empire was compelled to fight on several fronts, or when the fleet and the land forces were waging war simultaneously, the gunpowder mills had to produce far greater quantities of gunpowder in order to meet a sudden rise in demand. However, the saltpeter works operating within the *ocaklık* system were incapable of satisfying this increased demand. To make up for this shortfall, the Ottoman government had no choice but to purchase saltpeter.

The purchase of saltpeter at a specified price: a form of extraordinary taxation

The two terms the sources used for purchases of saltpeter are *iştira* and *mübayaa*, words whose exact meanings have been the subject of scholarly debate. Lütfi Güçer found that *iştira* meant purchase of specified volumes at a fixed price, and thus considered it a kind of extraordinary tax. Working mainly on Balkan sources, Avdo

---

[128] In 1577, the saltpeter workshops in Tembleque, Priorato de San Juan, Murcia, Lorca and Almería, as well as the gunpowder mills of Cartagena, were forced to abandon production owing to a lack of funds. By mid-1579 production had been at a standstill for more than fourteen months at the saltpeter works in Catalonia and for more than a year at the workshops in Murcia and Lorca. In May of the following year, the workshops in Priorato de San Juan also ceased production. By September saltpeter and gunpowder production had been at a standstill for at least six months throughout Spain. See I. A. A. Thompson, *War and Government in Habsburg Spain, 1560–1620* (London, 1976), pp. 246–47.

Table 4.1 *Purchases* (iştira *and* mübayaa) *of saltpeter at fixed price*

Term	Date	Fixed price akça per okka	Market price akça per okka	Amount	Amount in kg	Purchasing baruthane
İştira	1664	25	50	500 *kantar*	27,000	Buda, Eger and Kanije
İştira	1679	30	60	46,968 *okka*	57,714	Temeşvar
İştira	1681	30	60	60,000 *okka*	73,728	Temeşvar
Mübayaa	1690s	40	60	20,000 *okka*	24,576	Gelibolu

Sources: 1664: MAD 3279, p. 141; 1679: KK Mevkufat 2682, fols. 22a–23b; 1681: ibid., fol. 53b; 1690s: MAD 3127, pp. 13, 45, 54; MAD 10305, pp. 120–21.

Sučeska also concluded that the *iştira* was a type of *avarız* tax, since provisions were purchased at fixed price. Unlike Güçer, however, Sučeska argued that the amounts were not specified. Gilles Veinstein concluded that in the case of the *iştira* it was quantity that was fixed, with purchases taking place at the local market price. Caroline Finkel, who has provided us with the most detailed study of provisioning of the Ottoman army during the Habsburg–Ottoman war of 1593–1606, and has also reviewed the above cited works, found that *iştira* meant purchase at the local ruling price (*narh-i ruzi*). Consequently, she argued that "this takes *iştira* out of the ambit of irregular taxation."[129] Data related to saltpeter production also use the term *iştira* frequently, but, unlike sources concerning provisioning in the 1593–1606 war, they generally refer to purchases made at fixed prices, always well below the market price. In a great majority of cases, however, the sources use the term *mübayaa* for purchases, referring to purchases at the official price and also at the market price. This shows that there is little point in searching for general definitions of these terms. Instead we should always try to interpret them according to the given situation.

The growing importance of purchases at the market price

The sources also use the term *mübayaa* for purchases made at the market price. In these cases the authorities bought the peter from merchants (*rencberan, bazirgan*) or from certain individuals (*bazı kesan*). Despite the fact that saltpeter counted as prohibited goods, called *merces prohibitae* in European countries and *memnu eşya* in the Ottoman Empire, sources indicate that neither the Ottomans nor their Christian adversaries could enforce the prohibition. In the 1570s, Hungarian merchants around Gyula and Çanad offered saltpeter to the Ottomans at the market price.[130]

[129] Finkel, *Administration*, p. 140.
[130] MD 14, no. 483. One local *kantar* (48 *okka* or 59 kg) of saltpeter was traded at a price of 600 *akça*s at the local markets of Gyula and Çanad. This apparently followed prices on the other side of the military frontier, where market price in Ottoman Hungary for an *okka* of saltpeter was 12.5 *akça*s.

The market price fluctuated considerably even in the case of saltpeter bought by one *baruthane* in the course of one year, which proves that the gunpowder mills really did have to adjust to the market. For example, the Izmir gunpowder works purchased saltpeter for 45, 60 and 80 *akças* in 1694–95. It is very difficult to find any logical reason for changes in price. At first sight sources appear to suggest that the *baruthane* obtained the saltpeter more cheaply when it bought a larger quantity. However, if we examine a large enough number of sources, we find this attractive assumption does not hold up.

Furthermore, it seems that as time passed the gunpowder mills could purchase saltpeter at lower and lower prices. Thus, while in 1693–94 one *okka* of saltpeter cost 70 *akças*, in subsequent years the purchase price was on average 48 *akças*. Indeed, at the very beginning of the eighteenth century the purchase price was 40 *akças* and in 1720 just 32 *akças*.[131] If we also consider the depreciation in value of the *akça* over this period, it becomes evident that the market price of saltpeter underwent an even greater fall. Of course the above set of data might encourage us to think that the term *mübayaa* changed over the course of time, meaning in the latter period purchase at the official price rather than the market price, which would explain the decrease. The sources, however, contradict this: they clearly state that the peter was bought from merchants and emphasize that the purchases were made at local market prices (*cari olan narh*).[132]

Conclusion

Unlike many of their adversaries, the Ottomans managed to achieve self-sufficiency in saltpeter production. In territories where conditions were suitable, the Istanbul government established large saltpeter works run either by state-appointed and state-paid officials or by members of its ruling elite who operated the plants within the *iltizam* or tax-farming system as entrepreneurs. To cover the operational costs, Istanbul allocated special funds for the purpose, called *ocaklıks*, usually state revenues to be collected in the same area in which the plants were situated. In other areas the task of manufacturing peter was distributed among hundreds of villages which enjoyed tax-exemptions in return for their services. While at first sight the methods examined in the preceding pages might seem unfamiliar to non-Ottomanists, they were not that dissimilar from the means used by other early modern empires and states.

In France, for instance, the king placed saltpeter production under exclusive royal control and appointed the first saltpeter commissioners in the fifteenth

---

[131] See Appendix.

[132] Raw saltpeter was, of course, cheaper than refined saltpeter. For example, in 1696–97 the commissioner (*mübaşir*) of the gunpowder workshop in Selanik, a certain Ömer aga, purchased raw saltpeter at a price of 45 *akças* per *okka*, whereas he paid 58 *akças* per *okka* for the refined variety (MAD 3620, p. 85).

century; he authorized them to collect saltpeter wherever they found it.[133] Francis I created a grand master of artillery in 1515, giving this officer and the provincial royal commissioners who served under him command over the munitions industry. As in the Ottoman Empire, unauthorized manufacture of saltpeter and gunpowder was prohibited, and in France it was punishable by death and by confiscation of the workshops, equipment and tools.[134] We have also noted that the domestic needs of peter in France were determined by royal officials, and that the quotas were, as they were in the Ottoman Empire too, assigned to the provinces.

In King Philip II's Spain, the major rival of the Ottoman Empire in the Mediterranean, state enterprise played a central role in the armaments industry, but the results of the system were unsatisfactory. As did the Istanbul government, the Spanish crown also declared the production of weapons and munitions a royal monopoly and took an active part in the direct management of its own armament industries. The state initiated the establishment of new saltpeter works (like the one in Lérida, 1577), but it obtained most of its saltpeter from saltpeter-men in Granada, Murcia and La Mancha.[135] Since Spain had enough natural saltpeter deposits, a couple of government-owned gunpowder works might have been able to satisfy the national demand, especially in the mid-sixteenth century, when domestic needs of saltpeter seem to have been not particularly high, around 2,000 quintals or 92 metric tons in the mid-1550s through the late 1570s. By the 1570s, however, the old evil of illegal private manufacturing and contraband trade had reached the Spanish saltpeter and gunpowder industry, and only some 7 metric tons (150 quintals) of the 138 metric tons (3,000 quintals) of peter that could have been produced yearly reached the royal storehouses. General prohibitions, like the one issued in 1576, had only modest results, and by the end of the 1580s, when the gunpowder demand had risen to 184 metric tons, Spain had again become dependent on foreign gunpowder, despite the country's abundant saltpeter deposits.[136]

By contrast, the methods the Istanbul government employed were capable of ensuring a regular supply of peter to the major gunpowder works, and the Empire was self-sufficient in saltpeter and gunpowder until the end of the seventeenth century, when the yearly gunpowder need was estimated at 10,000 *kantar* or 540 metric tons.

---

[133] Nef, *Industry*, pp. 59–61; O. F. G. Hogg, *Artillery: Its Origins, Heyday and Decline* (London, 1970), p. 130. However, Marshall, *Explosives*, p. 53, mentions the first commissioner from 1540.

[134] John A. Lynn, *Giant of the Grand Siècle: The French Army, 1610–1715* (Cambridge, 1997), p. 99.

[135] Thompson, *War and Government*, pp. 234–35.

[136] Ibid., pp. 238, 241–42. Venice, the Ottomans' traditional enemy in the eastern Mediterranean, also lacked sufficient saltpeter resources on the mainland and relied on imports from Apulia and Crete or acquired peter from merchants who, depending on demand, charged from 32 to 95 ducats for the *miara* in the sixteenth century. The production of peter on the Terraferma was in the hands of private entrepreneurs or small firms. According to their contracts with the Council of Ten, such saltpeter-producers had the right to enforce labor and to dig in anybody's house or animal sheds. The government provided them with an advance to buy equipment and also paid the transport costs. M. E. Mallett and J. R. Hale, *The Military Organization of a Renaissance State: Venice c. 1400 to 1617* (Cambridge, 1984), pp. 399–400.

However, as already noted, the Ottoman system had its own drawbacks. At the time of protracted wars the quantity of saltpeter purchased at market price grew, and the annual purchases of saltpeter made up an increasing percentage of the total costs of the various *baruthanes*. In 1668–69, during the final stage of the Cretan war, the Ottoman authorities purchased more than 417 metric tons (339,400 *okka* or 7,713.6 *kantar*) of refined saltpeter which represented most of the saltpeter procured in that year.[137]

In 1693–94, during the Long War against the Holy League, 65 percent of the peter delivered to the gunpowder mills in Istanbul had to be purchased; only 208 metric tons (169,127.5 *okka*) of peter or 35 percent of the total came from the *ocaklıks*.[138] Similar conditions prevailed in the gunpowder works of Gelibolu and Selanik, where an increasing share of the saltpeter had to be purchased from merchants. In Gelibolu in the 1690s, for instance, this share amounted to 43 percent of total saltpeter requirements. Since this saltpeter had to be bought on the open market, the cost of purchase was 54 percent of the total operational cost of the gunpowder works.[139] By the 1720s, the proportion of saltpeter purchased at market price had grown further still, and its cost had continued to increase as well. While 75–80 percent of the *baruthane*'s total annual purchases of saltpeter were made at market price, the costs of purchases amounted to 82–86 percent of the total sum spent on acquiring saltpeter. The sums spent on saltpeter comprised 68 percent of the annual operating costs of the *baruthane*.[140] In the gunpowder works of Selanik the percentage of purchased saltpeter was already between 49 and 74 percent in the 1690s. In the 1720s the situation remained similar, and in 1723–24 the *baruthane* bought 72 percent of its saltpeter requirements, whereas only 28 percent was provided by the service or *ocaklık* villages.[141] The change in the proportion of saltpeter purchased vis-à-vis peter obtained via *ocaklıks* is noteworthy and reflects the general trend in the Ottoman economy, that is, the monetarization of the Ottoman war industry. However, it seems that until the mid-eighteenth century the Ottoman powder works got their necessary requirements of peter through the combined means of *ocaklık* and purchase.

Although saltpeter purchases made up a substantial part of the annual costs of the gunpowder mills, we should not overstate their importance. When compared with other military costs, the amounts spent on saltpeter were not too great and financing them could hardly have been a problem for the treasury. For the 7,713 *kantar* of refined saltpeter bought in 1668–69, which was enough to cover the production of the 10,000 *kantar* or 540 metric tons of powder that the authorities believed were necessary per annum, the treasury paid 10,182,000 *akças*.[142] In relation to the other war-related costs this amount does not seem excessive, for it roughly corresponds to the cost of one month's salaries paid to the 53,849 Janissaries in the

---

[137] KK 2647, p. 21.   [138] MAD 3127, p. 181.   [139] See Appendix.

[140] MAD 10312, pp. 194. See also Appendix.

[141] MAD 3127, p. 180; MAD 3620, pp. 16–19, 26–29, 32–37, 42–46, 52–55, 58–60, 68, 84–89, 92–94; MAD 10305, p. 194; MAD 10312, pp. 202, 121, 326–28, and 408. See also Appendix.

[142] KK 2647, p. 21.

financial year of 1669–70.[143] That is to say, the saltpeter that satisfied the powder requirements of major late seventeenth-century campaigns could be bought for the amount paid out to the Janissaries in just one month.

Regarding the quality of peter manufactured in the Empire there is no indication in the sources that the Ottomans faced more serious difficulties than their contemporaries. Europeans and Ottomans of the early modern era were aware that saltpeter became purer and more refined each time it was boiled. Indeed, one of the most highly regarded experts on artillery, Pietro Sardi, was of the opinion that all the vigor of the powder depended on the quantity and perfection of its main constituent, that is, of the saltpeter.

> If the saltpeter is put in use after the first boiling, the powder would not be so strong and perfect, as need would require, for the quantity of terrestrial material, common salt, and the unctuosity, which reside with the saltpeter, do hinder its virtue and strength. Therefore the producers refine it several times, and purge from it every extraneous matter as much as is possible, so that they may obtain the most strenuous effects of the powder.[144]

We know from Luigi Ferdinando Marsigli, the author of the best treatise on the seventeenth- and early eighteenth-century Ottoman military, that Sardi's book was available for the Ottoman authorities in translation and that they did use it.[145] It is also evident from the account books of the Ottoman saltpeter works that the Ottomans refined saltpeter several times.[146]

Because of its abundant saltpeter deposits and the various means the Ottoman government introduced to produce and obtain peter, the Ottoman Empire was self-sufficient in this essential ingredient of gunpowder, and sources unearthed so far do not indicate that Istanbul was dependent on foreign supply. The availability of peter, however, was only a precondition of self-sufficiency in gunpowder, and it was the task of the Ottoman gunpowder works to satisfy the gunpowder needs of the Empire's land forces, fleets and fortresses.

---

[143] Ömer Lütfi Barkan, "1079–1080 (1669–1670) Malî Yılına ait Bir Osmanlı Bütçesi ve Ekleri," *IFM* 17 (1955–56), 227.

[144] Pietro Sardi, *L'Artiglieria* (Venice, 1621), p. 121. For this seventeenth-century English translation of the relevant section of Sardi's work, see Henry Stubbe, *Legends no Histories: or a Specimen of some Animadversions upon History of the Royal Society* (London, 1670), p. 102.

[145] V. J. Parry, "Barud, IV: The Ottoman Empire," *EI*, vol. I, p. 1064.

[146] In the province of Karaman, for example, in 1673–74 and 1674–75, the process of reboiling resulted in the loss of 33 percent of the raw saltpeter (MAD 4527, p. 13). In Selanik, in the late 1690s the loss during the distillation (*keser-i kali* or *kal keseri*) of the raw saltpeter (*ham güherçile*) was only 20 percent (MAD 3620, pp. 29, 94). Of course, the purity of the saltpeter also depended on its fat content. Our sources seem to indicate that saltpeter from Morea was particularly greasy, and that the Ottomans were unable to refine it properly.

CHAPTER 5

Gunpowder industries

In order to maintain an adequate supply of gunpowder for the army, navy and the fortresses, the Ottoman government established a number of gunpowder works (*baruthane*s) throughout the Empire. In the sixteenth century, important gunpowder mills operated in Istanbul, Cairo, Baghdad, Aleppo, Yemen, Buda, Belgrade and Temeşvar (Temesvár). Less important powder manufacturing centers were located in Erzurum, Diyarbekir, Oltu and Van in Asia Minor, in Estergon (Esztergom) and Peç (Pécs) in Hungary. In addition to these plants, in the seventeenth century the Ottoman authorities set up major gunpowder works in Bor (in the province of Karaman), Selanik (Salonica), Gelibolu (Gallipoli) and Izmir. Selanik and Gelibolu together with the Istanbul gunpowder works remained the main producers of gunpowder in the eighteenth century. Apart from these gunpowder works, smaller powder mills, driven by either animals or manpower, operated in almost all the major fortresses of the Empire.

Gunpowder works in Istanbul

The Ottomans operated several gunpowder works in Istanbul. The city was an ideal location for the manufacture and storage of gunpowder. It was not only the seat of government but also a natural logistical center for military campaigns. It was the location of most of the central troops, the place at which troops from the provinces assembled prior to military campaigns, and the base of the Ottoman navy. Ships sailing from the Istanbul docks could transport gunpowder to the fleet, as it battled against the Venetians and the Spanish Habsburgs along the Dalmatian coast, in the Mediterranean or off the North African coast. Istanbul was also the point of departure for galleys bound for the Black Sea that were loaded with gunpowder – sometimes several hundred tons of it – for use in the Ottoman campaigns against Hungary, Poland, Russia and the Safavid Empire. The rooms beneath the domes of the Theodosian walls offered a secure location for the storage of gunpowder that had been manufactured in Istanbul or delivered to the city from the provinces.

128

The gunpowder works of the city were established at different points in time and are referred to in the sources according to their locations. In addition to the major gunpowder works, there were also several smaller workshops producing finer musket powder for the Janissaries.[1] The first known *baruthane* in the capital was built in the district of Atmeydanı during the reign of Mehmed II. It became known as the *baruthane* of Atmeydanı, which the Ottomans called the Hippodrome. Although this plant was destroyed in a fire in 1489 or 1490,[2] either it had been rebuilt or a new gunpowder factory had been established at the same site and was producing some 8,100 kg (150 *kantar*) of gunpowder per month in the early 1570s.[3] It was soon overshadowed by other powder works, not least because of its unfavorable location: it was rather close to Istanbul's most important public square, the Atmeydanı, where the Ottomans – following the traditions of the Byzantines – held their festivals.[4]

In the sixteenth and seventeenth centuries, the three important powder works in the capital city were the *baruthane*s of Kağıthane, Şehremini and Bakırköy. The *baruthane* of Kağıthane was built in that district of the city in the 1490s, perhaps using the facilities of a former Byzantine powder mill, which gave the name to the site (Kağıthane means paper mill or papermaking workshop). Situated beyond the city walls and several miles to the north of Pera, the original building was made of wood, but Süleyman I (r. 1520–66) had the factory rebuilt of stone and brick. The mills of the *baruthane* were driven by water, supplied by a nearby stream.[5] In 1571, 16,200 kg (300 *kantar*) of gunpowder were manufactured in the *baruthane* monthly,[6] but production levels at the turn of the century were remarkably lower,[7] and powder manufacturing must have ceased soon afterwards.[8] In the seventeenth century, however, the *baruthane* was reactivated. Indeed, when

---

[1] In the seventeenth century, gunpowder was manufactured in the new barracks of the Janissaries (Yeni odalar) and in the musket factory (Tüfenghane) in the district of Unkapanı on the Golden Horn. Whereas in the latter site gunpowder was pounded in just ten mortars, in another Istanbul powder plant, near the market of Macuncular, powder was manufactured in thirty mortars using horse-powered pounders. Another smaller *baruthane* in the capital city was located in the Ayasofya quarter, and was part of the armory (Cebehane), the site of several small-arms manufacturing workshops, which also housed the barracks of the armorers (*cebeci*s). See *Evliya Çelebi Seyehatnâmesi*, vol. I. Ed. Orhan Şaik Gökay (Istanbul, 1995), p. 257.
[2] Muzaffer Erdoğan, "Arşiv Vesikalarına Göre İstanbul Baruthaneleri," *İED* 2 (1956), 120.
[3] The source mentions an unnamed municipal workshop (*şehir karhanesi*). While one might assume that it refers to the Şehremini *baruthane*, all available data concerning the Şehremini gunpowder works stem from the seventeenth century. Another source (MAD 383, p. 79) also seems to refer to this powder works, stating that between September 16, 1594 and March 11, 1595 a rather modest sum of 9.2 metric tons (170 *kantar* and 82 *lodras*) of powder was manufactured here.
[4] It would hardly have been wise to manufacture and store large amounts of gunpowder close to the site of firework displays, mass sporting events and festivals marking ceremonies such as Ibrahim Pasha's wedding (1524) and the circumcisions of the Sultanic princes (1530, 1539 and 1582).
[5] *Evliya Çelebi Seyehatnâmesi*, p. 207; Erdoğan, "İstanbul Baruthaneleri," 120; Semavi Eyice, "Baruthane," *TDVİA*, vol. V, p. 95; MD 14, no. 1551.
[6] MD 16, p. 375, no. 656; Erdoğan, "İstanbul Baruthaneleri," 120.
[7] In the six months between September 16, 1594 and March 11, 1595, somewhat more than 4 metric tons (76 *kantar*) of gunpowder were manufactured in the Kağıthane works. MAD 383, p. 79.
[8] In 1601, the *baruthane* was disused, and Ali Topçıbaşı, the commander of the artillery, suggested that bombshells should be manufactured there. Ali Emiri, III. Murad no. 210.

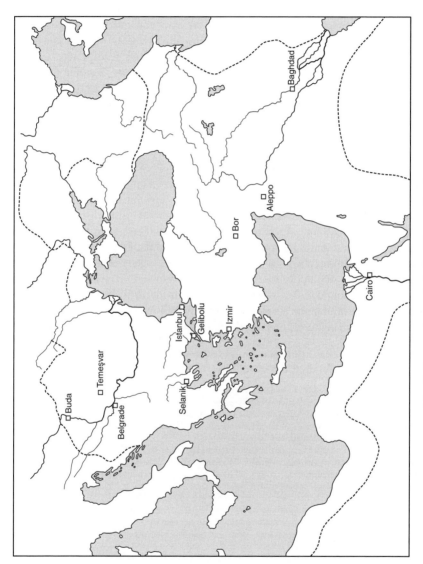

Map 2 Gunpowder works in the Ottoman Empire.

Evliya Çelebi visited it, there were 200 men working in the plants, who pounded the powder in 100 mortars with heavy metal pestles.[9] Despite claims in the literature that the factory was closed down at the end of the reign of Sultan Ibrahim (r. 1640–48),[10] sources indicate that it still produced powder for both muskets and cannons in the 1660s.[11] In the early 1680s, when the Empire was fighting against the Austrian Habsburgs in Hungary, production output levels were especially high. Between 1683 and 1685 almost 339 metric tons (6,275.27 *kantar*) of powder were manufactured at the *baruthane*.[12] When production at the Kağıthane works ceased towards the end of the century, its role was taken by the *baruthane* of Şehremini.

The Şehremini *baruthane* was built either in 1678–79 or a decade later, in 1687, in the district of Şehremini, close to the Topkapı Gate, inside the Theodosian walls that defined the western boundary of the city. It produced powder until September 1698.[13] Production fluctuated in the 1690s and the annual average output was 94 metric tons.[14] When the *baruthane* burnt to the ground in September 1698,[15]

[9] *Evliya Çelebi Seyehatnâmesi*, p. 207, who claims that the pestles weighed 50–61 kg (between 40 and 50 *okka*). Although Evliya Çelebi's data should be treated with caution, his figure concerning the number of mortars appears to be plausible: according to the 1683 inventory of the *baruthane* of Kağıthane there were forty bronze mortars and thirty-two wooden mortars in the gunpowder works (MAD 2936, p. 4).

[10] Erdoğan, "İstanbul Baruthaneleri," 120; Eyice, "Baruthane," p. 95; *Dünden Bugüne İstanbul Ansiklopedisi*, vol. II (Istanbul, 1994), p. 68.

[11] The output was modest compared with that of the Empire's major powder factories: between August 5, 1663 and July 24, 1664 a total of 338 *kantar* of gunpowder were produced in the Kağıthane and Şehremini gunpowder factories. See Gábor Ágoston, "Gunpowder for the Sultan's Army: New Sources on the Supply of Gunpowder to the Ottoman Army in the Hungarian Campaigns of the Sixteenth and Seventeenth Centuries," *Turcica* 25 (1993), 93–94.

[12] DBŞM 449. The accounts cover the period from February 28, 1683 through December 15, 1685, and reveal the operational costs of the *baruthane*. Although the largest item was the amount spent on the purchase of saltpeter, 89 percent of the saltpeter acquired by the *baruthane* stemmed not from purchases but from the *ocaklık*s and from the imperial saltpeter works: 129,786 kg (105,619.5 *okka*) from the *ocaklık* of Selanik, 118,598 kg (96,515.5 *okka*) from the *ocaklık* of Filibe, and a substantial amount (78,457 kg or 63,848.5 *okka*) from Aleppo.

[13] Defterdar Sarı Mehmed Paşa, *Zübde-i Vekayiat*. Ed. Abdülkadir Özcan (Ankara, 1995), p. 647, gives the date as 1687, and it is usually accepted by historians (Erdoğan, "İstanbul Baruthaneleri"; Eyice, "Baruthane," p. 95). The Cairo and the Revan copies of the *Zübde-i Vekayiat* (ibid., 647, footnote) claim that the construction took place ten years earlier in 1678–79. This earlier date also appears in one of the account books of the plant (MAD 2736, pp. 134–35), which repeats almost verbatim the sentence of the Ottoman chroniclers. In addition, MAD 12764 contains detailed data concerning the construction of the *baruthane* from the years 1681 through 1685. Unfortunately, this *defter* was not accessible during my repeated research trips in the 1990s. If the dates given in the catalogue are correct, the *defter* could settle the dispute and would support 1678 as the date of construction. However, gunpowder in small quantities was being manufactured there as early as 1663–64. See MAD 3279, pp. 170 and 175, and Ágoston, "Gunpowder for the Sultan's Army."

[14] For 1689–90: DBŞM 598; 1690–92: DBŞM 642; 1693–94: MAD 3620, pp. 80–81; 1694–95: MAD 10142, pp. 238–39; 1696–97: DBŞM 844; 1697–99: DBŞM 19085; cf. also Appendix. Secondary sources give no data regarding the *baruthane*'s output and assume that it was destroyed by fire right after its construction. See, for instance, Birol Çetin, *Osmanlı İmparatorluğu'nda Barut Sanayi, 1700–1900* (Ankara, 2001), p. 22.

[15] Sarı Mehmed Paşa, *Zübde-i Vekayiat*, p. 648; Mehmed Raşid, *Tarih-i Raşid* (2 vols., Istanbul, 1282/1865–66), vol. II, pp. 441–42; Erdoğan, "İstanbul Baruthaneleri," 121. In addition, DBŞM 19085 gives interesting details regarding the incident. We learn, for instance, that only 17,940 kg

the authorities decided to seek out a more secure location for the construction of a new gunpowder factory, instead of rebuilding it.

The destruction caused by fires at the *baruthane*s of Atmeydanı and Şehremini reminded the Ottoman authorities of the dangers of operating gunpowder factories within the walls of the city. In order to prevent further such calamities, a decision was taken to build the new *baruthane* outside the city walls. Although the old site of the Kağıthane had also been considered, for safety reasons the authorities decided to build the new powder factory at a different place.[16]

It was constructed in the garden of İskender Çelebi, on the shores of the Sea of Marmara between Kazlıçeşme and Bakırköy, after which the *baruthane* was named. The choice of what is today the district of Ataköy seemed to be an ideal one for several reasons: the garden of İskender Çelebi, the famous *defterdar* of Sultan Süleyman the Magnificent, lay beyond the city walls; the waters of a nearby brook provided enough energy to drive the wheels of the mill; and the proximity of the sea facilitated the delivery of the necessary raw materials and firewood, as well as the dispatch of the finished powder; additionally some of the old buildings could be used, too. Construction of the *baruthane* began in 1700,[17] and by 1701 gunpowder was already being manufactured at the new site.

Between 1701 and 1703 the *baruthane* of Bakırköy, also known as the Imperial Gunpowder Factory in Istanbul (Baruthane-i Amire der İstanbul), produced 137,160 kg (106,922 *okka* or 2,430 *kantar*) of powder, slightly less than the *baruthane* of Şehremini at the end of the century.[18] Four years after the *baruthane* was opened, a fire broke out in the gunpowder works, but the damaged equipment was soon repaired. In January 1706 it was expected that the factory would again achieve its former annual output of 56,440 kg (1,000 *kantar*), manufacturing high-quality English-type powder in two installments of 500 *kantar*.[19] Elhac (Hacı) Mehmed Efendi, the superintendent of the Imperial Cannon Foundry, was appointed superintendent of the Bakırköy gunpowder works and was expected to oversee the manufacturing of 141,100 kg (2,500 *kantar*) of powder. This aim, however, was only partially met.[20] Fires damaged the works in 1707 and 1725, and although the buildings were quickly rebuilt,[21] it seems that the baruthane could

---

(14,600 *okka*) of powder were destroyed in the fire, which was only 7.2 percent of the powder produced, for the bulk of the powder had already been delivered to the Cebehane, to the navy and to Kefe (Caffa).

[16] Some of the buildings of the old factory were still intact, and a further advantage of Kağıthane had been the presence of enough water to drive the wheels of the mill. Despite these advantages, the authorities rejected it for safety reasons. Over the years the Kağıthane and its neighborhood had become increasingly popular among the inhabitants of Istanbul and the surrounding villages as a place for excursions. Any fires caused by the day-trippers would have had disastrous consequences.

[17] Sarı Mehmed Paşa, *Zübde-i Vekayiat*, p. 648; Erdoğan, "İstanbul Baruthaneleri," 122.

[18] MAD 7488, pp. 2–14. The account book covers the period between November 3, 1701 and November 9, 1703, under the tenure of Yeğen Mustafa Pasha, *nazır* of the *baruthane*, who a decade earlier (between 1690 and 1692) had been the superintendent of the *baruthane* of Şehremini.

[19] CA 8406.   [20] MAD 2652.

[21] Erdoğan, "İstanbul Baruthaneleri," 122–24; MAD 7829, p. 465; CA 9031.

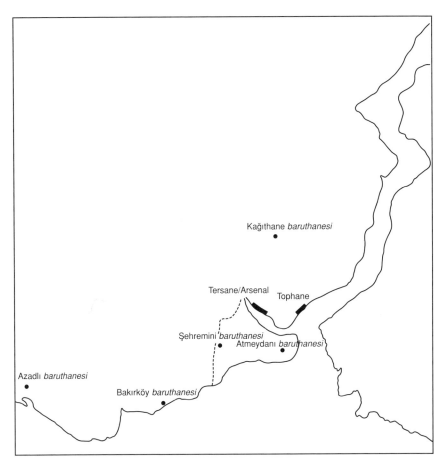

Map 3 War industry plants in Istanbul.

produce only some 66 percent (93,670 kg or 1,659 *kantar*) of the expected 141,100 kg of powder in 1734–35 under the tenureship of Elhac Süleyman Efendi.[22] However, in the second half of the eighteenth century production levels fell significantly. Powder shortages and quality problems were especially felt in the Russo-Ottoman war of 1768–74 and the campaign of 1787–92, prompting major reforms within the Ottoman powder industry. By 1793 the results of the reorganization and modernization of powder production were becoming apparent: in 1793 and 1794 the *baruthane* was producing 84,600 kg (1,500 *kantar*) of gunpowder per year. This level of production still fell short of the annual target of 112,800 kg (2,000 *kantar*), but it was 50 percent higher than production levels at the beginning

---

[22] DBŞM BRG 18250, the *defter* that contains the accounts of the *baruthane* of Istanbul in the year of 1147 (from June 3, 1734 through May 23, 1735), which is mistakenly classified as the account book of the *baruthane* of Gelibolu.

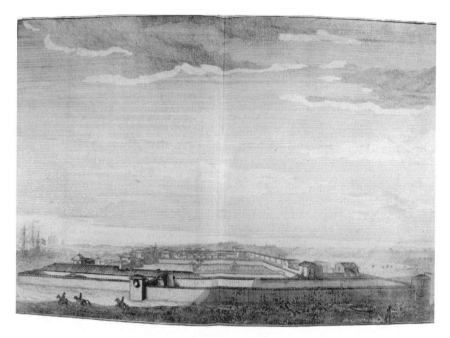

Figure 15 The old Imperial Gunpowder Factory in Bakırköy (Istanbul) was active between 1701 and the late 1790s. Often damaged by fires, its annual output varied between 56 and 94 metric tons of powder. Mahmud Raif Efendi, *Tableau des nouveaux reglemens de l'empire ottoman*, Constantinople, 1798.

of the century. The quality of the gunpowder improved, too: the mixture of ingredients suggests that by this time the powder manufactured here was approaching the quality of English and Dutch gunpowder, which both served as the model.[23] Although similar changes at the Empire's two other major eighteenth-century gunpowder works in Gelibolu and Selanik also resulted in production improvements, the government nevertheless decided to establish a new hydraulic gunpowder factory, the first modern powder factory in the Empire. Production at the new Azadlı gunpowder works in Küçükçekmece proceeded so rapidly that by 1797 the factory at Bakırköy was merely used to store gunpowder.[24]

While it was hazardous to have such a dangerous military-industrial facility in the capital city, Istanbul's strategic location prompted the Ottoman government to replace the destroyed gunpowder factories with newer ones in and around the city. The production output levels of the Istanbul plants were considerable.

Based on the data in Table 5.1, it is not unreasonable to suppose that in critical years during the sixteenth and seventeenth centuries, the Istanbul powder works

---

[23] DBŞM BRİ 18319 and 18321.
[24] Production resumed in the Bakırköy works, and in 1841 the facilities were expanded. See Eyice, "Baruthane," p. 95.

Table 5.1 *Output of the Istanbul gunpowder works*

Gunpowder works	Active	Date of production	Production (*kantar*/year)	Production (kg/year)
Kağıthane	1490?–early 1690s?	1571	1,800–3,600	97,200–194,400
Şehir karhanesi?	1570s	1571	900–1,800	48,600–97,200
Istanbul combined		1571	2,700–5,400	145,800–291,600
Kağıthane	1490?–early 1690s?	1683–85	2,215	119,610
Şehremini	1678?–1698	1689–99	1,666	89,964
Istanbul combined		1680s	3,881	209,574
Bakırköy	1701–late 1790s	1701–03	1,215	68,500
Bakırköy	1701–late 1790s	1734–35	1,660	93,690
Bakırköy	1701–late 1790s	1793–94	1,500	84,600

Notes: Figures in kg are rounded. Figures for 1571 are estimates based on monthly production output levels and calculated by six-month and twelve-month production periods. For sources and detailed figures see Appendix.

were capable of manufacturing some 200 metric tons of powder. Indeed, in the 1680s the combined yearly output of the gunpowder mills at Kağıthane and at Şehremini could have reached 205 metric tons (3,800 *kantar*) per year, and in some years it even approached 270 metric tons (5,000 *kantar*).

Gunpowder factories in the European provinces

After the consolidation of Ottoman power in the Balkans, the authorities began to establish military-industrial plants in their newly acquired lands. Gunpowder production was a priority for several reasons. First, local production of powder could reduce transport costs, which were particularly high because of the large volumes – 400–500 metric tons per campaign – needing to be transported. Second, the establishment of the technological infrastructure necessary for gunpowder production was a relatively straightforward task, because existing flour mills could be converted into powder mills. In each case, the work of conversion was supervised either by an expert from a nearby provincial gunpowder works or by master craftsmen brought from Istanbul. Local carpenters and workers performed the tasks at hand. In general, these provincial gunpowder works were able to meet the gunpowder needs of the local fortresses and the provincial armies. Furthermore, the most important provincial factories could supply powder for the imperial campaigns and specifically for the Ottoman navy.

Ottoman powder works in Hungary

The most far-flung gunpowder factory in the European provinces was established in Buda, seat of the westernmost frontline province of the Ottoman Empire between

1541 and 1686. Although new conquests led to the creation of new provinces in Hungary,[25] Buda remained the foremost Hungarian province, because (along with Belgrade) it was an important port on the Danube and the principal logistical base during the campaigns against Vienna. The fortress had a dual purpose: to defend the province and to support Ottoman campaigns in Europe by supplying the army with cannons, weaponry and military hardware.[26]

It was expected that the Buda gunpowder works, established through the conversion of a working flour mill under the governorship of Arslan, *beylerbeyi* of Buda (1565–66), would meet the Hungarian provinces' powder needs. The *baruthane* of Buda – situated to the north of the town, outside its walls – was a stamp mill where the pounders were operated by an undershot wheel, powered by the waters of the local hot springs.[27] Although production at the factory was interrupted temporarily each summer to avoid explosions and fires, it was capable of manufacturing about 54 metric tons (1,000 *kantar*) per annum, while stocks ranged between 54 and 162 metric tons in the latter part of the sixteenth century.[28] The level of stocks permitted the factory to send, in the 1570s, substantial amounts (54–162 metric tons) to other fortresses in the region, as well as to Istanbul and to the Ottoman army and navy fighting in the Mediterranean against the Venetians.[29] In the late sixteenth century, during the Hungarian wars of 1593–1606, the *baruthane* played an important role in supplying the troops with powder, whereas in the 1680s Buda became the most important logistical base for the Hungarian campaigns: in 1684 alone no fewer than 540 metric tons (10,000 *kantar*) of powder were stored there.[30]

In addition to Buda, in Ottoman Hungary gunpowder was also manufactured in Temeşvar, which was the center of an Ottoman province between 1552 and 1718. Temeşvar's strategic location facilitated Ottoman efforts to keep the vassal principality of Transylvania in check and Temeşvar assisted Ottoman military

[25] Temeşvar in 1552, the short-lived *vilayet*s of Sigetvar/Szigetvár, Yanık/Győr and Papa/Pápa at the end of the sixteenth century, Eğri/Eger in 1596, Kanije/Kanizsa in 1600, Varad/Várad in 1660, and Uyvar/Érsekújvár in 1663.

[26] Gábor Ágoston, "Ottoman Conquest and the Ottoman Military Frontier in Hungary," in Béla Király and László Veszprémy eds., *A Millennium of Hungarian Military History* (Boulder, CO, 2002), pp. 85–110.

[27] The building was square in shape and strengthened by a tower in each corner. It survived the siege of 1686 intact and continued to function as a gunpowder factory for a time afterwards.

[28] Gábor Ágoston, "Ottoman Gunpowder Production in Hungary in the Sixteenth Century: The *Baruthane* of Buda," in Géza Dávid and Pál Fodor eds., *Hungarian–Ottoman Military and Diplomatic Relations in the Age of Süleyman the Magnificent* (Budapest, 1994), pp. 154–55. In 1568, gunpowder in Buda was produced in forty-one mortars, and two men worked alongside each mortar for a daily wage of 10 *akça* (MD 7, p. 316, no. 908). A year later, fifty-one persons were paid 450 *akça* per day (DBŞM 66, p. 5). The number of skilled workers in the Buda works remained at around fifty in the 1570s (MAD 1561).

[29] MD 24, p. 2, nos. 2, 3, 4, 5; ibid., p. 76, no. 208; ibid., p. 7, nos. 210, 211, 212. The gunpowder was taken by boat down the Danube to Belgrade, Semendire and Rusçuk. In Rusçuk it was loaded onto carriages and taken to Varna. Here it was loaded onto boats and transported via the Black Sea to Istanbul.

[30] MAD 177, fol. 19a; MAD 3527, p. 48.

campaigns against the Habsburgs and Poland.[31] The *baruthane* of Temeşvar was built in 1568–69, and by 1571 it had sixteen working mortars, and produced 864 kg (16 *kantar*) of gunpowder every turn, or shift (*nevbet/nöbet*). There were five turns each month and thus 4,320 kg (80 *kantar*) of gunpowder could be produced monthly. If production was constant, annual output levels in Temeşvar could reach 43,200 kg (800 *kantar*). In March 1574, the amount of gunpowder accumulated in Temeşvar exceeded 97,200 kg (1,800 *kantar*).[32] In the seventeenth century, production levels appear to have fluctuated,[33] but accounts of the *baruthane* stemming from 1679–80 show that the annual production was 74,520 kg (1,380 *kantar*).[34] The main function of the *baruthane* of Temeşvar – as in the case of gunpowder works of similar size in eastern Anatolia and in the Middle East – was to provide gunpowder to the neighboring garrisons, the provincial troops, and (less frequently) to the imperial armies operating in the area, which it successfully accomplished.[35]

In the latter part of the seventeenth century, a smaller regional powder mill in Ottoman Hungary functioned in Eğri (Eger), another provincial center between 1596 and 1687. Located at the site of what later became a salt mill, the *baruthane* was surrounded on all four sides by water. It was a square-shaped building with six towers, and was equipped with wheels and three sluices. Five mortars operated on each of the sluices, and thus gunpowder could be prepared in fifteen mortars simultaneously. Powered by the water of the Eger brook, this *baruthane* manufactured some 27,000 kg (500 *kantar*) of powder per annum in the 1670s. Production levels could, however, be increased during major campaigns, although saltpeter had to be brought in from as far away as Filibe and Tatarpazarı, as in 1664 when production levels at the Hungarian gunpowder factories needed to be increased.[36]

The powder factories of Buda, Temeşvar and Eğri, along with the smaller powder mills built in Ottoman Hungary, played an important role in satisfying the powder demand of the Ottoman garrisons in these faraway frontier provinces as

---

[31] Pál Fodor, "Das Wilayet von Temeschwar zur Zeit der osmanischen Eroberung," *Südost-Forschungen* 55 (1996), 25–44, and Géza Dávid, "The Eyalet of Temeşvar in the Eighteenth Century," in Kate Fleet, ed., *The Ottoman Empire in the Eighteenth Century, Oriente Moderno* 18 [79] (1999), 113–28.

[32] MD 24, p. 19, nos. 52, 53, 54, 55; ibid., p. 22, nos. 65, 66; ibid., p. 85, no. 229.

[33] This can be seen from the amount of saltpeter that the *baruthane* purchased. In 1669, that is in the final year of the Cretan war, the *baruthane* purchased (*iştira*) 73,728 kg (60,000 *okka*) of saltpeter (KK 2647, pp. 19–20). Ten years later, in 1679–80, it bought just two-thirds of this amount, i.e., 54,714 kg (46,968 *okka*) (KK Mevkufat 2682, p. 22a). In 1681, however, the amount of refined saltpeter purchased was once again 73,728 kg (60,000 *okka*) (ibid., p. 53b).

[34] KK Mevkufat 2682, p. 23b. In July 1672, in just one delivery, the *baruthane* supplied 800 *kantar* of powder to the most important fortress in the area, Varad (MAD 1497, p. 9).

[35] MAD 2720, p. 858, indicates that in 1662, during Küçük Mehmed Pasha's Transylvanian campaign, 21,600 kg (400 *kantar*) of powder were transported from Temeşvar to the Ottoman army. This amount was 43,200 kg (800 *kantar*, see MAD 1497, p. 9) in November 1662, and 27,000 kg (500 *kantar*, see MAD 3527, p. 141) in the spring of 1684.

[36] MAD 3774, p. 96. After the re-conquest of Eger by the Holy League (December 18, 1687) the allied troops continued to use the *baruthane*, but it did not survive much longer. Indeed, on July 31, 1691, it was destroyed in a large explosion.

well as in assisting the Empire's other powder mills in supplying the Ottoman armies fighting against the Hungarians and the Austrians. However, in order to meet the increased levels of demand for powder in the 1660s, when the Ottomans waged war on both the Cretan and the Hungarian fronts, the Istanbul government decided to construct a new *baruthane* in Selanik (Salonica), which soon became one of the Empire's foremost powder factories in the late seventeenth and the eighteenth centuries.[37]

Selanik

The *baruthane* of Selanik was built of brick in 1663–64, outside the town close to a river by the name of Söğütlü, and gunpowder started being produced here in 1666–67.[38] In the late seventeenth century some 300 men were working in the *baruthane*,[39] and it can be seen from the relevant account books that annual production was significant: 134,190 kg (2,485 *kantar*) in 1686 through 1688.[40] Between early September 1693 and late August 1694 saltpeter deliveries to the *baruthane* amounted to 207,576 kg (3,844 *kantar*), which – bearing in mind the loss of saltpeter as a result of re-dehydration – was sufficient for the production of at least 216 metric tons (4,000 *kantar*) of gunpowder.[41] The real level of production, however, was probably somewhat lower, even though production figures for subsequent years imply that attempts were being made to increase output. Given the availability of raw materials, in the late 1690s the *baruthane* was in fact capable of producing 135–162 metric tons (2,500–3,000 *kantar*) of mainly cannon powder per annum, but also produced quality English-type fine gunpowder (*İngiltere/ İngiliz perdahtı*).[42] Stocks often exceeded annual production volumes because each year some gunpowder, along with considerable amounts of raw materials, were left in store. In 1695–96, for instance, stocks rose to 166 metric tons (3,081 *kantar*).[43]

The *baruthane* contributed substantial supplies of powder to the Ottoman armies fighting against the allied troops of the Holy League: in 1685, 81 metric tons (1,500

---

[37] MAD 3774, pp. 19–20; Erdoğan, "İstanbul Baruthaneleri," 116.

[38] DBŞM 240. Repairs were carried out also in 1666–67, and the cost of these repairs was set at about 1.2 million *akças*, which was to be covered by the poll-tax revenues of the province.

[39] M. Tayyib Gökbilgin, "Selanik," *İA*, vol. X, p. 343.

[40] DMKF 27627/189-A, pp. 2–4; however, production dropped to 54,000 kg (1,000 *kantar*) in 1691–92, which was one of the very lowest output levels in the period under study (MAD 3127, p. 133).

[41] MAD 3127, pp. 180–81.

[42] In 1695–96, under the supervision of Ömer Ağa, 136 metric tons (2,520 *kantar*) of powder were manufactured, including 11,610 kg (215 *kantar*) of *İngiltere perdahtı*, 49 metric tons (907.5 *kantar*) of gunpowder for muskets, and 75.5 metric tons (1,397.5 *kantar*) of cannon powder.

[43] This included 30,294 kg (561 *kantar*) of gunpowder from the previous year's production. Of this stock, 103,950 kg (1,925 *kantar*) were sent to Belgrade as well as several other fortresses. Almost 40 percent of the gunpowder produced remained in storage. The accounts also reveal that the Selanik gunpowder works suffered three minor fires during Ömer Ağa's tenure (MAD 3620, pp. 16, 19, 26–29).

Table 5.2 *Output of the* baruthane *of Selanik*

Date	Output in *kantar*	Output in kg	Stock in *kantar*	Stock in kg
1098–99/1686–88	4,970	268,380		
1103/1691–92	1,000	54,000		
1107/1695–96	2,520	136,080	3,081	166,374
1108/1696–97	2,035.5	109,917	3,231	174,474
1109/1697–98	3,078.5	166,239	3,315	150,363
1110/1698–99	1,713.5	92,529	2,784.5	
1129/1716–17	3,000	169,200		
1130/1717–18	3,000	169,200		
1131/1718–19	1,500	84,600		
1132/1719–20	2,000	112,800		
1133/1720–21	1,500	84,600		
1134/1721–22	1,500	84,600		
1135/1722–23	1,500	84,600		
1136/1723–24	2,000	112,800		
1145–46/1732–34	3,000	169,200		
1147/1734–35	2,000	112,800		
1148/1735–36	2,000	112,800		
1149/1736–37	2,000	112,800		
1154/1741–42	1,200	67,680		
1155–64/1742–51	1,800[a]	101,520[a]		
1164/1751	1,800	101,520	5,520	311,328
1165–67/1751–54	1,500[a]	84,600		
1167/1754	1,500	84,600	7,609	429,147.6
1168/1754–55	750	42,300		
1169/1755	1,500	84,600	7,208	406,531.2
1170/1756–57	1,500	84,600		
1171/1757–58	1,500	84,600	8,607.5	485,463
1172/1758–59	1,500	84,600	6,500.5	366,628.2
1173–76/1759–62	1,500[a]	84,600		
1176/1762–63	1,500	84,600		
1179/1765–66	1,500	84,600		
1184/1770–71	3,000	169,200		
1191/1777	2,000	112,800		

Note: [a] In each individual year.

Sources: 1686–88: DMKF 27627/189–A, pp. 2–4, MAD 3620, pp. 16, 19, 26–29; 1690s: MAD 3620, pp. 37–38, 42–46, 92–94, MAD 10305, p. 194, MAD 2732, p. 67; 1732–37: DBŞM BRS 18356, p. 4; 1759–62: DBŞM BRS 18362, p. 2; 1770–71: DBŞM BRS 18364, p. 2.

kantar) of gunpowder were transported by camel from Selanik to the troops in Hungary.[44] In 1693–94 and 1694–95, once more the same amounts of powder were supplied to Belgrade.[45]

In the eighteenth century, production at the Selanik *baruthane* fluctuated in line with demand. In 1716–17 and 1717–18, at the time of renewed wars against

---

[44] MAD 4428, pp. 25–26.   [45] MAD 3127, p. 153; MAD 10142, p. 236.

the Habsburgs, annual production was more than 169 metric tons (3,000 *kantar*) before falling back to just half of this amount per annum after the signing of the Treaty of Passarowitz in July 1718. In the following year, production rose to almost 113 metric tons (2,000 *kantar*), stabilizing in the early 1720s at almost 85 metric tons (1,500 *kantar*) per year.[46] In the period between 1741 and 1751, annual production reached 101.5 metric tons (1,800 *kantar*). In the following years, including the period of the Russo-Ottoman war of 1768–74, the level of production remained fairly steady at around 85 metric tons, and it was only in 1777 that it rose once again to around 113 metric tons.[47]

The *baruthane* continued to operate after the Russo-Ottoman war,[48] but there emerged serious problems with the quality of the powder manufactured in Selanik. After 1793, under the leadership of Mehmed Şerif Efendi, superintendent of the Ottoman gunpowder works, production improved considerably in all the major *baruthanes* of the Empire, including Selanik. However, when the modern Azadlı gunpowder factory in Istanbul proved capable of producing good quality powder in large enough quantities to meet the Empire's needs, the authorities decided to close the Selanik works.[49] Those *ocaklık* villages that had supplied Selanik with saltpeter in the course of the seventeenth and eighteenth centuries thereafter provided the *baruthane* in Azadlı with peter.[50]

In short, Selanik was one of the most significant powder factories of the Empire, from the 1680s through the 1770s. In the 1750s and early 1760s, there were years when production outputs and stocks together reached 564 and 705 metric tons (10,000 and 12,500 *kantar*), although this quantity was never at the *baruthane*'s disposal. In accordance with instructions from Istanbul, Selanik constantly supplied powder to the army, the fleet and the fortresses. Actual stock levels were still very substantial: around 169 metric tons (3,000 *kantar*) in the 1690s and between 310 and 485 metric tons (5,500–8,600 *kantar*) from the early 1740s through the early 1760s.[51]

---

[46] MAD 10312, pp. 200–03, 212, 326, 328, 408.

[47] CA 9814, 9595.   [48] CA 45731.

[49] CA 45774; Erdoğan, "İstanbul Baruthaneleri," 130–31.

[50] Even in 1804 saltpeter was still being stored in Selanik, which then had to be transported to the Azadlı works (Cevdet Askeriye 45765), and some gunpowder continued to be manufactured in Selanik, because in 1835 an order concerning the closure of the *baruthane* was reissued (Erdoğan, "İstanbul Baruthaneleri," p. 132).

[51] Total production during Abdurrahman Ağa's tenureship (from 1741 through 1751) was almost 1,083 metric tons (19,200 *kantar*). After subtracting deliveries, Abdurrahman Ağa passed more than 311 metric tons (5,520 *kantar*) of powder to his successor, Ahmedpaşazade Ali Bey. Ali Bey served as the *baruthane*'s *nazır* for just three years (from 1751–52 until 1753–54). Under his supervision almost 254 metric tons (4,500 *kantar*) of gunpowder were produced. Together with the 311 metric tons of gunpowder received from Ali Bey's predecessor, the *baruthane*'s total stocks rose to 565 metric tons (10,020 *kantar*). In the four-year period between 1759–60 and 1762–63, more than 338 metric tons (6,000 *kantar*) of gunpowder were produced in total. Together with the almost 367 metric tons (6,500.5 *kantar*) of powder brought forward from the previous year, total stocks plus production amounted to 705 metric tons (12,500.5 *kantar*). Nevertheless, under instructions received from Istanbul, almost half of this amount (335 metric tons or 5,933 *kantar*) was dispatched from Selanik (KK 6691, pp. 3–4).

Gelibolu

Situated on an island of the same name, the fortress of Gelibolu (Gallipoli) was vital to the defense of the Dardanelles. The Ottomans recognized the strategic location of the fortress immediately, and in 1354, assisted by an earthquake that had reduced the defense system of the fortress to ruins, occupied the town. The conquerors transformed the town into the center of a new *sancak*, but within a short time it had also become the military and logistical center for Ottoman campaigns against the Balkan states. Gelibolu was the site of the first Ottoman naval arsenal, and a storehouse for the stockpiling of powder and military supplies was built there at the very beginning of Ottoman rule. It is difficult to ascertain the exact date when the *baruthane* was established, but it was already manufacturing some 54 metric tons (1,000 *kantar*) of powder in 1668, that is, during the final stages of the Cretan war.[52]

However, production was not without difficulties. In 1697–98 – when the *baruthane* received an order for the production of 54 metric tons (1,000 *kantar*) – it soon became obvious that Ahmed Efendi, then supervisor of the powder works, knew little of gunpowder manufacturing. The situation was made even worse by the fact that the fleet's need for gunpowder was greater than normal. Thus, gunpowder production was taken out of Ahmed Efendi's hands and entrusted to Ali Ağa, under whose leadership production levels had previously (in 1696) already reached 1,000 *kantar*. Now, he was expected to manufacture 108 metric tons (2,000 *kantar*). Ali Ağa planned to meet the challenge by undertaking production in the form of a business partnership. He chose as his business associate Davud Ağazade Mehmed, who was not only an expert in gunpowder manufacturing but had also been the inspector (*nazır*) of the *baruthane* on several occasions. Since the *ocaklık* saltpeter was not enough to meet the new levels of demand, the fact that Davud Ağazade Mehmed was in possession of saltpeter was, no doubt, an important consideration in the eyes of the Istanbul authorities.[53]

In the eighteenth century, production output levels at the Gelibolu powder works fluctuated between 56.4 and 112.8 metric tons (1,000–2,000 *kantar*); the smaller amount of powder was manufactured during peace time, while the larger figure indicates wartime output levels.

At the very beginning of the 1720s, production fell to 84.6 metric tons (1,500 *kantar*) and then rose again to 112.8 metric tons (2,000 *kantar*), which may have

---

[52] KK 2647, pp. 9–12. In 1668, 54,190 kg (44,100 *okka*) of refined saltpeter were purchased for the Gelibolu *baruthane* at a price of 1,323,000 *akça*s from the nearby *livas* of Gelibolu, Çirmen and Pasha in Europe, and of Biga and Karasi in Asia Minor, as well as from the island of Midilli in the Aegean. Based on a conservative estimate, this amount was sufficient for the manufacture of at least 54 metric tons (1,000 *kantar*) of gunpowder. KK 4738, p. 1, indicates that from time to time powder was sent from Gelibolu to the Hungarian frontier, as was the case in October 1688 when 450 *kantar* of gunpowder were shipped to Transylvania.

[53] MAD 10305, pp. 126–27. It is not clear from the sources whether in the end the *baruthane* proved capable of fulfilling twice the normal level of production. MAD 8880, p. 66, claims thus, but see also MAD 10305, pp. 120–21, which mentions that only 1,000 *kantar* of gunpowder were produced in this year.

Table 5.3 *Output of the* baruthane *of Gelibolu*

Date	Output in *kantar*	Output in kg
1108/1696–97	1,000	54,000
1109/1697–98	1,000	54,000
1110/1698–99	1,000–2,000	54,000–108,000
. . .		
1133/1720–21	1,500	84,660
1134/1721–22	1,500	84,660
1135/1722–23	2,000	112,880
1136/1723–24	2,000	112,880
1137/1724–25	2,000	112,880
1138/1725–26	3,000	169,320
1139/1726–27	3,000	169,320
. . .		
1140/1727–28	3,000	169,320
1141/1728–29	3,000	169,320
1142/1729–30	2,000	112,880
. . .		
1151/1738–39	1,000	56,440
. . .		
1160/1747	1,000	56,440
1161/1748	1,000	56,440
1162/1748–49	1,000	56,440
1163/1749–50	1,000	56,440
1164/1750–51	1,000	56,440
1165/1751–52	1,000	56,440
1166/1752–53	1,000	56,440
1167/1753–54	1,000	56,440
1168/1754–55	1,000	56,440
1169/1755–56	1,000	56,440
. . .		
1191/1777	2,000	112,880
1196/1781–82	2,000	112,880

Sources: 1696–98: MAD 3127, p. 45; 1698–99: ibid., p. 54; 1720–21: MAD 10312, p. 194; 1721–22: ibid., p. 218; 1722–23: ibid., p. 318; 1723–24: ibid., p. 414; 1724–27: DBŞM BRG 18248, p. 11; 1727–30: DBŞM BRG 18249, p. 10; 1738–39: DBŞM BRG 18251; for the years between 1747 and 1756: KK 6691, pp. 1–2; 1777: Erdoğan, "İstanbul Baruthaneleri," p. 117; 1781–82: CA 9594.

been linked to the campaigns against Georgia and Persia. Between 1747 and 1756 production fell once again to 56.4 metric tons (1,000 *kantar*) per year, which is hardly surprising since the Ottomans signed a peace treaty with Iran in September 1746, which was followed by a period of relative tranquility until the outbreak of the Russo-Ottoman war in 1768.[54] Then, towards the end of the century, beginning in 1777 production rose again to 112.8 metric tons (2,000 *kantar*), which might

[54] In the first four years following the peace treaty with Iran in 1746 the *baruthane* was supervised by İskemleci Mustafa Ağa, in the course of whose tenure 225,600 kg (4,000 *kantar*) of gunpowder

be linked to the wars against Persia (1776–77) and later against Russia (1787–92) and Austria (1787–91).

In the mid-1780s the workers of Gelibolu were already quite capable of producing quality, English-type powder. However, as it turned out, powder was not to be manufactured in Gelibolu for very much longer. The new modern gunpowder factory at Azadlı in Istanbul soon became capable of meeting all the Empire's gunpowder requirements. Thus, in the years after 1795, there was no longer a need for gunpowder to be produced in Gelibolu, and – just like the *baruthane*s of Selanik and Izmir – the works were closed down.[55]

Gunpowder production in Asia Minor and the Arab provinces

Bor

A major center of gunpowder production in Asia Minor was the *baruthane* in Bor in the province of Karaman. In the 1630s this *baruthane* produced 110.6 metric tons (90,000 *okka*) of gunpowder every year, which it dispatched to Istanbul. In the late 1630s and early 1640s, thanks to the innovations and investments introduced by the *nazır* of the time, production increased for a short time to 162 metric tons (3,000 *kantar*). Soon afterwards, however, the entrepreneur, Yakub Efendi, then the *defterdar* of the province, was unable to fulfill even the earlier amount of 110.6 metric tons. Moreover, he was accused of stealing the funds that had been entrusted to him.[56]

In 1642–43, output levels dropped to 98 metric tons, but since there were no major Ottoman campaigns – apart from a minor action to retake the fortress of Azak (Azov) – and thus no urgent need in Istanbul for greater amounts of powder, it seems that this lower level of production was acceptable for Istanbul.[57] Murad Efendi was *defterdar* of the province in 1644, and it was he who managed the gunpowder works of Bor, which continued to produce around 98 metric tons (1,818 *kantar*) of powder. The gunpowder stocks of the *baruthane* at the time amounted to almost 400 metric tons (7,393 *kantar*), a rather substantial amount.[58] However,

were produced, of which 191,760 kg (3,400 *kantar*) were dispatched to places designated by the Porte. In the following years, however (with the exception of the years 1750–51 and 1753–54 when the same person, İsmail Beğ Efendi, managed production), the *baruthane* had a different *nazır* every year. It would come as no surprise to find out that in these relatively tranquil years of peace the *nazır*s were using the *baruthane* primarily as a source of income. At the same time the authorities failed to examine the accounts of the *nazır*s and had no knowledge of the expenditures or of the general financial situation of the *baruthane* (KK 6691).

55 Erdoğan, "İstanbul Baruthaneleri," 118.
56 MAD 5392, p. 49. A subsequent inquiry revealed that the *defterdar* had even concealed 24,576 kg (20,000 *okka*) of good-quality musket gunpowder, with the aim of enriching himself by selling it to merchants. Further documents indicate that he also used other financial scams to increase his revenue from powder production.
57 MAD 5685, pp. 2, 8–9. This perhaps explains why Murad Efendi sent just 5,515 kg (4,488 *okka*) of gunpowder to the capital, placing the rest in storage in Bor.
58 In addition to the gunpowder produced by Murad Efendi, there were still 153,949 kg (125,284 *okka*) remaining from earlier years, half of which were stored in Konya and half in Bor. An additional

Table 5.4 *Output of the* baruthane *of Bor*

Date	Production in *okka*	Production in kg
1630s	90,000	110,592
1637/38–1640/41	90,000[a]	110,592
1642/43–1651/52	80,000[a]	98,304
1673/74	80,000	98,304
1674/75	80,000	98,304

Note: [a] In each individual year.
Sources: 1630s: MAD 5392, p. 49; 1641–42: ibid., p. 26; 1673–75: MAD 4527, p. 13.

in the first year of the Venetian–Ottoman war of 1645–69, which broke out over control of Crete, the gunpowder requirements of the Ottoman fleet were greater than ever before: almost all of the powder stored at Bor, more than 376 metric tons (6,968 *kantar*), was ordered to be made available for use in the campaign.[59] In the second half of the seventeenth century, annual production targets at the gunpowder works of Bor fluctuated between 98 and 110 metric tons, but actual deliveries from Bor to Istanbul may have differed. In times of peace, deliveries were smaller, whereas during campaigns the amount of gunpowder sent from Bor to Istanbul was greater.[60]

It seems that in the second half of the 1670s saltpeter production became rather neglected in Karaman. Deliveries of saltpeter were often delayed, which had a negative effect on the production of gunpowder. However, in the late 1680s Bor still produced some powder, and on three occasions between November 1687 and November 1688, almost 85 metric tons (1,573 *kantar*) of powder were sent from Bor to Istanbul. Yet, the supply of saltpeter had become a problem by the 1690s, for many of the saltpeter-producing villages in the province of Karaman began manufacturing saltpeter for their own benefit. Instead of selling the peter to the state gunpowder works, they sold it for a higher price to private manufacturers and merchants. Since in 1694–95, peter had to be sent to Istanbul rather than to Bor, it is likely that by that time the gunpowder works at Bor was no longer operating.[61]

Izmir

We do not know exactly when the *baruthane* of Izmir was established.[62] There is ample indication that by the end of the Cretan war the gunpowder works at Izmir

147,456 kg (120,000 *okka*) were kept in the Niğde warehouse. This quantity was left over from the period of Yakub Pasha, the former *defterdar* of the province and former supervisor of the gunpowder mills. This latter piece of data reminds us that Yakub Pasha, who received so much criticism, did in fact make good use of the funds that were entrusted to him, placing in storage a substantial amount of powder.

[59] MAD 7512, pp. 10–11.   [60] KK 4738, p. 1.   [61] MAD 10142, p. 242.
[62] Muzaffer Erdoğan ("İstanbul Baruthaneleri," 119) found no data on Izmir, and it is also missing from Birol Çetin's *Barut Sanayi*.

Table 5.5 *Output of the* baruthane *of Izmir*

Date	Output in kantar	Output in kg	Kantar per year	Kg per year
1685–86 and 1686–87	3,144	169,776	1,572	84,888
January 17, 1694–February 19, 1695	2,248.5	121,419	2,075	112,050
1694–95, 1696–97 and 1697–98	5,422	294,570	1,807	97,578
July 10, 1698–June 28, 1699	2,081	112,374	2,081	112,374

Sources: 1685–86 and 1686–87: MAD 885, pp. 10–14; 1694–95: MAD 3620, p. 70; 1694–95, 1696–97 and 1697–98: ibid., p. 24; 1698–99: ibid., pp. 16–20.

was making significant contributions to the Ottoman war effort. In 1668–69, the *baruthane* received 86,016 kg (70,000 *okka*) of saltpeter, an amount sufficient for the production of at least 108 metric tons (2,000 *kantar*) of powder. From later sources, we see that the *baruthane*'s annual production quota for the fleet was indeed about 108 metric tons.[63]

Gunpowder production in Izmir was particularly important at the end of the seventeenth century, when a large part of the gunpowder requirement of the Ottoman fleet and that of the Ottoman fortresses in the Mediterranean was met by the Izmir powder works. In 1685–86 and 1686–87, 169,776 kg (3,144 *kantar*) of gunpowder were produced in the *baruthane* – that is, on average almost 86,400 kg (1,600 *kantar*) per year. Judging by the mixture ratio (saltpeter 75 percent, sulfur 12 percent, charcoal 13 percent), the gunpowder that was manufactured was in line with European standards and of good quality. The loss was merely 3 percent, which was particularly favorable in comparison with factories in other parts of the Empire or even in Europe.[64]

We do not know the extent of the damage (if any) sustained by the *baruthane* in the earthquake of July 1688, which ruined many of the town's public buildings as well as the fort of Sancakburnu situated at the entrance of the Gulf of Izmir on a peninsula three kilometers from the city, but it seems that at the time of the earthquake the *baruthane* was still in operation in Izmir.[65] In the 1680s and 1690s, on average the *baruthane* was capable of manufacturing almost 102 metric tons (1,883 *kantar*) of powder per annum.

Detailed accounts of the *baruthane* and correspondence between the central authorities and the superintendents of the Izmir gunpowder works indicate that

[63] KK 2647, already used by İdris Bostan, *Osmanlı Bahriye Teşkilatı: XVII. Yüzyılda Tersane-i Amire* (Ankara, 1992), pp. 172–73.

[64] MAD 885, pp. 10–14. The gunpowder stocks must have been slightly higher. In total 185,652 kg (3,438 *kantar*) were supplied from Izmir to fortresses on the islands of the Aegean and in western Anatolia as well as to the Imperial Armory. The accounts also indicate a minor fire in the *baruthane*, in the course of which 32 *kantar* of gunpowder went up in smoke.

[65] On the earthquake see N. N. Ambraseys and C. F. Finkel, *The Seismicity of Turkey and Adjacent Areas: A Historical Review, 1500–1800* (Istanbul, 1995), pp. 90–93. We do know, however, that the reconstruction of the fort was supervised by the then *nazır* of the *baruthane*, and that he contributed – from his own wealth – a sum of 1,000 *guruş* towards the repair costs, which amounted to 20,000 *guruş*. See Defterdar Sarı Mehmed Paşa, *Zübde-i Vekayiat*, p. 301.

Izmir, like other powder mills in the Empire, had to purchase some 40 percent of peter because the *ocaklık* villages could not satisfy its needs. From the sources, one can easily detect the deliberate attempt at increasing both the quantities and the quality of domestically manufactured powder. Izmir seems to have been successful in both regards and, as will be seen later, produced the highest quality powder in the Empire. The *baruthane* was still producing gunpowder at the end of the eighteenth century, although by then it was unable to meet the requirements of either quantity or quality. It was closed around 1795, corresponding to the closures of the gunpowder works in Selanik and Gelibolu.

Cairo

Conquered by the Ottomans in 1517, Egypt was important for strategic, economic and religious reasons. Its ports in the eastern Mediterranean were major naval bases that could be used to ward off Spanish invasion. Together with Greater Syria, by the late 1520s, Egypt already accounted for more than one-third of the Empire's revenues. Moreover, Egypt was a historic center of Islamic education and culture. Nevertheless, a revolt in 1523–24, which was led by the new province's governor (Hain) Ahmed Pasha, served as a warning to the Ottoman government in Istanbul that Egypt would always be difficult to control. The land route was too long, while the sea route had its seasonal limitations: Mediterranean naval technology did not make seafaring possible during the winter, and thus naval activity was restricted each year to a period lasting from the spring until the late autumn and called in Ottoman sources "Sea season" (*Derya* or *Deniz mevsimi*). More importantly, Egypt's rich countryside could generate enough resources for an anti-Ottoman rebellion, and Cairo, with a long tradition and legitimacy as a capital, was a natural center for any such uprising. All this led to the prompt adjustment of Ottoman administrative strategies and to a reinforcement of the Ottoman military presence.[66] As in Hungary – another distant province outside the core zones – in Egypt the establishment of a local armaments industry was an essential task and one that was initially aimed at meeting local needs.

The primary purpose of the gunpowder factories in Egypt was to supply gunpowder to the fortresses and armies defending the Arab provinces as well as to the Mediterranean fleet. Of course, gunpowder had been produced in Egypt prior to Ottoman rule, and the very first Ottoman governor of the province, Hayir Bey, sent supplies of gunpowder to the imperial troops during the campaign against Rhodes.[67] A provincial law book or *kanunname*, dating from 1524 and issued in connection with the reorganization of the province's administration after the rebellion of 1523, shows that the Ottoman authorities had placed gunpowder production

---

[66] Seyyid Muhammed es-Seyyid Mahmud, *XV Asırda Mısır Eyaleti* (Istanbul, 1990), pp. 77–90.
[67] Ibid., p. 62.

in Egypt under the control of the state. All other local gunpowder works had been closed down and, in order to ensure a state monopoly of gunpowder production, raw materials and cauldrons from these sites had been carried off to the Imperial Armory in Cairo.[68]

By the mid-sixteenth century Egypt had become one of the Empire's major gunpowder producers. The province possessed rich deposits of saltpeter: in December 1564, when preparations were underway for the Malta campaign, the *beylerbeyi* of the province was ordered to prepare 216 metric tons (4,000 *kantar*) of it.[69] Saltpeter was produced in seventy villages for the gunpowder works of Cairo. Every week, two caravans of saltpeter were taken from these villages to the Cairo armory. The quality of the saltpeter was checked by the *beylerbeyi*, who would reject deliveries of unrefined saltpeter.[70] By mid-century, Cairo was supplying between 162 and 216 metric tons (3,000–4,000 *kantar*) of gunpowder annually to the Ottoman fleet and army, and by the beginning of the seventeenth century, this amount had risen to 270 tons (5,000 *kantar*).[71]

Supplies of gunpowder from Egypt made an important contribution to the European campaigns. In the first year of the Hungarian wars of 1593–1606, 378 metric tons (7,000 *kantar*) of powder were sent from Cairo to Hungary. In 1599, the shipment was 216 tons, while in 1604 a further consignment of 270 metric tons from Cairo arrived at the Hungarian front.[72] Although the above figures provided by Abdülkadır Efendi's chronicle may appear somewhat exaggerated, the information has been confirmed by archival sources.[73]

At the time of the Ottoman campaigns of the seventeenth century, the Cairo gunpowder works regularly dispatched gunpowder supplies to the Ottoman armies and the fleet: in 1663–64, for instance, five deliveries of gunpowder – amounting to 198,774 kg or 3,681 *kantar* – were received from Egypt for use in the Hungarian campaign.[74] Gunpowder was also continuously supplied to the campaign in Crete.[75] In 1685 and 1688, Cairo sent 141,558 kg (3,200 Egyptian *kantar*) and

---

[68] Ömer Lütfi Barkan, *XV ve XVIıncı Asırlarda Osmanlı İmparatorluğunda Ziraî Ekonominin Hukukî ve Malî Esasları. I. Kanunlar* (Istanbul, 1943), p. 356.

[69] MD 6, p. 200, no. 420.

[70] Erdoğan, "İstanbul Baruthaneleri," 118. The *baruthane* of Cairo was a building with two cupolas that stood in a corner of the courtyard of the Pasha's seraglio. The wheels of the mill were driven by horses.

[71] Turgut Işıksal, "Gunpowder in Ottoman Documents of the Last Half of the 16th Century," *JTS* 2, 2 (1981–82), 82; es-Seyyid Mahmud, *Mısır Eyaleti*, p. 194, n. 93. In addition to local production, the *beylerbeyi* of Egypt also received gunpowder from Yemen by way of Suez. For example, in 1565, while preparations were underway for the Hungarian campaign, 27,000 kg (500 *kantar*) of gunpowder were brought in from Yemen.

[72] AK fols. 7a, 11b, 113b, 190a.

[73] The command sent to the *beylerbeyi* and *defterdar* of Egypt in June 1595 ordered the immediate delivery of 324 tons (6,000 *kantar*) of gunpowder (MD 73, p. 221, no. 518). Meanwhile a decree issued in August provided for the delivery of an additional 54 tons (1,000 *kantar*) (ibid., p. 353, no. 775). In late 1604 and early 1605 the governor of Egypt was repeatedly urged to send the requested amount of gunpowder to Selanik as soon as possible (MD 75, p. 65, no. 103; p. 108, no. 192; p. 325, no. 675), which might indicate that not all the needs could have been satisfied by Egypt.

[74] MAD 3279, pp. 169–70.   [75] DPYM 35141.

73,035 kg (1,352.5 *kantar*) of powder, respectively.[76] By the latter half of the
eighteenth century, however, production in Egypt had fallen back. During the
Russo-Ottoman war of 1768–74, it seems that the Porte urged the delivery of
gunpowder from Egypt, to no avail.[77]

Baghdad

Baghdad was conquered in 1534, and the city was transformed into the foremost
provincial center on the eastern frontier, but it remained contested as a result of
the Ottoman–Safavid imperial rivalry. In order to retain Baghdad, the Ottomans
were required to make considerable military commitments. In recognition of this,
Istanbul laid special emphasis on developing local military-industrial facilities,
including gunpowder workshops and a cannon foundry, so that neither the fortress
nor the province of Baghdad should be dependent on Istanbul.

The *baruthane* and the saltpeter works of Baghdad lay at the Shaykh Omar gate
to the city. By the latter half of the sixteenth century the *baruthane*'s output had
risen so greatly that it could satisfy local demand and afford regular deliveries of
powder to the European fortresses and the Mediterranean fleet. In 1566, when the
gunpowder factory in Buda had still to be built, some of the gunpowder produced
in Baghdad found its way to Buda and Belgrade.[78] In 1573 fourteen gunpowder
workshops were in operation and by 1575–76 their number had risen to sixteen,
with annual production supposedly reaching 270 metric tons (5,000 *kantar*).[79] In
the mid-1570s gunpowder stocks in Baghdad were around 216 metric tons (4,000
kantar), and at least 108 metric tons (2,000 *kantar*) of gunpowder were transported
each year from Baghdad to Istanbul or the European fortresses via Tripoli (Trablus-i
Şam) and Rhodes.[80]

Production, however, seems to have been rather uneven, and there were times
when Baghdad was unable to supply the desired quantities. Occasionally, the repair

[76] MAD 4428 p. 24; note that the Egyptian *kantar* was only 36 *okka*, that is, prior to the eighteenth
century it weighed 44.2 kg. For the shipment in 1688, see KK 4738, p. 1.
[77] The local authorities cited a lack of workers as well as the absence of wheels to operate the pestles.
As a further excuse, they mentioned the likelihood of the gunpowder, which was to be sent by sea,
becoming damp and therefore useless by the time it reached the Ottoman armies. Rejecting these
excuses, in April 1769 the Porte ordered the governor of Egypt to send his men out to the saltpeter
villages, where they were to collect as much saltpeter as possible. Production of gunpowder was
then to begin, the costs of which the governor was to cover from the province's taxes. The Porte
anticipated that Egypt would soon dispatch 10,000 *kantar* of gunpowder to Gelibolu. See Erdoğan,
"İstanbul Baruthaneleri," 119.
[78] Işıksal, "Gunpowder," 83.
[79] Cengiz Orhonlu, "Dicle ve Fırat Nehirlerinde Nakliyat," in his *Osmanlı İmparatorluğunda Şehircilik
ve Ulaşım* (Izmir, 1984), p. 132; Işıksal, "Gunpowder," 83–84; MD 24, p. 11, no. 29.
[80] In April 1570, at the time of the Cyprus campaign, the *beylerbeyi* of Baghdad was ordered to arrange
for the transport of 3,000 *kantar* of powder to Tripoli. From there the delivery was to be taken to
Cyprus. By 1574, stocks of gunpowder in Baghdad had once again risen to 216 metric tons, half of
which were then dispatched to the campaign. The remaining 108 metric tons, however, were kept
in storage, owing to a shortage of camels (MD 26, p. 6, no. 16; Işıksal, "Gunpowder," 89.)

of cauldrons became necessary, for which there appears to have been a lack of local copper and lead. A further problem was firewood, which was in short supply in the immediate vicinity of Baghdad and thus had to be brought in from the neighboring province of Şehrizol. On the other hand, the transport of raw materials and firewood was greatly facilitated by the Tigris and the Euphrates. For instance, firewood from southern Anatolia was brought in along the Euphrates.[81] Although Istanbul's power in Iraq weakened towards the end of the century, the gunpowder factory was still operating at the time of the Hungarian wars of 1593–1606.[82]

In the early seventeenth century, Istanbul's power in the region weakened still further, and when Shah Abbas (1587–1629) occupied the city in 1623, the Porte lost a source of gunpowder that was not to be recouped until the city's re-conquest in 1638. In the sources on the supply of armaments and ammunition during the campaigns of the late seventeenth and early eighteenth centuries, I have found no data for powder shipments from Baghdad. This may indicate that Ottoman gunpowder production in Baghdad was still rather insignificant in terms of the Empire as a whole.

Smaller and temporary *baruthane*s

In addition to the major *baruthane*s surveyed briefly above, there were numerous smaller powder works in the Empire that mainly satisfied local demand. Among them, gunpowder works along the Empire's frontiers were of special importance, given the logistical difficulties, as well as cost and time constraints, involved in transporting substantial quantities of powder from the core zones to the frontier garrisons. Their yearly output levels seldom exceeded 54 metric tons and their stocks were around this level too. On the eastern frontier, Erzurum, Van and Aleppo can be mentioned among the smaller powder plants of regional importance. Of these, Aleppo seems to have been the most important. In addition to satisfying local needs, Aleppo was occasionally capable of supplying some powder to the Ottoman navy as well. In 1570, for instance, the *beylerbeyi* of Aleppo was instructed to bring 54 metric tons (1,000 *kantar*) of powder with him to Cyprus and to arrange for the production of as much gunpowder as possible from any remaining saltpeter.[83]

In Erzurum, saltpeter production was attempted as early as the 1560s. By 1576, despite difficulties resulting from the shortage of water needed for the distillation of the peter,[84] gunpowder production was soon underway there.[85] The case of

[81] Işıksal, "Gunpowder," 84.   [82] MD 73, p. 221.
[83] MD 9, p. 46. In 1605, the final year of the long Hungarian wars, gunpowder from Aleppo was very much relied upon (MD 75, p. 99, no. 171).
[84] MD 27, p. 375, no. 897.
[85] MD 28, p. 189, no. 441. By October 1576, a gunpowder expert and fifteen mortars were en route from Istanbul. In the same month a further eleven mortars were sent via the Black Sea.

the gunpowder works in the province of Van, in an area controlled by the *kadı* of Ahtar, illustrates the difficulties of operating these smaller and often temporary gunpowder works which often lacked the necessary workforce. Gunpowder experts, dispatched to the scene either from Istanbul or from other major fortresses of the province, usually ran such smaller factories. The workers were local inhabitants or soldiers serving in the fortresses of the area.[86]

Some of the smaller *baruthane*s were established when demands for powder increased substantially as a consequence of protracted wars. Examples are the gunpowder works in Eğriboz (Egripos/Negroponte) and at Hanya (Chania) on Crete, both of which were manufacturing powder during the Cretan war and may have been established to aid the Empire's permanent plants in satisfying the much higher requirements of powder. The saltpeter necessary for production of powder in Eğriboz was bought from the sub-provinces (*liva*s) of Eğriboz, Tırhala and İnebahtı (Naupactus/Lepanto), and the amount purchased was enough for the production of approximately 64,800–75,600 kg (1,200–1,400 *kantar*) of powder.[87] The works at Hanya, where sources suggest production in 1669, that is, in the final year of the Cretan war, played a disproportionately important role, because the Venetians tried to prevent powder supplies from reaching the Ottoman troops fighting on the island. Although the powder works produced probably no more than 50,000 kg of powder, under the circumstances, even this amount was a godsend to the armies laying siege to Candia.[88] Even after the conquest of the island, there was still a need for the gunpowder works at Hanya.[89]

Types of Ottoman powder mills

The great majority of the Ottoman gunpowder works were stamp mills. The number and size of the mortars, even within one gunpowder works, changed over time. In 1567 the gunpowder works in Buda operated just twenty mortars, each with a maximum capacity of 61–68 kg (50–55 *okka*). Later on, however, in order to avoid the frequent explosions caused by the large size of the mortars and pestles, smaller

[86] The *kadı* of Ahtar indicated to the Porte the need for day laborers in the gunpowder works. The Porte then ordered the *beylerbeyi* of Van to assign garrison soldiers from major fortresses in the province, such as Bitlis, Ahtar and Ahlat, to the gunpowder factory. Gunpowder manufactured in the province of Van was taken via Erzurum to the port of Trabzon, whence it was shipped to Istanbul. MD 27, p. 263, no. 618; Işıksal, "Gunpowder," 89.

[87] KK 2647, pp. 1–3. In total 1,419,000 *akça*s were paid for 47,300 *okka* of saltpeter.

[88] In 1669 just 36,864 kg (30,000 *okka*) of saltpeter were purchased for the gunpowder works from the *liva* of Mora. This quantity of saltpeter was sufficient for the production of about 48,600 kg (900 *kantar*) of powder.

[89] In addition to the threat posed by pirates throughout the Mediterranean, until 1715 the Ottomans were also fearful of a counter-attack by the Venetians, who, under the peace treaty of 1669, retained the three rocky islands of Souda, Spinalonga and Grambousa, just off the northern coast of Crete. See Molly Greene, "Ruling an Island without a Navy: A Comparative View of Venetian and Ottoman Crete," in Kate Fleet ed., *The Ottomans and the Sea, Oriente Moderno* 20 (81), 1 (2001), 193–207.

mortars, each with a capacity of 25 kg (20 *okka*), replaced the larger ones. At the same time, there was a corresponding increase in the number of mortars: in 1568 forty-one mortars were being used in Buda;[90] by 1577 their number had grown to forty-four.[91] As regards the major gunpowder mills in the capital, there were – according to Evliya Çelebi – a hundred mortars in the *baruthane* at Kağıthane, each weighing 540 kg (10 *kantar*). Meanwhile, an inventory stemming from 1683 mentions seventy-two mortars (forty bronze and thirty-two wooden ones). At the same point in time, more than twice as many mortars – 120 bronze and 120 wooden mortars – were recorded in the Şehremini gunpowder works, although we do not know how many of these mortars were being used for the grinding of powder.[92] After the reconstruction of the *baruthane* at Bakırköy, which was destroyed by fire in 1725, gunpowder was manufactured in 216 mortars. The *baruthane* was divided up into eighteen units, with gunpowder being produced in twelve mortars per unit.

Wherever circumstances allowed, the Ottomans preferred to use mills powered by water (e.g., in Buda and Eğri). In the majority of cases, however, water energy was not a viable option. Thus, in the main, horses drove the wheels of the powder mills. In the late seventeenth century, almost a hundred horses were employed in the works of Istanbul, but their rate of exhaustion was high. In the early 1690s, during Yeğen Mustafa Paşa's nineteen-month tenure as superintendent of the *baruthane* of Istanbul, thirty-five horses perished.[93] Between 1697 and 1700, sixty-nine of ninety-two horses perished.[94] Even though the presence of water was one of the criteria for the establishment of a gunpowder mill at Bakırköy, in the end horses were used to drive the wheels.

Production capacity and output

Based on the data summarized above, I estimate the quantity of gunpowder produced annually in the major gunpowder works of Egypt, Baghdad, Aleppo, Erzurum, Istanbul, Buda and Temeşvar at the end of the sixteenth century to be 12,000–18,600 *kantar*, or 648–1,000 metric tons. These estimates were substantial, especially considering the estimated production levels of some of the Ottomans' main adversaries. All the factories in Castile were capable of producing only 920 kg (20 quintals) of powder per day in 1580, and even this very modest output had dropped to 552 kg (12 quintals) by 1587.[95] Assuming that all the plants were able to work for some 300 days per annum, which is an optimistic estimate for the sixteenth century, the total output of the Castilian gunpowder works would have been only 276 and 165.6 metric tons each year respectively.

---

[90] MD 7, p. 316, no. 908.   [91] MD 31, p. 93, no. 230.
[92] MAD 2936, p. 4.   [93] DBŞM 642.   [94] DBŞM 19085, p. 14.
[95] I. A. A. Thompson, *War and Government in Habsburg Spain, 1560–1620* (London, 1976), p. 241.

Table 5.6 *Estimated output of the Ottoman powder works, 1570s–1590s*

Gunpowder works	Date of production/ inventory	Production kantar/year	Production kg/year	Stock in kantar	Stock in kg
Kağıthane	1571	1,800–3,600*	97,200–194,400	1,600	86,400
Şehremini	1571	900–1,800*	48,600–97,200		
Istanbul	1594–95			4,460	240,840
Buda		1,000–2,000*	54,000–108,000	3,000–4,000	162,000–216,000
Temeşvar		800–1,200*	43,200–64,800	1,500–2,000	81,000–108,000
Baghdad	1570s	2,500–5,000	135,000–270,000	3,000–4,000	162,000–216,000
Egypt	1574	4,000	216,000		
Egypt	1593–95			7,000	378,000
Egypt	1599			4,000	216,000
Aleppo	1570	1,000	54,000	1,000	54,000
Erzurum	1579			2,000	108,000
Total		12,000–18,600	648,000–1,004,400		

Notes: * Figures are estimates, based on figures of stocks or of imperial orders. Lower figures for Istanbul (1571) take into consideration the fact that the powder works operated only for six months a year.
Sources: Istanbul: MD 16, p. 375, no. 656; Istanbul 1594–95: MAD 383; Buda and Temeşvar: Ágoston, "Ottoman Gunpowder Production"; Egypt 1593 and 1599: AK fols. 7a and 113b; 1595: MD 73, p. 221, no. 518; p. 353, no. 775; Baghdad: Işıksal, "Gunpowder"; Aleppo: MD 9, p. 46; Erzurum: MD 32, no. 579.

It appears that in the seventeenth century there was a modest increase in the gunpowder output of the Ottoman Empire. The importance of some of the earlier *baruthane*s declined, while several gunpowder works established in the seventeenth century gained in significance. In the seventeenth century, major gunpowder mills operated in Istanbul, Cairo, Bor, Buda, Temeşvar, Selanik, Gelibolu and Izmir, of which the *baruthane*s at Bor, Selanik, Gelibolu and Izmir were established in the seventeenth century. At the end of the seventeenth century, the accounts of the major *baruthane*s provide us with a relatively accurate impression of their operational capacities and accumulated stocks.

In the mid-seventeenth century annual production at Bor stood at about 108 metric tons, but, as we have seen, production occasionally rose to between 162 and 178 tons. In the 1680s, however, it fell back to a level of 81 to 97 tons, and by the turn of the century production appears to have been halted. In the 1680s gunpowder production in Istanbul, i.e., the combined output of the gunpowder mills at Kağıthane and Şehremini, rose to no less than 162–216 metric tons per year. Indeed, in some years, the combined production of the two gunpowder mills even approached 270 tons. Production in Temeşvar fluctuated between 54 and 75.6 metric tons per year, while average annual gunpowder production reached 124 metric tons at Selanik, 54 metric tons at Gelibolu, and between 86.4 and 108 metric tons at Izmir. One of our sources claims that in Egypt annual production

Table 5.7 *Estimated output of the Ottoman powder works in the 1680s*

	Minimum in *kantar*	Minimum in kg	Maximum in *kantar*	Maximum in kg
Istanbul	3,000	162,000	4,700	253,800
Buda	1,000	54,000	1,000	54,000
Temeşvar	1,000	54,000	1,400	75,600
Selanik	2,300	124,200	2,300	124,200
Gelibolu	1,000	54,000	1,000	54,000
Izmir	1,600	86,400	2,000	108,000
Bor	1,200	64,800	1,800	97,200
Cairo/Egypt	3,000	162,000	5,000	270,000
Total	14,100	761,400	19,200	1,036,800

stood at 270 metric tons, but data relating to stock inventories suggest a somewhat lower level of production (162–216 metric tons).

We have also noted that at times of war and during major campaigns production at the larger gunpowder mills increased or the Porte raised output at mills that had previously satisfied merely local demand for gunpowder. At times of greater military commitment, it was not unusual for the authorities to reactivate disused gunpowder mills or to establish new mills operating merely for the duration of a particular conflict. Several of the *baruthane*s falling into this latter category were of a significant capacity. We have noted, for instance, that at the time of the Cretan war the Ottomans were able to produce some 64.8–237.6 metric tons of gunpowder at Eğriboz and 48.6 metric tons of gunpowder per year at Hanya. Based on all this, we may estimate total annual gunpowder production in the 1680s in the *baruthane*s of Istanbul, Buda, Temeşvar, Selanik, Gelibolu, Izmir, Bor and Cairo at between 761 and 1,037 metric tons (14,100–19,200 *kantar*).

Actual gunpowder stocks and shipments

There was a great need for this amount of gunpowder, because the campaigns of the seventeenth century required even larger quantities than those of the six-teenth century. According to contemporaneous estimates, in the late seventeenth century, 540 metric tons (10,000 *kantar*) of gunpowder had to be mobilized for each campaign.[96] Judging by the surviving accounts, the author of the above esti-mate was well informed about levels of demand for gunpowder. These accounts also reveal that in the mid-seventeenth century, this quantity was still available for the Ottoman troops. The accounts of the Imperial Armory show that between March 1663 and May 1664 a total of almost 565 metric tons (10,459 *kantar*) of gunpowder was ordered to be dispatched from the armory to the campaigns. In

[96] Süheyl Ünver, "XVII. Yüzyıl Sonunda Padişaha Bir Layıha," *Belleten* (1969), 25.

the same period, gunpowder deliveries to the armory amounted to more than 605 metric tons (11,211 *kantar*).[97]

The amount of gunpowder distributed in the course of the Érsekújvár (Uyvar) campaign of 1663 and used at the time of the siege of the castle, as well as the gunpowder delivered to the various fortresses in the region, was almost 357 metric tons (6,611 *kantar*). At the time of the siege of Érsekújvár, more than 184 metric tons (about 3,410 *kantar*) of gunpowder were used.[98] In December 1663, in a command sent to the *defterdar* of Karaman, 162 metric tons (3,000 *kantar*) of gunpowder were requested just from Bor for the campaign in the following year.[99]

The long war at the end of the century required even greater quantities of powder. After repeated demands by the *beylerbeyi* of Buda, in March 1684 the Ottoman authorities accumulated a large amount of gunpowder at Buda. The detailed accounts show that the Ottomans brought 540 metric tons (10,000 *kantar*) of gunpowder to the fortress.[100] After the siege that had lasted three and a half months, the Ottomans began once again to replenish their stocks of powder. In 1685 and in early 1686 substantial amounts of military equipment were brought by boat and on camels from Belgrade to Buda. By the end of February 1686, more than 371 metric tons (6,874.5 *kantar*) of cannon powder and 28 metric tons (521 *kantar*) of musket powder had been brought to the fortress.[101]

Between November 1687 and November 1688, that is, during the fifth year of the Hungarian war, the total gunpowder input of the Imperial Armory was still almost 388 metric tons (7,183 *kantar*). This amount was doubtless sufficient in the late 1680s, for after their defeat in the battle of Nagyharsány (near Mohács) the Ottoman forces withdrew from Hungary, and during the subsequent domestic political crisis (execution of the Grand Vizier, the forced abdication of Sultan Mehmed IV, and the accession to the throne of Sultan Süleyman II), there were no major troop deployments. The withdrawal from Hungary of the main Ottoman forces may explain why during the period under discussion just 81,972 kg (1,518 *kantar*) of gunpowder were allocated from the armory, while almost 305,910 kg (5,665 *kantar*) remained there.[102]

In the late 1690s, the combined demand for gunpowder of a war that was being fought on several fronts on land and at sea placed an even heavier burden upon the gunpowder works. In 1697–98, for example, as the Ottoman fleet set out in the Mediterranean against the Morea and in the Black Sea against Özi and Kerç, there was a need for 461.7 metric tons (8,550 *kantar*) of gunpowder. The relevant accounts appear to show that the powder mills of the Empire were able to

[97] MAD 3279, pp. 171, 175.   [98] MAD 15877, pp. 1–2.

[99] MAD 3774, p. 14.   [100] MAD 177, fol. 19a; MAD 3527, p. 48.   [101] DBŞM 489.

[102] MAD 15758, p. 2. A partial account (KK 4738, p. 7) recording some of the gunpowder deliveries arriving in the Cebehane during a fifteen-month period between November 1687 and January 1689 reveals the delivery of 402,111 kg (7,446.5 *kantar*) of gunpowder, of which only 192,861 kg (3,571.5 *kantar*) were used, while the remaining 209,250 kg (3,875 *kantar*) were kept in storage in the Cebehane.

satisfy this demand.[103] In 1698–99, the authorities calculated that they would need 648 metric tons (12,000 *kantar*) of gunpowder.[104]

The quality of Ottoman powder

Available narrative sources provide contradictory accounts of the quality of Ottoman gunpowder. In a passage relating to the siege of Baghdad of 1630, the Ottoman chronicler Mustafa Naima (1655–1716) noted that the poor quality of the powder had damaged the touch holes (*falya*) of cannons. Similar complaints also appear in the writings of Katib Çelebi (1609–57) and Mehmed Raşid (d. 1735) with regard to the events of 1656 and 1669, respectively. Katib Çelebi added that, owing to the poor quality of Ottoman gunpowder, the European cannons measuring just 12 palms in length could achieve a greater range than the Ottoman cannons measuring 16 palms in length, even though generally speaking longer cannons usually had greater range.[105] While similar complaints occasionally appear in archival sources[106] and in Marsigli's work on the Ottoman army, one should remember that other observers contested the above opinions and praised the quality of the gunpowder used by the Sultan's troops. Montecuccoli, a contemporary of Marsigli, found that the Ottomans' powder was "excellent, as is evident from the noise of the discharge, and the velocity and range of the shot."[107]

Such opinions should remind us that citing a few arbitrarily selected passages from the readily available narrative sources can be very misleading. It is quite possible that both the negative and positive appraisals regarding the quality of the Ottoman powder were correct. Given the decentralized nature of Ottoman gunpowder production, it was impossible to maintain uniform standards. Discrepancies in the purity of the components of gunpowder and in the mixture ratio,

---

[103] MAD 8880, p. 66; cf. also Bostan, *Bahriye*, p. 173.

[104] MAD 10305, p. 140. The sources also clearly show that during protracted wars there was a need for as much gunpowder as could be extracted, and that the authorities tried to seek out and utilize new sources of gunpowder. In April 1685, for example, the Porte discovered that 300 *kantar* of gunpowder, which had been sent to the castle of Akkerman six years earlier during the Çehrin campaign, were still being stored at the castle. Since the commander-in-chief of the campaign, Süleyman Pasha, was short of gunpowder at the time, Istanbul ordered the shipment of 250 *kantar* of the powder (MAD 4428, p. 27).

[105] Rhoads Murphey, *Ottoman Warfare, 1500–1700* (New Brunswick, 1999), p. 215, n. 5; Henry Kahane, Renée Kahane and Andreas Tietze, *The Lingua Franca in the Levant: Turkish Nautical Terms of Italian and Greek Origin* (Urbana, IL, 1958; reprint Istanbul, 1988), p. 208. We find similar complaints in Hüseyn Hezarfen's chronicle, where Hezarfen repeats word for word Katib Çelebi's complaint. See Rhoads Murphey, "The Ottoman Attitude towards the Adoption of Western Technology: The Role of the Efrencî Technicians in Civil and Military Applications," in Jean-Louis Bacqué-Grammont and Paul Dumont eds., *Contributions à l'histoire économique et sociale de l'Empire ottoman* (Leuven, 1983), p. 293, n. 16, where Murphey quotes Hezarfen. This is hardly surprising given the fact that Hezarfen drew extensively from Katib Çelebi's work.

[106] See, for example, Ahmet Refik, *Onikinci Asr-i Hicri'de İstanbul Hayatı* (Istanbul, 1988), pp. 73–74, no. 102, regarding the poor quality of powder manufactured in Selanik in 1720.

[107] Quoted in Christopher Duffy, *Siege Warfare: The Fortress in the Early Modern World 1494–1660* (London, 1979; reprint London, 1996), p. 213.

Table 5.8 *Mixture of gunpowder in selected European countries and in the Ottoman Empire, 1546–1795*

Date	Country	Saltpeter	Sulfur	Charcoal
1546	Germany	50	33.3	16.7
1550s	France	75	11.5	13.5
1555	Germany	66.7	22.2	11.1
1560	Sweden	66.6	16.6	16.6
1571	Ottoman Empire/Temeşvar	72.4	9.8	17.8
1595	Germany	52.2	21.7	26.1
1598	France	75	12.5	12.5
1608	Denmark	68.3	8.5	23.2
1642–43	Ottoman Empire/Bor	75	12.5	12.5
1644–45	Bor (for cannon)	72	14	14
1644–45	Bor (for muskets)	75	12.5	12.5
1649	Germany	69	14.6	16.5
1650	France	75.6	13.6	10.8
1650s	Austria (for muskets)	70	13	17
1650s	Austria (for cannons)	66.9	14.3	18.8
1673–74	Ottoman Empire/Bor	69	15.5	15.5
1679–80	Ottoman Empire/Temeşvar	75	12.5	12.5
1686	France	76	12.0	12.0
1686–89	Ottoman Empire/Selanik	71.4	14.3	14.3
1689–90	Ottoman Empire/Istanbul	75	12.5	12.5
1690s	Ottoman Empire/Izmir	77	13.4	9.6
1696	France	75	12.5	12.5
1696–97	Ottoman Empire/Istanbul	75	12.5	12.5
1697	Sweden	73	10	17
1699–1700	Ottoman Empire	75	12.5	12.5
1700	Sweden	75	16	9
1742	England and Europe	75	12.5	12.5
1793–94	Ottoman Empire	77.1	10.4	12.5
1794–95	Ottoman Empire	75.8	10.5	13.7

Sources: Bor: MAD 5685, p. 7, MAD 4527, p. 13, MAD 7512, p. 10; Temeşvar: MD 12, p. 198, no. 418, KK Mevkufat 2682, p. 23a; Selanik: DMKF 27627, p. 4, MAD 3127, MAD 3620; Izmir: MAD 6880, p. 26. Istanbul: DBŞM 844, p. 6, DBŞM 598, pp. 4–5, Ágoston, "Gunpowder for the Sultan's Army," p. 89, and Ágoston, "Osmanlı İmparatorluğu'nda Harp Endüstrisi," p. 630; Dolleczek, *Geschichte*, p. 175.

as well as local differences affecting each phase of the production process, could significantly influence the quality of the finished product.[108] Nevertheless, such discrepancies were hardly unique to the Ottoman Empire. Similar problems were present in all the early modern states, and even the introduction of quality controls in the eighteenth century failed to ensure uniform quality. Having accepted all this, the researcher has no choice but to work through a large number of archival sources covering a substantial period of time and relating to several different provinces, with the aim of drawing conclusions about the composition of Ottoman powder.

[108] Murphey, *Ottoman Warfare*, p. 14.

The mixture of the various ingredients varied over time even at individual *baruthane*s. However, in the latter half of the seventeenth century, the composition of Ottoman gunpowder was very similar to that of the best European powder. It appears that until the latter part of the seventeenth century, Ottoman powder manufactured in Bor contained 69 percent of saltpeter, 15.5 percent of sulfur and the same percentage of charcoal. Generally speaking, however, Ottoman powder works produced powder according to the new mixture (*be ayar-i cedid*) or to the so-called English proportion (*be ayar-i perdaht-i İngiliz*). Such powder contained 75 percent of saltpeter and 12.5 percent of charcoal and sulfur. With the exception of Selanik, in 1686–89, this combination remained the usual mixture in Istanbul and elsewhere in the 1680s and 1690s.[109] This was also the most common proportion in England and in most of the European countries until the mid-eighteenth century.

Attempts by the superintendent of the *baruthane* at Izmir in the 1690s to improve the mixture and the quality of Ottoman powder clearly illustrate the importance both of local initiatives and of the value of possible acculturation. While the ratios of peter, sulfur and charcoal were already quite satisfactory in the 1680s, in the mid-1690s they were altered in order to produce gunpowder of even higher quality: the mixture contained 77 percent saltpeter, 13.4 percent sulfur and 9.6 percent charcoal. In the course of mixing the various ingredients, the loss was merely 3.8 percent, which was considered a very favorable percentage.[110] Elhac Yahya Ağa, then *nazır* of the powder works, tried, however, to improve the quality of powder further and to manufacture gunpowder of a higher quality than the so-called "English powder" (*İngiltere barutu*), previously produced in Izmir. This he attempted to do by boiling it twice and making further improvements to the mixture ratio. To every 10 *okka* (12.3 kg) of refined saltpeter, he now added just 1.25 *okka* (1.5 kg) of sulfur and just 0.75 *okka* (0.9 kg) of charcoal dust. The new powder manufactured in this way thus contained 83.3 percent saltpeter, 10.4 percent sulfur and 6.3 percent charcoal, and was also called "English powder." Just 11.5 *okka* of gunpowder could now be produced from 10 *okka* of saltpeter. In the course of manufacturing the gunpowder, half an *okka* was lost from every 12 *okka* of gunpowder, that is, the loss amounted to 4.2 percent – a slightly higher percentage than in previous years but still an outstandingly favorable ratio.[111]

It was the Grand Admiral of the Ottoman navy, that is, the Kapudan Pasha who suggested to the superintendent that he change the mixture ratios. This was almost certainly Mezemorta ("Half Dead") Hüseyn Pasha, the well-known reformer of the Ottoman navy, who held this post from 1695 until his death in 1701, and who placed particular emphasis on modernizing the fleet, increasing the number of galleons (*kalyon*), provisioning of boats with weapons and munitions, and improving the quality of weaponry. As the former governor general of Algiers and the commander of the Danube, Black Sea and Mediterranean fleets, he had considerable knowledge

[109] DBŞM 844, p. 6; DBŞM 598, pp. 4–5. The expected loss during the manufacturing process was also 12.5 percent.
[110] MAD 3620, p. 70.
[111] MAD 6880, pp. 24–26. The mixture was the same in the years between 1693 and 1698.

of the naval and weapons technology that the French, Spanish, Austrians and Russians possessed.[112] It was in applying this knowledge that he ordered the *nazır* of the *baruthane* of Izmir to change the mixture ratio for gunpowder and to produce gunpowder of a better quality for the cannons of the fleet. In the second half of the eighteenth century, Ottoman gunpowder was still manufactured according to this formula. At the end of the eighteenth century (1794–95) the Ottomans produced a better quality of gunpowder mixed in the proportions of 76:14:10 that closely followed the then-standard European proportions (75:15:10).[113]

In Western Europe more than twenty types of powder were being produced in the mid-sixteenth century, with the saltpeter content varying between 50 and 85 percent. In the seventeenth and eighteenth centuries the ratios of ingredients, though still varied from country to country, became more similar. These ratios also were much closer to what modern experts consider to be the ideal mixture for gunpowder (74.64 percent saltpeter, 11.85 percent sulfur and 13.51 percent charcoal). The Ottomans followed suit, and the mixture of the Ottoman gunpowder resembled that of the powder produced in France and England.

Of course, it was almost impossible to achieve the desired mixture. At each stage of production (during the refinement, weighing and grinding of each of the three ingredients and again during the mixing, granulation and drying processes) changes in the prescribed ratio might easily occur. Perhaps the weighing process constituted the most critical phase, because if the three ingredients were not properly dried out, then the finished product was bound to be slightly off-mark. It was only at the very end of the eighteenth century that it became known that, depending on atmospheric conditions, charcoal that had been fully dried out could reabsorb moisture from the air at a volume of up to one-eighth of its own weight.[114]

Also, the quality of the finished product could be greatly influenced by the purity of its various constituent elements. The Ottomans, just like their European contemporaries, purified and refined the saltpeter and sulfur several times. Even though the Ottomans' mixture of ingredients resembled that of their European adversaries, by the latter half of the eighteenth century the quality of their gunpowder had declined considerably. This view was shared by both European military experts of the time and the Ottoman authorities themselves.

Conclusion: decline in production, import and early reform

It is obvious from the material provided above that the Ottomans were self-sufficient in the production of gunpowder well into the eighteenth century. The Empire possessed the necessary raw materials and created the various financial and organizational means, as well as the required infrastructure, by which the Ottoman

[112] Cengiz Orhonlu, "Mezemorta Hüseyin Paşa," *İA*, vol. VIII, pp. 205–08.
[113] DBŞM BRİ 18321.
[114] Jenny West, *Gunpowder, Government and War in the Mid-Eighteenth Century* (London, 1991), pp. 175–76.

powder works were capable of manufacturing all the powder needed for the army and the fleet. Production output levels at the *baruthane*s fluctuated according to demand. They were considerably higher in times of war, whereas after major wars and in times of relative peace there was a certain decrease in output in many of the major powder works. The lack of demand might occasionally have caused the abandonment of powder production, as in the case of Bor in the second half of the 1670s, a period which saw no major conflict. More importantly, the central government might have lost oversight over its powder mills and often had no infor-mation regarding production even in the major powder works, as we have seen in the case of Gelibolu in the mid-eighteenth century. The *nazırs* often used their position to generate more income and ignored duties regarding production and record-keeping.[115]

I have previously noted these issues briefly, but the case of the *baruthane* of Izmir will illustrate the problems sufficiently. In the 1690s, the villages in the *sancak*s of Aydın, Saruhan, Menteşe and Sığla were to supply some 98 metric tons (80,000 *okka*) of refined saltpeter to Izmir each year. This amount would have been more than enough to produce the 108 metric tons (2,000 *kantar*) of powder that were required of the *baruthane*. The saltpeter had to be purchased from the *sancak*s mentioned under the supervision of the local *kadı*s, at the official price (30 *akça*s), to which transport costs (about 3 *akça*s per *okka*) had then to be added. Orders concerning purchases to be made in the year 1697–98 were sent out in the middle of the previous year. It soon became obvious, however, that the villages in question were incapable of producing the anticipated quantities. Thus, the *baruthane* received orders to buy the missing quantities on the open market, but the merchants of Izmir did not dispose of this amount of peter and it proved impossible to obtain the required amount from them. The *nazır* thus asked for permission to buy saltpeter from the merchants of Selanik. At the same time, however, he informed the Porte that even if he received such permission, he would still be unable to produce the 108 metric tons of gunpowder due in that year, because at his disposal was just a small fraction of the total funds allocated for the purchase of saltpeter.[116] Despite all these difficulties, the *nazır* finally managed to produce 97.2 metric tons (1,800 *kantar*) of gunpowder annually, which was sufficiently close to the quantity prescribed by Istanbul.

Sources at our disposal suggest that, against all odds, the Empire remained self-sufficient in powder well into the eighteenth century and that it was not until the Russo-Ottoman war of 1768–74 that powder shortages significantly hindered the operational capabilities of the Ottoman armies. This war, however, drew the attention of the Ottoman government to the problems regarding powder manufac-turing and supply. By this time shortage of peter had become critical, which in turn was the result of an increase in the number of unauthorized private gunpowder

---

[115] KK 6691.

[116] MAD 10305, pp. 138–39. In addition, sulfur had to be brought in from Selanik and deliveries of sulfur were often delayed, causing hold-ups in powder production. See MAD 10142, p. 236 and MAD 6880, p. 25.

producers,[117] the evil that had already reached the Spanish powder industry in the 1580s. The discrepancy between the market price and the fixed price paid by the Ottoman authorities to the peter producers also encouraged the latter to conceal their peter from the authorities.[118]

While in the seventeenth century the Ottoman powder mills could manufacture some 761–1,037 metric tons of powder, this amount had fallen to 169 metric tons (3,000 *kantar*) by the second half of the eighteenth century. Although the gunpowder mills at Selanik and Gelibolu were supposed to produce 112.8 metric tons (2,000 *kantar*) of powder each, both gunpowder works had serious difficulties in fulfilling these expectations.[119]

By this time it had become obvious that the domestic supply could not meet the demand. Therefore, from the 1770s Istanbul started to import substantial quantities of powder from Europe. While the amount of powder imported from England in 1770 (12,126 kg or 215 *kantar*)[120] was not yet significant, by the end of the decade imports of European powder amounted to 50 percent of domestic production. In 1778, with the assistance of the Swedish ambassador to Istanbul, the Ottomans bought 84,600 kg (1,500 *kantar*) of gunpowder from Sweden at 55 *guruş* per *kantar*.[121] It seems that the Ottomans purchased further shipments of gunpowder from Sweden. In November 1782, the Imperial Armory received 95,485 kg (1,693 *kantar*) of gunpowder from this source.[122] In 1783 a further shipment of 39,198 kg (695 *kantar*) arrived from England, while the largest ever quantity, 133,386 kg (2,365 *kantar*) of powder, was imported from Spain in that same year.[123] Unlike in the sixteenth and seventeenth centuries, when the import of gunpowder was negligible compared with domestic production,[124] by the end of the eighteenth century import had become a major source of powder without which the provisioning of the Ottoman troops would have been unthinkable.[125]

The problems of gunpowder supply were soon brought to the attention of Selim III (r. 1789–1807), who, as an integral part of his military modernization measures, made attempts to reorganize and modernize gunpowder production in order to improve output and quality. His first attempt, however, ended rather disastrously: in 1791 a Venetian adventurer, who like many of his European fellows

---

[117] In the late 1770s, after the Russo-Ottoman war of 1768–1774, gunpowder was being produced in many places outside the imperial *baruthanes*, such as Filibe, Pazarcık and Karlova. Therefore, between 1776 and 1778, many decrees were issued banning these places from producing gunpowder (CA 45657).

[118] Mehmet Genç, "18. Yüzyılda Osmanlı Ekonomisi ve Savaş," in his *Osmanlı İmparatorluğunda Devlet ve Ekonomi* (İstanbul, 2000), p. 219.

[119] CA 9594 and 9595.   [120] Ibid. 51076

[121] MAD 10398, p. 102.   [122] MAD 10405, p. 99.

[123] CA 13157, 45730; cf. also Çetin, *Barut Sanayi*, p. 137.

[124] On this see my "Merces Prohibitae: The Anglo-Ottoman Trade in War Materials and the Dependence Theory," in Kate Fleet ed., *The Ottomans and the Sea, Oriente Moderno* 20 (81), n.s. 1 (2001), 177–92.

[125] In 1784 it appears that the Porte bought 230 *kantar* of gunpowder from an English boat, paying the English 60 *guruş* per *kantar*. This relatively meager amount indicates that the Porte must have been very short of gunpowder and thus eager to take any opportunity to replenish stocks (CA 46900).

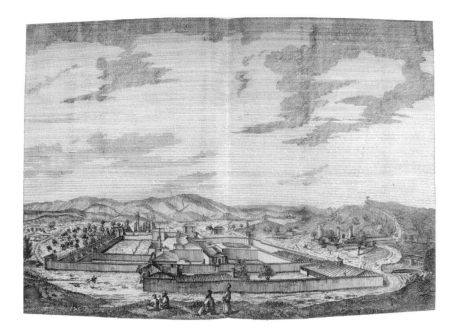

Figure 16 The new gunpowder works at Azadlı (Istanbul). Visited right after its completion by Sultan Selim III, this state-of-the-art gunpowder factory was able annually to produce some 560 metric tons of powder in 1800 leading to the closure of the Empire's older gunpowder works in Gelibolu, Selanik and Istanbul. Mahmud Raif Efendi, *Tableau des nouveaux reglemens de l'empire ottoman*, Constantinople, 1798.

merely purported to be a military expert, persuaded the Sultan to give him large sums of money to cover the cost of his constructing a modern gunpowder mill at Yeşilköy (San Stefano). Having taken the money, the Venetian subsequently failed even to begin construction of the gunpowder mill, and thus the Porte had him arrested and, in January 1791, imprisoned.[126] The same year, renewed consultations were held concerning methods of increasing production and improving the quality of the gunpowder in order that it might reach that of imported English and Dutch gunpowder. With this aim in mind, the authorities merged the administration of the Empire's three major *baruthane*s in Istanbul, Gelibolu and Selanik, and appointed Tevkii Ali Raik Efendi as superintendent of the new conglomerate. Raik Efendi was instructed to modernize production, so that 282 metric tons (5,000 *kantar*) of high-quality English- and Dutch-type powder could be produced every year in the three major gunpowder works. Since, however, the reorganization failed to bring about the expected result, in 1793 the supervision of the gunpowder works was entrusted to the former treasury chief (*defterdar*), Mehmed Şerif Efendi.[127]

[126] Stanford J. Shaw, *Between Old and New: The Ottoman Empire under Sultan Selim III, 1789–1807* (Cambridge, MA, 1971), p. 143.
[127] Ibid., and Erdoğan, "İstanbul Baruthaneleri," 125.

Figure 17 The interior of the Azadlı gunpowder works shows a modern and
well-organized facility. The new-type mill-structure of this hydraulic *baruthane* was made
by Arakil Efendi and was considered at the time to be a masterpiece of functionality.
Mahmud Raif Efendi, *Tableau des nouveaux reglemens de l'empire ottoman*,
Constantinople, 1798.

By the late eighteenth century, the Porte considered horse-driven gunpowder
works to be incapable of ensuring uniform quality because of the differences in
the strength of the animals. For this reason, Mehmed Şerif Efendi was instructed
to search for a place where a water-powered new factory could be built. In addition to quality, another advantage of the hydraulic mill was greater efficiency:
water could be used instead of animals, whose care and replacement – particularly
given the high rates of mortality – amounted to a substantial share of operating
costs. The use of water energy would allow for the dismissal of half the workers,
leading to further savings. A suitable site for the new *baruthane* was found in
Küçükçekmece, to the north of a lake by the same name. The site was close to the
Sea of Marmara, which facilitated the transport of raw materials and gunpowder by
ship, and there was also a local stream for generating power. Since there were no
settled communities in the chosen vicinity, the new gunpowder factory was safer
than its predecessors, endangering neither Istanbul nor other communities. Thus, it
was here that Mehmed Şerif Efendi built the new and up-to-date *baruthane* whose
new-type mill-structure was made by Arakil (Erakil) Efendi and was considered
at the time to be a masterpiece of functionality. The mills were operated by water
flowing along a newly built canal that connected the factory with the stream. In

order to ensure a steady supply of water, Mehmed Şerif Efendi also arranged for the construction of a reservoir, whose waters could even be used for extinguishing fires, thereby increasing the security of the factory. The construction of the powder factory, known as the *baruthane* of Azadlı, was completed within several months and production began in 1794.

It seems that the authorities were satisfied with production output levels of the reconstructed *baruthane* in Istanbul (Bakırköy) and that of Azadlı. By the end of the eighteenth century, the gunpowder works at Azadlı were able to manufacture sufficient quantities of gunpowder of much better quality,[128] and thus the other gunpowder works in the Empire (the *baruthane*s at Gelibolu, Selanik and Istanbul) were closed down – though, it seems, only temporarily.[129] In 1800, the Azadlı gunpowder works apparently produced 564 metric tons (10,000 *kantar*) of gunpowder of good quality,[130] although there were some difficulties with regard to the supply of sufficient amounts of saltpeter. By the end of the eighteenth century, the Empire had become once again largely self-sufficient in the production of gunpowder. Mahmud Raif Efendi claimed that by merely increasing the number of mills and the number of day laborers, production output could have reached 1,692–2,256 metric tons (30,000–40,000 *kantar*) a year.[131] No doubt with some exaggeration and with the intention of impressing foreign observers, he wrote that the gunpowder produced in the *baruthane* was eight times stronger than any other Ottoman gunpowder. With satisfaction he added: "We are no longer dependent on foreign gunpowder, our stores are full, and there is enough for military campaigns too; indeed, we have even started to export."[132]

[128] Ekmeleddin İhsanoğlu, "Ottoman Science in the Classical Period and Early Contacts with European Science and Technology," in Ekmeleddin İhsanoğlu ed., *Transfer of Modern Science and Technology to the Muslim World* (İstanbul, 1992), pp. 28–29; Shaw, *Between Old and New*, pp. 143–44.
[129] CA 45774; Erdoğan, "İstanbul Baruthaneleri," pp. 130–31; Shaw, *Between Old and New*, p. 144; S. Mübahat Kütükoğlu, "Baruthane-i Amire," *TDVİA*, vol. V, p. 96.
[130] CA 9756.
[131] Mahmud Raif Efendi, *Osmanlı İmparatorluğun'da Yeni Nizamların Cedveli*. Trans. and ed. Arslan Terzioğlu and Hüsrev Hatemi (Istanbul, n.d.), p. 17; Erdoğan, "İstanbul Baruthaneleri," 130–31; Shaw, *Between Old and New*, p. 144.
[132] Mahmud Raif Efendi, *Osmanlı İmparatorluğun'da Yeni Nizamların Cedveli*, 17. Major renovations of the *baruthane* were undertaken in 1819 and in 1836. Together with the gunpowder works at Bakırköy, the factory was considered one of the greatest military-industrial plants of the Empire. In the Russo-Ottoman war of 1877–78, Russian forces destroyed the factory, and the Porte never rebuilt the works (*Dünden Bugüne İstanbul Ansiklopedisi*, 69).

CHAPTER 6

Munitions and ordnance industries

The study of Ottoman munitions and ordnance industries is of outmost importance for understanding Ottoman military capabilities. In the general literature there are three related theories regarding this subject: (1) the notion of the Ottomans' supposed inability, from the late sixteenth century onward, to cast ordnance in quantities sufficient to meet the Empire's pressing military needs and the related idea of Ottoman dependence on foreign supplies of raw materials and ordnance; (2) associated with this is the view of Ottoman giant guns, that is, the claim that because of their lack of mass-production capabilities the Ottomans continued to cast a handful of large cannons instead of following the general European trend which, from the mid- or late fifteenth century onward, was characterized by the mass production of medium- and small-caliber guns; and finally, (3) the assertion that Ottoman artillery pieces were technologically inferior to those manufactured in Europe.[1] A cursory look at the literature on the above views will show that such assertions are based on random evidence, usually gained from contemporaneous European and Ottoman narrative sources. Archival records, most notably the account books of Ottoman mines, ironworks and cannon foundries, however, present a rather different picture, one that suggests much greater self-sufficiency regarding the production and supply of munitions and ordnance in the Empire. Thus, the primary aim of this chapter is to present and analyze these hitherto unused sources in order to provide the reader with sounder ground from which some general conclusions can be drawn. On the basis of this new archival material, the chapter not only challenges the above theories, but for the first time in the related literature seeks to give a comprehensive evaluation of the Ottoman ammunition and ordnance industries by concentrating on both quantitative and qualitative characteristics of Ottoman artillery. I start with an overview of the availability of strategic ore deposits and their exploitation. Because of the lack of any comprehensive work on Ottoman mining,[2] it is impossible at this stage to estimate the production levels of the Empire's copper and iron mines whose main

---

[1] See Introduction and chapter 3.
[2] The literature regarding Ottoman mining is mainly concerned with legal and social issues, and has almost no data on output levels. One of the pioneering works in this regard is Robert Anhegger, *Beiträge zur Geschichte des Bergbaus im osmanischen Reich* (Berne, 1945). Ahmed Refik's *Osmanlı*

consumers were, apart from the naval shipyards, the Ottoman cannon foundries and ironworks. Therefore, in order to gain a clearer impression regarding the possible sources and the supply of copper used in the foundries, as well as to appreciate possible production levels of the Ottoman iron mines and ironworks that manufactured the bulk of ammunition the Ottoman armed forces and navy consumed, it is necessary to present some preliminary data concerning the output levels of the Ottoman copper and iron mines, however incomplete they may seem. The second part of the chapter is concerned with the mass production of cannons. Since chapter 3 provides a comparative classification of Ottoman guns and discusses their main characteristics, those results are used, with additional statistical data, for further qualification with regards to the composition of the Ottoman ordnance.

Strategic ore deposits and mines

Unlike many of its rivals, the Ottoman Empire possessed rich ore deposits that were crucial in establishing domestic weapons production capabilities. While in the early modern era the Ottomans were self-sufficient in almost all the raw materials necessary for their weapons and ammunition industries, from time to time they were also successful in obtaining ore from abroad. In this regard tin – the only metal of which the Empire lacked sufficient deposits – assumed especially great significance, since the majority of Ottoman cannons were cast of bronze, a copper-tin alloy. Tin, along with copper and iron ore, was considered *merces prohibitae* or prohibited goods in Europe, exportation of which to the enemies of Christendom was strictly prohibited. However, due to political divisions among the European states and because of the high profits traditionally involved in the illicit trade in weaponry and war materials, the Ottomans were able to obtain such commodities from Europe. Despite repeated Papal bulls that forbade the export of strategic goods and weapons to Islamdom, threatening those who broke the embargo with excommunication and anathema, there were always European merchants who were eager to gain profit by supplying prohibited goods to the "infidels."[3] Except for

---

Devrinde Türkiye Madenleri (967–1200) (Istanbul, 1931) is still a valuable source that contains several important imperial decrees from the Mühimme Collection of the Ottoman Archives and has long been the main source for historians on Ottoman mining. In contrast to mining in Ottoman Anatolia, a subject that has only recently received some attention (see Fahrettin Tızlak *Osmanlı Döneminde Keban-Ergani Yöresinde Madencilik (1775–1850)* [Ankara, 1997]), the Balkan mines, especially the silver mines, are better studied. See, for example, Vasilje Simić, *Istoriski razvoj našeg rudarstva* (Belgrade, 1951); Mihailo Dinić, *Za istoriju rudarstva u srednjevekovnoj Srbiji i Bosni* (2 vols., Belgrade, 1955, 1962) and Adem Handžić, "Rudarstvo u Bosni XV do XVII stolječe," *İFM* 41, 1–4 (1985), 321–60; "Rudnici u Bosni u drugoj polovini XV stolječa," *POF* 26 (1976), 7–41; Rhoads Murphey, "Silver Production in Rumelia According to an Official Ottoman Report Circa 1600," *Südost–Forschungen* 39 (1980), 75–104, and the literature cited there. The best short summary to date is Rhoads Murphey, "Ma'din 3. Mineral Exploitation in the Ottoman Empire," *EI*, vol. V, pp. 973–85.

[3] Prohibition of the supply of weaponry and raw materials of military importance was not, of course, an invention of the early modern states. It was already a practice at the time of the Roman Empire,

tin, however, the Ottomans possessed abundant ore deposits within the borders of their Empire, and imported war material played an insignificant role vis-à-vis domestic ore deposits.

Several of the ore deposits found on the territory of the Empire had been mined in ancient times, under the Selçuks and the Byzantines. The Ottomans, too, placed special emphasis on the exploitation of these sites. Ore deposits – especially those containing silver and gold – were the principal targets of Ottoman imperial policy in the fourteenth and fifteenth centuries, and the attempts at conquering the rich silver and gold mines of Serbia and Bosnia started as early as the reign of Murad I (r. 1362–89).[4] Of these, Srebrenica (Ottoman Srebreniçe) in present-day Bosnia-Herzegovina, a mining center whose name is a reminder of its principal ore (*srebro* or silver), and Novo Brdo (New Hill, Ottoman Novaberda) in Kosovo were of special importance. Both mining centers were inhabited by Sase, that is, miners from Saxony, who in the thirteenth and fourteenth centuries had introduced the Saxon mining technology and terminology to the Balkans. Around 1450, the mines of Novo Brdo were producing about 6,000 kg of silver, known as *argentum glame* (an alloy of silver containing one-sixth gold), per annum, whereas the yearly silver output of the mines of Srebrenica is estimated at 1,200 kg around the same time.[5] Although Balkan historians maintain that the Ottoman conquest brought major disruptions to the indigenous mining industries in the Balkans, recent research has shown that the question is more complex. In fact, the Ottomans were very much interested in continuing the exploitation of existing mining centers,[6] and local Ottoman officials in the Rumelian and Anatolian provinces of the Empire were responsible for identifying old mines and for discovering and exploiting new sites containing ore deposits. While the output of the Balkan silver mines had somewhat declined by the end of the sixteenth century, partly as a consequence of the influx of cheaper silver from the Americas, the mines of Serbia and Thrace continued to produce large quantities of silver until about the 1630s. The effects of American silver in the Mediterranean world seem to have been overstated in earlier studies. The operation of several of the Ottoman mines in the Balkans was discontinued only under the reign of Sultan Ibrahim I (1640–48) as a result largely of centralizing monetary reforms. Ottoman sources indicate that we cannot speak about an overall decline in production levels of the Balkan mines until the 1630s and 1640s. Despite the negative effects of the influx of American silver, felt more

and had been formulated in the Codex Justinianus. Rival Christian and Muslim states in the Middle Ages also maintained such embargoes against each other. Embargoed goods, mentioned under the terms of *merces prohibitae, merces inlicitae* in Latin, and *memnu'at* in Arabic sources, included, among other things, guns, metal, timber suitable for the building of fortresses and ships, canvas, horses and other draught animals, servants and food. See Gábor Ágoston, "Merces Prohibitae: The Anglo-Ottoman Trade in War Materials and the Dependence Theory," Kate Fleet ed., *The Ottomans and the Sea, Oriente Moderno* 20 (81), n.s. 1 (2001), 177–92.

[4] Halil İnalcık and Donald Quataert eds., *An Economic and Social History of the Ottoman Empire, 1300–1914* (Cambridge, 1994), p. 58.

[5] Nenad Lockic, "Mining in Medieval Serbia: The *Sasi* Story," *Slovo: The Newsletter of the Slavic Interest Group* 8, 3 (37) (Spring 2003), http://slavic.freeservers.com/slovo/news30.html.

[6] Murphey, "Ma'din," p. 976.

drastically in Europe than in the Ottoman Empire, some of the Balkan mines still produced more notable quantities of silver around 1600 than prior to Ottoman rule. This was the case, for example, in the Srebreniçe mines, which produced some 2,534 kg of silver in 1585, that is, twice the amount of the estimated output in 1450. In other mining centers, however, output fell radically, like in Novaberda, whose mines produced only 1,034 and 1,285 kg of silver in 1582 and 1615, respectively; that is, only one-sixth to one-fourth of their 1450 output level. The overall silver production of the sub-Danubian region around 1600 is estimated at 50,515 kg (1,624,077 troy ounces), which is more than one-half of the total silver output of the Central European mines around 1530, that is, during the peak of their production.[7] Judging from these data, it is more accurate to talk about regional reorganizations and shifts in production levels than about overall decline regarding the sixteenth-century Balkan mines under Ottoman rule.[8]

In addition to silver and gold, which were crucial for generating more cash to pay the growing armed forces and bureaucracy of an expanding Empire, copper, iron and lead were also greatly valued as essential raw materials of the Ottoman ordnance industry. When in 1391 Bayezid I (r. 1389–1402) defeated Süleyman Pasha, the ruler of Kastamonu, the Ottomans seized the copper deposits of Kastamonu, southwest of Sinop. Although these territories were lost after the battle of Ankara in 1402, the ruler of Sinop, İsfendiyaroğlu, ceded the revenues of the copper mines of Kastamonu and that of Sinop to Mehmed I (r. 1411–21) in 1417. However, it was not until 1423 that the Ottomans established firmer control over the copper mines of Kastamonu under Murad II (r. 1421–51), who conquered the region from İsfendiyaroğlu.[9] In the fourteenth and fifteenth centuries, the copper deposits of Kastamonu were well known not only in Asia Minor, but also in Europe, and Italian merchants traded with Kastamonu copper in the Levant on a regular basis.[10]

The conquest of mines and the control over ore deposits remained a major objective of Ottoman military campaigns in the sixteenth and seventeenth centuries, too. An Ottoman spy report from 1583 claimed that the estate of Murány in Gömör county in northern Hungary "was so rich in iron ore that wherever people started to dig they found rich iron mines and iron ore in abundant quantities." In the neighboring Csetnek, the report continued, "iron ore of the best quality was to be found in such abundant quantities that there existed hardly any mine that possessed so much iron ore." That the spy report did not exaggerate the richness of the iron mines concerned can be seen from an official opinion, prepared by the Chamber

---

[7] Murphey, "Silver Production in Rumelia."

[8] Declining figures do not necessarily indicate declining output levels, for these figures might simply reflect the results of administrative reorganizations. When the boundaries of these units changed so did the number of mines belonging to them.

[9] Speros Vryonis, "The Question of the Byzantine Mines," *Speculum* 37 (1962), 9–10; Colin Imber, *The Ottoman Empire, 1300–1481* (Istanbul, 1990), pp. 38, 88, 96.

[10] In Selçuk Anatolia, thriving copper workshops operated in Konya, Mardin, Hasankeyf, Diyarbekir, Cizre, Siirt, Harput, Erzincan and Erzurum. See İ. Gündağ Kayaoğlu, "Bakır Kap Yapım Teknikleri, I. Dövme Tekniği," *Folklor ve Etnografya Araştırmaları* (Istanbul, 1984), p. 217.

of Besztercebánya (Banská Bystrica), that compared the iron mines of Gömör County to that of Erzberg in Styria, and claimed that they could supply ore to at least a hundred furnaces.[11] Since the Ottomans could not capture the mines, they destroyed most of the furnaces in the Murány valley and burned down the Dobsina ironworks in 1556, following their conquest of the Hungarian fort of Fülek that guarded access to the mines. Subsequently, the remaining ironworks of the region had to supply the Ottoman fortress of Fülek with iron bars and tools. It seems that in the latter part of the sixteenth century the town of Rozsnyó acted as a mediator between the Ottoman garrison and the ironworks, supplying the Ottomans not only with iron bars, shovels, hoes, chains and nails, but occasionally also with cannons.[12] The access to the ironworks and their products became easier from the 1640s when the whole Murány valley, Csetnek and its environs came under Ottoman rule.[13]

Another example that shows that the Ottomans treated the mines as strategic targets as late as the end of the sixteenth century is recorded by Ibrahim Peçevi, the Ottoman chronicler who spent a good deal of his life on the Hungarian frontier. Writing around 1640, Peçevi claimed that during the 1596 Hungarian campaign the Ottomans decided to besiege and capture Eger, instead of Komárom further to the west, because they wanted to seize the mines lying beyond Eger in northern Hungary.[14]

Similarly to their European opponents, the Ottomans also protected the ore deposits of their realms. They regarded copper, iron, and lead – along with saltpeter and sulfur – as mineral resources of strategic significance. Following medieval Islamic practice, Istanbul declared these mineral resources prohibited goods or *memnu eşya* (*memnu olan meta* from the Arabic *memnu'at*), and forbade their exportation to foreign countries.[15] In his handbook on Islamic law, Molla Hüsrev, Mehmed the Conqueror's famous Grand Mufti, considered arms, horses and iron as prohibited goods even in peace time, since these commodities, if in the hands of the Empire's enemies, could have been used for waging war against Muslims.[16] Export prohibitions were incorporated into the peace treaties concluded with foreign states, as well as into the passports issued to foreign travelers.[17] Ottoman

[11] Gusztáv Heckenast, "A török hódítás és a felső-magyarországi vasipar," in Péter Nagybánky and Gábor Németh eds., *V. Kézművesipartörténeti Szimpózium* (Veszprém, 1985), p. 45.

[12] On at least one occasion, the town of Rozsnyó acquired two cannons from Kassa, the seat of the commander of the Habsburg forces in northeastern Hungary, and sent them to the *sancakbeyi* of Fülek.

[13] Heckenast, "A török hódítás," pp. 46–47. On Fülek see Markus Köhbach, *Die Eroberung von Fülek durch die Osmanen 1554* (Vienna, 1994).

[14] İbrahim Peçevi (Peçuylu), *Tarih-i Peçevi* (2 vols., Istanbul, 1283/1866–67), vol. II, p. 191.

[15] The list of prohibited goods in the Ottoman Empire is rather lengthy and includes grain (*tereke*), arms (*yarak*), gunpowder (*barut*), saltpeter (*güherçile*), sulfur (*kükürt*), copper (*nuhas*), iron (*demir*), lead (*kurşun*), cotton (*penbe*), cotton yarn (*rişte-i penbe*), beeswax (*balmumu*), different kinds of leather, canvas (*kirpas-i sefine*), tallow (*don yağı*), pitch (*zift*), horses (*at*), etc. See Ágoston, "Merces Prohibitae," 182.

[16] Molla Hüsrev, *Gurrer ve Dürer Tercümesi* (2 vols., Istanbul, 1980), vol. II, p. 11.

[17] See, for instance, J. M. Mordtmann, "Zwei osmanische Paßbriefe aus dem XVI. Jahrhundert," in Friedlich Kraelitz and Paul Wittek eds., *Mitteilungen zur osmanischen Geschichte* (Vienna, 1922;

craftsmen working with such strategic materials were closely scrutinized. Coppersmiths who wanted to purchase copper ore from the mines had to prove their good intentions, presenting letters of accreditation regarding their legitimate business from the *kadı*s of their hometowns.[18] Merchants of the Empire's vassals were also prohibited from trading with goods designated as *memnu eşya*,[19] and even exporting such commodities to some Muslim states was banned.[20] The Ottoman authorities tried to block the export of strategic raw materials and other prohibited goods to enemy territories (*Darü'l-harb*), and watched their borders carefully, but it was impossible to intercept all shipments.[21] It was particularly difficult to do so when the Ottoman authorities faced organized attempts at mass imports, especially on the part of their eastern enemy, Safavid Persia, which lacked most of the raw materials necessary for its own domestic ordnance and ammunition industries. This was the case, for example, in September 1568, when some 400–500 Iranian merchants are reported to have purchased large quantities of copper around Kastamonu and Küre, and also in Istanbul, willing to pay well over the market price for this strategic ore.[22] Although local officials occasionally managed to confiscate sizeable quantities of copper already bought by Persian merchants,[23] given the porous nature of the eastern military frontier the latter must have been successful in obtaining significant quantities of copper ore.

Ottoman iron ore and finished goods made of iron were also sought-after commodities in Persia. Around 1570, for example, the Shah of Persia had at least three representatives (*halife*s) in the Divriği area, who were all local Ottoman residents and subjects of the Sultan. Their task was to supply the Shah with horseshoes and other goods. One of them is reported to have been able to procure more than 100,000 horseshoes for the Safavids annually. Angered by the smuggling of what was considered *memnu eşya* of obvious strategic significance, Istanbul instructed its local officials secretly to assassinate the Shah's man. Although the Porte usually did not refrain from persecuting and openly killing Safavid agents, this time

reprint Osnabrück, 1972), pp. 177–201; S. A. Skilliter, *William Harborne and the Trade with Turkey 1578–1582: A Documentary Study of the First Anglo-Ottoman Relations* (Oxford, 1977), pp. 22, 56. A similar ban concerning the Habsburg ambassador is mentioned in an order issued to the *kadı*s along the road from Istanbul to Buda, on October 31, 1574 (MD 26, no. 289).

[18] Suraiya Faroqhi, *Towns and Townsmen of Ottoman Anatolia: Trade, Crafts and Food Production in an Urban Setting, 1520–1650* (Cambridge, 1984), p. 181.

[19] MD 26, nos. 273, 291, 296, imperial orders concerning Transylvania, an Ottoman vassal. Occasionally, Istanbul did grant permission for its vassals. See, e.g., MD 5, p. 483, no. 1170, which allowed the men of the *voyvoda* of Moldavia to take out from the Empire 27,000 kg (500 *kantar*) of lead, purchased in Istanbul, for a newly built bathhouse in Jassy. Despite various decrees the shipment was stopped in Semendire, and Istanbul had to instruct the *emin* of the local port not to interfere. See MD 5, p. 546, no. 1497.

[20] MD 7, p. 483, no, 1396, an imperial order prohibiting the export of copper, silver, lead and muskets to India; MD 27, p. 174, nos, 396, 397, imperial decrees banning the exportation of copper and lead to Yemen and India.

[21] MD 5, p. 425, no. 1130, order to the *beylerbeyi* of Buda banning the export of horses, leather, leather goods and other prohibited goods to enemy territory.

[22] MD 7, p. 737, no. 2021; ibid., p. 763, no. 2086.

[23] MD 7, p. 793, no. 2168, regarding the confiscation of more than 8,300 kg (82 *yük*) and 8 ingots (*külçe*) of copper.

Istanbul took care to cover its operation and suggested that the Shah's man be attacked on the road, so that the targeted assassination of the enemy of the state would appear as ordinary highway robbery, thus not affecting Ottoman–Safavid relations, which were relatively calm in the early 1570s.[24]

In the period under discussion, the two basic forms in which Istanbul operated the Empire's mines were the same as those that the government used in saltpeter and gunpowder production, first, *emanet*, that is, direct administration through state-appointed superintendents, and second, *iltizam*, which meant farming out the right to mining for shorter periods (typically three to six years) to investors and entrepreneurs.[25] Similarly to the saltpeter and gunpowder works, the mines and furnaces operated seasonally. Most of the work took place during summer, usually in the six months from May 6 through November 7.[26] The miners worked normally in two-hour shifts and only five days a week because of the extremely hard nature of the job. Regarding the Küre copper mines, Katib Çelebi noted that since the mines lacked ventilation most slaves who were working in the mines looked like corpses rather than living men.[27] By using revolving shifts the mines could be operated on a twenty-four-hour basis.[28]

While the methods by which the Ottoman authorities exploited the Empire's mines were similar to those employed in the saltpeter and gunpowder works, and are familiar to the reader from the previous chapters, in terms of the numbers of workers involved, the mining industry outpaced the gunpowder works. It is especially true if we take into consideration the workers employed in the smelting works attached to the major mining centers. These plants were undoubtedly among the largest military-industrial complexes the Ottoman authorities had to operate and oversee. While the mining community in the Küre mines is estimated at between 130 and 150 workers in the early 1580s,[29] and that at the Pravişte works in 1702 at around 200,[30] if one counts all the officials charged with running and overseeing the mines (entrepreneurs/*mültezim*, intendants/*emin*, supervisors/*mutemed*, scribes/*katib*, scribes of expenditures/*sarf*, seal-bearers/*mühürdar-i hazine*, accountants/*şumari*, weighers/*vezzan*, guards), the mine and furnace operators (*küreci* and *fırıncı/furuncu*), smelters (*kalcı*), as well as the wood-cutters (*baltacı* and *teberci*), wood-carriers (*oduncu*) and charcoal-burners (*kömürcü*) living in nearby villages, and the hundreds of slaves and military auxiliaries (*yaya* and *müsellem*) charged with transporting the ore, soil and wood fuel, the total number employed in the mines and related activities must have been considerably

[24] Faroqhi, *Towns*, p. 188.   [25] Murphey, "Ma'din," p. 974.

[26] Contemporaneous Ottomans considered the period between November 8 and May 5 a season unsuitable for mining, transportation and sailing. Thus, the mines usually operated only for six months, between Ruz-i Hızır (May 6) and Ruz-i Kasım (November 7). This was the case, among others, in Banaluka in the 1680s, in Pravişte in 1702, and in the Keban-Ergani mines in the eighteenth century. See MAD 683, p. 14; DBŞM 483, p. 150; Tızlak, p. 108, respectively. Murphey ("Ma'din," p. 976), however, contends that the work in the mines took place during the seven and a half months from Nevruz (March 21) through Ruz-i Kasım.

[27] Faroqhi, *Towns*, p. 180.   [28] Murphey, "Ma'din," p. 976.   [29] Faroqhi, *Towns*, p. 176.

[30] DBŞM 483, p. 150, gives the number of workers as 198, not counting day laborers and auxiliaries.

higher. This is supported by data relating to other mines and smelting works. In 1684 the Banaluka mines employed 240 wood-cutters, 180 charcoal-burners, 40 extractors of iron ore (*cevher-keşan*), 35 woodmen working with ax (*teberciyan*), 18 soil-carriers (*toprakçıyan*), two families (*baştina*s) of shovellers, 50 ordinary workers, and an unspecified number of pit workers, swelling the total number of employees to more than 560.[31]

Copper for the cannon foundries

Copper (*nuhas*) was of especially great significance because most of the cannons in the Ottoman Empire – except for the smallest-caliber guns such as *prangı*, *eynek*, *saçma* and the like – were cast of bronze, whose main constituent is copper. The Empire possessed rich copper ore deposits in its Balkan and Anatolian provinces.[32] In the sixteenth and seventeenth centuries, the most important copper mines in Asia Minor were those of Küre-i mamure (also referred to in the sources as Küre-i nuhas), between the Black Sea port of İnebahtı and Kastamonu in the *sancak* of Kastamonu.[33] Substantial quantities of copper were mined also in Gümüşhane, some 60 kilometers southwest of Trabzon, but references to these mines come mainly from the late seventeenth century. In the eighteenth century, the production in Küre declined, while the Ergani-Keban region, northwest of Diyarbekir, had become the foremost place for copper mining. In the Balkans, copper ore was excavated in considerable quantities in Kratova (Kratovo, east of Skopje in present-day Macedonia),[34] and Maydanek (Majdanek in eastern Serbia).[35] In addition, at least until the mid-sixteenth century copper was mined in Foyniça (Fojinica) and Kreşevo (Kreševo, northwest of Sarajevo in Bosnia); however, it seems that later (in 1575 and 1604) mining of copper continued only in the latter site and only in small quantities.[36] The Hungarian copper mines that produced copper of exceptionally good quality lay outside Ottoman Hungary and copper usually had to be sent from Istanbul whenever bronze cannons were cast in Buda. However, it

---

[31] MAD 628, p. 13, summarized by Halil İnalcık "The Socio-Political Effects of the Diffusion of Fire-arms in the Middle East," in V. J. Parry and M. E. Yapp eds., *War, Technology and Society in the Middle East* (London, 1975), p. 213.

[32] According to a comprehensive list compiled by the Turkish Mineral Research and Exploration Institute, some 500 sites with copper deposits were to be found in the Republic of Turkey around 1981. See N. Apaydın and N. Erseçen, *Türkiyenin Bilinen Maden ve Mineral Kaynakları* (Ankara, 1981), pp. 4–7. Several of these mines had been known from ancient times. See P. S. de Jesus, *The Development of Prehistoric Mining and Metallurgy in Anatolia* (2 vols., Oxford, 1980), vol. II, pp. 211–76, and map 8.

[33] Refik, *Türkiye Madenleri*, p. 9. Talat Mümtaz Yaman, "Küre Bakır Madenine Dair Vesikalar," *Tarih Vesikaları* 1, 4 (1941), 266. Copper from Kastamonu was considered of high quality and its price was higher (60 *akça* per *okka*) than that of the copper mined in Bosnia (55 *akça* per *okka*). See Mübahat S. Kütükoğlu, *Osmanlılarda Narh Müessesesi ve 1640 Tarihli Narh Defteri* (Istanbul, 1983), p. 195.

[34] MD 28, p. 299.

[35] Vernon J. Parry, "Materials of War in the Ottoman Empire," in M. A. Cook ed., *Studies in the Economic History of the Middle East* (London, 1970), p. 225.

[36] Handžić, "Rudarstvo," 326.

was impossible to seal off the mineral resources of Hungary from the Ottomans who, from time to time, managed to acquire sizeable quantities of copper as can be seen from several transactions in 1559, in which the Ottomans acquired 51,891 kg (882.5 *mázsa* or Hungarian quintals).[37] That it was not an isolated case and that Hungarian copper found its way even to Anatolia can be seen from an order dated 1576–77, in which Istanbul instructed its local officials to prevent the sale of Hungarian copper in Asia Minor, because the cheaper Hungarian copper hurt the business of the entrepreneurs (*mültezim*) of the Küre copper mines.[38]

Although there is no comprehensive study of Ottoman mining available in any language, some sense of production capacity can be gained from the data in Table 6.1 regarding some of the Anatolian mining centers. As can be seen, estimates in kilograms are often uncertain because of the great variations in Ottoman units of weight according to locality and time. Despite these difficulties, it is safe to say that the Anatolian mines supplied only a fraction of the copper ore needed for casting cannons for the Sultan's military machine. A significant portion of the mines' output was used to satisfy other war industry-related demands and was consumed by the flourishing copper works of the Empire. As an example for the first category one can mention the case of the Küre craftsmen who in the spring of 1572 prepared forty-seven kettles and seventeen kettle bottoms for the saltpeter works using up 9,800 kg (7,976 *okka*) of copper.[39] While it is difficult to estimate the amount of copper that the hundreds of coppersmiths, itinerant tinkers and kettle-makers used up, judging from the great number of cities known for their copper works, one can assume that the quantity was not insignificant.[40]

However, the main consumers of Anatolian copper were the Ottoman cannon foundries, above all the Istanbul Imperial Foundry. In 1695, the Istanbul foundry requested 54,000 kg of copper from Gümüşhane,[41] whereas in 1697 it received some 32,800 kg (26,693 *okka*) of copper from the Gümüşhane mines in three shipments via Trabzon and the Black Sea. At the same time, an additional 31,556 kg (25,680 *okka*) of copper came from Kastamonu, making the total copper shipments of the Istanbul foundry from these two sources 64,356 kg (52,373 *okka*).[42]

These shipments, however, constituted only a fraction of the copper needed for the Istanbul foundry, for which substantial quantities were stored in the city. Huge stockpiles, ready to be sent to the foundry, were kept in the underground stores in front of the royal ward of the Sultan's Palace that are often referred to in the sources as "storerooms for raw copper" (*nuhas-i ham mahzeni*), in the private garden of the Sultan (*Has Bahçe*) and in the Imperial Armory. Between June 27, 1684 and March 6, 1685 no less than 849,150 kg (15,725 *kantar*) of copper was delivered to

---

[37] Parry, "Materials of War," p. 225.   [38] Faroqhi, *Towns*, p. 179.

[39] Faroqhi, *Towns*, p. 180; Refik, *Türkiye Madenleri*, p. 10.

[40] In Ottoman Asia Minor, the copper workshops and coppersmiths of Antep, Maraş, Mardin, Diyarbekir, Siirt, Malatya, Elaziğ, Erzurum, Trabzon, Giresun, Ordu, Sivas, Tokat, Kayseri, Çankırı, Çorum, Amasya, Kastamonu, Gerede, Konya, Burdur, Denizli, Afyon, Kütahya, Balikesir and Bursa were renowned for their artifacts and utensils produced for everyday markets. See Kayaoğlu, "Bakır Kap Yapım Teknikleri," p. 219.

[41] Refik, *Türkiye Madenleri*, p. 21.   [42] MAD 2730, p. 10.

Table 6.1 *Copper production in Asia Minor and copper shipments to the Tophane*

Mines/region	Date	Production or shipment	Production or shipment in kg
Gümüşhane	1695	1,000 *kantar*	54,000 (O)
Gümüşhane	1697	26,693 *okka*	32,800 (S)
Gümüşhane	1712–14	31,263 *okka*	40,104 (S)
Gümüşhane	1737–38	82,472 *okka*	105,795 (S)
Gümüşhane	1743–44	40,597 *okka*	52,077 (S)
Gümüşhane	1744–45	128,957 *okka*	165,426 (S)
Gümüşhane	1746–47	79,678 *okka*	102,211 (S)
Gümüşhane	1747–48	69,510 *okka*	89,167 (S)
Gümüşhane	1751–52	44,370 *okka*	56,917 (S)
Gümüşhane	1757–58	174,001 *okka*	213,812 (S)
Gümüşhane	1784–85	135,740 *okka*	174,127 (S)
Küre	1513	28,638 *okka*	35,190 (P)
Küre	1582	26,228 *men*	193,300–302,147 (P)[a]
Küre	1670	3,500 *batman*	26,939 (P)
Küre	late 17th century	20,000 *batman*	142,000–221,184 (P)[b]
Küre-i Kastamonu	1697	25,680 *okka*	31,556 (S)
Küre	1712–14	53,978 *okka*	69,243 (S)
Küre-i Kastamonu	1737–38	17,840 *okka*	22,885 (S)
Küre-i Kastamonu	1743–44	18,122 *okka*	23,247 (S)
Küre-i Kastamonu	1744–45	17,689 *okka*	22,692 (S)
Küre-i Kastamonu	1746–47	7,111 *okka*	9,122 (S)
Küre-i Kastamonu	1747–48	12,413 *okka*	15,923 (S)
Küre-i Kastamonu	1751–52	26,162 *okka*	33,561 (S)
Küre-i Kastamonu	1757–58	11,763 *okka*	15,089 (S)
Küre-i Kastamonu	1758–59	20,575 *okka*	26,394 (S)
Black Sea region	18th century	12,000 quintals	676,800[c]
Black Sea region	1785–86	431,466 *okka*	553,485[d]
Ergani	1780		6,400,000 (P)
Ergani	1792–93	200,000 *batman*	1,539,360 (P)
Ergani	1793–94	107,000 *batman*	823,558 (P)
Asia Minor	1799	3–4 million *okka*	3,848,400–5,131,200 (P)

Notes: [a] I calculated the minimum figure with the 6-*okka men* (cf. Notes on weights and measurements). The maximum figure is from Faroqhi, *Towns*, p. 179, who assumes that the *men* consisted of 9 *okka* (of 1.28 kg) and thus puts the output at 302,147 kg, which, however, seems too high a figure in comparison with other data.

[b] Faroqhi, *Towns*, p. 179, based on Katib Çelebi whose data probably relate to the late seventeenth century. The first figure in kg is calculated with 1 *batman* = 7.1 kg; the second is that of Faroqhi who follows Katib Çelebi, who claimed that the *batman* used in the mines consisted of 9 *okka*.

[c] Regarding the shipments from Trabzon in the Black Sea region in the eighteenth century, I have assumed that the foreign source used the word *quintal* for the Ottoman *kantar*, which by then equaled 56.4 kg.

[d] The shipments of copper made from the Black Sea region to the Imperial Cannon Foundry do not represent the total output of the copper mines of the Black Sea region. The source gives the amounts of copper both in *batman*s and *okka*. Based on these figures it seems that in the eighteenth century 1 *batman* equaled 6 *okka* or 7.6968 kg, which was used in the above calculations. Murphey, who gave the above piece of information, calculates the *batman* at 7.1 kg, whereas Tızlak gives its kg equivalent as 7.962 kg.

Abbreviations: O = annual obligation; P = actual production; S = actual shipment to the Tophane.

Sources: Küre and the Black Sea region: Murphey, "Ma'din," p. 977, and Faroqhi, *Towns*, p. 179; Gümüşhane, 1695: Refik, *Türkiye Madenleri*, p. 21; Gümüşhane and Kastamonu, 1697: MAD 2730, p. 10; 1712–14: DBŞM TPH 18617, p. 5, DBŞM TPH 18618, p. 13; 1737–38: DBŞM TPH 18645, p. 7; 1743–44: DBŞM TPH 18652, p. 6; 1744–45: DBŞM TPH 18655, p. 8; 1746–47: DBŞM TPH 18656, p. 6; 1747–48: DBŞM TPH 18658, p. 4; 1751–52: DBŞM TPH 18663; 1757–58: DBŞM TPH 18668, p. 12; 1758–59: DBŞM TPH 18671, p. 10; Gümüşhane, 1784–85: DBŞM TPH 18723, p. 5; Ergani: Tızlak, *Keban-Ergani*, p. 131; Asia Minor and the Black Sea region in the eighteenth century: Parry, "Materials of War," p. 225.

the foundry from these storehouses.[43] Judging from the latter figure, it is apparent that the overall copper output of the Empire's mines was considerably more than one may assume on the basis of table 6.1.

Iron, lead and the ammunitions industry

Iron (*demir*) was an ore of great strategic significance, used extensively in the Ottoman weapons industry as well as in fortifications and in the imperial naval yards. As noted earlier, the Ottomans cast most of their small-caliber artillery pieces of iron. In addition, hundreds of thousands of cannon balls were made every year out of this metal. Iron was the main material for manufacturing various tools and chains employed by the artillery corps for guns, as well as shovels, picks and axes used in the trenches, nails for fortresses and bridges, horseshoes, and so forth.

In Asia Minor, the closest iron mines to the capital were those of Bilecik near Eskişehir, but iron was also excavated in great quantities in Kiği in the vicinity of Erzurum, and in Keban. In the Balkans, the most important iron mines operated in Samakov (south of Sofia in present-day Bulgaria), but smaller quantities of iron ore were to be found in Çiproviç (Čiprovic) and Etropole, too. Iron was also excavated in Rudnik (north of Kosovo), in northwestern Macedonia (near Eridere), in the Rhodope Mountains, and in Samakovcuk in Thrace. In Bosnia, Banaluka (Banja Luka, north of Jajca on the river Vrbas) and Kamengrad (west of Banaluka) produced iron in considerable quantities, but there were dozens of smaller mining towns and villages nearby to major mining centers.[44]

Lead (*kurşun*) was also an ore of great military value because the projectiles for both hand firearms and small-caliber guns were made of this metal. The major suppliers of lead were the Empire's silver mines. In the Balkans, the most important mining centers with substantial lead deposits were to be found in Srebreniçe and Olovo (north of Sarajevo) as well as in several smaller mining villages[45] and Banaluka.[46] Substantial lead ore was also found in Rudnik,[47] Novaberda,

---

[43] MAD 4039, p. 153.
[44] The best known were those of Fojnica, Kreševo, Vareš, Ostruznica, Busovaca, Šebešic, Večerička, Vladiči, Varci, Krupanj, Daljegošta, Sase, Hladilo (Vrha Prača), Čelopek, Grabovica, Buševac and Čajnice. See Handžić, "Rudarstvo," MD 10, p. 200.
[45] Olovo was already an important lead producer in the fifteenth century, as can be seen from the town's revenue estimates. While in 1489 the inhabitants of Olovo had to pay 65,843 *akça* annually for the lead they mined, those of Foyniça paid only 21,000 *akça* after the silver they excavated in the local silver mines. See Handžić, "Rudnici u Bosni," 21, and Handžić, "Rudarstvo u Bosni," 326.
[46] MAD 2728, p. 4, regarding a shipment of 5,400 kg (100 *kantar*) of lead from Banaluka to the fortress of Kanije, in Hungary.
[47] MD 5, p. 623, no. 1737, imperial decree dated May 29, 1566 that ordered the *kadı* of Rudnik to cast 7,020 kg (130 *kantar*) of lead bullets and to send them to Belgrade. Cf. also MD 5, p. 644, no. 1804.

Kratova[48] and Kuçanya[49] in Serbia whereas in present-day Greece Sidrekapsa had lead deposits. While the lead mined in Olovo was known in Europe as *plumbum dulce*, that is, soft lead, the lead produced in Srebreniçe and Kuçanya is referred to in European sources as *plumbum durum* or hard lead. In Asia Minor, lead was obtained from the mines of Gümüşhane, Ergani, Keban, also from Bulgarmaden in the Taurus Mountains, and from Hakkari.[50]

The ironworks of Samakov were particularly important for the Ottoman shipyards, producing hundreds of anchors and iron parts as well as great quantities of nails for bridges every year.[51] The system used to produce the required quantities of iron was that of the *ocaklık*, discussed in the previous chapters, whereby the *reaya* of the mining towns and villages had to produce fixed quantities of iron and were, in turn, granted exemptions from paying the extraordinary *avarız* taxes. Their obligation changed over time: whereas in 1565, 300 anchors and 108,000 kg (2,000 *kantar*) of nails were ordered from Samakov for the Istanbul Naval Arsenal,[52] in the seventeenth century, the annual obligation of the *reaya* of Samakov for the arsenal seem to have declined substantially, fluctuating between 43,200 and 54,000 kg (800–1000 *kantar*).[53] However, annual production levels at the Samakov ironworks probably did not decline, and in the middle of the seventeenth century at least seventeen furnaces were active there that dispatched some 8,000 carts of finished iron to Selanik every year, the total weight of which was probably over 400,000 kg.[54]

Contrary to general assumptions, the Ottoman mining industry, and the economy in general, did quite well in the eighteenth century, at least until the 1760s. In the early decades of the century, production output in the Samakov mines increased considerably, and around 1720 there were some eighty active furnaces to be found in the Samakov–Sofia region, as opposed to the seventeen such installations some seventy years earlier. In the 1730s and 1740s further furnaces were opened, and mining and smelting activities were so intensive that by 1760 forest lands decreased

[48] MAD 2728, p. 4, refers to a shipment of 27,000 kg (500 *kantar*) of lead from Üsküb and Kratova to Kanije.
[49] MD 5, p. 623, no. 1737, imperial order dated May 29, 1566, which instructed the *kadı* of Kuçanya to cast 7,398 kg (137 *kantar*) of lead bullets.
[50] Parry, "Materials of War," p. 223.
[51] MD 12, p. 94, no. 203; ibid., p. 116, no. 251, orders dated in March 1571 regarding anchors for ships built in Ahyolu.
[52] Colin Imber, "The Navy of Süleyman the Magnificent," *ArchOtt* 6 (1980), 234.
[53] Their obligation was 1,000 *kantar* between 1651 and 1676, but it was only 945 *kantar* between 1676 and 1690, and only 935.5 *kantar* after 1693. See İdris Bostan, *Osmanlı Bahriye Teşkilatı: XVII. Yüzyılda Tersane-i Amire* (Ankara, 1992), pp. 121–22. A similar decline in production capabilities at the end of the seventeenth century can be observed with regard to Samakovcuk: until 1690, the inhabitants of that region had to produce 350 *kantar* per annum and transport it to the imperial naval yards in Istanbul. From this time onward, however, their obligation was just 200 *kantar* of iron, owing to their inability to maintain previous production levels (ibid., p. 122).
[54] Afet Inan, *Aperçu général sur l'histoire économique de l'empire turc-ottoman* (Istanbul, 1941), p. 68. See also table 6.2. Apart from anchors, chains and nails, the ironworks of Samakov also produced horseshoes, shovels, picks and axes, as well as axles for cannons. See MD 12, p. 12, no. 23; ibid., p. 94, no. 203, regarding axles for cannons to be cast in İskenderiye (Škodra).

substantially. As a result of wood shortages, the *kadı* of Samakov petitioned the Istanbul government to deny permission to entrepreneurs to open new mines and furnaces. Another indication of increased smelting and mining activities is the shortage of labor, mentioned frequently in the sources. However, after the 1760s production output levels started to decline, and owing to deforestation, emigration of workers and recurring epidemics, most of the furnaces of Samakov had become idle by the 1790s. Deterioration of public safety and banditry made mining and smelting almost impossible, and most of the abandoned mines had become the refuge of bandits by the end of the century.[55]

Whereas in the sixteenth and seventeenth centuries, the Samakov ironworks produced iron mainly for the shipyards, those of Bilecik and Kiği in Asia Minor were known for their production of cannon balls,[56] as were the mines and ironworks of Rudnik, Bac,[57] Banaluka, İskenderiye (Škodra) and Pravişte (near Kavala in Greece).[58] The ironworks of Pravişte were established in 1697 with the specific intention to meet the increasing demand for ammunition during the protracted wars at the turn of the century.[59]

While it is impossible, in the absence of any comprehensive work on Ottoman mining, to give reliable estimates concerning the output of the Empire's ironworks, the data in Table 6.2 will give some sense regarding possible production levels of both raw iron and of cannon balls.

Although output levels fluctuated in the Ottoman ironworks according to military demands and local production capabilities, the records of the Imperial Armory do not indicate that the Ottomans were in need of imported iron in any significant quantities. The only references in this regard are those to "Frankish steel" (*çelik-i firengi*). However, it is difficult to tell from the records whether they meant European steel or specially refined steel of "European quality" made domestically.[60] It is apparent from all the sources consulted that the bulk of raw

[55] Mehmet Genç, "18. Yüzyılda Osmanlı Ekonomisi ve Savaş," in Mehmet Genç, *Osmanlı İmparatorluğunda Devlet ve Ekonomi* (Istanbul, 2000), pp. 213–14.

[56] MD 5, p. 162, no. 389; MD 7, p. 517, no. 1486; İsmail Hakkı Uzunçarşılı, *Osmanlı Devleti Teşkilatından Kapukulu Ocakları, vol. II: Cebeci, Topçu, Top Arabacıları, Humbaracı, Lağımcı Ocakları ve Kapukulu Suvarileri* (Ankara, 1984), p. 73.

[57] İsmail Hakkı Uzunçarşılı asserted that Bac was another name for Rudnik and his identification has gained general acceptance in Turkish-language literature. However, Yugoslav historians have rejected Uzunçarşılı's identification and suggested that the Bac of Ottoman sources in the *kaza* of Rudnik was Bah, and probably is identical with the settlement today known as Ba. See Đurctica Petrović, "Neki podaci o izradi topovskih kugli u Srbiji i Bosni u XV i XVI veku," *VVM* 12 (1966), 172–73.

[58] MD 7, p. 378, no. 1084 (for Rudnik); MD 75, p. 291, no. 608, and MAD 628, and İnalcık "The Socio-Political Effects," p. 213 (for Banaluka); AK fols. 3b, 51b, 54a, 190a (for Bac).

[59] Mehmed Raşid, *Tarih-i Raşid* (2 vols., Istanbul, 1282/1865–66), vol. II, p. 396; Defterdar Sarı Mehmed Paşa, *Zübde-i Vekayiat.* Ed. Abdülkadir Özcan (Ankara, 1995), pp. 610–11. Another advantage of the newly established ironworks of Pravişte was that they were able to produce cannon balls in the winter, unlike the works in Banaluka that operated only during the summer months.

[60] As previously noted, the situation was similar with "English gunpowder" (*İngiliz perdahtı*). When the source of such *çelik-i firengi* was the customs officials of Izmir and Istanbul, the likelihood that the steel was imported from Europe or purchased from European ships on Ottoman waters is greater. Cf. e.g., MAD 3279, p. 170, which shows that for the 1663–64 campaign 162 kg (3 *kantar*) of *Firengi çelik* was acquired from such a source.

Table 6.2 *Estimated levels of annual iron production in selected ironworks*

Region	Date	Production, annual obligation or shipment	Production, annual obligation or shipment in kg
Samakov	1565	2,000 *kantar*	108,000 (P)[a]
Samakov	Mid-17th century	8,000 *araba* (wagonload)	432,000 (S)[b]
Bilecik	1568	35,000 cannon balls	692,272–835,584 (O)[c]
Banaluka	1663	29,300 cannon balls	356,180 (P)
Banaluka	1664–65	100,000 *okka* of cannon balls	122,880 (O)
Banaluka	1684	162,000 *okka*	199,066 (P)
Banaluka	1684	100,000 *okka* of cannon balls	122,880 (P)
Bac/Bah	1680–86	201,471 *okka*	247,568 (P)[d]
Kağıthane	1696–97	64,456 cannon balls	287,339 (P)
Tophane	1697	2150 cannon balls	19,968 (P)
Kağıthane	1697–98	30,444 cannon balls	118,338 (P)
Kağıthane	1697–98	64,840 bombshells	79,675 (P)
Pravişte	1702	3,500 *kantar*	197,400 (P)
Pravişte	1708–09	125,000 *okka*	160,350 (P)[e]
Pravişte	1713–14	97,558 cannon balls	255,195 (P)
Pravişte	1714–15	177,586 cannon balls	386,041 (P)
Pravişte	1715	57,532 shots + 12,579 bombs	481,756 (P)

Notes: [a] This was just part of the total output.

[b] MAD 920; MAD 2758 indicates that the Ottomans usually loaded 10 *kantar*, or approximately 540 kg, of munitions on each cart (*araba*).

[c] MD 7, p. 513, no. 1475 ordered the casting of 35,000 cannon balls whose breakdown is unspecified. MD 7, p. 559, no. 1580 specified that 15,000 shots should have been of 16, 14 and 11 *okka* in weight. From MD 5, p. 162, no. 389 (dated 1565) we learn that in Bilecik they usually cast cannon balls ranging from 11 to 22 *okka* in weight. Thus, regarding the 15,000 cannon balls I calculated with both 11 and 16 *okka*, assuming that all shots weighed either 11 or 16 *okka*, which, of course, was not the case, but it seemed the only logical method to estimate the theoretical minimum and maximum output levels in kg, namely 202,752 and 294,912 kg, respectively. Assuming that the remaining 20,000 cannon balls weighed either 20 or 22 *okka*, the levels are 491,520 and 540,672 kg. The table shows the estimates for the combined minimum and maximum output for 35,000 shots.

[d] The total output and purchase for the seven years between 1680 and 1686 (that is, for the Hicri years of 1091, 1092, 1093, 1094, 1095, 1096 and 1097) was 2,540,000 cannon balls that weighed 1,410,000 *okka* or 1,732,976 kg.

[e] Using this amount of iron to cast cannon balls, some 15 percent of iron was wasted and the weight of the final product was 136,298 kg (106,250 *okka*). See KK Maden 5185, p. 1.

Abbreviations: O = annual obligation; P = actual production; S = annual shipment.

Sources: Samakov: see footnotes 52 and 54; Bilecik: MD 7, p. 513, no. 1475; Banaluka, 1663: MAD 3279, p. 101; Banaluka, 1664–65: MAD 3774, p. 102; 1684: MAD 683, p. 14, and İnalcık, "The Socio-Political Effects," p. 213; Bac: MAD 5448, p. 2; Kağıthane and Tophane, 1696–97: MAD 4578, p. 8; Pravişte, 1702: DBŞM 483, p. 150; Pravişte, 1708–09: KK Maden 5185, pp. 4–6; 1713–15: MAD 4456, pp. 12–13.

iron needed in the Ottoman foundries to cast hundreds of small-caliber artillery pieces and hundreds of thousands of cannon balls came from domestic sources. Such self-sufficiency was not, however, the case with regard to tin, a metal that usually needed to be imported from abroad, most notably England.[61] Similarly, it

---

[61] Parry, "Materials of War," p. 225.

seems that during protracted wars in the middle and at the end of the seventeenth century, the Empire's mines were not able to satisfy the army's pressing need for lead either, and that the missing quantities had to be purchased. It was usually the task of the *emins* of the Izmir and Istanbul customs to acquire the necessary amounts.[62] While the source of these purchases is not always known, it is possible that the officials bought, at least partly, from foreign merchants. Foreign sources had certainly become important by the end of the seventeenth century. In January and May 1688, after the exhausting campaigns of 1687 and 1688 on the Hungarian front, the Imperial Armory in Istanbul purchased 209,520 kg (3,880 *kantar*) of lead from a European merchant.[63] While the amount was considerable in itself, the significance of the transaction becomes more apparent when we learn that the two consignments purchased represented almost 90 percent of the total supply of lead (236,520 kg or 4,380 *kantar*) to the Imperial Armory in this period.

Mass production of cannons and the Tophane

Ottoman as well as European sources agree that it was Mehmed II (r. 1451–81) who, in the years following the conquest of Constantinople in 1453, founded the Tophane-i Amire, that is, the Ottoman Imperial Cannon Foundry in the city. It is not clear, however, whether Mehmed established a new military compound without antecedents or inherited a Genoese foundry which he later expanded.[64] Whatever the answer to this question may be, it is certainly safe to say that the foundry gained its importance only under the Ottomans. In the late fifteenth and early sixteenth centuries, the Imperial Cannon Foundry, Armory (Cebehane-i Amire), Gunpowder Works (Baruthane-i Amire) and Naval Arsenal (Tersane-i Amire) gave Istanbul what was probably the largest military-industrial complex in early modern Europe, rivaled only by the Venetian Arsenal. Some of the earliest account books of the Tophane illustrate Ottoman production capabilities.

Before the establishment of the Tophane in Istanbul, the most important foundry operated in Edirne, where most of the guns used during the 1453 siege of Constantinople were made, as were the cannons used in the 1456 siege of Belgrade. From the mid-fifteenth century onward, besides Istanbul, the Ottomans cast cannon in their provincial capitals and mining centers, as well as in foundries

---

[62] MAD 3774, p. 53, shows that in 1664, during Köprülüzade Ahmed Pasha's Hungarian campaign, the *emins* of the Izmir and Istanbul customs purchased (*iştira*) 27,000 and 16,200 kg (500 and 300 *kantar*) of lead, respectively, which they had to send to the Hungarian front via the Black Sea and Rusçuk. Another example is provided in MAD 9879, p. 13, which reveals that in October 1694, the *kaymakam* of Istanbul was instructed to purchase 81,000 kg (1,500 *kantar*) of lead from either Istanbul or Izmir with the help of the local customs officials for the army fighting on the island of Sakiz.

[63] KK 4738, p. 1. In January, the armory bought 135,000 kg (2,500 *kantar*) of lead, whereas in May it purchased a further consignment of 74,520 kg (1,380 *kantar*).

[64] Regarding the debate see Colin Heywood, "Notes on the Production of Fifteenth-Century Ottoman Cannon," in Colin Heywood, *Writing Ottoman History: Documents and Interpretations* (Aldershot, 2002), article XVI, pp. 12–16, 19.

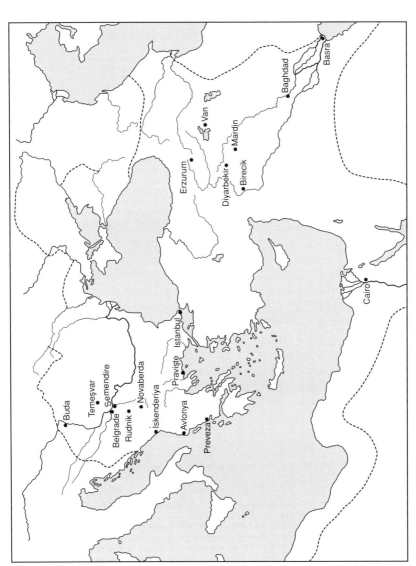

Map 4 Cannon foundries in the Ottoman Empire.

Table 6.3 *Output of the Imperial Cannon Foundry in Istanbul, 1513–28*

Date	Length of operation	Number of cannons cast	Material used (metric tons)
1513	4 months	188	27.4
1515–18	32 months	2 large cast iron	6.3
1517–18	8 months	24 (of which 22 cast iron)	185
1517–19	28 months	699 (+428 repaired)	550
1522–26	38.5 months	1,029	483
1527–28	9 months	148	65
Total	119.5	2,090	1,316.7

Sources: KK 4726, first used by İdris Bostan in his "A szultáni ágyúöntő műhelyben"; MAD 7668, first used by Colin Heywood in his "The Activity of the State Cannon-Foundry."

established during campaigns. Of these, the foundries of Avlonya and Preveza in the Adriatic (also important naval bases), Rudnik, Semendire, İskenderiye,[65] Novaberda, Pravişte and Belgrade in the Balkans, Buda and Temeşvar in Hungary, Diyarbekir, Erzurum, Birecik, Mardin and Van in Asia Minor, Baghdad[66] and Basra[67] in Iraq, and Cairo in Egypt[68] were among the most important and were active from time to time.[69] The production output of some of these foundries could easily match that of the Istanbul foundry, especially in the late fifteenth and early sixteenth century. For example, during the Venetian–Ottoman war of 1499–1503, from October 31, 1499 until August 26, 1500, that is, within ten months, the Ottomans cast 288 cannons in Avlonya for the imperial navy. Of those, 53 were large and medium-caliber cannons, 29 smaller ones to be used on board of *caiques*, and 206 small guns called *prangı*.[70] This volume of production was considerable. It took almost two years for William Lewett to manufacture 120 cast-iron cannons in his foundry in Sussex in 1543–45, though they were most certainly much larger than the Ottoman *prangıs* cast in Avlonya. As late as 1679, Seville's foundry, perhaps the most important ordnance factory in seventeenth-century Spain, could hardly manufacture more than 36 cannons of medium caliber per year.[71]

[65] MD 14, p. 345, no. 492. The foundry was capable of casting large *şaykas* firing cut stone cannon balls. See ibid., p. 707, no. 1020.

[66] MD 27, p. 198, no. 454, an imperial decree dated January 14, 1576, regarding the casting of new shipboard ordnance for the local galleys (*kadırga*s) using copper sent from Istanbul and broken guns. For other examples see ibid., p. 193, no. 441.

[67] MD 5, p. 317, no. 828; ibid., p. 318, no. 830; ibid., p. 319, no. 832; MD 27, p. 202, no. 466.

[68] It appears that the foundry was either newly built or rebuilt right after the conquest of Cairo by an Ottoman foundryman called Ayas Bey. Cf. the brief accounts dated 1517: AE, I. Selim, no. 23.

[69] AK fols. 3b, 53a–b, 55b, 57b, etc.; Uzunçarşılı, *Cebeci, Topçu*, pp. 45–46. In addition, the Ottomans also cast guns in smaller numbers in their fortresses. MD 28, p. 47, no. 114, refers to cannon casting in Akkirman in the mouth of the Dniester.

[70] İdris Bostan, "A szultáni ágyúöntő műhelyben (Tophane-i Amire) folyó tevékenység a 16. század elelyén," *Aetas* 18, 2 (2003), 8, based on AE, Bayezid II, no. 41.

[71] Corlo M. Cipolla, *Guns, Sails and Empires: Technological Innovation and the Early Phases of European Expansion 1400–1700* (New York, 1965, reprint New York, 1996), pp. 39, 155.

The production level of the other provincial foundries, however, cannot be compared to that of Avlonya. In the sixteenth and seventeenth centuries, the main function of these local foundries was confined to repairing the guns deployed in the respective provincial garrisons, and to casting new cannons mainly for the same forts. Occasionally, however, before major imperial campaigns the provincial foundries were charged with casting guns to be used by the imperial Ottoman army operating in the region. Although no account book of these provincial foundries has been found during my research, it is still possible to gain a sense of the potential production levels of these local foundries from scattered data gathered mainly from imperial decrees.

Despite the temporary importance of local foundries, Istanbul remained the center of the Ottoman weapons industry. The number of technicians working at the Tophane at a given time was not too great. In 1695–96, for instance, when 208 guns were cast, only sixty-two cannon founders or casters (*rihtegan*) along with five specialists who supervised the furnaces (*fırıncıyan*) were paid. In addition to them, there were other technicians whose work was closely related to the manufacturing of guns and gun carriages. The total workforce at the Tophane, however, was much more numerous, for the number of day laborers (*ırgad*) alone varied between 40 and 200.[72] With the help of the latter, the Istanbul foundry was capable of casting hundreds of cannons annually, as shown in Table 6.5. As can be seen from the table, the Tophane was able to increase its output considerably in the years that saw unusual military commitments. The peak years coincide with the long Hungarian wars at the end of the sixteenth and seventeenth centuries, and with the Russo-Ottoman war of 1768–74. The output was surprisingly low in 1604 because cannons cast in that year were meant for a single campaign on the eastern front while the bulk of the army was tied up still in Hungary.[73] There is an obvious decline in production levels during the relatively peaceful middle decades of the eighteenth century. However, the above figures should be considered together with the more detailed information provided in the Appendix, for the total number of artillery pieces in itself does not tell the whole story. The account books include all types of guns from the smallest cast-iron *saçma*s and *eynek*s to the largest *şayka*s, and so does the table. The composition of the output varied from year to year according to the military needs of the Empire. Sieges, land and sea campaigns all required different types of ordnance. Similarly, artillery pieces needed for newly constructed ships varied greatly according to ship types. During those years when guns were to be deployed aboard smaller ships at the Black Sea, Shatt al-Arab or the Danube, the majority of the pieces usually consisted of small-caliber and light *saçma*s and *eynek*s. This was the case, for instance, in 1704 when 93 percent (156 of 167 pieces) of the newly cast guns were small cast-iron *saçma*s and *eynek*s. In the next couple of years, however, one can observe a rather different trend.

---

[72] KK 5654, pp. 7–8.
[73] It is unfortunate that this is the only published account book of the Tophane. The fact that data regarding 1604 hardly reflect the overall output figures of the Istanbul foundry again shows that we have to be very careful not to draw far-reaching conclusions on the basis of few published sources.

Table 6.4 *Output of selected provincial cannon foundries*

Foundry	Date	Number of guns cast
Cairo	1537–38	90[a]
Cairo	1576	70[b]
Cairo	1576	30[c]
Basra	1552	61
Diyarbekir	1556	50
Semendire	1552	20
Semendire	1568	10
Semendire	1574	12
Buda	1566	30[d]
Buda	1592	15 *bacaloşka*
İskenderiye	1570	one 20-*okka şayka*
İskenderiye	1570	3[e]
İskenderiye	1571	2[f]
Belgrade	1593	50 *prangı*
Belgrade	1663	230[g]

Notes: [a] Cengiz Orhonlu, *Osmanlı İmparatorluğun Güney Siyaseti: Habeş Eyaleti* (Ankara, 1996), p. 17, mentions twenty pieces of 20-*okka* caliber *balyemez*, thirty pieces of *miyane darbzen*, and forty pieces of *ziyade darbzen* and *kolunburna* aboard the Ottoman navy that left for the Indian Ocean in 1538. While the ships were constructed in the shipyards of Suez, the guns were probably cast in Cairo.
[b] MD 28, p. 166, no. 385, an imperial decree dated August 17, 1576, ordered the casting of ten *bacaluşkas* of 14-*okka* caliber, twenty *kolunburnas* firing cut stone balls, and forty *darbzens* of medium size.
[c] MD 28, p. 286, no. 713, an imperial decree dated October 18, 1576, reveals the fact that most of the guns in Cairo were old, broken (*meksur*) and unsuitable for use (*amel-mande*). Therefore the chief gunner requested that twenty pieces of 80-*dirhem* and ten pieces of 100-*dirhem* caliber *darbzens* be sent to Cairo. However, Istanbul instructed the *beylerbeyi* of Egypt to cast the required number of guns at Cairo.
[d] The imperial decree instructed the *beylerbeyi* of Buda to arrange the preparation of thirty pieces of guns (*otuz kıt'a top hazır itdirirsin*), which does not necessarily mean that all the guns had to be cast anew. The breakdown of the pieces was as follows: five pieces of 16-*okka* caliber, nine pieces of 14-*okka* caliber, five pieces of 11-*okka*, six pieces of 10-*okka* caliber, and finally five pieces of 8-*okka* caliber guns.
[e] The decree also indicates that the material used to cast the three guns in question came from a fifteenth-century giant bombard, probably unsuitable for military use, which had to be cut into pieces and reused in the process of casting the new guns.
[f] In fact, the local foundrymen were required to cast four cannons; however, due to a shortage of raw material they managed to manufacture only two 14-*okka* caliber pieces.
[g] The breakdown of guns to be cast in Belgrade was as follows: 30 *balyemez* and *kolunburna*, and 200 *darbzen*.
Sources: See notes. Also Basra 1552: TSMK Koğuşlar 888, fol. 161b; Diyarbekir: Nejat Göyünç, "Diyarbekir," *TDVİA*, vol. IX, p. 467: Semendire 1552: TSMK Koğuşlar 888, fol. 61b; Semendire 1568: MD 7, p. 239, no. 663; Semendire 1574: MD 25, p. 330; Buda 1593: MD 5, p. 667, no. 1874, ibid., p. 670, no. 1879; Buda 1592: AK fol. 3b; İskenderiye 1570: MD 14, p. 647, no. 937, ibid., 654, no. 950; İskenderiye 1571: MD 12, p. 133, no. 293; Belgrade 1593: AK fol. 3b; Belgrade 1663: Uzunçarşılı, *Cebeci, Topçu*, p. 55.

Table 6.5 *Output of the Imperial Cannon Foundry in Istanbul, 1596–1798*

Date	Length of operation (days/months)[a]	Number of guns and mortars cast	Total weight of pieces (kg)	Note
1596	3–4 months	300	?	The long Hungarian war of 1593–1606
1604		52	28,134	Campaign against Shah Abbas
1676	5.5 months	46	?	
1684–85	326	785	626,967[b]	The long war of 1683–99
1685–86	281	324	135,000[b]	"
1691–92	140	298	?	"
1693–94	174	458⎱	401,322[c]	"
1694–95	312	221⎰		"
1695–96	134	207	218,862	"
1696–97	421	1,322[d]	361,962	"
1697–98	308	271	263,437	"
1704	119	167	?	No major campaign
1704–06	260	130	148,240	"
1706–07	468	177	242,580	"
1711–12	70	211	118,665	The Prut campaign
1712–14	140	103	127,353	Peace with Russia in 1711
1715–16	210	100	165,651	War against Venice and Austria, 1714/16–18
1717	158	177	115,353	"
1731–32	255	83	174,532	War against Iran, 1730
1732–33	260	386	172,510	"
1734–35	250	235	197,659	"
1737–38	355	648	271,007	War against Russia and Austria, 1736–39
1743–44	150	127	108,969	War against Iran, 1743–46
1744–45	149	117	113,840	"
1746–47	112	176	82,963	"
1747–48	296	22	20,748	Peace with Iran, 1746
1749–50	123	58	83,432	"
1751–52	150	99	101,663	"
1756–57	121	47	83,947	"
1757–58	187	111	125,310	"
1758–59	166	76	90,245	"
1760–61	158	82	95,590	"
1769–70	322	350	206,424	Russo-Ottoman war of 1768–74
1771–72	386	188	?	"
1775–76		36	?	Peace with Russia in 1774
1776–81	1,798	246	?	War against Iran, 1776–77
1781–82	63	33		
1782	140	76		
1784–85	298	173	221,510	Russian annexation of the Crimea, 1783

(*cont.*)

Table 6.5 (*cont.*)

Date	Length of operation (days/months)[a]	Number of guns and mortars cast	Total weight of pieces (kg)	Note
1788–92	1,357	324	261,694	Wars against Russia and Austria, 1787–92
1796–97	531	182	192,648	
1797–98	354	197	309,947	

Notes: [a] Arriving at the length of operation should be done cautiously since the dates given in our sources correspond to the start and end dates of a certain *nazir*'s term of office for which he submitted his accounts. In other cases, however, the accounts differentiate between the *nazir*'s term of office and the period devoted to actual casting. When the latter information is given, it is preferred in the table. The table accounts for figures for all the guns and mortars of various calibers cast at the Tophane in a given period of time. For details see the relevant tables in the Appendix. Figures for the total weight of pieces are rounded up.
[b] The figure is the weight of the material used during the process of casting and it is not the actual weight of the pieces.
[c] This is the weight of the 679 pieces (458 + 221) cast from October 12, 1693 through July 12, 1695.
[d] The total of 1,306 guns of various caliber and 16 mortars.
Sources: 1596: AK fols. 53a–b, 55b, 57b; 1604: Aydüz, "Tophane-i Amire'nin 1012 (1604) yılı gelir-gider muhasebesi," p. 157. From 1676 through 1785 see tables in the Appendix. 1788–92: DBŞM TPH 18734; 1796–97: TPH 18747; 1797–98: TPH 18750.

Although the total number of guns cast in 1704–06 was just 130, the majority (81 percent) of these pieces consisted of guns of 3-*okka* caliber and larger, including several large 44- and 22-*okka* caliber *şayka*s. Thus, one ought to be careful not to draw conclusions solely on the basis of random evidence regarding output figures of selected years.

Distribution of guns according to sizes

As noted in the Introduction, several Europeanist historians are of the opinion that the Ottoman artillery was characterized by its giant cannons, partly because the Ottomans were incapable of casting smaller guns in large quantities. We have seen that production output figures disprove the alleged lack of Ottoman ability in mass production. Archival records similarly challenge the gigantism theory of Ottoman artillery, put forward by Carlo Maria Cipolla and others.[74]

The account books of the Tophane suggest that the overwhelming majority of guns cast at the foundry consisted of small and medium-caliber pieces. Contrary to the general view, siege guns, that is, guns of the cannon class in European

[74] Cf. Gábor Ágoston, "Early Modern Ottoman and European Gunpowder Technology," in Ekmeleddin İhsanoğlu, Kostas Chatzis and Efthymios Nicolaides eds., *Multicultural Science in the Ottoman Empire* (Turnhout, 2003), pp. 13–27.

terminology, comprised only a small fraction of the Ottoman ordnance cast in a given year. Of the 1,027 pieces cast at the Tophane between 1523 and 1526, a period that witnessed intensive Ottoman military activity in Europe, 97 percent consisted of small and medium-sized guns. Small *darbzen*s, on average weighing 162 kg, accounted for 61 percent of all the pieces.[75]

Similar conclusions can be drawn from the late seventeenth- and eighteenth-century account books of the Tophane. Sixteenth- and seventeenth-century Ottoman military experts considered guns firing projectiles of between 8 and 22 *okka* (10–27 kg) suitable for both campaigns and sieges. However, in contemporaneous Ottoman terminology only the 12-, 14-, 15- and 16-*okka* caliber guns were regarded as siege cannons and only these were designated by the Persian term of *kale-kob* (fort-smasher). In chapter 3 we saw that the Ottoman *kale-kob*s were very similar to the *Halbe* and *Dreiviertel Karthauns* deployed in the Austrian armies and considered by European military experts as guns best suited for sieges. However, in the seventeenth century, 12-*okka* caliber guns seem to have been rare. Instead, 11-*okka* guns were favored. Consequently, in my classification I, too, considered guns firing projectiles of 11 *okka* (13.5–14 kg) in weight and above as large siege guns of the cannon class. On the other hand, Ottoman guns that fired cannon balls of 1.5 *okka* (1.8–1.9 kg) or less ought to be regarded as small pieces. Ottoman cannons that used shots weighing more than 1.5 *okka* but less than 11 *okka* are classified in this book as medium-caliber guns.

As can be seen from Table 6.6, late seventeenth-century data are fairly consistent. The data for 1685–86 and 1693–96 are especially valuable, for they reflect the largest inventory and output figures of the Imperial Cannon Foundry at the end of the seventeenth century. In the 1680s and 1690s, the great majority (62–90 percent) of newly cast guns consisted of very small caliber pieces, except for 1695–96 when their proportion was only 44 percent. Medium-caliber guns were the second largest group, except again for 1695–96 when they comprised the majority with 55 percent. The proportion of large siege guns of the cannon class is surprisingly small, except for the years 1691–92. This might partly be explained by the Ottoman practice by which large fortress guns, suitable for sieges, were mobilized during campaigns. Since most of these guns were deployed in frontier garrisons close to enemy territory, the difficulties of transporting large siege guns and the associated costs could somewhat be reduced by mobilizing such fortress pieces. The data support the notion that contrary to the general view suggested in earlier studies, the majority of guns cast throughout our period in the Ottoman foundries were small and medium-caliber pieces.

While large guns remained the minority in the early eighteenth century, there is a change between the proportions of the smallest and medium-caliber pieces. The latter category had become the dominant one, medium-caliber guns comprising the majority of newly cast cannons in 1704–06, 1712–13 and 1731–32. However, by

---

[75] Colin Heywood, "The Activity of the State Cannon-Foundry (Tophane-i Amire) at İstanbul in the Early Sixteenth Century According to an Unpublished Turkish Source," *POF* 30 (1980), pp. 214–16.

Table 6.6 *Distribution of Ottoman guns cast or kept in the Tophane*

Date	Total	Small no.	%	Medium no.	%	Large no.	%	Mortars no.	%
1685–86	416[a]	376	90.4	38	9.1	2	0.5	–	–
1691–92	298	187	62.4	61	20.5	50	16.8	1	0.3
1693–94	679	524	77.2	125	18.4	6	0.9	24	3.5
1695–96	208	92	44.2	115	55.3	1	0.5	–	–
1696–97	1,322	1169	88.4	111	8.4	26	2.0	16	1.2
1704	167	164	98.2	–	0.0	3	1.8	–	–
1704–06	130	25	19.2	105	80.8	–	0.0	–	–
1706–07	177	91	51.4	53	29.9	26	14.7	7	4.0
1712–13	103	28	27.2	58	63.3	2	1.9	15	14.5
1731–32	83	–	0	79	95.2	4	4.8	–	–
1732	486[a]	147	30.2	208	42.8	95	19.6	36	7.4
1748	22	20	90.9	2	9.1	–	0.0	–	–
1769–70	350	290	82.9	60	17.1	–	0.0	–	–
1771–72	188	140	74.5	20	10.6	–	0.0	28	14.9
1776–79	137	80	58.4	54	39.4	3	2.2	–	–
1779–81	41	1	2.4	39	95.2	1	2.4	–	–
1784–85	173	30	17.3	121	70.0	6	3.5	16	9.2

Notes: Small = 1.5-*okka* caliber or smaller; medium = more than 1.5 *okka* but smaller than 11-*okka* caliber; large = 11-*okka* caliber and above.
[a] Figures represent inventory; all other figures are actual production output levels.
Sources: See Appendix.

mid-century the pattern of the late seventeenth century had returned, with small-caliber guns dominating the output. The output figures during the Russo-Ottoman war of 1768–74 are understandable, as the Ottoman army needed large quantities of small field pieces in order to confront the Russian artillery that by then possessed very powerful artillery, with hundreds of deployed guns.[76]

The question of Ottoman technological inferiority

Recent research on the supposed "metallurgical inferiority" of Ottoman cannon,[77] which is based on the superficial assessment of random evidence, begs for re-evaluation. According to chemical analysis, an Ottoman gun-barrel cast in 1464 for Mehmed II was composed of excellent bronze containing 10.15 percent tin and 89.58 percent copper. Bronze of almost the same composition was recommended

---

[76] One might arrive at similar conclusions by examining weapons inventories of certain Ottoman garrisons. While Ottoman narrative sources and especially European travelers were often obsessed with the giant Ottoman cannons found in some key forts of the Sultan, archival evidence suggests a more complex and rather different picture. Cf. Ágoston, "Ottoman Artillery and European Military Technology in the Fifteenth to Seventeenth Centuries." *AOH*, 1–2 (1994), 15–48.

[77] Suggested by Geoffrey Parker, *The Military Revolution: Military Innovation and the Rise of the West, 1500–1800* (Cambridge, 1988; rev. 3 edition, 1999), p. 128.

Table 6.7 *Composition of Ottoman bronze cannons*

Date	Copper (%)	Tin (%)
1464	89.58	10.15
1517–23	91.0	9.0
1522–26	90.5	9.5
1604	90.8	9.2
1685–86	91.4	8.6
1693–94	89.5	10.5
1704–06	89.6	10.4
1704–06	89.5	10.5
1704–06	88.7	11.3
1706–07	89.5	10.5

Source: Ágoston, "Ottoman and European Gunpowder Technology," p. 24.

by Vanoccio Biringuccio (1480–1539), and was used in contemporary Europe. Ottoman techniques of cannon casting, as described in Michael Kritovoulos's account of a large cannon casting for the siege of Constantinople (1453), seem to have been similar to the technology applied in contemporary Europe.[78] Further-more, Ottoman production data suggest that, at least until the end of the seventeenth century, Ottoman cannon founders used the typical tin bronze, which contained 8.6–11.3 percent tin and 89.5–91.4 percent copper.

The data in Table 6.7 ought to be handled with caution. Chemical analysis of extant pieces would eventually be required in order to arrive at more accurate figures regarding the composition of Ottoman cannons.

Conclusion

In the light of evidence presented in this chapter, the ideas regarding the Ottomans' alleged "third-tier" weapons manufacturer status as well as their supposed techno-logical inferiority are hardly tenable. Hopefully, the data presented here are exact enough to show that such opinions are not supported by the evidence available from archival records.

Unlike many of their opponents, the Ottomans were fortunate to have had abun-dant ore deposits within the borders of their Empire to establish strong ammunition and ordnance industries. The only ore they lacked was tin which they imported from Europe. In the early years of Sultan Süleyman I's reign, the main supplier of tin was Lodovico (Alvise) Gritti, the natural son of the Venetian doge Andrea

---

[78] V. J. Parry, "Barud IV; The Ottoman Empire," *EI*, vol. I, p. 1061; Jerzy Piaskowski, "The Technology of Gun Casting in the Army of Muhammad II (Early 15th Century)," in *I. International Congress on the History of Turkish–Islamic Science and Technology, 14–18 September 1981. Proceedings*, vol. III (Istanbul, 1981), pp. 163–68.

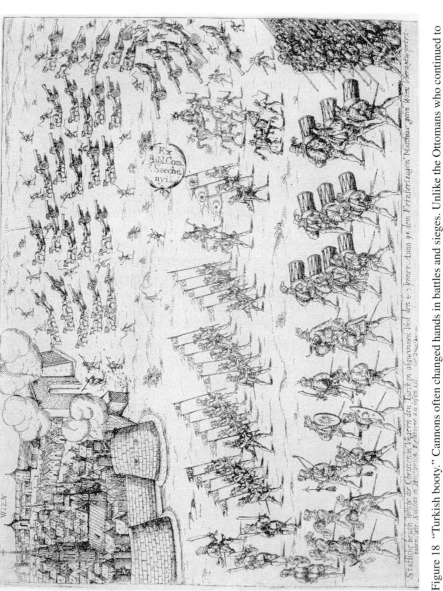

Figure 18 "Turkish booty." Cannons often changed hands in battles and sieges. Unlike the Ottomans who continued to use captured Venetian, Austrian, etc. cannons, the Europeans usually melted down and recast the Ottoman pieces. Unknown German artist.

Gritti and the confidant of Grand Vizier Ibrahim Pasha. Between 1523 and 1526, the Istanbul foundry obtained 10,800 kg (200 *kantar*) of tin from Gritti.[79] While the Empire possessed mines with lead deposits, from the mid- or late seventeenth century Istanbul purchased substantial quantities on the open market, increasingly from foreign merchants. Before that, however, it seems that the Porte was able to acquire from domestic sources most of the lead it needed for casting bullets and small cannon balls. Unlike tin and lead, copper was in abundant supply throughout the period under discussion. This may explain the Ottomans' choice of casting their medium and large cannons of bronze, which contained 89–91 percent copper. Although bronze guns were much more expensive than cast-iron pieces of the same caliber, they were considered much safer and of better quality. Iron ore was also available in abundant quantities in the Empire, but, unlike in Europe, the Ottomans did not cast large and medium pieces of iron. Nevertheless, they did use this metal to cast hundreds of small pieces, usually for the use of their navy, especially the river flotillas, and in forts.

Despite widespread claims to the contrary, the Ottomans were largely self-sufficient in the production of ammunitions and ordnance. They established mass-production capabilities both in their capital and in major provincial centers. The output of some of the provincial foundries, especially in the late fifteenth and early sixteenth century, rivaled that of the Istanbul Imperial Foundry. In the sixteenth and seventeenth centuries, some of these local foundries were capable, albeit usually only on a temporary basis, of casting several dozen cannons, thus making invaluable contributions to the Ottoman war effort during protracted military conflicts. In terms of the volume of its ammunition and ordnance industries the Ottoman Empire was certainly not a third-tier producer country.

Archival records show that the composition of Ottoman bronze cannons was very similar to those cast in Europe and that the proportions of copper and tin were very close to those suggested by Vanoccio Biringuccio, the most respected expert on the subject in sixteenth-century Europe. While chemical analyses might provide more precise figures in the future, it is worth remembering that there were only very modest technical advances in weapons design and effectiveness during the period covered by this investigation, and thus guns in 1800 were very similar to those made in 1500.[80] Thus it would be a mistake to place too much emphasis on the composition of alloy when comparing sixteenth- and seventeenth-century Ottoman and European ordnance.

[79] Heywood, "The Activity of the State Cannon-Foundry," p. 212.
[80] Bert S. Hall, *Weapons and Warfare in Renaissance Europe: Gunpowder, Technology, and Tactics* (Baltimore, 1997), 156.

CHAPTER 7

Conclusions: guns and empire

The age of gunpowder

There are two dangers I have tried to avoid throughout this book. The first is the obvious trap of technological determinism, while the second is the other extreme, the hyper-skepticism towards weapons technology. Although the first has lost its appeal among most historians in recent decades, the fascination with super weapons in certain policy-making circles and the overconfidence regarding the (as-yet) uncontested American military power may change this attitude in the near future.[1] As for the second, it has become fashionable to downplay the importance of military technology and that of weaponry in military conflicts. The skepticism towards all-encompassing theories – such as "gunpowder empire" – is warranted, because too much emphasis is placed on a single factor in explaining the complex processes of the rise and fall of empires. Recent scholarship has challenged notions concerning "war-winning weapons" in the early modern era and has qualified the significance of weapons for the outcome of military conflicts.[2] With regard to the Ottomans, Rhoads Murphey has pointed out the inconsistencies in the quality of Ottoman weaponry and gunpowder and emphasized the vulnerability of employed weapons technologies, arising, among other things, from weather conditions or physical and human constraints on warfare.[3] Yet, there was nothing particularly Ottoman in this, since vulnerability of weapons technologies and the conditions

---

[1] The shift in attitude towards the notion of "empire" among historians, political scientists and politi-cians is noteworthy. Following the demise of the last colonial empires after WWI (and II), "empire" as a topic of scholarly investigation was neglected and often despised. Empire was a fundamentally negative concept for both the political (and scholarly) Left and Right. While the former empha-sized the exploitative nature of empires, the latter also used it in a pejorative sense (recall President Ronald Reagan's labeling the USSR as the "evil empire"). By the 1990s, empires and "imperial endings" had again become fashionable, largely brought on by the dissolution of the Soviet Union and by the emergence of the USA as a dominant power in international politics. Politicians, the-orists and historians no longer seem to shy away from using the word "empire" with regard to the USA.

[2] Jeremy Black, *War and the World: Military Power and the Fate of the Continents, 1450–2000* (New Haven and London, 1998).

[3] Rhoads Murphey, *Ottoman Warfare, 1500–1700* (New Brunswick, 1999), pp. 14–16.

190

that created it were affecting all early modern states that tried to tackle these problems as best they could.

In spite of the obvious limitations of early modern gunpowder weapons, contemporaries were fascinated with them and regarded guns as indispensable for both conquest and defense: "Without these munitions and artillery one cannot preserve any state, nor defend it, nor attack the enemy," argued the Venetian Senate in 1489.[4]

Few historians would deny that gunpowder weapons changed the way states waged war in the early modern era. An impressive body of literature on the Gunpowder or Military Revolution, however contested certain elements may be, has also demonstrated the importance of gunpowder weapons. While individual pieces did have technological and tactical deficiencies – were often prone to burst, imprecise, slow and clumsy and so forth – deployed en masse firearms proved decisive. On the other hand, the lack of gunpowder weapons in the required quantities could and did jeopardize the military and political goals of monarchs. Even the most cautious literature acknowledges the significance of the aggregate firepower at the disposal of monarchs both in domestic policy and in inter-state and inter-cultural conflicts. Without guns, cannon-proof fortifications and shipboard artillery, states were vulnerable against enemies that possessed them. While other factors (diplomatic, geographical, economic, socio-political constraints and so forth) could and did alter inter-state relations, in the long run the availability and deployability of state-of-the-art weaponry in quantities never seen before was a sine qua non of military success.[5]

It was the age of gunpowder in the Ottoman context, too. It is true that military conflicts along the Empire's frontiers, from Hungary to the Black Sea littoral and Iraq, in general were characterized by minor skirmishes and raids – aptly called "little war" (*Kleinkrieg*) by contemporaneous Habsburg military men and politicians. However, only major military campaigns and costly and exhausting investments in sieges had the potential drastically to change the status quo between the competing parties. All these major military undertakings (sieges in Hungary and Iraq under Süleyman; in Hungary during the Long War of 1593–1606, against Baghdad in 1625–26 and 1638; against the Venetians in Crete between 1645 and 1669; against Hungary in 1663–64; and the siege of Vienna in 1683) required especially serious commitments of troops, weaponry and material. As one Grand Vizier reminded the Sultan, warfare and defense were made with gunpowder and firearms. Thus, the major topics with which this book has been concerned are the introduction and integration of firearms technology in the Ottoman Empire and the methods and war industry capabilities by which the Sultans ensured the steady supply of weapons and ammunition.

[4] Quoted by Michael Mallett, "Siegecraft in Late Fifteenth-Century Italy," in Ivy A. Corfis and Michael Wolfe eds., *The Medieval City under Siege* (Woodbridge, 1995), p. 247.
[5] Geoffrey Parker, *The Military Revolution: Military Innovation and the Rise of the West, 1500–1800* (Cambridge, 1988; rev. 3rd edition, 1999); William H. McNeill, *The Pursuit of Power: Technology, Armed Force, and Society since AD 1000* (Chicago, 1982).

Ottoman flexibility and pragmatism

Despite allegations to the contrary, Islam played a negligible role in the process by which the Ottomans (and other Muslim empires such as the Mamluks and Safavids) adopted and integrated gunpowder weapons into their military. While religious rhetoric was occasionally used to justify political decisions regarding the military, imperial ambitions, social pressure, military challenges, economic and geographical conditions and the like were more important than religion in the processes that shaped the evolution of the armed forces of Islamic empires. The history of Ottoman, Mamluk and Safavid experiences with firearms suggests that the integration of gunpowder technology was a complicated matter that cannot be explained by any one factor. As elsewhere in Europe, the modes, timing and success (or failure) of incorporating weapons technologies depended on various elements. Historical challenges, social and economic conditions and cultural attitudes all played a significant role in it. It was exactly these factors that forced the Ottomans to adopt firearms and to keep pace with the evolution of the European militaries from the late fourteenth century on. Facing Byzantine, Balkan and Hungarian fortresses, as well as enemies already in possession of gunpowder weapons, the Ottomans were quick to realize the advantages of firearms. The pragmatism and flexibility of the Ottoman ruling elite led to the relatively smooth integration of gunpowder weapons in the Ottoman army. By the mid-fifteenth century, the Ottomans had become militarily competent rivals to their European and Middle Eastern adversaries. The oft-cited counter-evidence, the reluctance of the *sipahis* to adopt firearms, can be explained by the mentality, social status and military tradition of the light-armed *sipahi* horsemen, with the inadequacy of early firearms for the mounted warrior as well as with the military need for light cavalry on the Empire's eastern front, rather than by invoking Islam. On the whole, the Ottomans preceded both their European and Middle Eastern adversaries in establishing centralized and permanent troops specialized in the manufacturing and handling of firearms. Between the fifteenth and seventeenth centuries, direct military conflicts, the employment of European military experts and, to a lesser degree, illegal trade in weaponry ensured relatively easy dissemination of up-to-date technologies and military know-how in the Sultan's realms. While the degree of Ottoman receptivity and the intensity of European–Ottoman military acculturation varied from ruler to ruler, the channels of military acculturation remained open throughout the period under investigation.

The nature of European–Ottoman military acculturation

Eurocentric and Orientalist historiography has generally overstated the role of European experts in the Ottoman Empire and suggested that the Ottomans had been dependent on European military know-how throughout the early modern period.

We have seen that there was nothing particularly Ottoman in this dependency. Hiring foreign military experts was the prime means throughout Europe for acquiring new technology. The assistance of technicians from countries that were considered to be on the cutting edge of military technology at the time was a general practice in countries not yet familiar with the techniques. The Ottomans were no exception; rather, they were very much part of this diffusion of early modern weapons technology. The diffusion of military technology and know-how through a common pool of experts across societies with different religions is a reminder that we should not overstate the importance of the Muslim–Christian religious divide and that notions such as "Islamic conservatism" – not to mention the currently fashionable idea of a "clash of civilizations" – have very little value in understanding the cross-cultural interactions of the Ottomans with Europe from the fifteenth through the eighteenth centuries.

In one respect, though, Keith Krause is correct. For the most part European–Ottoman military acculturation involved European military experts who sold their expertise to the Ottomans and not vice versa. Linguistic evidence also supports this observation: Ottoman names for weapons and ships often come from Greek or from western languages, suggesting that ordnance and naval technology primarily flowed from Byzantium and Europe to the Ottomans. The Ottomans thus do not differ from their opponents in the use of foreigners. Where they do differ is that their indigenous experts do not seem to have been in much demand in the West. But this again appears not to be something that was characteristic to the Ottomans or other Islamic empires. Rather, it seems to have been the case in other countries classified by Krause as second- and third-tier arms producers, that is, countries that largely relied on foreign expertise. However, if one adopts a more global view that transcends Europe's boundaries, the picture is more complex and carries a couple of noteworthy features.

First is the Ottoman capital's ideal location for technological dialogue. Istanbul was more than a simple recipient of foreign technologies with its Turkish and Persian artisans and blacksmiths, Armenian and Greek miners and sappers, Turkish, Bosnian, Serbian, Hungarian, Italian, German, and later French, English and Dutch foundrymen and military engineers, as well as with its Venetian, Dalmatian, Greek and North African shipwrights and sailors. To give but one example: while miners from the mining centers of medieval Serbia, Bosnia, Greece and Asia Minor brought into Istanbul their knowledge of metallurgy, Turkish, Arab and Persian blacksmiths added to it their expertise of metallurgy techniques of the Islamic East that produced the world-famous Damascus blades. To what extent Europeans could and did profit from this technological dialogue must be the subject of further research. There is one, somewhat uncertain, example that may indicate such a case. We know of a cannon founder in Frankfurt in 1486 by the name of George who is said to have melted and cast cannons in a "wind-pot" or kiln; that is, he was able to cast his pieces without contact between metal and fuel. The invention is significant for "it was ancestral to all the reverberatory furnaces (puddling, open hearth, etc.) of European siderurgy." It is also known that George had worked for a long time in the Ottoman Empire as a cannon founder, and thus it is assumed that he may have learned the technique in the Istanbul foundry.[6]

The second notable feature regarding European–Ottoman military acculturation is the Ottomans' role in the diffusion of gunpowder technology in the Middle East and Asia. Ottoman experts played roles of varying importance in the transmission of gunpowder technology to the Khanates in Turkistan, the Crimean Khanate, Abyssinia, Gujerat in India and the Sultanate of Atche in Sumatra. Istanbul sent cannons and hand-held firearms to the Mamluk Sultanate, Gujerat, Abyssinia and Yemen (before the latter two were incorporated into the Empire). Ottoman experts (Ali Kulu, Rumi and Mustafa) played a significant role in the diffusion of firearms technology and the *Rumi* methods of warfare in Babur's Mughal India. Even the Safavids, the Ottomans' main rivals in the East, acquired Ottoman artillery and muskets as a consequence of Prince Bayezid's rebellion and of his escape to Iran. There were Rumlu Tofangchis, that is, Ottoman artillerists in Shah Tahmasp's (r. 1524–76) Safavid army. The conquest of Diu in 1531 was partly the result of Muslim firepower over the Portuguese deployed by Mustafa Bayram, an Ottoman expert. As a result of this victory, the Portuguese were repelled from Diu, although eventually the Ottomans failed to draw them off from the Indian Ocean.[7]

Lastly, and for Europe's future most importantly, there is the impact of Ottoman advance on the evolution of the European armies and societies. Until well into the seventeenth century, but especially in the fifteenth and sixteenth centuries, Ottoman artillery proved to be superior against European fortifications. In the Central European theater of war, by 1526 the Ottomans had conquered all the key forts of the Hungarian defense system that had guarded the southern borders of the kingdom and that successfully halted Ottoman advance in the fifteenth century. Between 1521 and 1566 only thirteen Hungarian forts were able to resist Ottoman firepower for more than ten days, merely nine castles for more than twenty days, and altogether four fortresses were able fully to withstand Ottoman assaults. However, only one fortress, Kőszeg, was besieged by the main military force of the Sultan. The others were attacked by Ottoman troops led either by the Grand Vizier or by the governor general of Buda, that is, by armies representing smaller numbers of deployed troops and firepower. Three of the four fortresses were later captured, within one, ten and forty-four years, respectively, despite Habsburg efforts at reinforcement and modernization.

In order to match Ottoman firepower Europeans took countermeasures. These included modernization of fortress systems (the introduction of *trace italienne*

---

[6] Joseph Needham, *The Development of Iron and Steel Technology in China* (London, 1958), p. 22. Could it be that George is the very same Jörg of Nuremberg? (See p. 44.)

[7] Halil İnalcık, "The Socio-Political Effects of the Diffusion of Fire-arms in the Middle East," in V. J. Parry and M. E. Yapp eds., *War, Technology and Society in the Middle East* (London, 1975), pp. 195–217; Salih Özbaran, "The Ottomans' Role in the Diffusion of Fire-arms and Military Technology in Asia and Africa in the Sixteenth Century," in his *The Ottoman Response to European Expansion* (Istanbul, 1994), pp. 61–66.

into Central and Eastern Europe); increasing the quality and production output of armaments industries; changing the cavalry–infantry ratio; improving the training and tactics of field armies; as well as modernizing state administration and finances. While all these were part of a larger phenomenon, often referred to as the European Military Revolution, and were undoubtedly fostered by the frequency of inter-state violence within Europe, in Central and Eastern Europe it was Ottoman duress and military superiority, of which firepower was a significant part, that constituted the greatest challenge and required adequate countermeasures.[8] In the long run, Ottoman military superiority fostered technological experimentation and the increase of industrial production of weaponry in Central and Eastern Europe. All this was most apparent in the Austrian Habsburg lands whose capital had already become the "Red Apple," the symbol of Ottoman imperial ambitions.[9] In short, Ottoman pressure played an important role in Habsburg military-fiscal modernization and in the creation of what became known as "Habsburg Central Europe."[10]

Weapons: similarities and differences

In an age when the flow of experts and military know-how from one place to the other was more or less incessant, it was virtually impossible to gain lasting technological superiority that had significant tactical implications. Despite such logical conclusions, the theory of Ottoman giant guns and that of an East–West/Muslim–Christian technological divergence has gained surprisingly broad acceptance.

It had become apparent very early in the course of my research that the lack of understanding of the bewildering terminology of Ottoman weapons has misled most historians writing about the Ottoman military. In the absence of such understanding it has until recently been impossible to compare Ottoman and European artillery pieces in any meaningful way, which in turn led to unfounded and erroneous generalizations regarding Ottoman weaponry and military technology. Based on Ottoman archival evidence, the present book provides the reader with a classification of Ottoman guns which in turn makes comparisons of Ottoman and European artillery pieces feasible. This endeavor has led to several important conclusions. First, it is obvious that the Ottomans matched their European adversaries in the production of various types of cannons. They produced all three main classes of guns used in early modern Europe: parabolic-trajectory mortars and howitzers, flat-trajectory large caliber siege and fortress guns of the cannon class, as well as medium- and small-caliber pieces of the culverin type.

---

[8] Parker, *Military Revolution*; Jeremy Black, *A Military Revolution? Military Change and European Society, 1550–1800* (London, 1991). On the Central European front see Gábor Ágoston, "Habsburgs and Ottomans: Defense, Military Change and Shifts in Power," *TSAB* 22, 1 (1998), 126–41.

[9] On which see Pál Fodor, "Ungarn und Wien in der osmanischeen Eroberungsideologie," *JTS* 13 (1989), 81–98.

[10] While the term is recent, the idea goes as far back as Arnold Toynbee. See Toynbee, *A Selection of his Works*. Ed. E. W. F. Tomlin (Oxford, 1975), pp. 23–27.

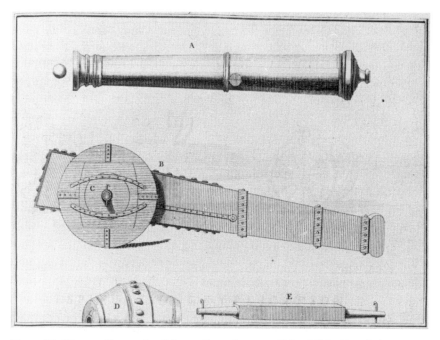

Figure 19 Ottoman 12-pounder. It is not clear what pound Marsigli had in mind. Calculating with the Venetian and Viennese pounds this 12-pounder could have fired projectiles of 3.6 kg and 6.7 kg in weight, respectively. Thus, it was probably an Ottoman *kulunburna* although it may also have been a large *şâhî* or *darbzen*. Luigi Marsigli, *L'état militaire de l'empire ottoman*, 1732.

By the latter part of the fifteenth century Ottoman foundrymen were casting the largest cannons known to contemporaries. While these large bombards were clumsy, difficult to maneuver, had a very low rate of fire (a couple of shots per day) and were of questionable usefulness, one must acknowledge that the production of such monsters required unusual technical and organizational skills that only the most advanced European states possessed. As so often in history, these gigantic pieces were the pride of the monarchs and the symbol of technological advancement of the period. In forging and casting huge bombards, the Ottomans followed suit. Unlike most of their European adversaries who had abandoned the production of such gargantuan cannons by the beginning of the sixteenth century, the Ottomans still manufactured a limited number of such massive pieces in the 1510s and perhaps even later.

Lying as abandoned pieces on the walls of Ottoman fortresses in Hungary or on the Dardanelles defenses, these giant and obsolete cannon were described and popularized by such European experts of the Ottoman military as Luigi Ferdinando Marsigli in the 1690s and Baron de Tott in the 1770s. As their descriptions captured

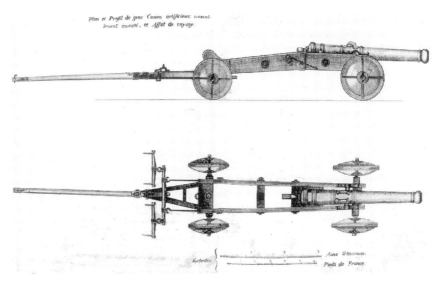

Figure 20 Late eighteenth-century Ottoman large cannon on new carriage. Throughout the early modern era Europeans observed the heavy Ottoman gun carriages. This new carriage is much lighter and more maneuverable than the old ones. Mahmud Raif Efendi, *Tableau des nouveaux reglemens de l'empire ottoman*, Constantinople, 1798.

the imagination of the European mind and found their way into European military and history books, the myth of the Ottoman giant guns was born. And the myth has survived to this day.

The systematic analysis of Ottoman gun names has shown that the Sultan's army employed a great variety of guns from the largest *şaykas* and *balyemezes* to the smallest *şâhî, saçma, prangı, eynek, misket* and *şakaloz* guns. Production output data and inventory figures of the Imperial Cannon Foundry in Istanbul from the 1520s, 1680s and 1690s, as well as from the eighteenth century, suggest that the overwhelming majority (80–100 percent) of the guns cast at the foundry consisted of small and medium-caliber pieces. Large siege and fortress cannons, that is, weapons that fired shots weighing 11 *okka* (13.5–14 kg) and more, usually comprised only a small fraction of the annual output, although the composition of ordnance cast in a given year was determined by actual military needs. In general, however, the examination of Ottoman cannons and hand firearms has revealed that Ottoman weapons were more similar to the European ones than previously thought. Similarities rather than differences with major ballistic implications are apparent in our comparisons between Ottoman and Habsburg mortars, as well as between Ottoman and European siege/fortress guns.

Although neither the gigantism nor the divergence theories of European histo-riography regarding Ottoman ordnance are supported by the evidence presented in this book, another kind of deficiency is obvious. The Ottomans used a greater variety of artillery pieces than their opponents, which suggests that they lagged behind the most advanced Western European nations in terms of standardization, even though real standardization was nowhere accomplished in the early modern period. This deficiency, that is, the perplexing variety of artillery pieces, was shared by some of the Sultan's adversaries, most notably by the two Mediterranean nations, the Venetians and the Spaniards. The sources also show, however, that during the eighteenth century the Ottomans considerably reduced the various types of any given cannon category.

As for the quality of Ottoman guns, production data of the Istanbul foundry suggest that, at least until the end of the seventeenth century, Ottoman cannon founders used the typical tin bronze, which contained 8.6–11.3 percent tin and 89.5–91.4 percent copper. Bronze of similar composition was used in many Western European countries and was recommended by Vanoccio Biringuccio, the uncontested authority on guns in the sixteenth century. Despite similar composition, sloppy foundry techniques or impurities in the metal may have caused significant porosity. However, it ought to be remembered that inconsistencies in the quality of weapons were also apparent everywhere in Europe, especially in countries where weapons and ammunition production was decentralized and where weapons were made in relatively small artisan workshops scattered in the monarchs' respective realms. Although standardization was attempted time and again, it was never really achieved in the period under discussion. The individuality of weapons remained, in spite of the fact that the workshops tried to adhere as closely as they could to the sample pieces or instructions and specifications with which the monarch (or other customers) provided them.

One main difference between Ottoman and European technology of cannon casting is apparent: whereas the Europeans cast all types of cannons of iron especially in the seventeenth century, the majority of medium- and large-caliber Ottoman guns were of bronze. The Ottomans experimented with cast-iron guns fairly early into the sixteenth century, but throughout the early modern period they usually cast only small guns of iron. In the absence of reliable evidence, it is difficult to know for sure whether the Ottomans continued to cast their larger pieces in bronze because bronze pieces were considered much safer by contemporaneous experts and because they had an abundant supply of copper, or because of the lack of Ottoman foundrymen skilled in iron casting. Further research is needed in order to answer this question.

With regard to hand firearms, Janissary *tüfenk*s closely resembled the muskets used by their Spanish and Venetian opponents. Well into the seventeenth century, the Janissaries used the matchlock musket, although from the late sixteenth century on more and more flintlock muskets were manufactured in the Empire with the Spanish *miquelet*-lock. Regarding the quality of Ottoman hand firearms further research is required. Sporadic sources suggest that *tüfenk*s manufactured in private workshops from the latter part of the sixteenth century onward were usually of better quality than those manufactured in state plants.

Self-sufficiency and mass production

We have also seen that unlike many of their rivals, such as the Spanish and the Austrian Habsburgs, the Ottomans possessed almost all the raw materials necessary for the production of ammunition and ordnance. Istanbul also created the various financial and organizational means, as well as the required infrastructure by which the Ottoman powder works and foundries were capable of manufacturing all the powder and weaponry needed for the army and the fleet.

In addition to smaller local powder plants, gunpowder was manufactured in at least a dozen major *baruthane*s or gunpowder works throughout the Empire. In the sixteenth century, important gunpowder mills operated in Istanbul, Cairo, Baghdad, Aleppo, Yemen, Buda, Belgrade and Temeşvar. In the seventeenth century, the Ottoman authorities established additional major gunpowder works in Bor (in the province of Karaman), Selanik, Gelibolu and Izmir. Of these, Selanik and Gelibolu together with the Istanbul gunpowder works remained the chief producers of gunpowder in the eighteenth century. The Ottomans were self-sufficient in the production of gunpowder well into the eighteenth century. In the sixteenth century Ottoman powder mills could manufacture some 648–1,000 metric tons (12,000–18,600 *kantar*) of powder whereas in the seventeenth this total was about 761–1,037 metric tons (14,100–19,200 *kantar*).

These amounts were more than sufficient, because contemporaneous sources estimated the powder need of seventeenth-century major campaigns at about 540 metric tons (10,000 *kantar*). That Istanbul was able to marshal the required quantities and ship them to the battlefront is evident from the account books of the Imperial Arsenal of the 1660s and 1680s. In 1684, for instance, anticipating a major Habsburg counter-offensive after the disastrous defeat at Vienna, the Ottoman authorities brought, in several shipments, about 540 metric tons of gunpowder to the fortress of Buda.

In the second half of the eighteenth century, irregular supplies of saltpeter caused production levels to fall considerably and in the 1770s a general shortage of raw materials forced the *baruthane*s to interrupt production on several occasions. Annual production levels fell to 169 metric tons by the second half of the eighteenth century. Powder shortage and quality problems were especially felt in the Russo-Ottoman war of 1768–74 and the campaigns of 1787–92, prompting major reforms within the Ottoman powder industry. By 1793, the results of the reorganization and modernization effected after these humiliating conflicts were becoming apparent in the Istanbul, Gelibolu and Selanik plants. Production levels increased and the quality of the powder also improved, approaching the quality of English and Dutch gunpowder, both of which served as models. Despite these improvements, the government decided to establish a new hydraulic gunpowder works, the first modern powder factory in the Empire. Production at the new Azadlı gunpowder works in Küçükçekmece proceeded so rapidly that by the end of the eighteenth century it was capable of manufacturing sufficient quantities of gunpowder of even better quality than before. Consequently the old factories at Gelibolu, Selanik and Bakırköy/Istanbul lost their importance and were generally used for gunpowder storage.

The history of weapons manufacturing is more complicated. The main producer of Ottoman cannons was the Istanbul Imperial Foundry, although the Ottoman government operated local foundries in many provincial capitals and mining centers. Of these, the foundries of Avlonya and Preveza on the Adriatic, Rudnik, Semendire, İskenderiye, Novaberda, Pravişte and Belgrade in the Balkans, Buda and Temeşvar in Hungary, Diyarbekir, Erzurum, Birecik, Mardin and Van in Asia Minor, Baghdad and Basra in Iraq, and Cairo in Egypt were among the important ones. While the Avlonya foundry was capable of casting 288 cannons within ten months in 1499–1500, rivaling the production levels of Istanbul, the output of the other provincial foundries was more modest, producing a couple of dozen small and medium-caliber guns usually for the forts of the province. Occasionally, and especially before major imperial campaigns, they were charged with casting guns of larger caliber to be used by the imperial Ottoman army. Ottoman stockpiles of weapons and ammunition greatly outnumbered (and often doubled) the weapons and ammunition supplies of their Hungarian and Habsburg adversaries as late as the 1680s. During the Russo-Ottoman war of 1768–74 the Istanbul foundry, unlike the Empire's powder mills, was operating at full steam, producing cannons in significant numbers. Nevertheless, contemporaneous sources noticed the poor quality of Ottoman artillery.[11]

Although the history of Ottoman *tüfenk* manufacturing and trade requires further research, it seems that despite occasional imports of hand firearms from Europe the Empire was largely self-sufficient in the manufacturing of these weapons. Because weapons technology was relatively static until the industrialization of warfare in the latter part of the nineteenth century, muskets could be used for decades. Since armies were seldom forced to surrender their hand weapons, once the troops had been equipped with muskets the manufacturing of hand firearms was limited to replacing losses or matching the increase in musket-bearing troops. Both narrative and archival sources suggest that it was not the lack of weapons, but rather the spread of hand firearms in Asia Minor, the Balkans and the Arab lands that caused problems for the Istanbul government, especially in the sixteenth and seventeenth centuries. With regard to pistols and lock mechanisms sporadic data point to a greater reliance on imports.

What went wrong?

Available evidence suggests that it was neither the Ottomans' "inferiority" in military technology nor their supposed shortcomings in ordnance production

---

[11] Virginia Aksan, *An Ottoman Statesman in War and Peace: Ahmed Resmi Efendi, 1700–1783* (Leiden, 1995), p. 128.

that brought on their first significant military failures at the end of the seventeenth century, and led to disastrous and humiliating defeats at the hands of the Russians in the latter part of the eighteenth. Such factors as double-front engagements and overstrained communications were obviously of greater significance in an empire where weaponry and ammunition manufacturing plants were scattered from Cairo to Buda, often thousands of kilometers from the theaters of war. More importantly, it became increasingly difficult to maintain a thriving manufacturing sector in an empire where the economy as a whole experienced the contractions plaguing the entire Mediterranean region. The Ottomans consequently started to lag behind the Western European economies in fields such as production capacity and productivity. In comparison with the European logistical systems, the Ottoman system proved more effective until the introduction of wide-ranging economic and administrative reforms in Europe. After these crucial administrative-bureaucratic reforms had taken place by the late seventeenth century, however, the European adversaries of the Porte were able to supply their ever-growing armies with the necessary weaponry and munitions. Furthermore, the Sultan's adversaries had by then outstripped their mighty rival, not only in the field of war industry and military know-how, but also in such fields as production capacity, finance, bureaucracy, scientific engineering and state patronage, to name a few. These factors had been of considerable importance for strengthening the European military machine since the Italian Renaissance. Yet, because of the sudden change in the nature of the Ottoman–European confrontation on land, all these improvements proved decisive at the end of the seventeenth century.

Between 1526 and 1683 there were only two major field battles (that of Mezőkeresztes in 1596 and Szentgotthárd in 1664) fought in Hungary, the main theater of Ottoman–European continental confrontation. Besides minor skirmishes of frontier forces, the Sultan's army and major provincial forces were engaged almost exclusively in siege operations. Consequently, they had to adapt the composition of their artillery and the training of their gunners. At the same time the Thirty Years War proved to be a fruitful "laboratory" for Christian armies in major field battles, as Gustavus Adolphus demonstrated. With the exception of the 1663 and 1664 wars of Köprülüzade Fazil Ahmed Pasha, the Ottomans had been given little opportunity to acquaint themselves with the intense firepower, disciplined tactics and continuous drilling of the reformed European forces. Familiarity with European battle tactics nevertheless became essential, given the changes after the Siege of Vienna in 1683. Siege warfare progressively gave way to field battles: at the Danubian frontier fifteen major field battles took place in as many years between 1683 and 1697. The Ottomans won just two of these battles; one battle ended in a stalemate, and all others were won by the European allies. By 1699 the Ottomans had lost Hungary, together with Transylvania, to the Habsburgs, the Morea to Venice, and Azov to Russia.

One should avoid the temptation to overemphasize the importance of these European victories. Technological developments, such as the adoption of the socket bayonet and flintlock musket, played an important yet limited role.[12] It was not better guns that ultimately gave the advantage to the Europeans, but better drill, command and control, and bureaucratic administration. Additionally, the Habsburgs were able to defeat their archenemy to the east only in coalition with the other forces of the Holy League, which comprised the German Princes of the Holy Roman Empire, Venice, Poland-Lithuania and Russia, all of which in effect represented all the Christian neighbors of the Sultan. The Habsburgs also had to mobilize the economic and human resources of half the continent. As a consequence of this Christian coalition, the Ottomans were forced to fight in four different theaters of war: in Hungary against the imperial forces; in Dalmatia, the Morea and the Mediterranean against the Venetians; and in Moldavia against the Poles; the Russians, who joined the Holy League in 1686, tied up the Tatars on the Eastern European and Black Sea frontier. None of the major states in seventeenth-century Europe would have been capable of waging wars simultaneously on four different frontiers and the Ottomans were no exception. Neither were the Habsburgs. After the Habsburgs were forced to withdraw their best forces from Hungary to the Rhine frontier to fight the French in the War of the League of Augsburg (1688–97), the Ottomans quickly recaptured Belgrade in 1690. Like the Ottoman Empire, the Christian archenemy of the Sultan was still too weak to engage successfully in alternative commitments. Because of the Treaty of Karlóca (Karlowitz) in 1699, the expansion of the Ottoman Empire was finally reversed. Yet the Habsburgs subsequently failed to push further south until the late nineteenth century, and plans to "liberate the Balkans" and conquer Istanbul remained unfulfilled.

It was the number of Ottoman weapons deployed on the battlefields, on the walls of Ottoman castles and aboard Ottoman ships that enabled the Empire to gain superiority in firepower. This, in turn, was a result of the availability of ample natural and human resources, as well as the efficient Ottoman administrative, financial and logistical systems through which the Porte was able to mobilize its resources and deploy its weaponry. It was only at the end of the seventeenth century that the adversaries of the Porte were able, for the first time, to match Ottoman firepower and logistics, albeit only in terms of weapon deployability in coalition warfare. Yet even this argument should not be overemphasized. Ottoman economic and military resurgence in the first half of the eighteenth century, and the success of Ottoman arms against Russia in 1711 and against Austria in the war of 1737–39, should not be forgotten.[13] In the latter war the Ottomans won back Belgrade and the northern Balkan territories. Thereafter the Habsburgs retreated behind the Military Frontier which had been (re)built along the southern border of Hungary. Subsequently, the two empires attempted to avoid open war. The Habsburg forces were preoccupied with the War of the Austrian Succession (1740–48) and the Seven

---

[12] Black, *War and the World*, pp. 60–95 (see especially p. 90).
[13] See also ibid., p. 104.

Years War (1756–63), while the Ottomans, who had fortified their own fortresses on the other side of the Military Frontier in the first decades of the century, were engaged in increasingly hopeless and costly wars against Russia, a country which had become their main adversary in the eighteenth century.

The Russo-Ottoman war of 1768–74 demonstrated the weaknesses of the Ottomans, although they were still capable of mobilizing large forces. At least on paper, the Ottomans mobilized some 12,000–60,000 troops of the standing army (Janissaries and cavalry) and allegedly had some 100,000–145,000 strong provincial light cavalry, assisted by the reputedly 100,000 strong undisciplined Tatar cavalry. However, these inflated numbers hardly reflect actual army strength and have recently been questioned. Russia, which was maintaining Europe's largest standing army (about 450,000 in the 1760s) on revenues which were equivalent in amount to just one-fifth of those of France, relied upon conscription. All male Russians were subject to the draft, and in the course of the century approximately 2.4 million were actually conscripted (24,000 per year on average). The Ottomans maintained two armies: the standing army, located in Istanbul and in the fortresses, and the *miri levend*, "a combination of volunteerism, village conscription and bribery." The transition to a system of conscription was still incomplete at the end of the century. A lack of leadership and problems of discipline continued to plague the Ottoman army. Although the Ottoman soldiers were better fed than the Russians, neither empire was immune to famine and disease.[14]

Despite the fact that the Ottomans (and the Russians) were making war on the cheap by Western European standards, the burden was still a large one for the weak Ottoman economy which was exhausted by the Russian wars. For instance, in the 1790s production at the Samakov furnaces came to a halt owing to the outbreak of epidemics, which habitually accompany wars and cause greater destruction than weapons. The forsaken mines fell into the possession of the "mountain rebels," who were the peculiar creation of war and disorder in the Balkans, and the center lost the furnaces for good. The export of raw materials was once again prohibited, and new prohibitions were placed on the export of dressed leather and various fabrics. Price increases between 1760 and 1800 reached 200 per-cent.[15] Although at the end of the eighteenth century the Imperial Cannon Foundry was occasionally still capable of casting several hundreds of cannons whose total weight approached late seventeenth-century figures (200,000 kg), especially in years that saw major troop and resource mobilization against the Russians, overall production levels lagged behind those of the peak years of the late seventeenth

[14] Aksan, *An Ottoman Statesman*, pp. 100–69; Virginia Aksan, "The One-Eyed Fighting the Blind: Mobilization, Supply, and Command in the Russo-Turkish War of 1768–1774," *IHR* 15, 2 (1993), 221–38, "Feeding the Ottoman Troops on the Danube, 1768–1774," *War and Society* 13, 1 (1995), 1–14, and "Whatever Happened to the Janissaries? Mobilization for the 1768–1774 Russo-Ottoman War," *War in History* 5, 1 (1998), 23–36.
[15] Mehmet Genç, "18. Yüzyılda Osmanlı Ekonomisi ve Savaş," in Genç, *Osmanlı İmparatorluğunda Devlet ve Ekonomi* (Istanbul, 2000), pp. 211–25.

century. Yet, the real problem occurred in the field of gunpowder production. In the decentralized late eighteenth-century Empire the central government had little control over powder production which had fallen to just 15–30 percent of the output levels of the sixteenth and seventeenth centuries. And as one Grand Vizier noted during the Long Hungarian Wars of 1593–1606, "where there is a shortage of gunpowder, even if there is a sea of gold coins, it cannot take the place of gunpowder, [for] the defense of the fortresses and warfare takes place with gunpowder." But the late eighteenth-century Ottoman government had no gold coins either.

Annual state expenditure rose by 30 percent between 1761 and 1785 (from 14,064,788 silver *guruş* in 1761 to 18,693,336 silver *guruş* in 1785), but in the war years there was a 100 percent increase. Soldiers' salaries comprised 75 percent of expenditure in 1784 and 74 percent in 1785. Meanwhile state revenues remained at much the same level, and efforts to increase revenue failed owing to the general economic stagnation. The lack of financial resources prevented the Ottomans from reacting immediately when the Russians annexed the Crimea in 1783. The Ottoman leaders fully understood that new troops were needed for the war, but the Imperial Treasury was unable to finance the payment of additional salaries. The senior accountant at the Imperial Treasury stated that 15 million *guruş* were needed to begin the war, an amount that was equal to the treasury's total annual revenue. Meanwhile the Grand Admiral estimated the costs of building a battle fleet at 6–7.5 million *guruş*; and he also considered the drafting of 36,000 troops necessary.[16] Under such circumstances, it is no surprise that the Porte waited until 1787 before launching its campaign.

Financial problems and the dislocation of the economy as a consequence of the weakening of the central administration's power vis-à-vis the provincial notables plagued the Ottomans' capabilities to wage war. To make things even worse, Ottoman troops not only were short of money, powder and adequate weaponry at the end of the eighteenth century, but, according to European and Ottoman observers, they lacked "order, discipline and technique," as early as the 1730s.[17] The secret of success, according to an Ottoman reform treatise published in 1734, was the reorganization of the Ottoman military and the transmission of order and discipline, in other words, the introduction of a new order (*nizam-i cedid*).[18] However, eighteenth-century Ottoman military reforms were limited to the technical branches of the army. The Ottoman leadership declined to implement fundamental reforms, fearing that they would endanger the entire social fabric. Drastic reforms were attempted only after the disastrous failures of the Russo-Ottoman war of 1787–92. Selim III put forward plans for the establishment of a new type of army on the European model. These plans met with the resistance of the traditionally

[16] Yavuz Cezar, *Osmanlı Maliyesinde Bunalım ve Değişim Dönemi* (Istanbul, 1986), pp. 89–97.
[17] Cf. Maréchal de Saxe's observation as quoted by Parker, *The Military Revolution*, p. 128.
[18] Ibrahim Müteferrika, *Milletlerin Düzeninde İlmî Usüller* (Istanbul, 1990), pp. 73–112.

privileged *askeri* class (particularly the Janissary–*ulema* alliance). Selim's "New Model Army" (which had been established with one regiment of 2,536 men, but had grown to some 25,000 men by 1808) was dissolved and the Sultan himself was deposed and killed. True reforms had to wait until after the liquidation of the Janissary Corps (1826). As had been predicted, these reforms sparked off profound and unforeseen social changes.

Appendix

Table 1 Ocaklık saltpeter acquired from the sancaks of Selanik and Pasha for the baruthane of Selanik, 1695–99

Kazas	H. 1107/AD 1695/96			H. 1108/AD 1696/97			H. 1109/AD 1697/98			H. 1110/AD 1698/99		
	hane	okka	okka/hane	hane	okka	okka/hane	hane	okka	okka/hane	hane	okka	okka/hane
In the *sancak* of Selanik												
Selanik	–	–	–	–	–	–	462.5	7,883.5	17	455	7,755.5	17
Yenice-i Vardar	–	–	–	–	–	–	193	4,172.5	21.6	103	2,223.5	21.6
Vodena	–	–	–	–	–	–	234	3,994	17	160	2,727.5	17
Avrat Hisari	–	–	–	–	–	–	185	3,153	17	185	3,152	17
Agustos (Njeguš)	–	–	–	–	–	–	75	1,278.5	17	75	1,278.5	17
Subtotal	–	–	–	–	–	–	1,149.5	20,481.5	17.6	978	17,137	17.5
In the *sancak* of Pasha												
Siroz (Ser)	350	–		350	–		350	7,000	20	350	7,000	20
Zihna	150	–		150	–		150	3,000	20	150	3,000	20
Florina (Lerin)	100	–		100	–		100	2,000	20	100	2,000	20
Nevrokop	133	–		133	–		133	2,667	20	133	2,666.5	20
Monastir (Bitola)	250	–		250	–		250	5,000	20	250	5,000	20
Drama	50	–		50	–		50	1,000	20	50	1,000	20
Temür Hisari	100	–	–	100	–	–	100	2,000	20	100	2,000	20
Subtotal	1,133	22,667	20	1,133	22,667	20	1,133	22,667	20	1,133	22,666.5	20
Total	1,133	22,667	20	1,133	22,667	20	2,282.5	43,148	18.8	2,111	39,803.5	18.9

Notes: 1. In H. 1107/AD 1695–96 the total saltpeter income was 110,000 *okkas* of which 87,333 *okkas* of saltpeter. From these data it is clear that the *kazas* of the *sancak* of Pasha gave their regular annual 22,667 *okkas* of saltpeter, rather they paid their taxes. This amount then was added to the cash fund that was used to purchase the necessary amount of saltpeter. The amount of saltpeter acquired from *ocaklık* (22,667 *okka*) in H. 1107 is given in MAD 3620, p. 16 as an aggregate.

2. In H. 1108/AD 1696–97 the *kazas* in the *sancak* of Selanik paid 17,150 *guruş* but the relevant section of the document is somewhat confusing since it mentions certain *kazas* of the *sancak* of Pasha among those who were paying *avarız* taxes instead of their saltpeter obligations, although it is obvious from this and other documents that these *kazas* in the *sancak* of Pasha did actually produce saltpeter. Since the total saltpeter income of the *baruthane* of Selanik was 88,000 *okkas* of which 65,333 *okkas* was purchased and 22,667 *okkas* gathered from the *sancak* of Pasha, it means that the *kazas* of the *sancak* of Selanik did not fulfill their saltpeter obligation in kind; rather they paid the corresponding tax in cash, which amount, again, was used to purchase saltpeter (ibid., pp. 84–85).

3. Note that MAD 3620, p. 32, gives a total of 42,821 *okkas* for the year H. 1109 instead of the correct total of 43,148 *okkas*. Also MAD 10305, p. 194, gives the usual 200 *avarız-hane* for Avrat Hisari and thus a subtotal of 20,737 *okkas* for all the saltpeter produced in the *sancak* of Selanik in H. 1109.

4. For the year H. 1110 our source (MAD 3620, p. 52) erroneously gives 988 *hanes* in the *sancak* of Selanik. According to our sources the total amount of saltpeter produced in the year of H. 1110 was only 39,603.5 *okkas*.

Sources: MAD 3620, pp. 16, 18 (for H. 1107); ibid., p. 87 (for H. 1108); ibid., pp. 33–34 (for H. 1109); ibid., pp. 52–53 (for H. 1110).

Table 2 Ocaklık saltpeter acquired from the sancaks of *Selanik* and *Pasha* for the baruthane of *Selanik*, 1720–24

Kazas	H. 1133/AD 1720–21					H. 1135/AD 1722–23					H. 1136/AD 1723–24				
	hane	akça	okka	okka/hane	akça/hane	hane	akça	okka	okka/hane	akça/hane	hane	akça	okka	okka/hane	akça/hane
In the *sancak* of Selanik															
Selanik	380.5	142,813	6492	17	375	380.5	142,813	6,492	17	375	380.5	142,813	6,492	17	375
Yenice-i Vardar	49	23,275	1,058	21	475	49	23,275	1,058	21	475	49	23,275	1,058	21	475
Vodena	165	61,875	2,812.5	17	375	165	61,875	2,812.5	17	375	165	61,875	2,812.5	17	375
Avrat Hisari	84	31,575	1,435	17	375	84	31,575	1,435	17	375	84	31,575	1,435	17	375
Agustos (Njeguš)	63	23,672	1,076	17	375	63	23,672	1,076	17	375	63	23,672	1,076	17	375
Subtotal	741.5	283,210	12,873.5	17.4	382	741.5	283,210	12,873.5	17.4	382	741.5	283,210	12,873.5	17.4	382
In the *sancak* of Pasha															
Siroz (Ser)	–		–			350		7,000	20		350		7,000	20	
Zihna	150		3,000	20		150		3,000	20		150		3,000	20	
Florina (Lerin)	–					–		–			–		–		
Nevrokop	133		2,666.5	20		133		2,666.5	20		133		2,667	20	
Monastir (Bitola)	250		5,000	20		250		5,000	20		250		5,000	20	
Drama	50		1,000	20		50		1,000	20		50		1,000	20	
Temür Hisari	100		2,000	20		100		2,000	20		100		2,000	20	
Subtotal	683		13,666.5	20		1,033		20,666.5	20		1,033		20,666.5	20	
Kaza of Köprülü	3.5	3905	144	20		3.5	3905	144	20		–				
Total			26,684			1,778		33,684			1,774.5		33,540		

Note: The *kazas* of the *sancak* of Selanik gave cash instead of saltpeter. Since 3.5 *hanes* in the *kaza* of Köprülü in the *sancak* of Üsküp (Skopje) also paid 3,905 *akças* as their *avarız* and *bedel-i nüzul* taxes, which was used to buy a further 144 *okkas* of saltpeter, the total saltpeter income from *ocaklıks* was 26,684 *okkas*, instead of the 26,540 given as total in the table. In the year H. 1134/AD 1721–22 the total amount of saltpeter acquired from *ocaklık* was 33,684 *okkas*. In the year H. 1035/AD 1722–23 the total *ocaklık* saltpeter (together with the 144 *okkas* from the *kaza* of Köprülü) was again 33,684 *okkas*.

Sources: 1720–21: MAD 10312, pp. 200–03; 1721–22: ibid., p. 212; 1722–23: ibid., pp. 326–28; 1723–24: ibid., pp. 408–10.

Table 3 *Sulfur acquired from* ocaklık *by the* baruthane *of Selanik 1695–1724*

Year (H/AD)	Ocaklık in okka	Ocaklık as percentage of total acquired	Purchased sulfur in okka	Purchased sulfur as percentage of total acquired	Cost of purchase	Total acquired sulfur
1107/1695–96	15,850.5	75.46	5,156	24.54	108,276	21,006.5
1108/1696–97	16,080	100.00	–	–	–	–
1109/1697–98	19,974.5	92.75	1,561	7.25	–	21,535.5
1110/1698–99	–	–	3,136.5	–	62,730	–
...	...	...	...	...	...	...
1133/1720–21	9,429	–	–	–	–	–
1134/1721–22	9,429	–	–	–	–	–
1135/1722–23	9,429	–	–	–	–	–
1136/1723–24	12,571	–	–	–	–	–

Note: In H. 1110/AD 1698–99 the total amount of sulfur used during the production of 1,713.5 *kantar* of powder was 11,968.5 *okka*, of which 3,136.5 *okka* (26.20 percent) had been purchased.
Sources: MAD 3620, pp. 27, 87, 32–33, 58 (in this order); MAD 10312, pp. 200, 212, 326.

Table 4 *Saltpeter acquired by the* baruthane *of Gelibolu, 1694–99*

Year (H/AD)	Saltpeter from the sancaks		Saltpeter purchased		Total acquired	
	in okka	in akça	in okka	in akça	in okka	in akça
1106/1694–95	20,000	800,000	15,000	900,000	35,000	1,700,000
1107/1695–96						
1108/1696–97	20,000	800,000	15,000	900,000	35,000	1,700,000
1109/1697–98	19,500	780,000	15,000	900,000	34,500	1,680,000
1110/1698–99	19,500	780,000	15,000	900,000	34,500	1,680,000

Sources: MAD 3127, pp. 13, 45, 54; MAD 10305, pp. 98–99, 120–21.

Table 5 *Expenditures of the* baruthane *of Gelibolu, 1695–1724*

Date	Expenditure (akça)	Cost of saltpeter (akça)	%
1108/1696–97		1,700,000	
1109/1697–98		1,680,000	–
1133/1720–21	3,450,583	2,328,990	67
1134/1721–22	3,446,990	2,325,397	67
1135/1722–23	4,665,486	3,173,985	68
1136/1723–24	4,652,562	3,173,985	68

Sources: 1108: MAD 10305, pp. 98–99, and MAD 3127, p. 45; 1109: MAD 10305, pp. 120–21; 1133: MAD 10312, p. 194; 1134: ibid., p. 218; 1135: ibid., p. 318; 1136: MAD 10312, p. 414.

Table 6 *Gunpowder stock in the* baruthane *of Istanbul, 1594–95*

Source	*Kantar*	Kg
Surplus from previous year	3,324.99	179,550
Surplus of the Imperial Navy	555.45	29,994
Egypt	333	17,982
Baruthane at Istanbul	170.82	9,224
Baruthane at Kağıthane	76	4,104
Total	4,460.26	240,854

Source: MAD 383, p. 79.

Table 7 *Operational costs of the imperial gunpowder works at Kağıthane, 1683–85*

	Amount	Amount in kg	Expenditure in *akça*
Saltpeter	32,347 *okka*	41,495	2,380,480
Sulfur	31,376 *okka*	40,249	714,400
Charcoal	44,370 *okka*		133,110
Firewood	4,472 *çeki*	1,009,769	227,047
Tools and repairs			1,000,694
Salaries			30,900
Given to Şabanzade Mehmed Ef.			700,000
Remained at his hand			914,160
Total			6,100,791

Source: DBŞM 449, pp. 2–5.

Table 8 *Production output of the Şehremini gunpowder works, 1689–99*

Period of production	Gunpowder produced		
	(*okka*)	(*kantar*)	(kg)
5 June 1689–2 December 1690	77,003.5	1,750	94,622
3 December 1690–15 June 1692	87,516	1,989	107,540
8 January 1693–7 January 1694	88,177	2,004	108,352
24 July 1694–12 June 1695	75,441.5	1,714.6	92,703
26 November 1696–23 March 1697	25,126	571	30,875
11 March 1697–24 October 1699	201,569	4,581	247,688

Sources: 1689–90: DBŞM 598; 1690–92: DBŞM 642; 1693–94: MAD 3620, pp. 80–81; 1694–95: MAD 10142, pp. 238–39; 1696–97: DBŞM 844; 1697–99: DBŞM 19085.

Table 9 *Gunpowder deliveries to the Cebehane,*
November 1687 through February 1689

Source of gunpowder	Amount in *kantar*
Fortress of Boğazkesen	1,010
Karaman	1,573.5
Baruthane of Istanbul	1,616.5
Egypt (Cairo)	1,352.5
Gelibolu	450
Total	6,002.5

Source: KK 4738, p. 1 (NB: the account is incomplete).

Table 10 *Operational costs of the* baruthane *of Izmir,*
January 17, 1694 through February 19, 1695

	Expenditure in *akça*	Percentage of total expenditure
Purchase of saltpeter, sulfur, charcoal	584,270	23
Purchase of equipment	299,336	12
Salaries	1,647,315	65
Total	2,530,921	100

Source: MAD 3620, p. 70.

Table 11 *Operational costs of the* baruthane *of Izmir in 1694–95, 1696–97 and 1697–98*

	Expenditure in *akça*	Percentage of total expenditure
Purchase of saltpeter	5,856,550	50.4
Purchase of *sulfur*	916,185	7.9
Purchase of charcoal	202,482	1.7
Salaries	4,652,330	40
Total	11,627,547	100

Note: Unfortunately, the accounts do not mention exact dates and therefore we have no idea whether they cover the whole year of 1106/ 1694–95 (partly covered by MAD 3620) or just the second half of that year. The year 1107/1695–96 is missing from the account. It is possible that production in that year was not under the control of Yahya Ağa, whose accounts MAD 6880 contains.
Source: MAD 6880, p. 24.

Table 12 *Output and costs of individual Karaman saltpeter works, 1641–42*

Plant	Output in *kantar*	Unrefined peter in *okka*	Costs in *akça*	Costs per *okka* in *akça*
Kilisehisar	670	29,480	254,600	8.6
Kayseri	450	19,800	171,000	8.6
Develi	230	10,120	87,400	8.6
Konya	160	7,040	60,800	8.6
Larende	170	7,480	64,600	8.6
Şarkışla	250	11,000	95,000	8.6
Akşehir	120	5,280	45,900	8.7
Aksaray	80	3,520	30,400	8.6
Budak Özü	70	3,080	26,600	8.6
Total	2,200	96,800	836,300	

Source: MAD 5392, p. 26.

Table 13 *Gunpowder production and gunpowder stocks in the Ottoman Empire,*
1644–99

Gunpowder work	Date of production	Production in *kantar*	Stock in *kantar*	Source
Istanbul	Mar. 25, 1663–June 1664		11,211	MAD 3279[a]
Istanbul	Nov. 7, 1687–Nov. 23, 1688		7,183	MAD 15758[b]
Istanbul	Mar. 30, 1683–June 10, 1686	6,275		DBŞM 449
Istanbul	June 5, 1689–Dec. 2, 1690	1,750		DBŞM 598
Istanbul	Dec. 3, 1690–June 15, 1692	1,989		DBŞM 642
Istanbul	Jan. 8, 1693–Jan. 7, 1694	2,004		MAD 3620, pp. 80–81
Istanbul	Nov. 26, 1696–Mar. 23, 1697	571		DBŞM 844
Istanbul	Mar. 11, 1697–Oct. 24, 1699	4,581		DBŞM 19085
Gelibolu	1668	1,000		KK 2647, pp. 9–12
Gelibolu	July 31, 1696–July 19, 1697	1,000		MAD 3127, p. 45
Gelibolu	July 20, 1697–July 9, 1698	1,000		MAD 3127, p. 45
Gelibolu	July 10, 1698–June 28, 1699	1,000		MAD 3127, p. 54
Izmir	1685–87	3,144		MAD 885, pp. 10–14
Izmir	Jan. 17, 1694–Feb. 19, 1695[c]	2,248.5		MAD 3620, p. 70
Izmir	July 31, 1696–July 9, 1698	3,534.4		MAD 6880, pp. 26–27
Izmir	July 10, 1698–June 28, 1699	2,081		MAD 6880, p. 17
Selanik	Nov. 17, 1686–Oct. 25, 1688	4,970		DMKF 27627/189-A
Selanik	1695/96	2,520	3,081	MAD 3620, p. 27
Selanik	1696/97	2,035.5	3,231	MAD 3620, p. 87
Selanik	1697/98	3,078.5	3,306	MAD 3620, p. 37
Karaman	1644/45		7,392.8	MAD 7512
Bor (in Karaman)	Second half of the 17th century	1,800–2,000/year[d]		
Temeşvar	1672		1,000[e]	MAD 1497
Temeşvar	1679/80	1,380		KK 2682
Egypt	1663/64		2,000	MAD 3279[f]
Buda	1684		10,000	MAD 177[g]

Notes: [a] The figure indicates the total gunpowder income of the imperial ammunition stores.

[b] The figure gives the total amount of gunpowder to be found in the Imperial Armory in this period.

[c] MAD 6880, p. 26 claims that the production in H. 1106 (Aug. 22, 1694–Aug. 11, 1695) was 1,887.6 *kantars*.

[d] The annual obligation of Karaman in this period was 80,000 *okka* (1,818 *kantars*). However, during campaigns such as the 1663–64 Hungarian campaign the officials in Karaman had to and did send more gunpowder than required by their obligation.

[e] In July 1672 800 *kantars* of gunpowder was delivered to Varad (MAD 1497, p. 9).

[f] On May 6, 1663 818 *kantars* and on June 25 a further shipment of 613 *kantars* arrived from Egypt for the 1663–64 Hungarian campaign. On October 15 again 613 and on April 17 another shipment of 818 *kantars* arrived from Egypt for the 1664 campaign.

[g] This was the shipment that reached Buda by the end of March.

The source of all notes, unless indicated otherwise, is Ágoston, "Gunpowder for the Sultan's Army."

Table 14 *Output of the Tophane, 1517–19*

Type of gun	Length of gun in *karış*	Note	Number of guns
bacaluşka	30		8
bacaluşka	25		8
bacaluşka	25	In two parts	1
şayka	20		8
şayka	18		6
darnzen	17		1
darbzen	14	In two parts	25
darbzen			550
prangı			64
havayî			2
Total			673

Sources: KK 4726; İdris Bostan, "A szultáni ágyúöntő műhelyben (Tophane-i Amire) folyó tevékenység a 16. század elején," *Aetas* 18, 2 (2003), 12.

Table 15 *Output of the Tophane, January 17, 1676 through May 23, 1676*

Name/caliber of piece	Number
9-*okka* gun	8
7-*okka* gun	7
3-*okka* gun	3
1.5-*okka* gun	22
Total	40

Source: DBŞM TPH 18596, p. 3.

Table 16 *Output of the Tophane, June 24, 1676 through August 13, 1676*

Name/caliber of piece	Number
14-*okka* gun	6

Source: DBŞM TPH 18596, p. 7.

Table 17 *Output of the Tophane, July 26, 1684 through June 16, 1685*

Name/caliber of piece	Number	Material used in *kantar*	Material used in kg
Guns cast under Elhac Mehmed Aga in the *firın*s			
14-*okka balyemez*	2		
7-*okka* gun	60		
5-*okka* gun	126		
3-*okka* gun	28		
1-*okka şâhî*	12		
0.5-*okka şâhî*	36		
mortars (*havan-i humbara*)	6		
Subtotal	270	7,791.5	420,741
Guns cast under Kul-zade in the new *ocak*s			
5-*okka* gun	29		
3-*okka* gun	45		
1.5-*okka* gun	13		
şayka	9		
1-*okka şâhî*	27		
0.5-*okka şâhî*	20		
Subtotal	143	2,709.5	146,313
Guns cast under Elhac Mehmed in the new *ocak*s			
3-*okka* gun	3		
1.5-*okka* gun	13		
şayka	21		
1-*okka şâhî*	17		
0.5-*okka şâhî*	14		
saçma	82		
eynek	222		
Subtotal	372	1,109.5	59,913
Total	785	11,610.5	626,967

Source: KK 5649, pp. 1, 7, 12.

Table 18 *Output of the Tophane, October 14, 1685*
through July 21, 1686

Name/caliber of piece	Number
Guns cast under Mustafa Efendi in the old *fırıns*	
14-*okka balyemez*	1
11-*okka balyemez*	1
9-*okka* gun	2
7-*okka* gun	2
5-*okka* gun	11
3-*okka* gun	11
1.5-*okka* gun	28
1-*okka şâhî*	16
0.5-*okka şâhî*	16
mortars (*havan-i humbara*)	16
Subtotal	104
Guns cast under Elhac Salih in the new *ocak*s	
1.5-*okka* gun	1
1-*okka* gun	8
0.5-*okka* gun	49
mortars	10
Subtotal	68
Guns cast under Bektaş in the new *ocak*s	
1-*okka şâhî*	4
0.5-*okka şâhî*	38
misket	40
saçma	30
eynek	40
Subtotal	152
Total	324

Note: The total weight of material used during the process of casting is given as 2,500 *kantar* or 135,000 kg.
Source: DMŞM TPH 18598, pp. 3, 8–9, 14.

Table 19 *Guns taken into inventory at the Tophane, October 14, 1685 through July 21, 1686*

Name/caliber of piece	Number (I)	Number (II)
14-*okka balyemez*	1	1
11-*okka balyemez*	1	1
9-*okka*	4	4
7-*okka*[a]	4	4
5-*okka*	11	12
3-*okka*	19	17
1.5-*okka*	43	44
şayka	15	15
1-*okka*	94	148[b]
0.5-*okka*	75	
100-*dirhem top-i misket*	48	40
saçma	30	30
eynek	40	40
havan-i humbara	26	26
top-i humbara	5	2
Total	416	384

Notes: [a] MAD 4028 gives them as 9-*okka* guns. However, it is clear from DBŞM TPH 18597 that these were 7-*okka* guns. (II) according to DBŞM TPH 18598, p. 14.
[b] 1-*okka* and 0.5-*okka* guns together.
Sources: (I) MAD 4028, p. 90; (II) DBŞM TPH 18597, p. 7; DBŞM TPH 18598, p. 14.

Table 20 *Output of the Tophane, December 12, 1691 through April 30, 1692*

Name/caliber of piece	Number
11-*okka*	50
7-*okka*	6
5-*okka*	25
3-*okka*	30
sefer	100
top-i şayka-i Tuna	34
various cannon for *kalyata*s and *firkate*s	26
*eynek*s for *kalyata*s and *firkate*s	26
havan	1
Total	298

Source: DBŞM TPH 18601, pp. 4–15.

Table 21 *Output of the Tophane, April 18,*
1693 through June 14, 1693

Name/caliber of piece	Number
11-*okka* gun	2
9-*okka* gun	6
7-*okka* gun	14
Total	22

Source: DBŞM TPH 18604, p. 2.

Table 22 *Output of the Tophane, October 12,*
1693 through April 4, 1694 and September 4,
1694 through July 12, 1695

Name/caliber of piece	Number
11-*okka*	6
9-*okka*	5
7-*okka*	63
5-*okka*	43
3-*okka*	14
1.5-*okka*	72
1-*okka*	157
100-*dirhem*	79
saçma	72
eynek	144
70-*okka* mortars	6
35-*okka* mortars	18
Total	679

Note: The total weight of pieces was 7,431.9 *kantar* or
401,323 kg.
Source: MAD 5432, p. 29b.

Table 23 *Output of the Tophane, September 24, 1695 through April 5, 1696*

Name/caliber of piece	Number cast	Average weight per gun in *kantar*	Average weight per gun in kg	Total weight in *kantar*	Total weight in kg
11-*okka*	1	56	3,024	56	3,024
9-*okka*	37	47	2,538	1,739	93,906
7-*okka*	1				
5-*okka*	42	33.5	1,809	1,407	75,978
3-*okka*	35	23	1,242	805	43,470
saçma	30	0.66	35.64	20	1,080
eynek	62	0.42	22.68	26	1,404
Total	208			4,053	218,862

Source: KK 5654, pp. 16, 30.

Table 24 *Output of the Tophane, April 6, 1696 through May 31, 1697 (guns)*

Name/caliber of piece	Number cast	Weight per piece in *kantar*	Weight per piece in kg	Total weight in *kantar*	Total weight in kg
44-*okka* gun	2	80	4,320	160	8,640
16-*okka* gun	22	75	4,050	1,650	89,100
11-*okka* gun	2	56	3,024	112	6,048
9-*okka* gun	7	47	2,538	327	17,658
7-*okka* gun	23	37	1,998	851	45,954
5-*okka* gun	45	33.5	1,809	1,485	80,190
3-*okka* gun	36	23	1,242	828	44,712
1.5-*okka* gun	62	13 and 9.5[a]	702 and 513	596	32,184
1-*okka* gun	38	9 and 5.5[b]	486 and 297	265	14,310
0.5-*okka* gun	2	6	324	12	648
100-*dirhem* gun	61	1	54	61	3,294
100-*dirhem* gun	4	–		4	216
cast-iron *saçma* gun	334			?	
cast-iron *eynek* gun	668			?	
Total	1,306			6,351[c]	342,954

Notes: [a] Two pieces weighed 13 *kantar*, while sixty pieces weighed only 9.5 *kantar*.
[b] Sixteen pieces weighed 9 *kantar*, while twenty-two pieces weighed only 5.5 *kantar*.
[c] Does not include the weight of the 1002 small cast-iron pieces.
It is interesting to note that the account refers to the guns other than *saçma* and *eynek* as cannon (*top*) and treats them separately at the heading, giving their number as 300 (the correct number is 304). While all the cannons were cast of bronze, the small-caliber *saçma* and *eynek* pieces were cast-iron guns.
Source: MAD 173, p. 16b.

Table 25 *Output of the Tophane, April 6, 1696 through May 31, 1697 (mortars)*

Name/caliber of mortar	Number	Weight per piece in *kantar*	Weight per piece in kg	Total weight in *kantar*	Total weight in kg
180-*okka* large mortar (*havan-i kebir*)	1	72	3,888	72	3,888
80-*okka havan-i kazgan*	8	22.5	1,215	180	9,720
36-*okka* medium mortar (*havan-i vasat*)	4	16	864	64	3,456
24-*okka* mortar	3	12	648	36	1,944
Total	16			352	19,008

Source: MAD 173, p. 16b.

Table 26 *Guns dispatched from the Tophane and deployed aboard various Ottoman ships, 1696–97*

- To the *kapudan paşa* for the *kalyon*s of the Imperial Armada, 113 pieces: 2 pieces of 44-*okka* caliber *şayka* guns, 22 pieces of 16-*okka*, 3 pieces of 9-*okka*, 21 pieces of 7-*okka*, 30 pieces of 5-*okka*, 29 pieces of 3-*okka* and 6 pieces of 1-*okka* caliber guns.
- To the *kadırga* of Süleymanpaşazade and Memipaşazade, 3 pieces: 1 9-*okka* caliber *koğuş* gun for Süleymanpaşazade and 2 pieces of 1.5-*okka* caliber *yan top* for Memipaşazade.
- To the *işkampoye*s of the Black Sea, 180 pieces: 60 pieces of iron *saçma*s and 120 pieces of iron *eynek*s.
- To the *kalyata*s of the Black Sea, 405 pieces: 15 pieces of 5-*okka* caliber *koğuş* guns, 60 pieces of 1.5 *okka* caliber *yan* guns, 110 pieces of iron *saçma*s and 220 pieces of iron *eynek*s.
- To the *şayka*s of the Black Sea, 225 pieces: 25 pieces of 1-*okka* caliber *koğuş* guns, 50 pieces of 100-*dirhem* caliber *yan* guns, 50 pieces of iron *saçma*s and 100 pieces of iron *eynek*s.
- To the *kalyon*s of the Black Sea, 303 pieces: 2 pieces of 5-*okka* caliber iron guns, 1 piece of 3 *okka* caliber iron gun, 100 pieces of iron *saçma*s and 200 pieces of iron *eynek*s.
- To the *sandal* of Mehmed Paşa, *baş buğ* in the region of Azak, 6 pieces: 2 pieces of iron *saçma*s and 4 pieces of iron *eynek*s.
- To the new *firkate* ships of the Black Sea, 36 pieces: 12 pieces of iron *saçma*s and 24 pieces of iron *eynek*s.

Source: MAD 173, pp. 16b–17a.

Table 27 *Cannon balls cast in the Kağıthane, April 4,*
1696 through May 31, 1697

	Number
Caliber (*okka*)	
9	1,720
7	7,955
5	15,427
3	14,374
2.5	5,992
2	2,800
1.5	12,307
1	1,881
0.5	2,000
Total	64,456
Total weight in *okka*	233,836
Total weight in kg	287,338

Note: Our source mistakenly gives the total number of shots as 65,457.
Source: MAD 4578, p. 8.

Table 28 *Cannon balls cast in the Tophane,*
February 7, 1697 through March 23, 1697

	Number
Caliber (*okka*)	
11	600
9	400
7	650
3	500
Total	2,150
Total weight in *okka*	16,250
Total weight in kg	19,968

Source: MAD 4578, p. 8.

Table 29 *Cannon balls cast in the Kağıthane, November 23, 1697 through May 20, 1698*

	Number
Caliber (*okka*)	
16	364
11	280
9	500
7	3,800
5	6,600
3	2,500
1.5	4,000
1	7,200
0.5	5,200
Total	30,444
Total weight in *okka*	96,304
Total weight in kg	118,338

Source: MAD 2732, p. 48.

Table 30 *Bombshells cast in the Kağıthane, November 23, 1697 through May 20, 1698*

	Number	Weight per piece in *okka*s	Total weight in *okka*s	Total weight in kg
Caliber (*okka*)				
80	283	60	16,980	
45	250	40	10,000	
36	818	30	24,540	
24	666	20	13,320	
Total	2,017		64,840	79,675

Source: MAD 2732, p. 48.

Table 31 *Cannon balls cast in the Tophane,
November, 23, 1697 through May 20, 1698*

	Number
Caliber in *okka*	
9	515
7	1,050
5	3,120
3	2,100
1.5	4,100
1	16,000
Total	26,885
Total weight in *okka*	62,261
Total weight in kg	76,506

Note: In addition to these newly cast shots, in the storehouses of the
Tophane there were 2,101 cannon balls of various calibers and 900
"infidel" bombshells of 80-*okka* caliber. From the Naval Arsenal
arrived 600 16-*okka* shots and from Pravişte came 17,400 cannon
balls from 16-*okka* through 1.5 *okka* caliber. The total number of
shots cast and amassed in the Tophane and Kağithane is given as
77,430 (see Tables 29 and 31), whereas that of bombshells is 2,917
(see Table 30, plus these 900).
Source: MAD 2732, p. 49.

Table 32 *Output of the Tophane, November 15, 1697
through September 18, 1698*

Name/caliber of piece	Number	Total weight in *kantar*	Total weight in kg
Guns of various caliber	237	4,627	249,858
Mortars	16	241	13,014
saçma	2	7	378
eynek	16	3.46	187
Total	271	4,878.46	263,437

Source: MAD 2732, p. 32. As can be seen there is some overlap
with the accounts of MAD 173. Also DBŞM TPH 18609 and 18610
contain valuable information for the same years.

Table 33 *Types and number of guns sent from the Tophane to Mehmed Pasha,* kapudan *of the Shatt al-Arab fleet, 1698–99*

Name/caliber of piece	Number
1.5-*okka koğuş* gun	41
1-*okka koğuş* gun	19
0.5-*okka* flanking (*yan*) gun	92
100-*dirhem* flanking (*yan*) gun	28
24-*okka* mortar	2
14-*okka* mortar	2
saçma	18
Cast-iron *saçma* gun	230
eynek	24
Cast-iron *eynek*	472
Total	928

Source: MAD 975, p. 16.

Table 34 *Types and number of projectiles sent from the Tophane to Mehmed Pasha,* kapudan *of the Shatt al-Arab fleet, 1698–99*

Type/caliber of projectile	Number of projectiles	Weight in kg
24-*okka* bombshell (*humbara*)	221	6,517
14-*okka* projectile	331	5,693
1.5-*okka* cannon ball (*yuvarlak*)	4,100	7,557
1-*okka* cannon ball	1,900	2,335
0.5-*okka* cannon ball	9,400	5,775
100-*dirhem* cannon ball	2,600	799
Total	18,552	28,676

Note: Weight in kg is calculated with the nominal weight.
Source: MAD 975, p. 16.

Table 35 *Output of the Tophane, June 20,*
1704 through October 15, 1704

Name/caliber of piece	Number
20-*okka* gun	1
14-*okka* gun	1
11-*okka* gun	1
0.5-*okka* gun	8
iron *saçmas*	52
iron *eyneks*	104
Total	167

Source: DBŞM TPH 18613, p. 4.

Table 36 *Output of the Tophane, October 16, 1704 through March 15, 1706*

Name/caliber of piece	Number	Average weight of piece in *kantar*	Average weight of piece in kg	Total weight of pieces in *kantar*	Total weight of pieces in kg
44-*okka* caliber şayka	8	72	3,888	576	31,104
22-*okka* caliber şayka	5	48.2	2,603	241	13,014
5-*okka* caliber guns	13	25.6	1,382	332.8	17,971
3-*okka* caliber guns	79	20	1,080	1580	85,320
1-*okka* caliber şâhî	1	9.1	491	9.1	491
saçma	8 ⎫			6.29	340
eynek	16 ⎭				
Total	130			2745.19	148,240

Note: The total weight of pieces is given as 2,744 *kantar*.
Source: MAD 2652, pp. 24–25.

Table 37 *Output of the Tophane, August 28,*
1706 through December 9, 1707

Name/caliber of pieces	Number
şayka	8
16-*okka* gun	3
14-*okka* gun	5
11-*okka* gun	10
7-*okka* gun	2
5-*okka kalyon*	30
3-*okka kalyon*	21
1.5-*okka* gun	1
1-*okka* gun	77
3-*okka kalyon*	3
1.5-*okka* gun	2
1-*okka şâhî*	2
300-*dirhem şâhî*	1
100-*dirhem misket*	5
85-*okka* mortar	4
24-*okka* mortar	3
Total	177

Note: The total weight of pieces was 4,301.07 *kantar* or
242,752 kg.
Source: MAD 2679, pp. 2–11.

Table 38 *Output of the Tophane, February 20,*
1711 through March 10, 1712

Name/caliber of pieces	Number
7-*okka* fortress gun	10
5-*okka* fortress gun	10
3-*okka* fortress gun	6
3-*okka kalyon*	14
1.5-*okka yan kalyata*	26
1-*okka koğuş-i firkate*	31
300-dirhem *koğuş-i firkate*	70
150-*dirhem misket*	18
85-*okka* mortar	2
45-*okka* mortar	2
18-*okka* mortar	22
Total	211

Note: The total weight of pieces was 2,102.49 *kantar* or
118,665 kg (DBŞM TPH 18615, pp. 14–19).
Source: DBŞM TPH 18615, p. 20.

Table 39 *Output of the Tophane, March 11, 1712, through June 22, 1714*

Name/caliber of pieces	Number	Total weight of pieces in *kantar*	Average weight per piece in *kantar*	Total weight of pieces in kg	Average weight per piece in kg
Guns cast in the *fırns*					
9-*okka* 16-*karış sefer*	4	196.4	49.1	11,085	2,771
7-*okka* 14-*karış sefer*	5	221.7	44.34	12,513	2,503
5-*okka* 16-*karış sefer*	7	234.6	33.51	13,241	1,892
5-*okka* 13-*karış kalyon*	18	535	29.72	30,195	1,678
3-*okka* 14-*karış sefer*	6	141	23.5	7,958	1,326
3-*okka* 12-*karış kalyon*	16	344.3	21.52	19,432	1,215
Guns cast in the *ocaks*					
22-*okka* 16-*karış şayka*	2	92.09	46	5,194	2,599
7-*okka* 11-*karış* . . . gun	1	32.04	32.04	1,808	1,808
3-*okka* 12- *karış kalyon*	1	21	21	1,185	1,185
1-*okka* 11-*karış şâhî*	28	309.1	11	17,446	623
85-*okka* mortar	3	40.66	13.55	2,295	765
45-*okka* mortar	2	43.2	21.6	2,438	1,219
20-*okka* mortar	5	36.74	7.35	2,074	415
14-*okka* mortar	5	8.6	1.72	485	97
Total	103	2,256.43		127,349	

Sources: DBŞM TPH 18617, p. 4. and 18618, pp. 20–25.

Table 40 *Output of the Tophane, October 13, 1731 through June 23, 1732*

Type/caliber of pieces	Number
11-*okka* 21-*karış* gun	4
9-*okka* 14-*karış* gun	30
5-*okka* 14-*karış* gun	10
3-*okka* 14-*karış* gun	23
3-*okka* 18-*karış* gun	16
Total	83

Source: MAD 2677, p. 20.

Table 41 *Average weight of Ottoman guns cast at
the Tophane for the imperial galleons, 1731–32*

Type/caliber of pieces	Average weight	
	in *kantar* and *lodra*	in kg
11-*okka* 21-*karış* gun	86 *kantar*, 42 *lodra*	4,878
9-*okka* 14-*karış* gun	46 *kantar*, 50 *lodra*	2,624
5-*okka* 14-*karış* gun	29 *kantar*, 81 *lodra*	1,682
3-*okka* 18-*karış* gun	34 *kantar*, 4 *lodra*	1,942
3-*okka* 14-*karış* gun	21 *kantar*, 72 *lodra*	1,226

Source: MAD 2677, pp. 16–20.

Table 42 *Types and number of guns in the
storehouse of the Tophane, June 1732*

Name/caliber of pieces	Number
28-*okka* gun	1
ağızlı	1
44-*okka şayka-i kalyon*	12
16-*okka kalyon*	22
14-*okka sefer*	4
14-*okka şayka-i sefer*	7
11-*okka kalyon*	48
9-*okka sefer*	13
9-*okka kalyon*	30
7-*okka sefer*	15
7-*okka kalyon*	33
5-*okka sefer*	15
5-*okka kalyon*	57
3-*okka sefer*	12
3-*okka kalyon*	33
1.5-*okka şâhî-i sefer*	40
1.5-*okka yan-i kalyata*	36
1-*okka şâhî-i sefer*	55
1-*okka koğuş-i fırkate*	9
0.5-*okka yan-i fırkate*	2
100-*dirhem misket*	2
50-*dirhem misket*	3
Total	450

Source: MAD 2677, p. 21.

Table 43 *Types and number of mortars in the storehouse of the Tophane, June 1732*

Caliber	Number
200-*okka*	2
120-*okka*	5
85-*okka*	6
45-*okka*	6
32-*okka*	4
20-*okka*	2
18-*okka*	7
Mortar for hand grenades (*havan-i deste*)	4
Total	36

Note: The source gives the total number of mortars as 44.
Source: MAD 2677, p. 21.

Table 44 *Output of the Tophane, September 21, 1732 through June 13, 1733*

Name/caliber of piece	Number
Guns	
14-*okka sefer*	6
11-*okka sefer*	10
9-*okka sefer*	2
3-*okka sefer*	3
14-*okka şayka-i sefer*	3
1.5-*okka şâhî-i sefer*	30
1-*okka şâhî-i sefer*	20
0.5-*okka şâhî-i sefer*	200
saçma	1
eynek	1
Subtotal	276
Mortars	
85-*okka*	4
45-*okka*	6
Small mortars	100
Subtotal	110
Total number of guns and mortars	386

Note: The total weight of pieces was 3,056.53 *kantar* or 172,510.44 kg (DBŞM TPH 18637, pp. 16–27).
Source: DBŞM TPH 18637, p. 27.

Table 45 *Output of the Tophane, March 24, 1734*
through March 20, 1735

Name/caliber of piece	Number
Guns cast in the *fırıns*	
11-*okka kalyon*	6
7-*okka kalyon*	8
5-*okka kalyon*	15
3-*okka kalyon*	9
1.5-*okka şâhî-i sefer*	15
Subtotal	53
Guns cast in the *ocaks*	
5-*okka kalyon*	14
3-*okka kalyon*	9
1-*okka şâhî-i sefer*	90
0.5-*okka şâhî*	58
45-*okka* field mortar (*havan-i sefer*)	2
32-*okka* field mortar	3
18-*okka* field mortar	4
18-*okka* . . . mortar	1
. . . mortar	1
Subtotal	182
Total number of guns and mortars	235

Note: The total weight of pieces was 3,502.11 *kantar* or 197,659 kg
(DBŞM TPH 18641, pp. 17–24).
Source: DBŞM TPH 18641, pp. 18, 24.

Table 46 *Output of the Tophane, March 8, 1737*
through April 20, 1738

Name/caliber of piece	Number
Guns	
5-*okka sefer*	10
3-*okka* gun	20
1.5-*okka şâhî*	50
1-*okka şâhî*	80
1-*okka şayka*	20
300-*dirhem firkate*	144
0.5-*okka şâhî*	80
0.5-*okka şayka ve firkate*	76
100-*dirhem çifte?* gun	4
Subtotal	484
Mortars	
45-*okka*	15
32-*okka*	52
18-*okka*	49
Small mortars	48
Subtotal	164
Total number of guns and mortars	648

Note: The total weight of guns and mortars was 4,801.68 *kantar* or
271,006.82 kg (DBŞM TPH 18645, pp. 12–22).
Source: DBŞM TPH 18645, p. 22.

Table 47 *Output of the Tophane, November 8, 1743 through November 26, 1744*

Name/caliber of piece	Number
11-*okka* 14-*karış* gun	4
9-*okka* 14-*karış* gun	8
7-*okka* 14-*karış* gun	4
5-*okka* 14-*karış* gun	4
3-*okka* 14-*karış* gun	4
1.5-*okka* 11-*karış* şâhî	6
1-*okka* 9-*karış* şâhî	50
0.5-*okka* 8-*karış* şâhî	25
45-*okka* mortar	10
32-*okka* mortar	3
18-*okka* mortar	9
Total	127

Source: DBŞM TPH 18652, p. 17.

Table 48 *Output of the Tophane, November 27, 1744 through November 15, 1745*

Name/caliber of piece	Number
14-*okka* 15-*karış* gun	4
14-*okka* 7-*karış* gun	2
11-*okka* 15-*karış* gun	2
5-*okka* 15-*karış* gun	9
3-*okka* 15-*karış* gun	12
1.5-*okka* 11-*karış* şâhî	30
1.5-*okka* 10-*karış* şâhî	6
1-*okka* 11-*karış* şâhî	14
1-*okka* 9-*karış* şâhî	24
32-*okka* mortar	2
18-*okka* mortar	6
14-*okka* mortar	6
Total	117

Source: DBŞM TPH 18655, p. 19.

Table 49 *Output of the Tophane, November 22,*
1746 through October 25, 1747

Name/caliber of piece	Number
11-*okka* 15-*karış* gun	1
1.5-*okka* 11-*karış şâhî*	30
1-*okka* 11-*karış şâhî*	14
1-*okka* 9-*karış şâhî*	39
0.5-*okka* 8-*karış şâhî*	65
0.5-*okka* 7-*karış şâhî*	19
18-*okka* mortar	8
Total	176

Source: DBŞM TPH 18656, p. 15.

Table 50 *Output of the Tophane, October 16, 1747*
through October 25, 1748

Name/caliber of piece	Number
3-*okka* gun	2
1.5-*okka şâhî*	6
1-*okka şâhî*	5
0.5-*okka şâhî*	5
120-*okka* mortar	2
85-*okka* mortar	2
Total	22

Source: DBŞM TPH 18658, p. 8.

Table 51 *Output of the Tophane, October 4, 1749*
through September 17, 1750

Name/caliber of piece	Number
9-*okka* gun	1
7-*okka* gun	3
5-*okka* gun	15
3-*okka* gun	15
1.5-*okka şâhî*	20
85-*okka* mortar	2
18-*okka* mortar	2
Total	58

Note: The total weight of pieces was 1,478.25 *kantar* or 83,432 kg
(DBŞM TPH 18660, pp. 12–17).
Source: DBŞM TPH 18660, p. 17.

Table 52 *Output of the Tophane, September 7,*
1751 through September 9, 1752

Name/caliber of piece	Number
5-*okka* 16-*karış* gun	12
3-*okka* 16-*karış* gun	15
1.5-*okka* 11-*karış şâhî*	50
1-*okka* 11-*karış şâhî*	22
Total	99

Note: The total weight of pieces was 1,801.26 *kantar* or
101,663 kg (DBŞM TPH 18663, pp. 10–14).
Source: DBŞM TPH 18663, p. 14.

Table 53 *Output of the Tophane, July 28, 1756*
through July 10, 1757

Name/caliber of piece	Number
7-*okka* 16-*karış* gun	12
5-*okka* 16-*karış* gun	12
3-*okka* 16-*karış* gun	16
45-*okka* mortar	2
18-*okka* mortar	5
Total	47

Note: The total weight of pieces was 1,487.36 *kantar* or
83,947 kg (DBŞM TPH 18666, pp. 13–15).
Source: DBŞM TPH 18666, p. 15.

Table 54 *Output of the Tophane, July 11, 1757*
through September 3, 1758

Name/caliber of piece	Number
132-*okka* large *şayka*	2
7-*okka* 16-*karış* gun	8
5-*okka* 16-*karış* gun	8
3-*okka* 16-*karış* gun	15
1.5-*okka* 11-*karış şâhî*	26
1-*okka* 9-*karış şâhî*	14
0.5-*okka* 8-*karış şâhî*	5
0.5-*okka* 5.5-*karış şâhî*	24
32-*okka* mortar	3
18-*okka* mortar	4
14-*okka* mortar	2
Total	111

Note: The total weight of pieces was 2,220.23 *kantar* or
125,310 kg (DBŞM TPH 18668, pp. 18–24).
Source: DBŞM TPH 18668, p. 24.

Table 55 *Output of the Tophane, September 4, 1758*
through August 24, 1759

Name/caliber of piece	Number
11-*okka* 16-*karış* gun	4
9-*okka* 16-*karış* gun	3
7-*okka* 16-*karış* gun	11
5-*okka* 16-*karış* gun	12
1-*okka* 6-*karış* *şâhî*	10
0.5-*okka* 6-*karış* *şâhî*	2
100-*dirhem* 6-*karış* *şâhî*	30
85-*okka* mortar	2
45-*okka* mortar	2
Total	76

Note: The total weight of pieces was 1,598.96 *kantar* or 90,245 kg
(DBŞM TPH 18671, pp. 15–18).
Source: DBŞM TPH 18671, p. 19.

Table 56 *Output of the Tophane, August 13, 1760*
through August 1, 1761

Name/caliber of piece	Number
Guns cast in the *fırıns*	
7-*okka* 16-*karış* gun	4
3-*okka* 16-*karış* gun	14
3-*okka* 13-*karış* gun	13
Subtotal	31
Guns cast in the *ocaks*	
3-*okka* 16-*karış* gun	6
3-*okka* 13-*karış* gun	15
1.5-*okka* 11-*karış* gun	20
1-*okka* 9-*karış* gun	6
0.5-*okka* 8-*karış* gun	4
Subtotal	51
Total	82

Note: The total weight of pieces was 1,693.66 *kantar* or 95,590 kg
(DBŞM TPH 18673 pp. 18–22).
Source: DBŞM TPH 18673, pp. 19, 22; DBŞM TPH 18674, p. 2.

Table 57 *Output of the Tophane, April 2, 1769 through June 29, 1770*

Name/caliber of piece	Number
5-*okka* 16-*karış* gun	10
3-*okka* 16-*karış* gun	10
3-*okka* 13-*karış* gun	40
1.5-*okka* 11-*karış şâhî*	40
1.5-*okka* 9-*karış şâhî*	68
1-*okka* 10-*karış şâhî*	50
1-*okka* 7-*karış şâhî*	120
0.5-*okka* 9-*karış şâhî*	10
14-*okka* gun	2
Total	350

Note: The total weight of the pieces cast was 3,660 *kantar* or 206,424 kg (DBŞM TPH 18687, pp. 10–24).
Source: DBŞM TPH 18687, pp. 10–24.

Table 58 *Minimum/maximum weight of guns cast at the Tophane, 1769–70*

Name/caliber of piece	Minimum weight	Maximum weight
5-*okka* 16-*karış* gun	35 *kantar*, 46 *lodra*	36 *kantar*, 60 *lodra*
3-*okka* 16-*karış* gun	27 *kantar*, 86 *lodra*	28 *kantar*, 96 *lodra*
3-*okka* 13-*karış* gun	17 *kantar*, 66 *lodra*	19 *kantar*, 6 *lodra*
1.5-*okka* 11-*karış şâhî*	9 *kantar*, 46 *lodra*	13 *kantar*, 66 *lodra*
1.5-*okka* 10-*karış şâhî*	8 *kantar*, 96 *lodra*	9 *kantar*, 66 *lodra*
1.5-*okka* 9-*karış şâhî*	8 *kantar*, 2 *lodra*	9 *kantar*, 10 *lodra*
1-*okka* 10-*karış şâhî*	8 *kantar*, 52 *lodra*	9 *kantar*, 96 *lodra*
1-*okka* 7-*karış şâhî*	4 *kantar*, 46 *lodra*	6 *kantar*, 2 *lodra*
0.5-*okka* 9-*karış şâhî*	7 *kantar*, 16 *lodra*	7 *kantar*, 82 *lodra*

Source: DBŞM TPH 18687, pp. 10–24.

Table 59 *Output of the Tophane, September 21, 1771 through October 12, 1772*

Name of piece	Caliber (*okka*)	Length (*karış*)	Number
–	5	16	2
–	3	16	8
–	3	6	10
şâhî	1.5	6	10
şâhî	1	6	15
şâhî	1	9	50
şâhî	0.5	6	15
şâhî	0.5	7	50
Total			160

Note: The Tophane had to cast 487 guns altogether. However, our account claims that by October 12, 1772 only 159 pieces had been cast. The remaining pieces were planned to be cast in the coming months. Guns firing projectiles of 5 and 3 *okka* are referred to as large (*kebir*) guns.
Source: DBŞM TPH 18693, p. 3.

Table 60 *Types and number of mortars cast in the Tophane, September 21, 1771 through October 12, 1772*

	Number
Caliber (*okka*)	
32	4
18	10
14	14
Total	28

Source: DBŞM TPH 18693, p. 3.

Table 61 *Output of the Tophane, March 4, 1775 through February 20, 1776*

Name/caliber of piece	Number
5-*okka* large (*kebir*) gun	2
3-*okka* gun	2
balyemez gun	1
7-*okka balyemez* gun	1
100-*dirhem* gun	9
18-*okka* mortar	4
1.5-*okka şâhî*	17
Total	36

Note: The source does not give the weight of the pieces. It considers all the guns except the *şâhî* ones as large (*kebir*) guns.
Source: DBŞM TPH 18696, p. 2.

Table 62 *Output of the Tophane, February 21, 1776 through September 11, 1779*

Name/caliber of piece	Number
22-*okka* large (*kebir*) gun	3
9-*okka* gun	2
7-*okka* gun	3
5-*okka* gun	8
3-*okka* gun	41
1.5-*okka şâhî*	54
1-*okka şâhî*	26
Total	137

Source: DBŞM TPH 18696, p. 2.

Table 63 *Output of the Tophane, September 23, 1781 through February 3, 1782*

Name/caliber of piece	Number
7-*okka* 16-*karış* gun	2
5-*okka* 16-*karış* gun	16
3-*okka* 16-*karış* gun	15
Total	33

Source: DBŞM TPH 18710, p. 6.

Table 64 *Output of the Tophane, January 31,*
1782 through September 11, 1782

Name/caliber of piece	Number
14-*okka* 14-*karış* gun	5
11-*okka* 14-*karış* gun	2
9-*okka* 14-*karış* gun	2
7-*okka* 16-*karış* gun	3
5-*okka* 16-*karış* gun	7
5-*okka* 14-*karış* gun	8
3-*okka* 16-*karış* gun	8
3-*okka* 13-*karış* gun	8
1.5-*okka* 10-*karış* *şâhî*	21
85-*okka* mortar	1
45-*okka* mortar	3
32-*okka* mortar	4
18-*okka* mortar	3
14-*okka* mortar	1
Total	76

Source: DBŞM TPH 18712, p. 9.

Table 65 *Output of the Tophane, August 21,*
1784 through September 13, 1785

Name/caliber of piece	Number
44-*okka* 14-*karış* *şayka kalyon-i miri*	6
For the castle of İsmail	
9-*okka* 14-*karış* gun	4
7-*okka* 16-*karış* gun	10
5-*okka* 16-*karış* gun	47
3-*okka* 16-*karış* gun	30
1.5-*okka* 10-*karış* *şahî* gun	24
1.5-*okka* 7-*karış* *sürat* gun	2
1.5-*okka* 5-*karış* *sürat* gun	1
32-*okka* mortar	2
18-*okka* mortar	6
14-*okka* mortar	8
For *şehtiye* boats	
3-*okka* 8-*karış* gun	30
1-*okka* 8-*karış* *şahî* gun	3
Total	173

Note: The total weight of pieces was 3,924.7 *kantar* or
221,510 kg (DBŞM TPH 18723, pp. 7–13).
Source: DBŞM TPH 18723, p. 13.

Table 66 *Types and number of shots cast in Pravişte, January 17,*
1714 through January 6, 1715

Caliber of shot	Actual weight of shots	Number of shots	Total weight of shots cast in *okka*
16-*okka*	15 *okka*	4,836	72,540
14-*okka*	13 *okka*, 300 *dirhem*	4,301	59,138
11-*okka*	9 *okka*	434	3,906
9-*okka*	7.5 *okka*	748	5,610
7-*okka*	5 *okka*, 100 *dirhem*	3,860	20,265
5-*okka*	3 *okka*, 250 *dirhem*	12,103	43,073
3-*okka*	2 *okka*, 80 *dirhem*	23,998	52,595
1.5-*okka*	1 *okka*, 150 *dirhem*	17,870	21,788
1-*okka*	340 *dirhem*	5,881	4,999
0.5-*okka*	190 *dirhem*	3,530	1,676.5
100-*dirhem*	100 *dirhem*	23,680	5,920
75-*dirhem*	75 *dirhem*	28,600	4,646.5
50-*dirhem*	50 *dirhem*	28,725	3,590.5
25-*dirhem*	25 *dirhem*	19,020	1,189
Total		177,586	300,936.5 (386,040 kg)

Note: The accounts give the total weight as 300,932.5, an obvious slip of the pen.
Source: MAD 4456, p. 23.

Table 67 *Types and number of shots in the storehouses of Pravişte*
and Kavala, 1715

Caliber	Actual weight of shots	Number of shots	Total weight of shots cast in *okka*
14-*okka*	13 *okka*, 300 *dirhem*	1,420	19,525
11-*okka*	9 *okka*	2,442	23,786
9-*okka*	7.5 *okka*	2,675	20,062
7-*okka*	5 *okka*, 100 *dirhem*	3,863	23,131.5
5-*okka*	3 *okka*, 350 *dirhem*	10,056	40,066
3-*okka*	2 *okka*, 150 *dirhem*	17,400	35,452.5
2-*okka*	1 *okka*, 270 *dirhem*	5,190	8,693.25
1-*okka*	340 *dirhem*	37,000	31,450
0.5-*okka*	190 *dirhem*	16,670	8,283
300-*dirhem*	300 *dirhem*	2,436	1,827
100-*dirhem*	100 *dirhem*	500	125
Total		99,652	212,401.3 (272,468 kg)

Source: MAD 4456, p. 24.

Table 68 *Total number of shots (cast and stored) in Pravişte and Kavala, 1715*

Caliber	Number of shots	Weight of shots cast in *okka*
16-*okka*	4,836	72,540
14-*okka*	5,721	78,662
11-*okka*	2,876	27,692
9-*okka*	3,423	25,672
7-*okka*	7,723	43,396
5-*okka*	22,159	83,139
3-*okka*	41,398	88,048.5
2-*okka*	5,190	8,693
1.5-*okka*	17,870	21,788
1-*okka*	42,881	36,449
0.5-*okka*	20,200	9,959.5
300-*dirhem*	2,436	1,827
100-*dirhem*	24,180	6,045
75-*dirhem*	28,600	4,646.5
50-*dirhem*	28,725	3,590.5
25-*dirhem*	19,020	1,189
Total	277,238	513,337
		(658,508.7 kg)

Note: The accounts give the total weight as 513,333, an obvious slip of the pen.
Source: MAD 4456, p. 24.

Table 69 *Production output of the workshops in Pravişte*

Date	Number of shots	Weight of shots		Number of shells	Weight of shells		Source
		okka	kg		*okka*	kg	
1697–1700	182,624						MAD 4275
Dec. 12, 1700–June 12, 1706	277,269	822,554	1,055,172	5,400	270,692	347,244	MAD 4415
Jan. 28, 1713–Jan. 16, 1714	97,558	198,936	255,195				MAD 4456
Jan. 17, 1714–Jan. 6, 1715	177,586	300,932	386,036				MAD 4456
Jan. 7, 1715–Dec. 26, 1715	57,532	168,655	216,350	12,579	206,895	265,405	MAD 4456
Dec. 27, 1715–Nov. 19, 1719	230,320	510,038	654,277	4,488	136,681	175,334	DBŞM TPH 18621

Notes on weights and measurements

Because no handbook on Ottoman weights and measurements exists, the conversion of Ottoman measures to the metric system is especially difficult, and, in the secondary literature, is often haphazard. The following notes are based on archival sources used in this book, as well as on data published so far.[1]

Araba = cartload

The actual weight of a cartload or wagonload varied according to the types of carts and the commodities they transported. Regarding transportation of munitions (*cebehane*), the usual weight with which the Ottoman authorities calculated varied between 9.5 and 10.5 *kantar*s,[2] but they generally calculated with 10 *kantar*s, that is, either 540 or 564 kg.[3]

Batman

According to İnalcık the standard *batman* was 23 kg, but it is not clear in what period this was the case. He also suggests that in the nineteenth century in Asia Minor 1 *batman* was equal to 7.694 kg.[4] However, a source from 1566, regarding

[1] Unless stated otherwise, Ottoman data are taken from Walter Hinz, *Islamische Masse und Gewichte umgerechnet ins metrische System* (Leiden, 1955); Halil İnalcık, "Introduction to Ottoman Metrology," *Turcica* 15 (1983), 311–48; Halil İnalcık and Donald Quataert eds., *An Economic and Social History of the Ottoman Empire, 1300–1914* (Cambridge, 1994), pp. 987–94. Data for Hungary and the Austrian Habsburg lands are from István Bogdán, *Magyarországi űr-, térfogat-, súly- és darabmértékek 1874-ig* (Budapest, 1991).

[2] MAD 920 contains detailed figures regarding the weight of bullets, cannon balls, gunpowder and various tools of ordnance that needed to be transported during the 1697 campaign. For instance, they loaded on one cart 420 pieces of 1-*okka* shot which weighed 9.5 *kantar*. However, they usually loaded on the same cart 1 *maymuncuk* that commonly weighed 1 *kantar*, making the total weight put on a cart 10.5 *kantar*. Gunpowder was transported in barrels (*varil/varul*), of which eight were loaded on one cart, weighing 9.5 *kantar*.

[3] MAD 2758, p. 45, regarding the transportation of munitions during the 1697 campaign from Varna to Rusçuk. The *cebehane* weighed 3,487 *kantar* for which the authorities requested 348 carts.

[4] İnalcık and Quataert eds., *An Economic and Social History*, p. 987.

the province of Dulkadır in Asia Minor, indicates that in that region 1 *batman* was about 7.2–7.5 kg, depending on whether one calculates with 54 kg or 56.4 kg per *kantar*.[5] An imperial decree sent to the *kadı* of Gümüşhane in late 1695 instructed the addressee to calculate with *batman* that weighed 6 *okka* and with *kantar*s that weighed 44 *okka*.[6] Consequently, in the 1690s, around Gümüşhane the *batman* was about 7.37 or 7.69 kg. Since the light *männ/men* used in Anatolia in the sixteenth and seventeenth centuries was also of this weight, this piece of information supports those who use the *batman* and *männ/men* as synonyms. However, both units of weight varied considerably according to time and locality, and the exact *okka* and kilogram equivalent of each *batman* and *männ/men* should be determined on an individual basis. A source from 1785–86 gives the equivalent of 1 *batman* as 6 *okka* or 7.6968 kg, which is close to the standard *batman* to be found in handbooks.[7] This case also shows that we cannot automatically calculate with the standard 23 kg *batman* regarding sixteenth-century data from Asia Minor.

Dulkadır (1566) = 7.2–7.5 kg
Gümüşhane (1694–95) = 6 *okka* = 7.37 or 7.69 kg

Center

German *Zentner*, Latin *centenarius, centenarium*, Hungarian *mázsa*: 70–144 pounds
Viennese = 100 Viennese pounds = 55.58–56 kg
    55.58 kg (until the end of the sixteenth century)
    56.12 kg (seventeenth century through 1756)
    56 kg (1756–1871)
Hungarian = 120 Hungarian pounds = 58.8 kg

Cwt = hundredweight (see also *Zentner*)

1 English (long) hundredweight = 50.80 kg
1 English (short) hundredweight = 45.36 kg

Dirhem

Rumi dirhem = 3.207 g
Tabrizi dirhem = 3.072 g

---

[5] MD 5, p. 469, no. 1259.
[6] Ahmet Refik, *Osmanlı Devrinde Türkiye Madenleri (967–1200)* (Istanbul, 1931), p. 21.
[7] Rhoads Murphey, "Ma'din 3. Mineral Exploitation in the Ottoman Empire," *EI*, vol. V, p. 977. In the source 431,466 *okka* is given as the equivalent of 71,911 *batman*, which gives us 6 *okka* = 1 *batman*, and not 5.5379 *okka* = 1 *batman* as Murphey suggests, unless there is a typing error in Murphey's article (i.e., 71,911 instead of 77,911 *batman*).

Kantar

Transylvania (1489–) = 44 *okka* = 55.44 kg
Ottoman = 100 *lodra* = 44 *okka* = 54 kg or 56.44 kg
Ottoman (in mines and ironworks) = 50 *okka*[8] = 61.44 kg or 64.14 kg

Karış (span)

The *karış* or span is the standard measurement used in weapon inventories to measure the length of Ottoman gun barrels. As in the case of European guns, the length of the barrel is often engraved on the upper side of it. Based on existing Ottoman guns on display in the gardens of the Military and Naval Museums in Istanbul, whose length is given in *karış* on the barrel as well as in centimeters in the relevant inventories, it seems that the *karış* used in these cases equaled 22–23 cm. In all my calculations I used 1 *karış* = 22 cm.

Kile

1 standard = 36 liters = 37 cubic decimeters
1 standard = 20 *okka* = 25.66 kg for wheat and 22.25 kg (of course, if one accepts the *Rumi dirhem*, see above) for barley since the *kile* originally was a measurement for volumes. It also varied greatly from region to region, being less than 12 *okka* (15.36 kg) in Bursa and as much as 80 *okka* (102.54 kg) in Tirnovo, Bulgaria. Even within a relatively small area, such as the *sancak* of Pojega in 1579, very different *kile*s of 30, 35, 66, 72, 84, 90 and 100 *okka* were in use.[9]

Libra

See pound

Lodra

1 *lodra* = 176 *dirhem* = 0.54 kg or 0.56 kg

Men (Männ)

1 *männ* (standard in Iran and Asia Minor) = 260 *dirhem* = 799 g or 834 g
Diyarbekir = 580 *dirhem* = 1.78 kg or 1.86 kg

---

[8] MAD 683, p. 14.
[9] Gyula Káldy-Nagy, *Magyarországi török adóösszeírások* (Budapest, 1970), pp. 27–28.

(heavy) = 12 *okka* = 14.75 kg or 15.39 kg
(light) = 6 *okka* = 7.37 kg or 7.69 kg

Okka

The related literature uses the standard English pound of 454 g and the *Rumi dirhem* of 3.207 g.[10] However, according to Halil Sahillioğlu's studies, "the official *dirhem* in use (in coinage) down to the end of the seventeenth century was the *Tabrizi dirhem* of 3.072 g and after that time the *Rumi dirhem* of 3.207."[11] Sahillioğlu's findings are supported by some European data published recently.[12] Hungarian data at my disposal also correspond with the *Tabrizi dirhem* of 3.072 g. The best sources in this regard are the Ottoman provincial law codes (*kanunname*s), especially those from the European provinces, for they often mention local and Ottoman measurements. If the *kanunname*s give us the weight of local measurements in Ottoman *dirhem* or *okka*, it becomes possible to establish the exact weight of the *dirhem* or *okka* used in that province at a given time period, provided we are familiar with the local measurement and know its exact weight in kilograms. While it might often be difficult, it was possible to establish beyond any doubt that in the *sancak*s of Buda and Szolnok the Ottomans used the *Tabrizi dirhem* as late as the 1590s.[13] For the above reasons, concerning pre-eighteenth-century data I follow 1 *okka* = 400 *Tabrizi dirhem* = 1.2288 kg. Consequently, 1 *kantar*, that is 44 *okka*, is calculated as 54 kg. However, regarding the eighteenth century I follow the usual calculations of 1 *okka* = 1.2828 kg and 1 *kantar* = 56.44 kg. In 1714 in Transylvania 1 *okka* weighed 2.25 Viennese pounds, that is, 1.26 kg. Sources from the 1770s and 1780s, as well as from the mid-nineteenth century, indicate that it was the standard *okka* used in Hungary and Transylvania throughout the eighteenth and nineteenth centuries.[14] *Okka*/kg/pound equivalents (until the end of the seventeenth century):

1 *okka* = 1.2288 kg (until the end of seventeenth century)
1 *okka* = 2.7 English pounds

Pound

Using the standard English pound of 454 g and the *Rumi dirhem* it would mean that the standard *okka* weighed 2.83 pounds.[15] However, since we assume that it was the *Tabrizi dirhem* that was used in the Empire until the end of the seventeenth century, the standard *okka* (1.2288 kg) would equal just 2.7 English

[10] Hinz, *Islamische Masse und Gewichte*, p. 24.
[11] İnalcık, "Introduction," 318–20.
[12] Edmund M. Herzig, "A Note on the Ottoman Lidre and Dirhem Around 1500," *Turcica* 20 (1988), 247–49.
[13] Gábor Ágoston, "A szolnoki szandzsák 1591–92. évi összeírása, I," *Zounuk* 3 (1988), 221–96.
[14] Bogdan, *Mayarországi űr-, térfogat-, súly- és darabmértékek*, p. 460.
[15] Rhoads Murphey, *Ottoman Warfare, 1500–1700* (New Brunswick, 1999), 201.

pounds, which is used in all my calculations in the main text. However, contemporary European armies used a variety of pounds. The Spanish (and Portuguese) pound or *libra* was about 460 g (about 1.011–1.016 English pounds). The Habsburg Imperial Armies usually calculated in the Nurenberger *Pfund*. However, modern historians disagree as to its actual weight. Some suggest that it was 682 g while others claim that one Nurenberger *Pfund* weighed 509 g.[16] Accordingly, 1 *okka* would have equaled either 1.8 or 2.4 Nurenberger *Pfund*, a substantial difference indeed. However, in the Habsburg armies and in ordnance inventories of fortresses held by the Habsburgs in Hungary the Viennese *Pfund* of 560 g was also widely used. Calculating the *okka* to pound ratio in Viennese *Pfund* would mean that the standard *okka* until the end of the seventeenth century would weigh 2.2 *Pfund*.

Standard English = 0.4536 kg
Hungarian (1549) = 0.4900 kg
Nurenberger = 0.682 kg
Nurenberger = 0.509 kg
Spanish = 16 *onzas* = 0.4589–0.4608 kg
Venetian = 0.303 kg
Viennese (sixteenth century) = 0.5612 kg
Viennese (1756–) = 0.5600 kg

Quintal = hundredweight (cwt)

1 Hungarian *mázsa* (1566) = 58.80 kg
1 Viennese *Zentner* (seventeenth century) = 56.12 kg
1 Viennese *Zentner* (1756) = 56.00 kg
1 Spanish = 100 Castilian pounds = 46 kg

Ton

1 metric ton = 1,000 kg
1 short ton = 2,000 pounds = 0.9072 metric ton

Varil = barrel, cask

*Varil*s used for transporting gunpowder usually weighed about 1.19 *kantar*, that is, 64 kg or 67 kg.[17]

---

[16] György Domokos, "Várépitészet és várharcászat Európában a XVI–XVII. században," *HK* 33, 1 (1986), p. 78.
[17] MAD 920, pp. 8–9.

Zentner

Zentner = 100 *Pfund*
Nurenberger = 68.2 kg
Nurenberger = 50.9 kg
Viennese (sixteenth century) = 56.12 kg
Viennese (1756-) = 56 kg

Zira

Zira or *arşun* of architects was 0.758 m

Bibliography

Archival Sources

İstanbul Başbakanlık Osmanlı Arşivi (BOA)

Maliyeden Müdevver Defterleri (MAD)

173, 177, 362, 383, 498, 628, 683, 885, 920, 975, 1031, 1361, 1497, 1561, 1951, 2113, 2426, 2515, 2652, 2670, 2677, 2679, 2720, 2728, 2730, 2731, 2732, 2736, 2758, 2764, 2843, 2931, 2936, 2962, 3127, 3150, 3182, 3279, 3448, 3527, 3560, 3620, 3774, 3992, 4028, 4031, 4039, 4040, 4275, 4321, 4415, 4428, 4456, 4457, 4527, 4578, 4629, 4688, 4875, 4959, 5392, 5432, 5448, 5449, 5472, 5685, 6147, 6151, 6188, 6419, 6616, 6880, 7488, 7512, 7539, 7668, 7829, 8880, 9829, 9879, 10142, 10305, 10312, 10378, 10384, 10398, 10405, 12764, 12778, 15758, 15877, 18162, 18215.

Bâb-i Defteri Başmuhasebe Kalemi Defterleri (DBŞM)

66, 240, 449, 478, 483, 489, 598, 642, 844, 18368, 18369, 19085, 40877

Bâb-i Defteri Başmuhasebe Kalemi Defterleri Gelibolu Baruthânesi (DBŞM BRG)

18248, 18249, 18250 (which is in fact an account of the *baruthane* of Istanbul), 18251

Bâb-i Defteri Başmuhasebe Kalemi Defterleri İstanbul Baruthânesi (DBŞM BRİ)

18319, 18321

Bâb-i Defteri Başmuhasebe Kalemi Defterleri Selanik Baruthânesi (DBŞM BRS)

18356, 18362, 18364

248

Bâb-i Defteri Başmuhasebe Kalemi Defterleri Tophane-i Âmire (DBŞM TPH)

18596, 18597, 18598, 18599, 18601, 18604, 18609, 18610, 18613, 18615, 18617,
    18618, 18620, 18621, 18622, 18637, 18641, 18643, 18645, 18652, 18655,
    18656, 18658, 18660, 18663, 18666, 18668, 18671, 18672, 18673, 18674,
    18677, 18687, 18693, 18696, 18706, 18707, 18710, 18712, 18713, 18723,
    18734, 18747, 18748, 18750

Bâb-i Defteri Başmuhasebe Kalemi Defterleri Cebehane-i Âmire (DBŞM CBH)

18368

Bâb-i Defteri Mevkufat Kalemi (DMKF)

22736, 27627, 27640

Bâb-i Defteri Piyade Mukabelesi Kalemi (DPYM)

35132, 35141, 35162, 35180, 35273

Kâmil Kepeci (KK)

2472, 2628, 2647, 2682, 4726, 4738, 5185, 5649, 5654, 6691

Mühimme Defterleri (MD)

Volumes 3, 5, 6, 7, 9, 10, 12, 14, 16, 22, 24, 26, 27, 28, 29, 31, 32, 46, 70, 73, 74,
    75, 77, 94 [Volumes 3, 5, 7 and 12 were published by the staff of the Prime
    Minister's Ottoman Archives after the completion of the manuscript and were
    occasionally used during the final revision of the book.]

Cevdet Askeri (CA)

8406, 9031, 9594, 9595, 9756, 9778, 9814, 9595, 13157, 45641, 45657, 45663,
    45730, 45731, 45765, 45774, 46189, 46900, 51076

Ali Emiri (AE)

Bayezid II no. 41
Mehmed IV nos. 1119, 2397
III. Murad no. 210
I. Selim no. 23

İstanbul Topkapı Sarayı Müzesi Kütüphanesi (TSMK)

Koğuşlar 888

Vienna, Österreichische Nationalbibliothek (ÖNB), Handschriftensammlung

Mxt. 130: Topçular Katibi Abdülkadir Efendi, *Tarih-i Al-i Osman* (AK)
Mxt 599

Published Sources

Agricola, Georgius, *De re metallica*. Trans. Herbert Clark Hoover and Lou Henry Hoover. New York, 1950.

A janicsárok törvényei. Trans. Pál Fodor. Budapest, 1989.

Barkan, Ömer Lütfi, "1070–1071 (1660–1661) Tarihli Osmanlı Bütçesi ve Bir Mukayese," *İFM* 17 (1955–56), 304–47.

"1079–1080 (1669–1670) Malî Yılına ait Bir Osmanlı Bütçesi ve Ekleri," *İFM* 17 (1955–56), 225–303.

XV ve XVIıncı Asırlarda Osmanlı İmparatorluğunda Ziraî Ekonominin Hukukî ve Malî Esasları. I. Kanunlar. İstanbul, 1943.

"H 933 934 (M 1527–1528) Mali Yılına ait Bir Bütçe Örneği," *İFM* 15 (1953–54), 251–329.

"İstanbul Saraylarına Ait Muhasebe Defterleri," BTTD 9, 13 (1979), 1–380.

Biringuccio, Vannoccio, *The Pirotechnia of Vannoccio Biringuccio: The Classic Sixteenth-Century Treatise on Metals and Metallurgy*. Trans. Cyril Stanley Smith and Martha Teach Gnudi. New York, 1990.

Defterdar Sarı Mehmed Paşa, *Zübde-i Vekayiat*. Ed. Abdülkadir Özcan. Ankara, 1995.

Evliya Çelebi, *Seyehatnâme*. 10 vols. İstanbul, 1314/1896–97.

Evliya Çelebi Seyehatnâmesi, vol. I. Ed. Orhan Şaik Gökay. Istanbul, 1995.

Evlia Cselebi török világutazó magyarországi utazásai 1660–1664. Trans. Imre. Karácson, ed. Pál Fodor. Budapest, 1985.

Hasan Kâfî, *Usûlü'l-hikem fi Nizâmi'l-âlem*. Ed. Mehmed İpşirli. *TED* 10–11 (1979–80 [1981]), 239–78.

Hertz, Allan Z., "Armament and Supply Inventory of Ottoman Ada Kale, 1753," *ArchOtt* 4 (1972), 95–171.

Istvánffy Miklós magyarok dolgairól írt históriája. Tallyai Pál XVII. századi fordításában, vol. I, pt. 1. Ed. Péter Benits. Budapest, 2001.

Marsigli, Luigi, *L'état militaire de l'empire ottoman*. 2 vols. The Hague and Paris, 1732.

Naima, Mustafa, *Ravzatü'l-hüseyn fî Hulasati Ahbari'l-hafikayn*. 6 vols. Istanbul, 1280/1863–64.

Orhonlu, Cengiz, *Osmanlı Tarihine Aid Belgeler: Telhisler (1597–1607)*. Istanbul, 1970.

Peçevi (Peçuylu), İbrahim, *Tarih-i Peçevi*. 2 vols. İstanbul, 1283/1866–67.

Raif, Mahmud Efendi, *Osmanlı İmparatorluğun'da Yeni Nizamların Cedveli*. Trans. and ed. Arslan Terzioğlu and Hüsrev Hatemi. Istanbul, n.d. *Tableau des nouveaux reglemens de l'empire ottoman*. Constantinople, 1798.

Raşid, Mehmed, *Tarih-i Raşid*. 2 vols. Istanbul, 1282/1865–66.

Refik, Ahmed, *Osmanlı Devrinde Türkiye Madenleri (967–1200)*. Istanbul, 1931.

Rycaut, Paul, *The History of the Present State of the Ottoman Empire*. London, 1686.

Sardi, Pietro, *L'Artiglieria*. Venice, 1621.

Selânikî, Mustafa Efendi, *Tarih-i Selânikî*. Ed. Mehmed İpşirli. 2 vols. Istanbul, 1989.

Szakály, Ferenc, ed., *Buda visszafoglalásának emlékezete, 1686*. Budapest, 1986.

Thúry, József, *Török történetírók*. 2 vols. Budapest, 1893–96.

Tott, Baron de, *Memoirs of Baron de Tott* (London, 1785; reprint New York, 1973).

Uzunçarşılı, İsmail Hakkı, "Osmanlı Sarayı'nda Ehl-i Hıref (Sanatkarlar) Defteri," *BTTD* 11, 15 (1981–86), 23–76.

Select list of secondary sources

Ágoston, Gábor, "Early Modern Ottoman and European Gunpowder Technology," in Ekmeleddin İhsanoğlu, Kostas Chatzis and Efthymios Nicolaides eds., *Multicultural Science in the Ottoman Empire*. Turnhout, 2003, pp. 13–27.

"Gunpowder for the Sultan's Army: New Sources on the Supply of Gunpowder to the Ottoman Army in the Hungarian Campaigns of the Sixteenth and Seventeenth Centuries," *Turcica* 25 (1993), 75–96.

"Habsburgs and Ottomans: Defense, Military Change and Shifts in Power," *TSAB* 22, 1 (1998), 126–41.

"Merces Prohibitae: The Anglo-Ottoman Trade in War Materials and the Dependence Theory," in Kate Fleet ed., *The Ottomans and the Sea, Oriente Moderno* 20 (81), n.s. 1 (2001), 177–92.

"Osmanlı İmparatorluğu'nda Harp Endüstrisi ve Barut Teknolojisi (1450–1700)," in Güler Eren, Kemal Çiçek and Cem Oğuz eds., *Osmanlı*, vol. VI: *Teşkilat*. Ankara, 2000, pp. 613–21.

"Ottoman Artillery and European Military Technology in the Fifteenth to Seventeenth Centuries," *AOH* 47, 1–2 (1994), 15–48.

"Ottoman Gunpowder Production in Hungary in the Sixteenth Century: The *Baruthane* of Buda," in Géza Dávid and Pál Fodor eds., *Hungarian–Ottoman Military and Diplomatic Relations in the Age of Süleyman the Magnificent*. Budapest, 1994, pp. 149–59.

"Ottoman Warfare in Europe, 1453–1812," in Jeremy Black ed., *European Warfare, 1453–1815*. London, 1999, pp. 118–44.

Aksan, Virginia, "Breaking the Spell of the Baron de Tott: Reframing the Question of Military Reform in the Ottoman Empire, 1760–1830," *IHR* 24, 2 (2002), 253–77.
  "Feeding the Ottoman Troops on the Danube, 1768–1774," *War and Society* 13, 1 (1995), 1–14.
  "Locating the Ottomans among Early Modern Empires," *Journal of Early Modern History* 3, 2 (1999), 103–34.
  "The One-Eyed Fighting the Blind: Mobilization, Supply, and Command in the Russo-Turkish War of 1768–74," *IHR* 15, 2 (1993), 221–38.
  An Ottoman Statesman in War and Peace: Ahmed Resmi Efendi, 1700–1783. Leiden, 1995.
  "Ottoman War and Warfare, 1453–1812," in Jeremy Black ed., *War in the Early Modern World, 1450–1815.* London, 1999, pp. 147–75.
  "Whatever Happened to the Janissaries? Mobilization for the 1768–1774 Russo-Ottoman War," *War in History* 5, 1 (1998), 23–36.
Ambraseys, N. N. and C. F. Finkel, *The Seismicity of Turkey and Adjacent Areas: A Historical Review, 1500–1800.* Istanbul, 1995.
Anhegger, Robert, *Beiträge zur Geschichte des Bergbaus im osmanischen Reich.* Berne, 1945.
Ayalon, David, *Gunpowder and Firearms in the Mamluk Kingdom: A Challenge to a Mediaeval Society.* London, 1956; 2nd edition London, 1978.
Aydüz, Salim, "Cıgalazade Yusuf Sinan Paşa'nın Şark Seferi için Tophane-i Amire'de hazırlanan toplar ve Tophane-i Amire'nin 1012 (1604) yılı gelir-gider muhasebesi," in Feza Günergun ed., *Osmanlı Bilimi Araştırmalrı,* vol. II, Istanbul, 1998, pp. 139–62.
Bartusis, Mark C., *The Late Byzantine Army: Arms and Society, 1204–1453.* Philadelphia, 1992.
Belinickii, A. M., "O poiavlenii i rasprostaneii ognestrel'nogo oruzhia v srednei Azii i Irane v XIV–XVI. vekah," *Izvestiia Tadzhiskogo Filiala Akademii Nauk SSSR* 15 (1949), 21–35.
Beskrovnyi, L. G., *Russkaia armiia i flot v XVIII veke: Ocherki.* Moscow, 1958.
Black, Jeremy, *European Warfare, 1494–1660.* London, 2002.
  A Military Revolution? Military Change and European Society, 1550–1800. London, 1991.
  War and the World: Military Power and the Fate of the Continents, 1450–2000. New Haven and London, 1998.
Bostan, İdris, *Osmanlı Bahriye Teşkilatı: XVII. Yüzyılda Tersane-i Amire.* Ankara, 1992.
  "A szultáni ágyúöntő műhelyben (Tophane-i Amire) folyó tevékenység a 16. század elején," *Aetas* 18, 2 (2003), 5–19.
Brummett, Palmira, *Ottoman Seapower and Levantine Diplomacy in the Age of Discovery.* New York, 1994.

"The Ottomans as a World Power: What We Don't Know about Ottoman Sea-power," in Kate Fleet ed., *The Ottomans and the Sea, Oriente Moderno* 20 (81) n.s. 1 (2001), 1–21.

Buchanan, Brenda J., ed., *Gunpowder: The History of an International Technology.* Bath, 1996.

Çetin, Birol, *Osmanlı İmparatorluğu'nda Barut Sanayi, 1700–1900.* Ankara, 2001.

Cezar, Mustafa, *Osmanlı Tarihinde Levendler.* Istanbul, 1965.

Cezar, Yavuz, *Osmanlı Maliyesinde Bunalım ve Değişim Dönemi.* Istanbul, 1986.

Chase, Kenneth, *Firearms: A Global History to 1700.* Cambridge, 2003.

Chernov, A. V., *Vooruzhennye sily russkogo gosudarstvo XV–XVII vv.* Moscow, 1954.

Christensen, Stephen, "European–Ottoman Military Acculturation in the Late Middle Ages," in Brian Patric McGuire ed., *War and Peace in the Middle Ages.* Copenhagen, 1987, pp. 227–51.

Cipolla, Carlo M., *Guns, Sails, and Empires: Technological Innovation and the Early Phases of European Expansion 1400–1700.* New York, 1965; reprint New York, 1996.

Çizakça, Murat, *A Comparative Evolution of Business Partnerships: The Islamic World and Europe, with Specific Reference to the Ottoman Archives.* Leiden, 1996.

"Ottomans and the Mediterranean: An Analysis of the Ottoman Shipbuilding Industry as Reflected by the Arsenal Registers of Istanbul, 1529–1650," in Rosalba Ragosta ed., *Le genti del mare Mediterraneo*, vol. II. Naples, 1981, pp. 773–88.

Collins, James B., *The State in Early Modern France.* Cambridge, 1999.

Contamine, Philippe, *War in the Middle Ages.* Trans. Michael Jones. Oxford, 1984.

Cook, Weston F., Jr., *The Hundred Years War for Morocco.* Boulder, CO, 1994.

Dağlı, Yücel and Cumhure Üçer, *Tarih Çevirme Kılavuzu*, vols. IV–V. Ankara, 1997.

Darling, Linda, *Revenue-Raising and Legitimacy: Tax Collection and Finance Administration in the Ottoman Empire, 1560–1660.* Leiden, 1996.

Daumas, Maurice, *A History of Technology and Invention.* Trans. Eileen B. Hennessey. 2 vols. New York, 1969.

Dávid, Géza and Pál Fodor eds., *Hungarian–Ottoman Military and Diplomatic Relations in the Age of Süleyman the Magnificent.* Budapest, 1994.

eds., *Ottomans, Hungarians, and Habsburgs in Central Europe: The Military Confines in the Era of Ottoman Conquest.* Leiden, 2000.

Delbrück, Hans, *History of the Art of War within the Framework of Political History.* Trans. Walter J. Renfroe, Jr. 4 vols. Westport, CN, 1975–85; reprint Lincoln and London, 1990.

DeVries, Kelly, "Catapults Are Not Atomic Bombs: Towards a Redefinition of 'Effectiveness' in Premodern Military Technology," *War in History* 4, 4 (1997), 454–70.

"Gunpowder Weapons at the Siege of Constantinople, 1453," in Yaacov Lev ed., *War and Society in the Eastern Mediterranean, 7th–15th Centuries*. Leiden, 1997, pp. 343–62.

Medieval Military Technology. Peterborough, Ontario, 1992.

Dolleczek, Anton, *Geschichte der österreichischen Artillerie von den frühesten Zeiten bis zur Gegenwart*. Vienna, 1887.

Duffy, Christopher, *Fire and Stone: The Science of Fortress Warfare, 1660–1860*. London, 1996.

Siege Warfare: The Fortress in the Early Modern World 1494–1660, London, 1979; reprint London, 1996.

Dupuy, Trever Nevitt, *The Evolution of Weapons and Warfare*. New York, 1985.

Emecen, Feridun, *İstanbulun Fethi Olayı ve Meseleleri*. Istanbul, 2003.

Erdoğan, Muzaffer, "Arşiv Vesikalarına Göre İstanbul Baruthaneleri," *İED* 2 (1956), 115–38.

Esper, Thomas, "Military Self-Sufficiency and Weapons Technology in Moscovite Russia," *Slavic Review* 28, 2 (1969), 185–208.

Faroqhi, Suraiya, *Towns and Townsmen of Ottoman Anatolia: Trade, Crafts and Food Production in an Urban Setting, 1520–1650*. Cambridge, 1984.

Finkel, Caroline, *The Administration of Warfare: The Ottoman Military Campaigns in Hungary, 1593–1606*. Vienna, 1988.

"French Mercenaries in the Habsburg–Ottoman War of 1593–1606," *BSOAS* 55, 3 (1992), 451–71.

Fleet, Kate, "Early Turkish Naval Activities," in Kate Fleet ed., *The Ottomans and the Sea, Oriente Moderno* 20 (81) n.s. 1 (2001), 129–30.

Floor, Willem, *Safavid Government Institutions*. Costa Mesa, CA, 2001.

Genç, Mehmet, "İltizam," *TDVİA*, vol. XXII, pp. 154–58.

Osmanlı İmparatorluğunda Devlet ve Ekonomi. Istanbul, 2000.

"Osmanlı Maliyesinde Malikane Sisitemi," in Genç, *Osmanlı İmparatorluğunda Devlet ve Ekonomi*, pp. 99–152.

"18. Yüzyılda Osmanlı Ekonomisi ve Savaş," in Genç, *Osmanlı İmparatorluğunda Devlet ve Ekonomi*, pp. 211–25.

Glete, Jan, *War and the State in Early Modern Europe: Spain, the Dutch Republic and Sweden as Fiscal-Military States, 1500–1660*. London and New York, 2002.

Goffman, Daniel, *The Ottoman Empire and Early Modern Europe*. Cambridge, 2002.

Gohlke, Wilhelm, *Geschichte der gesamten Feuerwaffen bis 1850*. Leipzig, 1911.

Goodman, David, *Spanish Naval Power, 1589–1665: Reconstruction and Defeat*. Cambridge, 1997.

Göyünç, Nejat, "Yurtluk-Ocaklık Deyimleri Hakkında," in *Prof. Dr. Bekir Kütükoğlu'na Armağan*. Istanbul, 1991, pp. 269–77.

Grant, Jonathan, "Rethinking the Ottoman 'Decline': Military Technology Diffusion in the Ottoman Empire, Fifteenth to Eighteenth Centuries," *Journal of World History* 10, 1 (1999), 179–201.

Greene, Molly, "Ruling an Island without a Navy: A Comparative View of Venetian and Ottoman Crete," in Kate Fleet ed., *The Ottomans and the Sea, Oriente Moderno* 20 (81) n.s. 1 (2001), 193–207.

Guilmartin, Jr., John Francis, "Early Modern Naval Ordnance and the European Penetration of the Caribbean: The Operational Dimensions," *The International Journal of Nautical Archeology and Underwater Exploration* 17 (1988), 35–53.

"The Early Provision of Artillery Armament on Mediterranean War Galleys," *The Mariner's Mirror* 59, 3 (1973), 257–80.

Gunpowder and Galleys: Changing Technology and Mediterranean Warfare at Sea in the Sixteenth Century. Cambridge, 1974; rev. edition Annapolis, MD, 2003.

Hale, J. R., "Gunpowder and the Renaissance: An Essay in the History of Ideas," in J. R. Hale, *Renaissance War Studies.* London, 1983, pp. 389–420.

War and Society in Renaissance Europe 1450–1620. London, 1985.

Hall, Bert S., *Weapons and Warfare in Renaissance Europe: Gunpowder, Technology, and Tactics.* Baltimore, 1997.

Hall, Bert S. and Kelly DeVries, "The Military Revolution Revisited," *Technology and Culture* 31 (1990), 500–07.

Handžić, Adem, "Rudarstvo u Bosni XV do XVII stoljeće," *İFM* 41, 1–4 (1985), 321–60.

"Rudnici u Bosni u drugoj polovini XV stoljeća," *POF* 26 (1976), 7–41.

al-Hassan, Ahmad Y. and Donald R. Hill, *Islamic Technology: An Illustrated History.* Cambridge, 1986.

Hess, Andrew C., "The Evolution of the Ottoman Seaborne Empire in the Age of Oceanic Discoveries, 1453–1525," *American Historical Review* 75, 7 (1970), 1892–919.

The Forgotten Frontier: A History of the Sixteenth-Century Ibero-African Frontier. Chicago, 1978.

Heywood, Colin, "The Activity of the State Cannon-Foundry (Tophane-i Amire) at Istanbul in the Early Sixteenth Century According to an Unpublished Turkish Source," *POF* 30 (1980), 209–16; reprinted in Heywood, *Writing Ottoman History.*

"Notes on the Production of Fifteenth-Century Ottoman Cannon," in *Proceedings of the International Symposium on Islam and Science, Islamabad, 1–3 Muharrem, 1401 A. H. (10–12 November, 1980).* Islamabad, Government of Pakistan, Ministry of Science and Technology, 1981, pp. 58–61; reprinted in Heywood, *Writing Ottoman History.*

Writing Ottoman History: Documents and Interpretations. Aldershot, 2002.

Hogg, O. F. G., *Artillery: Its Origin, Heyday and Decline.* London, 1970.

İhsanoğlu, Ekmeleddin, "Ottoman Science in the Classical Period and Early Contacts with European Science and Technology," in Ekmeleddin İhsanoğlu ed., *Transfer of Modern Science and Technology*, pp. 1–120.

ed., *Osmanlılar ve Batı Teknolojisi.* Istanbul. 1992.

ed., *Transfer of Modern Science and Technology to the Muslim World.* Istanbul, 1992.

İlgürel, Mücteba, "Osmanlı İmparatorluğunda Ateşli Silahların Yayılışı," *TD* 32 (1979), 301–18.

"Osmanlı Topçulugun İlk Devri," in *Hakki Dursun Yıldız Armağanı.* Ankara, 1995, pp. 285–93.

Imber, Colin H., "The Navy of Süleyman the Magnificent," *ArchOtt* 6 (1980), 211–82.

The Ottoman Empire, 1300–1481. Istanbul, 1990.

The Ottoman Empire, 1300–1650. New York, 2002.

İnalcık, Halil, "Military and Fiscal Transformation in the Ottoman Empire, 1600–1700," *ArchOtt* 6 (1980), 283–337.

"Osmanlılar'da Ateşli Silahlar," *Belleten* 83, 21 (1957), 508–12.

"The Socio-Political Effects of the Diffusion of Fire-arms in the Middle East," in V. J. Parry and M. E. Yapp eds., *War, Technology and Society in the Middle East.* London, 1975, pp. 195–217.

İnalcık, Halil and Donald Quataert eds., *An Economic and Social History of the Ottoman Empire, 1300–1914.* Cambridge, 1994.

Işıksal, Turgut, "Eski Türk Topları ve İstanbul Tophanesinde Bulunan bir Kayıt Defteri," *BTTD* 3 (1967), 61–63.

"Gunpowder in Ottoman Documents of the Last Half of the 16th Century," *IJTS* 2, 2 (1981–82), 81–91.

Jones, E. L., *The European Miracle: Environments, Economies, and Geopolitics in the History of Europe and Asia.* Cambridge and New York, 1987; 3rd edition 2003.

Kaçar, Mustafa, "Osmanlı İmparatorluğunda Askeri Sahada Yenileşme Döneminin Başlangıcı," in Feza Günergun ed., *Osmanlı Bilimi Araştırmaları.* Istanbul, 1995, pp. 209–25.

Kafadar, Cemal, *Between Two Worlds: The Construction of the Ottoman State.* Berkeley, 1995.

Kahane, Henry, Renée Kahane and Andreas Tietze, *The Lingua Franca in the Levant: Turkish Nautical Terms of Italian and Greek Origin.* Urbana, IL, 1958; reprint Istanbul, 1988.

Káldy-Nagy, Gyula, "The First Centuries of the Ottoman Military Organization," *AOH* 31 (1977), 147–83.

Kazancıgil, Aykut, *Osmanlılarda Bilim ve Teknoloji.* Istanbul, 1999.

Kennedy, Paul, *The Rise and Fall of the Great Powers: Economic Change and Military Conflict from 1500 to 2000.* New York, 1989.

Köhbach, Markus, *Die Eroberung von Fülek durch die Osmanen 1554. Eine historisch-quellenkritische Studie zur osmanischen Expansion im östlichen Mitteleuropa.* Vienna, 1994.

"Der osmanische Historiker Topçılar Katibi 'Abdü'l-qadir Efendi. Leben und Werk," *OsmAr* 2 (1981), 75–96.

Krause, Keith, *Arms and the State: Patterns of Military Production and Trade.* Cambridge, 1992.

Kütükoğlu, Mübahat S., "Baruthane-i Amire," *TDVİA*, vol. V, pp. 96–98.

Levy, Avigdor, "Military Reform and the Problem of Centralization in the Ottoman Empire in the 18th Century," *Middle Eastern Studies* 18 (1982), 227–48.

Lewis, Bernard, *Muslim Discovery of Europe.* London, 1982; reprint 1994.

What Went Wrong? The Clash between Islam and Modernity in the Middle East. New York, 2002.

Lynn, John A., *Giant of the Grand Siècle: The French Army, 1610–1715.* Cambridge, 1997.

Mallett, Michael, "Siegecraft in Late Fifteenth-Century Italy," in Ivy A. Corfis and Michael Wolfe eds., *The Medieval City under Siege.* Woodbridge, 1995, pp. 245–71.

Mallett, M. E. and J. R. Hale, *The Military Organization of a Renaissance State: Venice c. 1400 to 1617.* Cambridge, 1984.

Manucy, Albert, *Artillery through the Ages.* Washington, D.C., 1949; reprint 1985.

Marshall, Arthur, *Explosives I: History and Manufacture.* London, 1917.

Martin, Colin and Geoffrey Parker, *The Spanish Armada.* London, 1988.

Matthee, Rudi, "Unwalled Cities and Restless Nomads: Firearms and Artillery in Safavid Iran," in Charles Melville ed., *Safavid Persia: The History and Politics of an Islamic Society.* London, 1996, pp. 389–416.

McNeill, William H., *The Pursuit of Power: Technology, Armed Force, and Society since AD 1000.* Chicago, 1982.

Murphey, Rhoads, "The Ottoman Attitude towards the Adoption of Western Technology: The Role of the Efrencî Technicians in Civil and Military Applications," in Jean-Louis Bacqué-Grammont and Paul Dumont eds., *Contributions à l'histoire économique et sociale de l'Empire ottoman.* Leuven, 1983, pp. 287–98.

"The Ottoman Resurgence in the Seventeenth-Century Mediterranean: The Gamble and its Results," *Mediterranean Historical Review* 8 (1993), 186–200.

Ottoman Warfare, 1500–1700. New Brunswick, 1999.

Needham, Joseph, *Gunpowder as the Fourth Power: East and West.* Hong Kong, 1985.

Needham, Joseph J., Ho Ping-Yü, Lu Gwei-Djen and Wang Ling, *Science and Civilization in China, vol. V: Chemistry and Chemical Technology, pt. 7, Military Technology: The Gunpowder Epic.* Cambridge, 1986.

Nef, John U., *Industry and Government in France and England, 1540–1640.* Ithaca, NY, 1964.

Orhonlu, Cengiz, *Osmanlı İmparatorluğunda Şehircilik ve Ulaşım.* Izmir, 1984.

Ostapchuk, Victor, "The Human Landscape of the Ottoman Black Sea in the Face of the Cossack Naval Raids," in Kate Fleet ed., *The Ottomans and the Sea, Oriente Moderno* 20 (81) n.s. 1. (2001), pp. 23–95.

Özbaran, Salih, "The Ottomans' Role in the Diffusion of Fire-arms and Military Technology in Asia and Africa in the Sixteenth Century," in Salih Özbaran, *The Ottoman Response to European Expansion*. Istanbul, 1994, pp. 61–66.

Pacey, Arnold, *Technology in World Civilization: A Thousand-Year History*. Oxford, 1990.

Pamuk, Şevket, *A Monetary History of the Ottoman Empire*. Cambridge, 2000.

Panzac, Daniel, "Armed Peace in the Mediterranean 1736–1739: A Comparative Survey of the Navies," *The Mariner's Mirror* 84, 1 (1997), 41–55.

Parker, Geoffrey, *The Military Revolution: Military Innovation and the Rise of the West, 1500–1800* (Cambridge, 1988, rev. 3rd edition, 1999).

Parry, V. J., "Barud, IV: The Ottoman Empire," *EI*, vol. I, pp. 1061–66.

"La maniere de combattre," in V. J. Parry and M. E. Yapp eds., *War, Technology and Society in the Middle East*. London, 1975, pp. 218–56.

"Materials of War in the Ottoman Empire," in M. A. Cook ed., *Studies in the Economic History of the Middle East*. London, 1970, pp. 219–29.

Petrović, Djurdjica, "Fire-arms in the Balkans on the Eve of and After the Ottoman Conquest of the Fourteenth and Fifteenth Centuries," in V. J. Parry and M. E. Yapp eds., *War, Technology and Society in the Middle East*. London, 1975, pp. 164–94.

Piaskowski, Jerzy, "The Technology of Gun Casting in the Army of Muhammad II (Early 15th Century)," in *I. International Congress on the History of Turkish–Islamic Science and Technology, 14–18 September 1981. Proceedings*, vol. III. Istanbul, 1981, pp. 163–68.

Pitcher, Donald Edgar, *An Historical Geography of the Ottoman Empire from the Earliest Times to the End of the Sixteenth Century*. Leiden, 1973.

Pryor, John H., *Geography, Technology, and War: Studies in the Maritime History of the Mediterranean, 649–1571*. Cambridge, 1992.

Ralston, David B., *Importing the European Army: The Introduction of European Military Techniques and Institutions into the Extra-European World, 1600–1914*. Chicago, 1996.

Rogers, Clifford J., ed., *The Military Revolution Debate: Readings on the Military Transformation of Early Modern Europe*. Boulder, CO, 1995.

Sahin-Tóth, Péter, "À propos d'un article de C. F. Finkel: Quelques notation supplémentaires concernant les mercenaires de Pápa," *Turcica* 26 (1994), 249–60.

Schmidtchen, Volker, *Bombarden, Befestigungen, Büchsenmeister. Von den ersten Mauerbrechern des Spätmittelalters zur Belagerungsartillerie der Renaissance. Eine Studie zur Entwicklung der Militärtechnik*. Düsseldorf, 1977.

Setton, Kenneth Meyer, *Venice, Austria, and the Turks in the Seventeenth Century*. Philadelphia, 1991.

Shaw, Stanford J., *Between Old and New: The Ottoman Empire under Sultan Selim III, 1789–1807*. Cambridge, MA, 1971.

Singer, Charles, E. J. Holmyard and A. R. Hall eds., *History of Technology II. The Mediterranean Civilizations and the Middle Ages c. 700 BC to c. AD 1500.* Oxford, 1957.

Smith, Robert D. and Ruth Rhynas Brown, *Bombards: Mons Meg and her Sisters.* London, 1989.

Thompson, I. A. A., *War and Government in Habsburg Spain, 1560–1620.* London, 1976.

Tomlinson, H. C., *Guns and Government: The Ordnance Office under the Later Stuarts.* London, 1979.

Uzunçarşılı, İsmail Hakkı, *Osmanlı Devleti Teşkilatınaan Kapukulu Ocakları, vol. II: Cebeci, Topçu, Top Arabacilorı, Humbaracı, Lağımcı Ocakları ve Kapukulu Suvarileri*, Ankara, 1984.

Osmanlı Devletinin Merkez ve Bahriye Teşkilatı. Ankara, 1984.

Vasiliev, A., "Jörg of Nuremberg: A Writer Contemporary with the Fall of Constantinople (1453)," *Byzantion* 10 (1935), 205–09.

Vatin, Nicolas, *L' Ordre de Saint-Jean-de-Jérusalem, l'empire ottoman et la Méditerranée orientale entre les deux sièges de Rodes (1480–1522).* Paris, 1994.

West, Jenny, *Gunpowder, Government and War in the Mid-Eighteenth Century.* London, 1991.

Wittek, Paul, "The Earliest References to the Use of Firearms by the Ottomans," in David Ayalon, *Gunpowder and Firearms*, pp. 141–43.

Zdraveva, Milka, "Der Abbau von Schwefel und Salpeter in Makedonien zur Zeit der osmanischen Herrschaft und deren Verarbeitung zu Schwarzpulver," *Südost-Forschungen* 39 (1980), 105–15.

Zimmermann, Jörg, *Militärverwaltung und Heeresaufbildung in Österreich bis 1806. Handbuch zur deutschen Militärgeschichte, 1648–1939*, vol. III. Frankfurt am Main, 1965.

Index

Abbreviations: A. Albanian, Ar. Arabic, B. Bulgarian, G. German, Gr. Greek, H. Hungarian, It. Italian, O. Ottoman, P. Polish, R. Russian, S. Southern Slav/general Slavonic, Sl. Slovak, T. Turkish

The Mamluks in Egyptian Politics and Society
Thomas Philipp and Ulrich Haarmann (eds.)
0 521 59115 5

The Delhi Sultanate
A Political and Military History
Peter Jackson
0 521 40477 0

European and Islamic Trade in the Early Ottoman State
The Merchants of Genoa and Turkey
Kate Fleet
0 521 64221 3

Reinterpreting Islamic Historiography
Harun al-Rashid and the Narrative of the 'Abbāsid Caliphate
Tayeb El-Hibri
0 521 65023 2

The Ottoman City between East and West
Aleppo, Izmir, and Istanbul
Edhem Eldem, Daniel Goffman and Bruce Masters
0 521 64304 X

A Monetary History of the Ottoman Empire
Sevket Pamuk
0 521 44197 8

The Politics of Trade in Safavid Iran
Silk for Silver, 1600–1730
Rudolph P. Matthee
0 521 64131 4

The Idea of Idolatry and the Emergence of Islam
From Polemic to History
G. R. Hawting
0 521 65165 4

Classical Arabic Biography
The Heirs of the Prophets in the Age of al-Maʾmūn
Michael Cooperson
0 521 66199 4

Empire and Elites after the Muslim Conquest
The Transformation of Northern Mesopotamia
Chase F. Robinson
0 521 78115 9

Poverty and Charity in Medieval Islam
Mamluk Egypt, 1250–1517
Adam Sabra
0 521 77291 5

Christians and Jews in the Ottoman Arab World
The Roots of Sectarianism
Bruce Masters
0 521 80333 0

Culture and Conquest in Mongol Eurasia
Thomas T. Allsen
0 521 80335 7